SCIENCE
CHEMISTRY

NCERT/CBSE SYLLABUS

For Class-IX

By

Dr. S. P. JAUHAR
Formerly Professor of Chemistry
Department of Chemistry
Panjab University, **Chandigarh**

R. JAUHAR
B.Sc., B.Ed.

Nytra
Watch books come alive

Revised Edition
2020-21

MODERN PUBLISHERS
(Producers of ... Books)

OUR ADDRESSES IN INDIA

- **New Delhi:** MBD House, Gulab Bhawan, 6, Bahadur Shah Zafar Marg — Ph. 61312345, 23318301
- **Mumbai:** A-683, T.T.C. Industrial Area, M.I.D.C. Off. Thane-Belapur Road, Navi Mumbai — Ph. 32996410, 27780821, 8691053365
- **Chennai:** No. 26 B/2 SIDCO Estate, North Phase, Pataravakkam Ambattur Industrial Estate, Ambattur — Ph. 26359376, 26242350
- **Chennai:** Plot No. 3018, Old Y Block, 3rd Street, 12th Main Road, Anna Nagar West, Chennai — Ph. 23741471
- **Kolkata:** Satyam Building, 46-D, Rafi Ahmed Kidwai Marg — Ph. 22296863, 22161670
- **Jalandhar City:** MBD House, Railway Road — Ph. 2458388, 2459046, 2455663
- **Bengaluru:** 124/31, 1st Main, Industrial Town (Near Chowdeshwari Kalyan Mantap), West of Chord Road, Rajajinagar — Ph. 23103329, 23104667
- **Hyderabad:** 3-4-492, Varun Towers, Barkatpura — Ph. 27564788, 9985820001
- **Ernakulam:** Surabhi Building, South Janatha Road, Palarivattom — Ph. 2338107, 2347371
- **Nagpur:** Plot No. 231, Lendra Park, Behind Krims Hospital, Ramdaspeth, Nagpur — Ph. 0712-2447306, 2447330, 7410017938
- **Ahmedabad:** Godown No.10, Vedant Prabha Estate, Opp. ONGC Pumping Station, Sarkhej Sanand Road, Sarkhej — Ph. 26890336, 7600024542
- **Cuttack:** Badambadi, Link Road — Ph. 2367277, 2367279, 2313013
- **Guwahati:** Chancellor Commercial, Hem Baruah Road, Paan Bazar — Ph. 7637014051
- **Lucknow:** 173/15, Dr. B. N. Verma Road, Old 30 Kutchery Road — Ph. 4010992, 4010993
- **Patna:** Ist Floor, Annapurna Complex, Naya Tola — Ph. 2678732, 2678994
- **Bhopal:** Plot No. 137, 138, 139, Sector-I, Special Industrial Area, Govindpura — Ph. 2581540, 2601535
- **Goa:** MBD Group, H. No. 1644, Plot No. 100, Kranti Nagar, H.B. Colony, Nr. Nana Nani Park, Porvorim, Tal: Bardez, Dist. North Goa — Ph. 0832-2413982, 7028912261
- **Jaipur:** C-66A, In front of Malpani Hospital, Road No. 1, V.K. Industrial Area, Sikar Road — Ph. 4050309, 4020168
- **Raipur:** Behind Aligarh Safe Steel Industries, Vidhan Sabha Road, Avanti Bai Chowk, Lodhi Para Pandri — Ph. 2445370, 4052529
- **Karnal:** Plot No. 203, Sector-3, HSIDC, Near Namaste Chowk, Opp. New World — Ph. 2220006, 2220009
- **Shimla (H.P.):** C-89, Sector-I, New Shimla-9 — Ph. 2670221, 2670816
- **Jammu (J&K):** MBD, Khasra No. 417, Industrial Area, Gangyal, Near SICOP Office — Ph. 9419104035
- **Ranchi (Jharkhand):** MBD Group, Shivani Complex, 2nd Floor, Jyoti Sangam Lane, Upper Bazar — Ph. 7260813703, 7260813710
- **Sahibabad (U.P.):** B-9 & 10, Site IV, Industrial Area — Ph. 3100045, 2896939
- **Dehradun (Uttarakhand):** Plot No. 37, Bhagirathipuram, Niranjanpur, GMS Road — Ph. 2520360, 2107214

DELHI LOCAL OFFICES

- **Delhi (Shakarpur) :** MB 161, Street No. 4 — Ph. 22546557, 22518122
- **Delhi (Daryaganj):** MBD House, 4587/15, Opp. Times of India — Ph. 23245676
- **Delhi (Patparganj):** Plot No. 225, Industrial Area — Ph. 22149691, 22147073

ON THE SAME LINE FOR CLASS IX

- **Modern's** abc + of Chemistry
- **Modern's** abc + of Physics
- **Modern's** abc + of Biology
- **Modern's** abc + of Mathematics

We are committed to serve students with best of our knowledge and resources. We have taken utmost care and paid much attention while editing and printing this book but we would beg to state that Authors and Publishers should not be held responsible for unintentional mistakes that might have crept in. However, errors brought to our notice shall be gratefully acknowledged and attended to.

Published by : **MANIK JUNEJA**
MODERN PUBLISHERS
MBD House, Railway Road, Jalandhar

Printed at : **TECHNOVA PRINTERS**
C-57-58, Focal Point Extension, Jalandhar

D0303A3576

E info@mbdgroup.com
W www.mbdgroup.com
Toll Free No. : 1800 572 2233

Preface

We feel pleasure in bringing out our multicolour book **"Modern's abc + of Science (Chemistry)"** for class IX students. The book has been prepared according to the syllabus and the scheme of C.B.S.E.

Salient Features of the Book–

- Text matter has been presented in a simple language and interesting style and in tune with the N.C.E.R.T. textbook.
- The text has been supplemented with a large number of neatly well-labelled diagrams.
- The topics are supported by important notes, facts to know, do you know, key point that strengthen the fundamental concepts to young scholars.
- Assignments are provided in each chapter in the light of new pattern i.e., Practice Exercises and Activities.
- Assignments in each chapters provide specially designed questions (solved as well as unsolved) for covering all types of questions; very short answer type, short answer type, long answer type and multiple choice questions.
- **NCERT FILE** at the end of each chapter provides solutions to In-Text Questions, Exercise Questions and Exemplar Problems.
- A number of Higher Order Thinking Skills (**HOTS**) questions with answers are given at the end of each chapter.
- Multiple Choice Questions (**MCQs**) for competitive examinations are given in Revision Exercise.
- Latest **NTSE-SAT** Questions are given at the end of each chapter.

We hope that the book will be warmly received by the teachers and the students. Suggestions for further improvements of the book will be gratefully acknowledged.

Dr. S. P. Jauhar
R. Jauhar

SYLLABUS

Science-IX

Marks : 80

Unit No.	Units	Marks
I.	Matter – Its Nature and Behaviour	23
II.	Organisation in the Living World	20
III.	Motion, Force and Work	27
IV.	Our Environment	06
V.	Food; Food Production	04
	Total	80
	Internal assessment	20
	Grand Total	100

THEME : MATERIALS

Unit I : Matter-Nature and Behaviour (50 Periods)

Definition of matter: Solid, liquid and gas; characteristics - shape, volume, density; change of state-melting (absorption of heat), freezing, evaporation (cooling by evaporation), condensation, sublimation.

Nature of matter: Elements, compounds and mixtures. Heterogenous and homogenous mixtures, colloids and suspensions.

Particle nature, basic units: Atoms and molecules, Law of constant proportions, Atomic and molecular masses, Mole concept: Relationship of mole to mass of the particles and numbers.

Structure of atom: Electrons, protons and neutrons, valency, chemical formula of common compounds, Isotopes and isobars.

THEME : THE WORLD OF THE LIVING

Unit II : Organization in the Living World (45 Periods)

Cell - Basic Unit of life: Cell as a basic unit of life; prokaryotic and eukaryotic cells, multicellular organisms; cell membrane and cell wall, cell organelles and cell inclusions; chloroplast, mitochondria, vacuoles, endoplasmic reticulum, Golgi apparatus; nucleus, chromosomes - basic structure, number.

Tissues, Organs, Organ System, Organism: Structure and functions of animal and plant tissues (only four types of tissues in animals; Meristematic and Permanent tissues in plants).

Biological Diversity: Diversity of plants and animals – basic issues in scientific naming, basis of classification. Hierarchy of categories / groups, major groups of plants (salient features) (Bacteria, Thallophyta, Bryophyta, Pteridophyta, Gymnosperms and Angiosperms). Major groups of animals (salient features) (Non-chordates upto phyla and chordates upto classes).

Health and Diseases: Health and its failure. Infectious and non-infectious diseases, their causes and manifestation. Diseases caused by microbes (virus, bacteria and protozoans) and their prevention, Principles of treatment and prevention. Pulse polio programmes.

THEME : MOVING THINGS, PEOPLE AND IDEAS

Unit III: Motion, Force and Work (60 Periods)

Motion: Distance and displacement, velocity; uniform and non-uniform motion along a straight line; acceleration, distance-time and velocity-time graphs for uniform motion and uniformly accelerated motion, derivation of equations of motion by graphical method; elementary idea of uniform circular motion.

Force and Newton's laws: Force and Motion, Newton's Laws of Motion, Action and reaction forces, Inertia of a body, Inertia and mass, Momentum, Force and Acceleration. Elementary idea of conservation of Momentum.

Gravitation: Gravitation; Universal Law of Gravitation, Force of Gravitation of the earth (gravity), Acceleration due to Gravity; Mass and Weight; Free fall.

Floatation: Thrust and Pressure. Archimedes' principle; Buoyancy; Elementary idea of Relative Density.

Work, energy and power: Work done by a force, Energy, Power; Kinetic and potential energy; Law of conservation of energy.

Sound: Nature of sound and its propagation in various media, speed of sound, range of hearing in humans; Ultrasound; Reflection of sound; Echo and SONAR. Structure of the Human Ear (Auditory aspect only).

THEME : NATURAL RESOURCES: BALANCE IN NATURE

Unit IV: Our Environment (15 Periods)

Physical resources: Air, Water, Soil. Air for respiration, for combustion, for moderating temperatures, movements of air and its role in bringing rains across in India.

Air, water and soil pollution (brief introduction). Holes in ozone layer and the probable damages.

Bio-geochemical cycles in nature : Water, Oxygen, Carbon and Nitrogen.

THEME : FOOD

Unit V: Food Production (10 Periods)

Plant and animal breeding and selection for quality improvement and management; Use of fertilizers and manures; Protection from pests and diseases; Organic farming.

CONTENTS

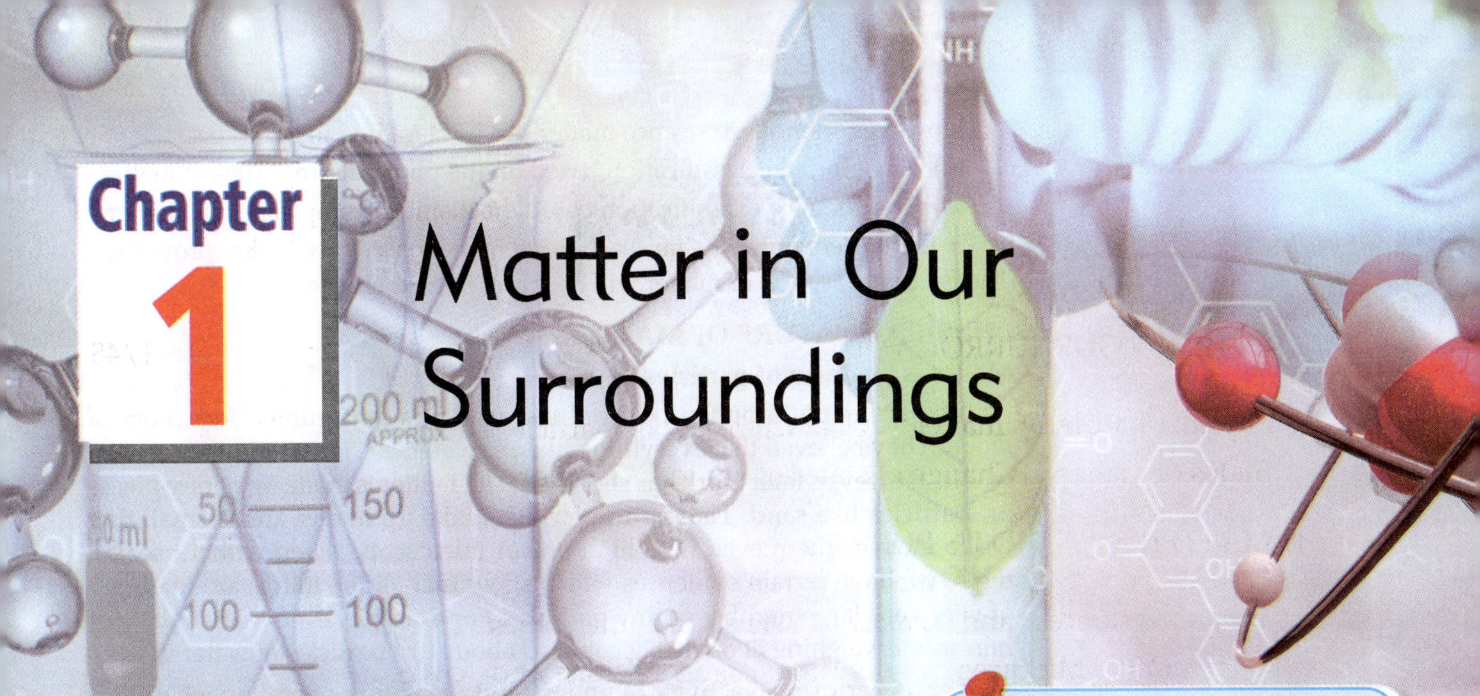

Chapter 1 Matter in Our Surroundings

As we look around our surroundings, we see a large variety of objects around us. The nature and behaviour of different types of substances around us are different. These substances differ in their shapes, sizes, colours, smells, textures etc. It is possible that two substances may have similar appearance but still they may be different. For example, sodium chloride (common salt) and powdered sugar on our dining table are white solids and have almost similar appearances, but both are different substances. As we all know, they have many different properties.

Do you ever thought that all the things around us are alike in one way. They all are made up of material to which the scientists have given the name **matter**. All the things around us; the air we breathe, the food we eat, the clouds, the stars, the plants and animals, the stone, sand, the everyday substances that we use like wood, salt, paper, steel, ice, water, etc. are matter. They all have mass and occupy space.

Anything that occupies space and has mass is called ***matter.***

Thus, we can say that all the objects around us are composed of matter. For example, a book occupies some space. If you pick up the book, you can feel its weight. Similarly, air, water, a cube of sugar, iron rod, have mass and occupy space.

Thus, to understand the world around you, it is *essential to know about matter.*

Since the early times, the human beings have been trying to understand their surroundings. The Greek and Indian philosophers and scientists have been trying to analyse and classify the matter. The early Greek philosophers suggested that there are **four basic elements :** fire, water, air and earth which constituted all materials.

Interestingly, almost same concept was developed by Indian philosophers. According to Indian philosophers, all matter (*padarth*), living or non-living, is made up of **five basic elements** called "*the panch tatva*". These are *sky, air, fire, water* and *earth*. According to them, everything living or non-living is made up of these five basic elements.

In this chapter

However, in modern science matter can be classified in two types:

(*i*) The physical classification based on the physical properties of matter.

(*ii*) The chemical classification based on chemical composition of matter.

In the present unit, we shall learn about matter based on physical properties. The chemical aspects of matter will be learnt in next chapters.

PHYSICAL NATURE OF MATTER

Matter is made up of particles

The earlier philosophers believed that **matter is continuous** like a block of wood. They believed that everything like air, water, etc. is a single element as a whole. However, later work has shown that all matter is made up of tiny pieces or particles like sand. The particles which make up matter are so small that we cannot see them even with high power microscope. Even without seeing them, we have certain evidences which show that all the things are made up of very very large number of tiny particles. For example, even a small drop of rain water weighing about 0.05g contains about 10^{21} particles of water in it.

Let us perform an activity to understand the nature of matter; whether it is continuous or particulate (discontinuous).

Activity 1

To demonstrate that matter is made up of particles

1. Take a 100 mL beaker.
2. Fill the beaker up to half with water and mark the water level.
3. Dissolve a small amount of sugar (or common salt) with the help of a glass rod.
4. Observe the change in water level and note your observation.

Now answer the following questions :

(*a*) What do you think has happened to sugar (or salt)?

(*b*) Where does it disappear?

(*c*) Does the level of water change?

We observe that the sugar (or common salt) has completely dissolved in water. Therefore, we are not able to see it. It must have spread completely in between water. This gives us the idea that matter must be made up of particles. The particles of sugar (or common salt) have spread throughout water. As we know, we can not spread the block of wood but we can easily spread saw dust obtained from the same block.

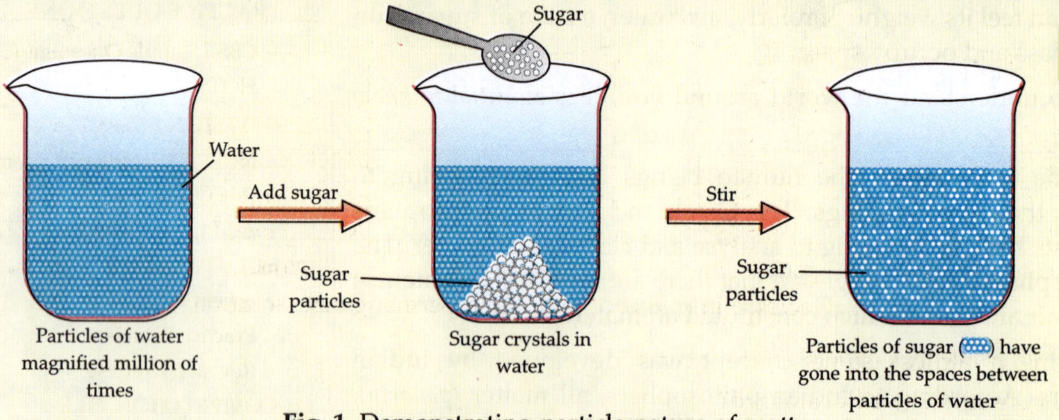

Fig. 1. Demonstrating particle nature of matter.

Thus, we can say that sugar (or common salt) is a collection of a large number of particles. When we dissolve sugar (or salt) in water, its particles get into the spaces between particles of water. Both the sugar crystals and water are made up of particles. The particles of sugar leave the crystal and mix with the particles of water.

The spreading of particles of coloured crystal can be easily seen by repeating the activity with a crystal of potassium permanganate. Potassium permanganate is purple coloured solid substance and water is colourless liquid. When we dissolve a crystal of potassium permanganate in water in a beaker, it is observed that water slowly turns purple on its own. The purple colour starts spreading through the water. This is because the particles of potassium permanganate go into the spaces between the particles of water.

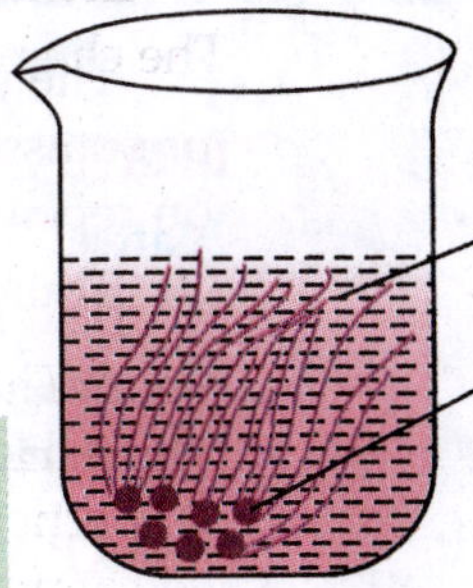

Fig. 2. Spreading of particles.

Thus, we can say that matter is particulate in nature *i.e.,* made up of particles. So, we can say that

everything around us is made up of particles.
Our body is made up of particles. So are our desks, our chairs, our books, our pens and all other things.

How small are the particles of matter?

The next question which comes to mind is "how small are the particles of matter?" This can be understood by the following activity :

Activity 2

To demonstrate that the particles of matter are very small

1. Take a 100 mL of water in a beaker. Add 2–3 crystals of potassium permanganate in it and stir to dissolve. The solution will become dark pink colour.
2. Take out about 10 mL of this solution and put it into 90 mL of clear water in another beaker the total volume up to 100 mL.
   Place your two solutions side by side on the table.
3. Now take 10 mL of the solution prepared in step 2 and put it into another 90 mL of clear water in another beaker.
4. Keep diluting the solution like this about 5 to 8 times.

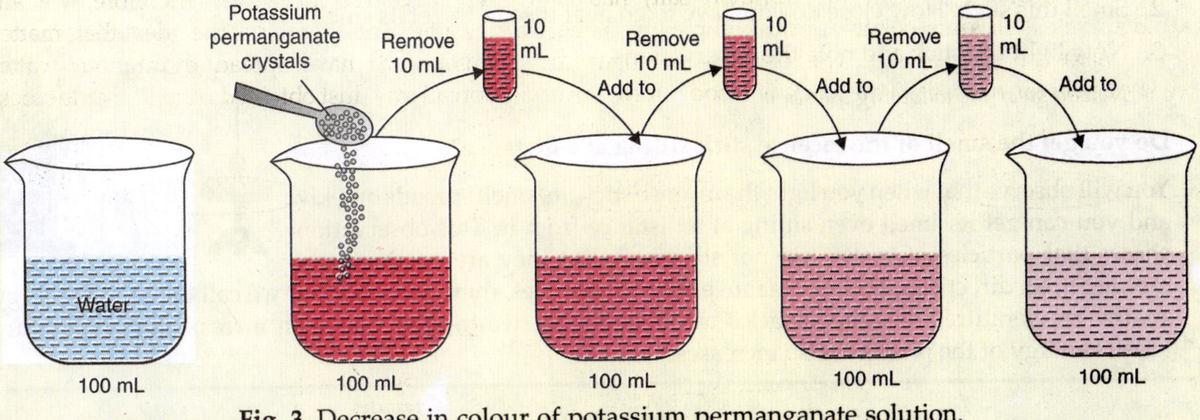

Fig. 3. Decrease in colour of potassium permanganate solution.

Now answer the following questions

(*a*) Is the solution still coloured?

(*b*) How many times you can dilute the solution so that you don't see the pink colour in the solution?

(*c*) What does this tell us about the particles in the crystal?

This experiment shows that a few crystals of potassium permanganate can colour a large volume of water as large as about 1000 L.

➡ We may conclude that there must be million and million of tiny particles in just one crystal of potassium permanganate which keep on dividing themselves into smaller and smaller particles. Ultimately, a stage may reach when these particle can not be divided further into smaller particles.

The same activity may be repeated by using about 2mL of Dettol instead of potassium permanganate. It is observed that the smell can be detected even on repeated dilution.

Thus, we may conclude that

the particles of matter are very small; they are small beyond our imagination.

CHARACTERISTICS OF PARTICLES OF MATTER

1. Particles of matter have spaces between them

The activities 1 and 2 show that particles of sugar, salt, potassium permanganate or Dettol get evenly distributed in water. Similarly, when we prepare tea, coffee or lemonade (*nimbu pani*) we observe that particles of one type of matter get into the spaces between particles of the other.

This show that there is large space between particles of matter.

2. Particles of matter are continuously moving

The particles of matter are continuously moving in all directions. Sometimes, when a beam of sunlight enters a dark room through a small hole, we can see tiny dust particles suspended in air which are moving in a haphazard way. The movement of particles can be understood by the following activity :

Activity 3

❑ **To demonstrate that particles of matter are continuously moving**

1. Take an incense stick (*agarbatti*) and place it in a corner of your classroom.
2. Smell this stick. How close do you have to go near it so as to get its smell ?
3. Now light the stick and note the observations.

Now answer the following question :

? **Do you get the smell of the incense stick sitting at a distance?**

You will observe that when you light the incense stick, its smell spreads quickly and you can get its smell even sitting at a distance from it. This observation shows that particles of matter are not stationary but they are continuously moving in all directions. Due to the movement of particles, they possess what we call the kinetic energy. As the temperature rises, the particles move faster. So, we can say that with increase in temperature, kinetic energy of the particles also increases.

Intermixing of particles : Diffusion

The particles of perfume in the incense stick mix with the particles of air around us and spread out. Due to spreading of particles, the smell of the perfume goes all over the room. Therefore, we can get its smell even sitting at a distance from it.

The intermixing of particles of two substances on their own is called ***diffusion.***

Leakage of cooking gas in our homes is detected due to diffusion of a strong smelling substance that is mixed with the liquefied petroleum gas (LPG). Similarly, if a bottle of ammonia is opened in one corner of the laboratory, its small can be felt in other corner of the laboratory after sometime.

It may be noted that on heating the rate of diffusion increases. This is the reason that when incense stick is lighted we get its smell even sitting at a distance from it.

Let us learn more about diffusion by performing the following activitiy :

Activity 4

To demonstrate that diffusion of different substances is different

1. Take two beakers filled with water.
2. Put a drop of blue (or red) ink slowly and carefully along the sides of first beaker and honey in the second beaker.
3. Leave the beakers undisturbed in a corner in the class.
4. Record your observations.

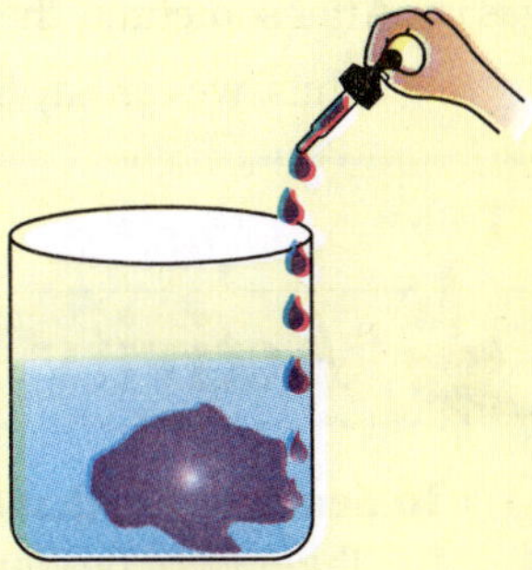

Now, answer the following questions :

(*a*) What do you observe immediately after adding the ink drop?

(*b*) What do you observe immediately after adding a drop of honey?

(*c*) How many hours or days does it take for colour of ink to spread evenly.

(*d*) How does diffusion vary with density of liquid?

You would observe that the ink spreads earlier than honey.

➡ The diffusion of honey is less than that of ink because honey has more density.

DO YOU KNOW?

The purity of honey can be checked by putting a drop of honey in water. If honey falls in the form of a streak, it is considered to be pure.

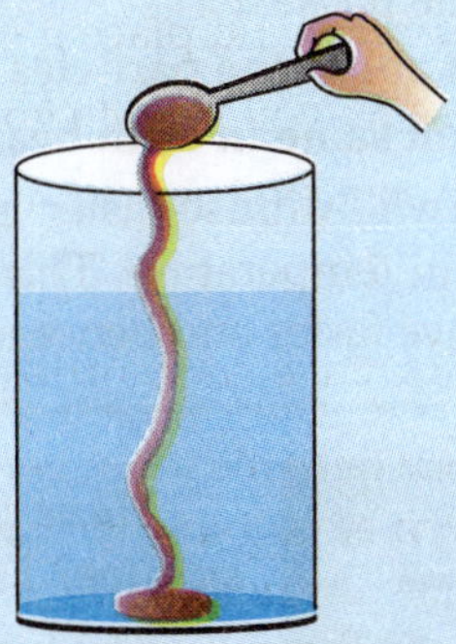

Gases have strong tendency to intermix or diffuse. When two gases are brought in contact, the particles of one gas go in between the empty spaces of the other gas. This can be shown by the following activity:

Activity 5

To demonstrate the diffusion of gases

1. Take a gas jar containing bromine vapour. Its colour is brown red.
2. Place a jar containing air (colourless) upside down on the jar containing bromine vapour.

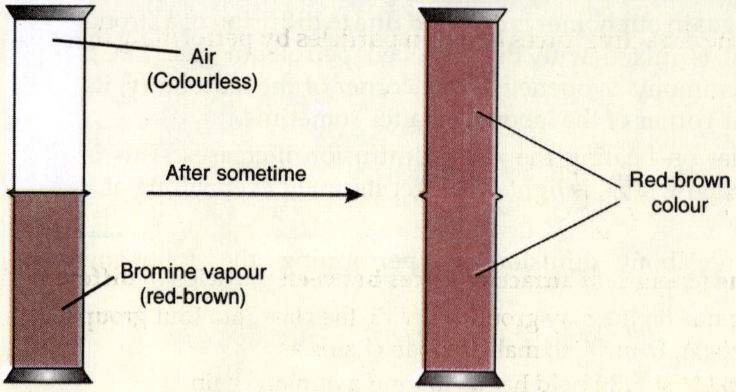

Fig. 4

What do you observe after sometime?

You would observe that red-brown vapour of bromine from the lower gas jar spread into the air in the upper gas jar. After sometime, the gas jar containing air also becomes completely red brown in colour.

Thus, we can say that gases have strong tendency to diffuse.

Activity 6

To demonstrate that the rate of intermixing increases with increase in temperature

1. Take two beakers. Put hot water in one beaker (Label A) and cold water in another beaker (Label B).
2. Drop a crystal of copper sulphate (or potassium permanganate) into a beaker of hot water (beaker A) and a beaker of cold water (beaker B).
3. Record the observations.

Now answer the following questions :

(*a*) What do you observe immediately above the solid crystal in the two beakers?

(*b*) What happens as time passes?

(*c*) What does it suggest about the particles of solids and liquids?

(*d*) Is the rate of diffusion same in both beakers. Why and how?

You will observe that solid will diffuse faster in hot water than in cold water. This suggests that rate of diffusion increases with increase in temperature. This is because the particles at higher temperature have large kinetic energy. Therefore, they move faster and hence intermix or diffuse quickly.

DO YOU KNOW?

Have you ever thought how do aquatic plants and animals survive? From where do they get oxygen for their lives?

The aquatic plants and animals survive because the gases from the atmosphere diffuse and dissolve in water. These gases mainly contain carbon dioxide and oxygen. These are taken by the animals and plants for their survival.

Thus, we conclude that solids, liquids and gases all diffuse into liquids. Due to presence of larger intermolecular spaces and higher kinetic energy of the particles of liquids as compared to solids,

the ***rate of diffusion in liquids is higher than in solids.***

3. Particles of matter attract each other

The particles of matter attract each other. There are some forces of attraction between the particles of matter which bind them together.

Let us learn about the attractive forces between particles by performing the following activity:

Activity 7

To demonstrate the strength of attractive forces between particles of different kinds of matter

1. Let us play a game on the play ground. Divide the class into four groups A, B, C and D of students. Ask the three groups A, B and C to make human chains as :
1. The first group (A) should hold hands to form a human chain.

2. The second group (B) should hold each other from the back and lock arms (like Bihu dancers : a folk dance of Assam).
3. The third group (C) should from a chain by touching each other only with their finger tips.
4. Ask the fourth group (D) students run around each human chain and try to break these human chains one by one into as many small groups as possible.

What do you observe ?

Which group was easiest to break and why ?

We observe that the human chain formed by students of group C is easiest to break because they cannot hold each other strongly. Now if we consider each student as a particle of matter than we can say that particles in group C are held together with weakest force.

Thus, the particles of matter are held together by the forces of attraction between the particles. These forces keep the particles together. However, the strength of these forces of attraction are different for different kinds of matter. Let us perform the following activity :

Activity 8

To demonstrate the strength of attractive forces between the particles of different kinds of matter

1. Take an iron nail, a piece of chalk and a rubber band.
2. Try to break each of these by hammering, cutting or stretching.

What do you observe?

We observe that it is very difficult to break an iron nail while it is very easy to break a piece of chalk. This suggests that the particles of an iron nail are held together by stronger force while the particles of a chalk piece are held by a weaker force. These activities suggest that particles of matter have forces acting between them. These forces keep the particles together. The strength of these forces of attraction depend upon the kind of matter. These forces are also called **interparticle forces or intermolecular forces of attraction.** We also observe that when we try to break, the stream of water from a tap with our fingers, it is not cut completely. The stream of water remains together suggesting forces of attraction between the particles of water.

STATES OF MATTER

If we observe matter around us, we can see that different substances in the universe can be classified into three states namely, solid, liquid and gas.

These three states may simply be classified as :

(*a*) **Solid state.** *A solid possesses a fixed volume and a definite shape.* Thus, solids are generally hard and rigid. Some common examples of solids are : wood, stone, common salt, sugar, iron, copper etc.

(*b*) **Liquid state.** *A liquid possesses a fixed volume but not definite shape.* A liquid takes up the shape of the container in which it is placed. Moreover, liquids also have a tendency to flow. Therefore, these are also called **fluids.** Common examples of liquids are : water, milk, oil, alcohol, etc.

(*c*) **Gaseous state.** *A gas neither possesses a fixed volume nor a definite shape.* A gas occupies the whole of the volume of the vessel in which it is placed. It also takes up the shape of the container. Common examples of gases are : air, oxygen, hydrogen, carbon dioxide, etc.

Fig. 5

Let us learn about the properties of these three states of matter.

1. THE SOLID STATE

The solid state is characterized by having definite shape, distinct boundaries and fixed volumes. These have rigidity and incompressibility. The solids are rigid and, therefore, they maintain their own shape when subjected to outside force. On applying force, the solids may break but it is difficult to change their shape. The pen in our hand is solid. It is rigid. However, it may break when dropped or hammered.

CURIOUS QUESTIONS ABOUT SOLIDS

1. Rubber band can change its shape when stretched. Is it a solid?
2. Sugar and salt when kept in different jars (or containers) take their shapes. Are they solids?

Rubber band, sugar and salt are solids.

- A rubber band changes its shape only under a force and regains its shape when the force is removed. However, if excessive force is applied, it breaks.
- Sugar and salt are solids because the shape of each individual crystal of sugar or salt remains fixed, whether we take it on our hand or put it on a plate or in a jar.

Let Us Learn Some More About Solids.

Properties of Solids

(*i*) Solids have fixed shapes

The solids have fixed shape and distinct boundaries because of strong forces of attraction between the particles which hold them together in fixed positions. The particles of a solid only vibrate about their fixed positions. They cannot move from one position to another. Therefore, the solids have fixed shapes. They donot change their shapes even when put in different containers.

(ii) Solids have fixed volume

All solids occupy a fixed volume. The space occupied by a substance is called volume.

(iii) Solids have higher densities

Many solids are dense. This suggests that the particles in solid state are tightly packed into a small volume (space). This is also expressed in terms of ***density.***

The mass per unit volume of a substance is called ***density.***

Since the particles in the solid state are tightly packed into a small volume, we say that ***solids have higher density as compared to other states of matter.***

(iv) Solids have strong intermolecular forces

The particles of matter exert attractive forces upon one another. These forces are called ***intermolecular forces*** or ***interparticle forces.*** These are attractive forces and depend upon the nature of the particles. The stronger the forces of attraction, closer the particles are. When the intermolecular forces are very strong, the particles are packed close together and matter takes the solid form.

(v) Compressibility

Due to strong forces of attraction between the particles of solid, the particles are tightly held in place. Therefore, they have fixed positions. The space between the particles of matter is called ***intermolecular space.*** In solid, the particles are very closely packed so the intermolecular space in solid is very less. Therefore, the solids are hard and cannot be compressed much.

DO YOU KNOW?

You must be knowing about a sponge. It is a solid but we can compress it easily. Why?

The sponge can be compressed easily because it has minute holes in which air is trapped. When we press it, the trapped air is expelled out and, therefore, we can easily compress it.

(vi) Rigidity

The particles of matter are constantly moving. ***The energy possessed by a particle due to its motion*** is called ***kinetic energy.*** The particles of solids are closely packed and the empty spaces between the particles are very small. Due to close packing of the particles, they can only vibrate about their fixed positions *i.e.* can have only ***vibratory motion.*** As a result, the kinetic energy of the particles in the solid state is very less. This is the reason that solids have fixed or rigid shape.

(vii) Diffusion

Since the particles of solids donot move much so solids donot have the property of diffusion into other solids. However, there are some rare examples where we observe some diffusion of solid into solid. For example, it becomes hard to clean a blackboard on which something has been written with chalk and left without cleaning for a long time (about 15–20 days). This may be due to diffusion of chalk (solid) into blackboard (solid). Similarly, it is observed that when two metal blocks are tightly bound together and left undisturbed for a few years, particles of one metal may diffuse into the other.

However, it may be noted that there are rare examples where you can see diffusion of solid into solid. The particles in solid state donot move much from their normal position. So solids, in general, donot have the property of diffusion into other solids.

Let us perform the following activity :

Activity 9

- **To understand the properties of solids**
  1. Collect the following articles:

     a pen, a book, a needle and a piece of thread.
  2. Sketch the shape of these articles in your note book by moving a pencil around them.

     (*a*) Do all these articles have a definite shape, distinct boundaries and a fixed volume?

     (*b*) What happens if these articles are hammered, pulled or dropped?

     (*c*) Are these capable of diffusing into each other.

     (*d*) Try compressing them by applying force. Are you able to compress these?

➡ We will observe that all the above articles are solids because these have definite shape, fixed boundaries and fixed volume. These are rigids and cannot be compressed. These donot have any tendency to diffuse into each other.

2. THE LIQUID STATE

The liquid state is characterized as ***having fixed volume*** but ***no definite shape*** or ***boundaries.*** Moreover, the liquids also have a tendency to flow. Therefore, these are also called ***fluids.*** If a glass of water is spilled on floor, it will change shape and form a layer on the floor. However, it may be noted that the particles of a liquid flow (or move) but attractive forces between them are weak. However, they are not weak enough to allow the particles to separate from one another. Thus, the liquids have definite volume. For example, if we take 1L milk, its volume remains 1L whether it is put in a jug, a glass or a bottle though its shape may change.

Let Us Learn Some More About Liquids.

Properties of Liquids

(i) Shape

Liquids donot have fixed shape. They take the shape of the container in which they are put. For example, if we put same amount of water in different types of containers such as beaker, glass tumbler, conical flask or flat bottomed flask, one by one, it is observed that water takes the shape of the container.

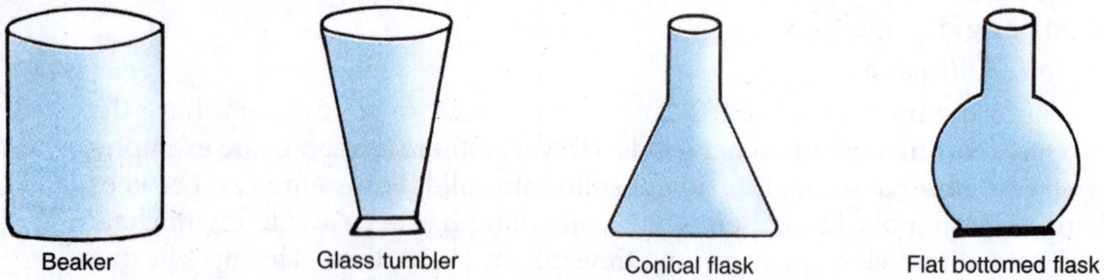

Fig. 6. Water (or a liquid) takes the shape of the container.

Thus we can say that a *liquid does not have a fixed shape.* It takes the shape of the container.

(ii) Fluidity

Liquids flow and they are not rigid. They are called fluids because they can easily flow and change their shape in response to outside forces.

(iii) Density

Liquids generally have lower density than solids. This is because the particles in the liquids are not closely packed as in case of solids. However, it may be noted that ice floats over water. This means that ice has unexpectedly lower density than water.

(iv) Solids have strong intermolecular forces

In liquids, the particles are loosely packed and the empty spaces between them are relatively large. Due to loose packing, attractive forces between them are weaker than in solids. The distance between the particles (intermolecular spaces) in liquids are more as compared to that of solids. Therefore, the *liquids are more compressible than solids.*

(v) Diffusion

Due to larger interparticle distances in liquids than in solids, the particles in liquid state move more freely and, therefore, have higher kinetic energy than the solids. However, their kinetic energy is less than that of gases. Being fluids, the liquids show the property of intermixing and therefore have diffusion properties.

Activity 10

To understand that liquids have definite volume but no definite shape

1. Collect the following :
   (*i*) Water, cooking oil, milk, juice and a cold drink.
   (*ii*) Containers of different shapes.
2. Put a 50mL mark on these containers using a measuring cylinder from the laboratory.
3. Make the following observations and record :

(*a*) What will happen if these liquids are spilled on the floor ?

(*b*) Measure 50 mL of any one liquid and transfer it into different containers one by one. Note the volume.

(*c*) Does the shape of the liquid remain the same ?

(*d*) When you pour the liquid from one container into another, does it flow easily ?

We will observe that all these liquids flow when spilled on the floor. Volume of the liquid remains same i.e., 50mL when it is transferred from one container to the other. We will observe that the shape of the liquid is not fixed and it takes the shape of the container in which it is put. When the liquid is poured from one container to another, it flows.

➡ All these observations show that liquids do not have definite shape but have definite volume. These easily flow.

3. THE GASEOUS STATE

The gaseous state is characterized by ***no definite volume and no definite shape***. They also have ***fluidity*** and high ***compressibility.***

In gases, the particles are very loosely packed and the intermolecular spaces between them are very large. The attractive forces between the particles are negligibly small. The particles can move at random in all the directions with high velocities. Thus, gases have neither definite shape nor definite volume. Since the molecules of a gas are free to move anywhere, it takes the shape and volume of its container.

You must have seen a balloon seller filling a large number of balloons from a single cylinder of gas. The gases have almost negligible density as compared to solids and liquids.

Let us learn more about gases.

(*i*) ***Compressibility***

We have learnt that gases have very weak intermolecular forces between the particles and the distance between the particles is very large as compared to the solids and liquids. Therefore, the gases are highly compressible as compared to solids and liquids.

Let us perform the following activity.

Activity 11

To understand the compressibility of solids, liquids and gases

1. Take three 100 mL syringes and close their nozzles by inserting them in a rubber cork as shown in Fig. 7. Remove the pistons from all the syringes.
2. Fill chalk pieces in the first syringe, water in the second syringe and leave third syringe as such. It already contains air.
3. Insert the pistons back into the syringes. You may apply a little vaseline on the pistons before inserting them into the syringes for their smooth movement.
4. Now try to compress all the syringes by pushing the pistons.

(*a*) **What do you observe?**

(*b*) **In which case has the piston easily pushed in?**

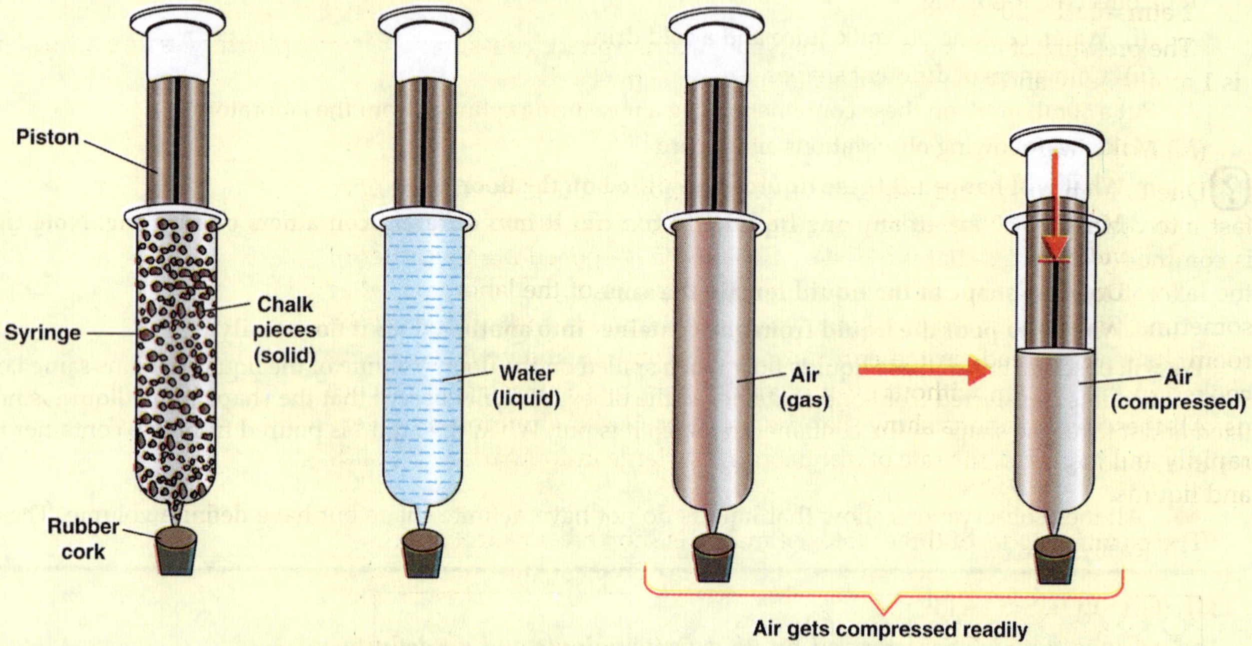

Fig. 7. Experiment to study the compressibility of solid, liquid and gas.

You can easily note the difference between the behaviour of a solid, a liquid and a gas.

You will observe that when the syringe containing air (third syringe) is compressed by applying pressure, the piston can move downward easily and it can be compressed to a larger extent. On the other hand, when the syringe containing water (second syringe) is compressed, it is compressed not easily and it can be compressed to much lesser extent than that of air. The first syringe containing chalk pieces (solid) is compressed with most difficulty.

This shows that ***gases are more compressible than liquids.*** Due to the compressibility of the gases, we can fill more and more air into a tyre which increases only slightly in volume. In fact, a given quantity of a gas can fill a container of any size. At the same time, a large quantity of gas can be compressed to fill any small space. For example, the liquefied petroleum gas (LPG) cylinder that we use at home for cooking purposes or the oxygen supplied to hospitals in the cylinders is compressed gas. The natural gas is compressed and is supplied as a fuel for vehicles in the name of CNG (Compressed Natural Gas). However, liquids are relatively incompressible.

(ii) ***Gas pressure***

The kinetic energy of the particles in the gaseous state is very large. It is maximum among the three states of matter. As a result, the molecules in the gaseous state are free to move randomly at high speeds. Due to their random movement, the particles collide with each other and also with the walls of the container. The constant bombardment of the molecules on the walls of the container exert as steady force and this results into the ***pressure of the gas.*** **The pressure is measured as the force exerted by the gas molecules per unit area on the walls of the container.**

The pressure of a gas is expressed in terms of unit atmosphere (atm) or cm of Hg or mm of Hg. These are related as :

1 atm = 76 cm of Hg = 760 mm of Hg

The another unit of pressure is pascal (Pa). It is related to atm as :

1 atm = 1.01×10^5 Pa

The pressure of air in atmosphere is called atmospheric pressure. The atmospheric pressure at sea level is 1 atmosphere and is called normal atmospheric pressure.

(iii) ***Diffusion***

Due to high speed and large intermolecular forces, the gases diffuse very fast into other gases. Therefore, the rate of diffusion of gases is very high. It is commonly observed that if a bottle of ammonia is opened in one corner of the laboratory, its smell can be felt in the other corner of the laboratory after sometime. Similarly, if we put a few drops of perfume in some corner of the room, its smell spreads in the entire room. We come to know what is being cooked in the kitchen without even entering there by the smell that reaches us. All these observations show that the particles of gases can intermix very rapidly and therefore, the rate of diffusion is very large in comparison to solids and liquids.

The particle model of three states of matter is shown below in Fig. 8.

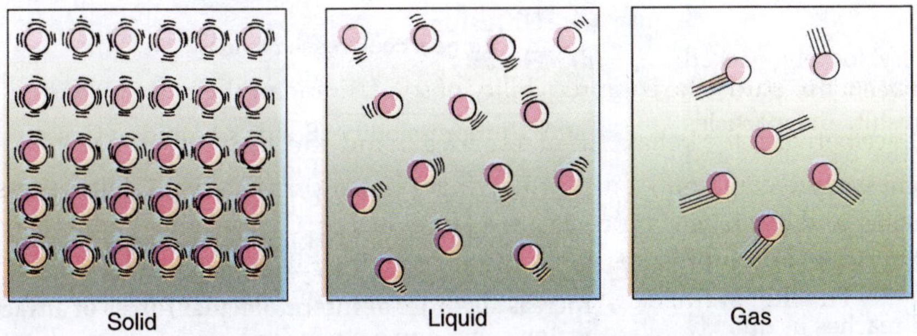

Fig. 8. Particle model of three states of matter.

The important characteristics of three states of matter are summarised below :

Table 1. Summary of characteristics of solids, liquids and gases.

Property	Solid	Liquid	Gas
1. Shape and volume	Solids have a fixed volume and a definite shape.	Liquids have a fixed volume but have no fixed shape. They take the shape of the container but they donot fill it.	Gases have neither a fixed shape nor a fixed volume. They take the shape and volume of the vessel. They fill the container.
2. Interparticle forces of attraction	The interparticle forces of attraction are strongest in solids.	Interparticle forces of attraction in liquids are weaker than those in solids but stronger than those in gases.	Interparticle forces of attraction are the weakest.
3. Compressibility	Solids are rigid and are not compressible.	Like solids, liquids cannot be compressed much.	Gases are easily compressible.
4. Density	Solids have high densities. They are heavy.	Liquids have moderate to high densities. They are generally less dense than solids.	Gases have very low densities. They are very light.
5. Fluidity	Solids donot flow.	Liquids generally flow easily.	Gases flow more easily.
6. Diffusion	Solids donot diffuse.	Liquids can diffuse more than solids.	Gases have strong tendency for diffusion.
7. Spreading	Solids stay where they are placed.	Liquids can be poured into another containers.	Gases spread out quickly.

Solved Examples

❑ **Example 1. Out of solids, liquids and gases, which one has :**

(a) minimum spaces between molecules?

(b) maximum intermolecular forces of attraction?

(c) maximum movement of molecules?

Solution :

(a) Solids

(b) Solids

(c) Gases

❑ **Example 2. Give reasons for the following :**

(a) A gas fills completely the vessel in which it is kept.

(b) We can get the smell of perfume sitting several meters away.

(c) The smell of hot sizzling food reaches you several meters away but to get the smell from cold food we have to go close.

Solution :

(a) In gases, the particles are very loosely packed and the attractive forces between the particles are negligibly small. As a result, the particles can move at random in all the directions and therefore can fill the vessel completely.

(b) This because the particles of the perfume have good tendency to intermix with particles of the air and reach to our nose.

(c) The smell of hot sizzling food reaches us quickly as compared to smell of cold food. This is because rate of diffusion increases with increase in temperature.

❑ **Example 3.**

(a) A spoonful of sugar is added to a beaker containing 500 mL of water and stirred for a while. State any two observations that you will make.

(b) Account for your observations.

(CBSE Sample Paper 2011)

Solution :

(a) Two observations are :

(i) Sugar dissolves in water

(ii) The volume of water does not increase.

(b) These observations are due to the fact that there is a lot of space between water molecules. The sugar molecules go into these spaces of water and therefore, dissolve in water or disappear.

❑ **Example 4. Arrange solids, liquids and gases in order of increasing:**

(a) Compressibility

(b) Density

(c) Diffusion

(d) Fluidity

Solution :

(a) Compressibility : Solids < Liquids < Gases

(b) Density : Gases < Liquids < Solids

(c) Diffusion : Solids < Liquids < Gases

(d) Fluidity : Solids < Liquids < Gases

❑ **Example 5. Arrange the following substances in the increasing order of intermolecular forces of attraction water, sugar and oxygen.**

Solution : The increasing order of intermolecular forces is

oxygen < water < sugar.

Practice Exercise 1A

Answers and Hints on Page 44

1. Which of the following are matter ?
   (*i*) book (*ii*) chair
   (*iii*) air (*iv*) love
   (*v*) smell of perfume (*vi*) almonds
   (*vii*) thought (*viii*) cold
   (*ix*) cold drink (*x*) hot coffee.
2. Name the three states of water.
3. Arrange the following substances in the increasing order of intermolecular forces of attraction :
   (*a*) Salt (*b*) Water
   (*c*) Carbon dioxide
4. Which of the following can be easily compressed? liquid water or steam
5. Which state of matter has neither definite shape nor volume?
6. Which of the two : liquid state or solid state is rigid?
7. Out of solid, liquid or gas, which state has
   (*a*) maximum spaces between molecules
   (*b*) maximum tendency for diffusion
   (*c*) minimum forces of attraction between molecules
   (*d*) minimum energy for molecules.
8. What is the physical state of water at
   (*a*) 0°C (*b*) 100°C
   (*c*) 50°C
9. Name the physical state of matter
   (*a*) which can be easily compressed
   (*b*) which is most rigid
   (*c*) which can flow but cannot fill the vessels completely.
10. Name the phase of matter in which the particles have the lowest density.
11. Which type of motion is associated with solids?
12. A rubber band changes its shape when stretched. Can it be regarded as solid? Say yes or no.
13. Arrange the following substances in the increasing order of forces of attraction between their particles :
    Water, ice, steam
14. Which of the two diffuses faster : a liquid or a gas?
15. Out of solid, liquid or gaseous state, which state has low molecular motion of its molecules?
16. Why are liquids called fluids ?
17. Give two reasons to justify:
    (*i*) Water at room temperature is liquid.
    (*ii*) An iron almirah is a solid at room temperature.
18. Explain why diffusion occurs more quickly in a gas than in a liquid?
19. Why does a gas exert pressure?
20. Write the correct choices
    (*a*) Gases have .... (more/less) intermolecular spaces than liquids.
    (*b*) Solids are .... (rigid/compressible).
    (*c*) Liquids have .... (more/less) interparticle forces of attraction than solids.
    (*d*) Gases have .... (larger/smaller) rate of diffusion than solids.
    (*e*) Liquids have .... (more/less) density than gases.

CHANGE OF STATES OF MATTER

A substance may exist in any of the three states of matter (*i.e.* solid, liquid or gas) depending upon the conditions of temperature and pressure. By changing the conditions of temperature and pressure, a substance can be made to exist as solid, liquid or a gas. A solid on heating usually changes into a liquid which on further heating changes into gas. Similarly, a gas on cooling condenses into a liquid which on further cooling changes into a solid. The most familiar and common example is water. It exists in all the three states :

- solid : ice
- liquid : water and
- gas : water vapour.

Ice is a solid state and may be melted to form water (liquid) which on further heating changes into steam (gas). These changes can also be reversed on cooling.

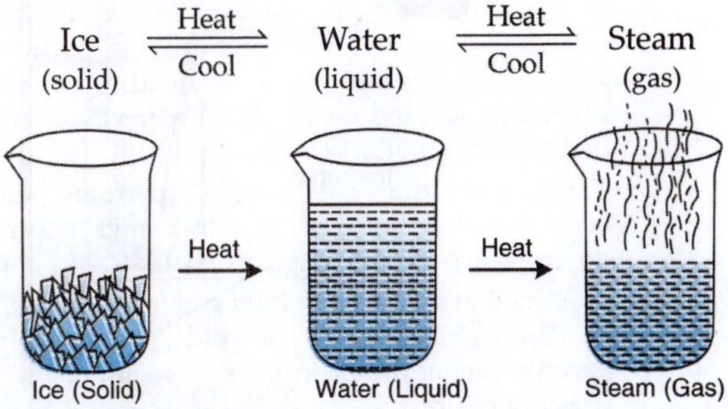

Fig. 9. Change in three states of matter.

Now many questions come to our mind :

1. **What happens during change of state inside the matter?**
2. **How does this change of state take place?**

To understand these questions let us learn about the effect of temperature and pressure on these states.

1. Effect of change of Temperature

Let us learn the effect of temperature on three states of matter by performing the following activity:

Activity 12

❑ To understand the change of state

1. Take a piece of about 100–150 g of ice in a beaker.
2. Hang a laboratory thermometer in it so that its bulb is in contact with ice.
3. Start heating the beaker slowly on a low flame.
4. Note down the temperature when ice starts changing to water.
5. Note the temperature when whole of the ice has been converted to water.
6. Record your observations for the conversion of solid ice into liquid water.
7. Now, place a glass rod in the beaker and slowly heat the beaker with constant stirring with the help of a glass rod.
8. Note the temperature when water starts changing into water vapour.
9. Keep a close look at the thermometer and note the temperature when most of water has vaporized.
10. Record your observations for the conversion of water in the liquid state to vapour state.

We observe that as temperature increases, the ice starts changing into water. This change is called melting. The temperature remains same till all the ice changes into water. The thermometer shows 0°C until all the ice has melted. On further heating, the temperature starts rising. At 373 K (or 100°C), water starts boiling. As the water continue boiling, the temperature remains almost constant.

Let us explain these results on the basis of particle nature of matter.

(*i*) Solid to Liquid

Ice is a solid. In solids, the particles are tightly packed together. When we heat a solid, its particles become more *energetic* and *kinetic energy of the particles increases.* Due to increase in kinetic energy, the particles start vibrating with greater speed. The energy supplied by heat overcomes the intermolecular forces of attraction between the particles. As a result, the particles leave their fixed positions and start moving more freely. Finally, a stage is reached when **the solid melts and converts into liquid.**

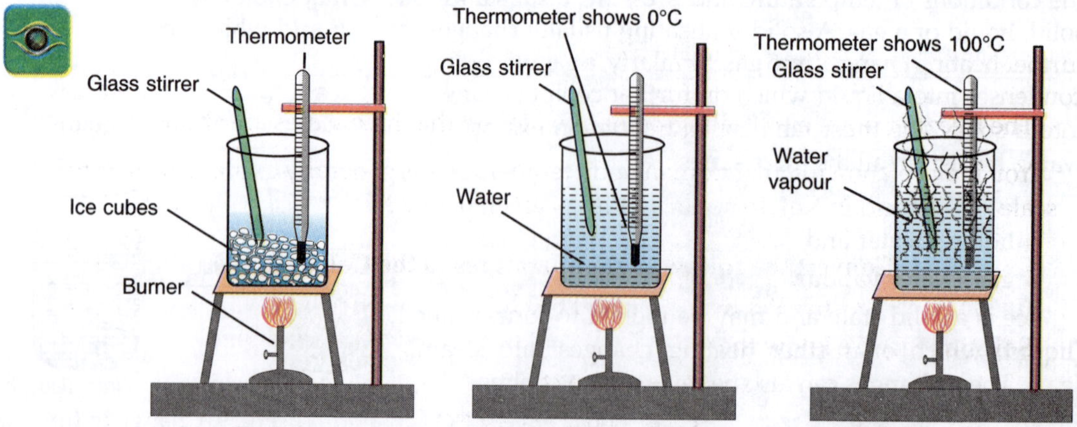

Fig. 10. Conversion of ice to water and water to water vapour

The temperature at which a solid melts to become a liquid at the atmospheric pressure is called its ***melting point.***

Therefore, the melting point of a liquid is an indication of the strength of the intermolecular forces of attraction. The melting point of ice is 0ºC. It may also be expressed as 273.16 K or simply as 273 K. The process of melting is also called fusion.

NOTE

SCALES OF MEASURING TEMPERATURE

We all know that temperature is measured with a thermometer. There are three scales for measuring the temperature. These are :

Celsius scale measuring in degree Celsius represented as °C.

Kelvin scale measuring in degree Kelvin represented as K.

Fahrenheit scale measuring in degree Fahrenheit represented as F.

Celsius scale. This is very common temperature scale. The thermometers with celsius scale are calibrated from 0° to 100°C where these two temperatures are the freezing point and boiling point of water respectively. The temperatures are expressed as 25°C, 50°C, 80°C, or 100°C.

Kelvin scale. This is the SI unit of temperature and is very common. The temperature on this scale is represented as 0K, 273K, 300K, etc.

It may be noted that **Kelvin temperature is written without a degree sign.**

On Kelvin scale, the freezing point of water is 273K and boiling point of water is 373K.

Conversions of Scales

To convert temperature on Celsius scale to Kelvin scale, add 273.16 to the given temperature. For simplicity 273.16 is rounded off to 273.

For example, $0°C = 0 + 273 = 273K$

$100°C = 100 + 273 = 373K$

Similarly, to convert temperature on Kelvin scale to Celsius scale, subtract 273 from the given temperature.

For example, $373\ K = 373 - 273 = 100°C$

In general

$$K = °C + 273$$

Thus,

Temperature in Kelvin = Temperature in °C + 273

Temperature in Celsius = Temperature in K – 273

The Fahrenheit scale is related to Celsius scale as

$$°F = \frac{9}{5}(°C) + 32°$$

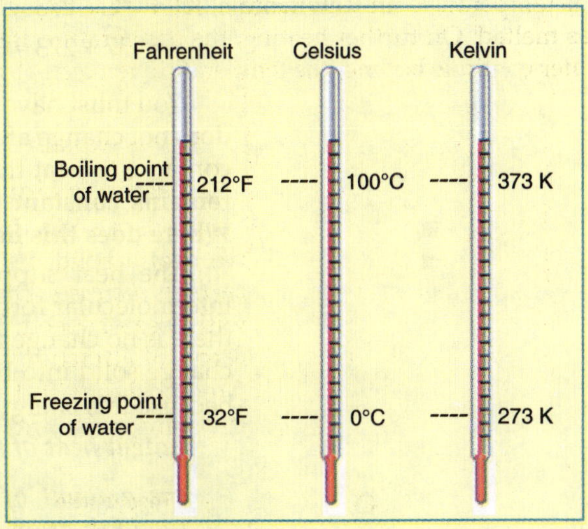

The freezing point and boiling point of water on the three scales are shown :

You may be knowing that human body temperature is generally expressed as 98.6°F. Its value in Celsius scale is 37°C and in Kelvin scale is 310K as given below :

Example 6. Convert the following temperatures to the Celsius scale :

(*i*) 300 K (*ii*) 353 K (*iii*) 800 K

Solution : (*i*) We know that

$$°C = K - 273$$

$$°C = 300 - 273 = 27°C$$

(*ii*) We know that

$$°C = K - 273$$
$$°C = 353 - 273 = 80°C$$

(*iii*)
$$°C = K - 273$$
$$\therefore \quad °C = 800 - 273 = 527°C$$

Example 7. The room temperature on Celsius scale is 25°C. Calculate its value in Kelvin scale.

Solution : We know that

$$K = °C + 273$$
$$K = 25 + 273 = 298 \text{ K}$$

Example 8. Liquid oxygen used in rocket engines boils at 92 K under normal atmospheric pressure. Express this temperature on Celsius scale.

Solution :

$$°C = K - 273$$
$$°C = 92 - 273 = -181°C$$

Example 9. The human body temperature is generally expressed in Fahrenheit scale as 98.6° F. Express its value in (*i*) Celsius scale and (*ii*) Kelvin scale.

Solution :

Temperature in Fahrenheit = 98.6°F

(*i*) We know that

$$°F = \frac{9}{5}(°C) + 32°$$
$$\frac{9}{5}(°C) = °F - 32$$
$$= 98.6 - 32 = 66.6°$$
$$\therefore \quad °C = \frac{66.6 \times 5}{9} = 37\ °C$$

In Kelvin scale, $K = °C + 273$
$$= 37 + 273 = 310 \text{ K}$$

You must have observed in Activity 12, that the temperature of the system does not change after melting point is achieved till all the ice melts, though we continue to heat the beaker. **Why does the temperature of the melting solid remains constant even though we continue heating (or supplying heat)? Where does this heat go?**

The heat supplied is used up in changing the state by breaking the intermolecular forces of attraction which hold them in solid state. As a result, there is no change in temperature till all the ice melts. This energy required to change solid into liquid is called **latent heat.** The word **latent** means **hidden** because this energy is hidden into the contents of the beaker.

Latent heat of fusion is defined as

the amount of heat energy required to change 1 kg of a solid into a liquid at atmospheric pressure without any change in temperature at its melting point.

Thus, the particles in water at 0°C (273 K) have more energy than the particles in ice at same temperature.

(*ii*) ***Liquid to gas***

In a liquid, most of the particles are close together. When we supply heat energy to the liquid, the particles of water start vibrating even faster. Some of the particles become so energetic that they can overcome the attractive forces of the particles around them. Therefore, they become free to move and escape from the liquid. When this happens, the liquid evaporates i.e., starts changing into gas.

The temperature at which a liquid changes into a gas or vapour at the atmospheric pressure** is called its **boiling point.

Boiling is a ***bulk phenomenon.*** In this process, the particles from the bulk of the liquid get enough energy to change into vapour state. For water, the boiling point is 100°C or 373 K. ***The particles in steam i.e., water vapour at 373 K have more energy than water at the same temperature.*** This is because the particles in steam have absorbed extra energy in the form of latent heat of vaporisation. Latent heat of vaporisation be defined as

the amount of heat energy that is required to change 1 kg of water into its vapour at atmospheric pressure without any change in temperature at its boiling point.

REMEMBER

- The heat energy required to change the state of a substance is called **latent heat.**
- Latent heat is of two types:
  - ➡ **Latent heat of fusion** (to convert solid into liquid state)
  - ➡ **Latent heat of vaporisation** (to convert liquid into vapour state)
- Latent heat of fusion of ice is 3.34×10^5 J/kg
- Latent heat of vaporisation of water is 2.25×10^6 J/kg

DO YOU KNOW?

Difference between a gas and a vapour?

The terms gas or vapour are the same. The word vapour is used to describe those gases which usually exist as liquid at room temperature. For example, water exists as liquid at room temperature. So when it is in the gaseous state it is called water vapour. On the other hand, oxygen or nitrogen exists as a **gas** at room temperature so we call it a **gas** and not vapour.

It is interesting to note that like melting, the temperature of a water or any other liquid remains constant once the liquid starts boiling even though it is still being heated. This is because the heat supplied is used up in changing the state from liquid water to water vapour by breaking the forces of attraction. As a result, there is no change in temperature till all the water evaporates.

The boiling point of a liquid also indicates the strength of intermolecular forces of attraction between particles. Volatile liquids such as alcohol, petrol and acetone have very weak intermolecular forces. Therefore, they boil at low temperatures. On the other hand, water has stronger intermolecular forces of attraction and therefore, it boils at higher temperature.

It may be noted that when steam is cooled, it condenses to water. When water is cooled, it changes to ice. So, the opposite changes may also be carried out by cooling as :

Steam —(Cool below 100°C / **Condensation**)→ **Condenses to water** —(Cool below 0°C / **Solidification**)→ **Frozen or solidifies to ICE**

Thus, we may write as :

Solid state ⇄ (Heat / Cool) **Liquid state** ⇄ (Heat / Cool) **Gaseous state**

The common example is

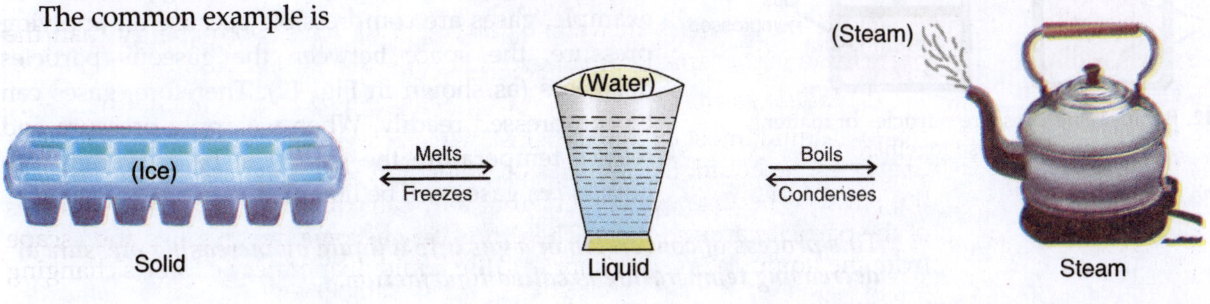

We have seen that

condensing (condensation) is opposite to evaporating (evaporation) and freezing (solidification) is opposite to melting.

Thus, we have observed that the state of matter can be changed into one another by changing the temperature.

We have seen that substances around us change state from solid to liquid and from liquid to gas by heating. But there are some substances which change directly from solid state to gaseous state and vice versa without changing into the liquid state.

To understand this, consider the following activity :

Activity 13

To understand the process of sublimation

1. Take some camphor or ammonium chloride.
2. Powder it and put in a china dish.
3. Place an inverted funnel over the china dish as shown in Fig. 11.
4. Heat the china dish slowly.

Now answer the following questions.

(a) What do you observe?

(b) What do you infer from this activity?

We observe that solid camphor on heating gets converted into vapour which gets condensed on the funnel.

This process of change of solid state directly to gaseous state without changing into liquid state or vice versa is called sublimation.

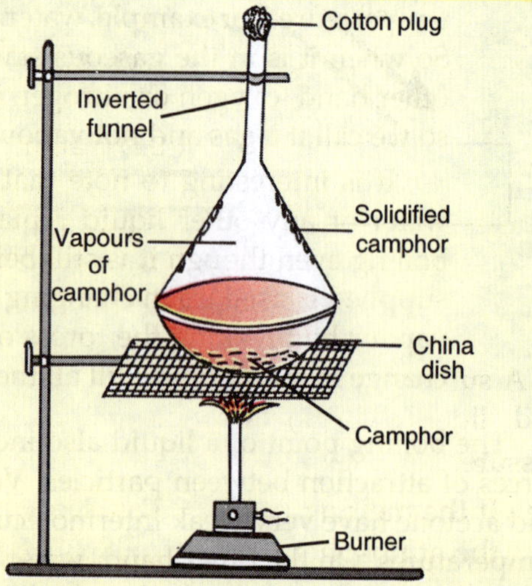

Fig. 11. Sublimation of ammonium chloride.

Many substances such as camphor, ammonium chloride, naphthalene sublime.

2. Effect of Pressure

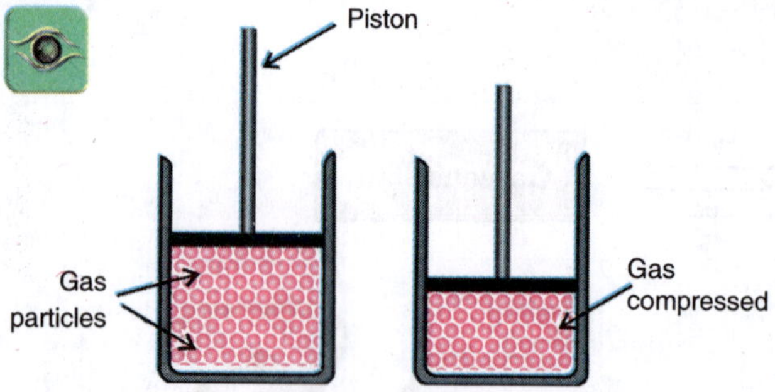

Fig. 12. By applying pressure particles of matter can be brought close together.

We have learnt that the three states of matter differ in the intermolecular forces and intermolecular distances of the constituent particles. If we start putting pressure and compress a gas enclosed in a cylinder, what will happen? Will the particles come closer? Will the state of matter change as increasing or decreasing pressure. For example, gases are compressible because on applying pressure, the space between the gaseous particles decreases (as shown in Fig. 12). Therefore, gases can be compressed readily. When we apply pressure and reduce temperature the gases can be converted into liquids *i.e.*, gases will be liquefied.

This process of conversion of a gas into a liquid by increasing pressure or decreasing temperature is called liquefaction.

DO YOU KNOW?

You must have learnt about solid carbon dioxide (CO_2). Solid carbon dioxide is also called **dry ice.** Solid CO_2 gets converted into gaseous state directly on decreasing pressure to 1 atmosphere without coming into liquid state.

Thus, we can conclude that temperature and pressure determine the state of a substance ; solid, liquid or gaseous.

The interchange between different states may be shown below :

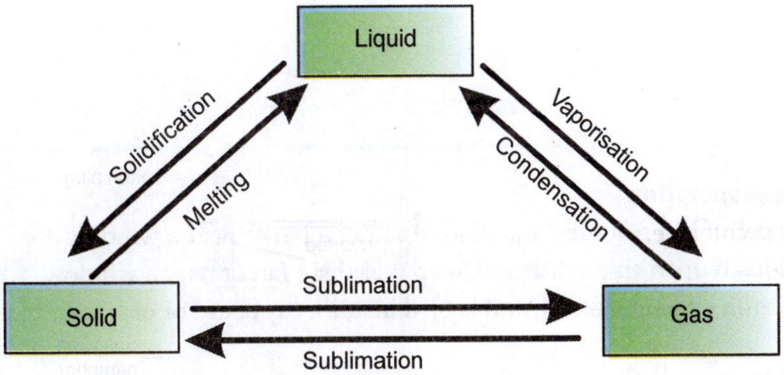

Fig. 13. Interconversion of three states of matter.

A substance may exist in any of the three different states of matter (i.e., solid, liquid or gas) depending upon the conditions of temperature and pressure.

- If the melting point of a substance is above the room temperature at the atmospheric pressure, it is said to be a ***solid.***
- If the boiling point of a substance is above room temperature under atmospheric pressure, it is classified as ***liquid.***
- If the boiling point of the substance is below the room temperature at the atmospheric pressure, it is called a ***gas.***

EVAPORATION

We have learnt that a liquid can be converted into gaseous state either by heating or by decreasing the pressure. But we observe many examples in our everyday life where change of state from liquid to vapour takes place without the liquid reaching the boiling point. For example,

- Water in ponds changes from liquid to vapour without reaching the boiling point.
- Water when left uncovered slowly changes into vapour.
- When we put wet clothes for drying, the water from the clothes goes to the atmosphere.

? What happens to water in the above examples?

We have learnt that particles are never at rest but are always moving. When left in open, the particles of water are constantly colliding with each other and with the particles of gases present in the atmosphere (Fig. 14). After sometime, the particles at the surface get sufficient kinetic energy to break away from the intermolecular forces of attraction. As a result, the particles of higher energy leave the surface and become water vapour. They go into the atmosphere.

This phenomenon of change of a liquid into vapour at any temperature below its boiling is called ***evaporation.***

This is a surface phenomenon because the particles of a liquid present on the surface gain energy and leave the surface.

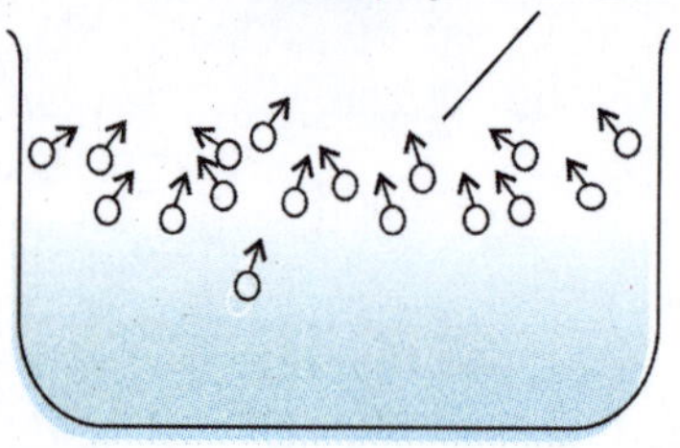

Fig. 14. Evaporation of a liquid in an open container

Factors Affecting Evaporation

Let us learn about the factors affecting evaporation by considering the following activity.

You would have noticed that rate of evaporation increases with the following factors :

Activity 14

To understand the factors affecting evaporation

1. Take about 5 mL of kerosene or petrol in a test tube and place it under a fan or near a window.
2. Take 5 mL of kerosene or petrol in an open china dish and keep it under a fan or near a window.
3. Take 5 mL of kerosene or petrol in an open china dish and keep it inside a cupboard or on a shelf in your class.
4. Take 5 mL of kerosene or petrol in an open china dish and put it outside in sun.
5. Observe the process of evaporation of kerosene or petrol in the above cases and record the time or days taken for the evaporation. What do you notice about the following aspects of evaporation?

What do you notice about the following aspects of evaporation ?

(*a*) Effect of surface area.

(*b*) Effect of wind velocity. (compare results of experiment B and C)

(*c*) Effect of temperature by comparing the results in steps 1, 2, 3 and 4

Repeat the above three steps of activity on a rainy day and note your observations.

1. Increase of surface area of the liquid

Rate of evaporation increases with increase in surface area. The evaporation depends upon the surface area. If the surface area is increased, the rate of evaporation increases. As we have learnt in the above activity, the rate of evaporation increases when we put kerosene or petrol in an open china dish than in a test tube (step 1 and 2). We also know that while putting washed clothes for drying up we spread them so that surface area for evaporation increases.

2. Increase of temperature

Rate of evaporation increases with increase in temperature. This is because with the increase in temperature more number of particles get enough kinetic energy to go into the vapour state (or gaseous state).

As we know, drying of clothes take place rapidly in summer than in winter.

3. Decrease in humidity

The rate of evaporation increases with decrease in humidity in the atmosphere. Humidity is the amount of water vapour present in air. Air around us cannot hold more than a definite quantity of water vapour at a given temperature. If the amount of water in air is already large *i.e.*, humidity is more, the rate of evaporation decreases. We know that it takes long time for drying of clothes on a humid day.

4. Increase of wind speed

The rate of evaporation also increases with increase in speed of the wind. This is because with increase in speed of wind, the particles of water vapour move away with the wind resulting decrease in the amount of vapour in the surroundings. This increases the rate of evaporation of water. We know, clothes dry faster on a windy day.

Similarly, you must have noticed that in hot and humid weather, we sweat more. Therefore, we usually sit under the fan. The fan increases the wind speed around us and thereby increasing the rate of evaporation and making us feel a bit cool and comfortable.

Thus, we may sum up

Evaporation increases with

- increase in surface area
- increase in temperature
- decrease in humidity
- increase in wind speed

- It may be noted that rate of evaporation also depends on the nature of liquid. This is because of different types of interparticle forces of attractions in different liquids. For example, interparticle forces in alcohol are less than in water. Therefore, alcohol evaporates faster than water.

Evaporation Causes Cooling

During evaporation, cooling is always caused. This is because evaporation is a phenomenon in which only the high energy particles leave the liquid surface. As a result, the particles having low energy are left behind. Therefore, the average molecular energy of the remaining particles left in the liquid state is lowered. As a result, there is decrease in temperature on the part of the liquid that is left. Thus, ***evaporation causes cooling.***

This can also be understood from the following examples from our daily life :

(*i*) When we pour some acetone (nail polish remover) on our palm, we feel cold. This is because the particles gain energy from our palm or surroundings and leave the palm feeling cool.

(*ii*) Sometimes, we sprinkle water on the roof or open ground after a sunny hot day. This cools the roof or open ground. This is because as water evaporates, it takes up the large latent heat of vaporisation from the surface. This helps to cool the hot surface.

Let Us Learn More About Evaporation

1. Why should we wear cotton clothes in summer?

We all prefer to wear cotton clothes during summer. This is because our body mechanism is such that we perspire more to keep our body cool. As we have learnt that during evaporation, the particles at the surface of liquid gain energy from the surroundings and change into vapour. For this, heat energy equal to the latent heat of vaporization is absorbed from the body. As a result body becomes cool. Now, cotton is good absorber of water and therefore, it helps in absorbing the sweat and exposes it to the atmosphere for easy evaporation.

Fig. 15. Droplets formed on the surface of the glass containing ice cold water.

2. Why do we see water droplets on the outer surface of a glass containing ice cold water?

You must have noticed that if we place some ice-cold water in a dry glass, we see small drops of water on the outer surface of the glass. From where has this water come ? The water vapour present in air touches the cold surface of the glass. They lose their energy and get converted to water (liquid state). These appear as water droplets outside the glass. This is also an example of condensation.

DO YOU KNOW?

Now scientists are talking about five states of matter. In addition to, solid, liquid and gaseous state, there is another state known as ***plasma.***

The ***plasma*** state consists of super energetic and super excited particles. These particles are in the form of ionized gases. The fluorescent tube and neon sign bulbs consist of plasma. The fluorescent tube contains a helium gas and neon sign bulbs contain neon gas. When electrical energy flows through these gases, it gets ionized *i.e.* get charged. This charging up creates a glowing plasma inside the tube or bulb. The plasma glows with a special colour depending upon the nature of gas. The sun and the stars also glow because of presence of plasma in them. The plasma is created in sun and the stars because of very high temperature.

In 1920, Indian physicst Satyendra Nath Bose has suggested fifth state of matter on the basis of certain calculations. On the basis of his calculations, Albert Einstein proposed a new state of matter called the **Bose-Einstein Condensate** (BEC). The BEC state is formed by cooling a gas of extremely low density, about one hundred-thousandth the density of normal air to super low temperatures. In 2001, Eric A. Cornell, W. Ketterle and Carle E. Wieman of USA recevied a noble prize for achieving "Bose-Einstein Condensation."

Solved Examples

❑ **Example 10. Which phenomenon occurs during the following changes :**

(*a*) Drying of wet clothes

(*b*) Decrease of size of naphthalene balls

(*c*) Formation of clouds

(*d*) Conversion of solid carbon dioxide into carbon dioxide gas

(*e*) Conversion of ammonia gas into liquid ammonia

Solution : (*a*) Evaporation

(*b*) Sublimation

(*c*) Condensation

(*d*) Sublimation

(*e*) Liquefication

❑ **Example 11. In the following examples state which factor is responsible for the change in rate of evaporation and is effective :**

(*a*) Wet clothes dry faster on spreading them.

(*b*) Clothes dry faster on a windy day.

(c) Clothes take longer time to dry on a rainy day.

(*d*) Clothes dry faster in sun than in the shade.

Solution : (*a*) Increase in surface area on spreading them.

(*b*) Increase in wind speed.

(*c*) Increase of humidity in wet air.

(*d*) Increase of temperature.

❑ **Example 12. Which of the following statements are true or false? Correct the false statements.**

(*a*) When we pour some nail polish remover on our palm, we feel warm.

(*b*) Evaporation increases by increase in humidity.

(*c*) Boiling point of a liquid is always constant irrespective of the atmospheric pressure.

(*d*) Solid CO_2 gets converted to gaseous state directly and the process is called sublimation.

(e) If the boiling point of substance is above room temperature under atmospheric pressure, it is classified as liquid.

Solution : (a) False : When we pour some nail polish on our palm, we feel cold.

(b) False: Evaporation decreases by increase in humidity.

(c) False : Boiling point of a liquid depends upon the atmospheric pressure.

(d) True (e) True

Practice Exercise 1 B

Answers and Hints on Page 44

1. Convert the following temperatures to Celsius scale :
   (i) 323 K (ii) 600 K
2. Convert the following temperatures to Kelvin scale :
   (i) 127°C (ii) 20°C
3. Complete the following conversions :
   (a) ....°C = 372 K
   (b) 82°C = ... K
   (c) 373°C = ... K
   (d) ....°C = 569K
   (e) 1 atm = ... Pascal
   (f) .... atm = 2.02×10^5 Pascal
   (g) 2000 mL = ... L
   (h) 1 L = ... dm^3
4. Name two substances which can sublime.
5. Complete the following figure by mentioning the process :

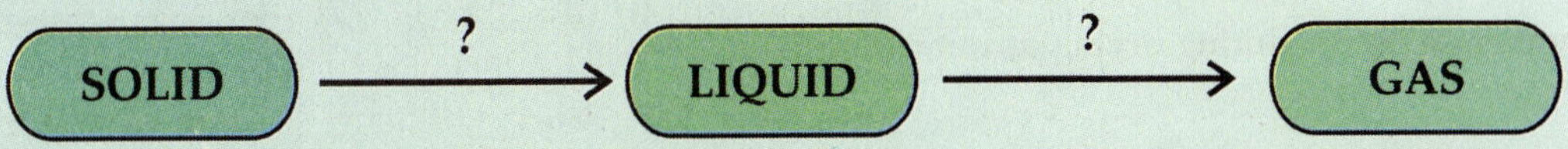

6. Two liquids A and B have boiling points 350 K and 375 K respectively. Which of the two has greater intermolecular forces of attraction ?
7. Name the process for the following changes :
   (i) liquid ⟶ solid
   (ii) solid ⟶ gas
   (iii) gas ⟶ liquid
   (iv) gas ⟶ solid
8. Liquid X has stronger intermolecular forces than liquid Y. Will it boil at lower or higher temperature than Y.
9. The melting points of three liquids are 280 K, 320 K and 360 K. The order of intermolecular forces of attraction between these three liquids A, B, C are in the order :
   B > C > A
   Label the boiling point for each liquid.
10. Which of the following processes require heating /cooling
    (i) solid ⟶ gas
    (ii) liquid ⟶ solid
    (iii) liquid ⟶ gas
11. Which of the following processes require heating
    (i) fusion
    (ii) condensation
    (iii) vaporisation
    (iv) solidification

12. Name the following phenomena :

(*a*) Conversion of liquid to gas ....

(*b*) Conversion of gas to solid directly ....

(*c*) Conversion of gas to liquid ....

13. Predict whether the process of evaporation increases/decreases with the following factors :

(*a*) decrease in humidity ....

(*b*) decrease in wind speed ....

(*c*) increase of temperature ....

(*d*) increase of surface area ....

(*e*) decrease of temperature ....

14. Label the changes (a) to (d) below :

$$\text{Ice } (s) \underset{(c)}{\overset{(a)}{\rightleftharpoons}} \text{Water } (l) \underset{(d)}{\overset{(b)}{\rightleftharpoons}} \text{Steam } (g)$$

15. Melting point of a substance is below room temperature. Predict its state at room temperature.

16. Name the process which is opposite to vaporisation.

17. Out of Celsius and Kelvin scales of temperature, which is considered better and why?

18. At what temperature does solid ice and liquid water co-exist?

19. Write full form of LPG and CNG.

20. Do we sweat more on a dry day or on a humid day?

21. What type of clothes should we wear in summer?

22. Name two factors which increase the rate of evaporation.

23. How is Celsius degree related to Kelvin degree?

24. What phenomenon occurs during drying of wet clothes?

25. Define :

(*i*) Latent heat of fusion

(*ii*) Latent heat of vaporisation

26. (*a*) Define :

(*i*) boiling point

(*ii*) melting point

(*b*) Why does temperature remain the same during melting till all the ice has changed to water?

27. Give two points of differences between evaporation and boiling.

28. (*a*) What is latent heat ? What are the two types of latent heat ?

(*b*) How much is the latent heat of fusion of ice ?

29. Give one word or term for the following descriptions:

(*i*) Changes from a vapour to a liquid.

(*ii*) The process during which ammonium chloride changes from a solid to a gas when it is heated.

(*iii*) A measure of average kinetic energy of particles.

(*iv*) The temperature at which a liquid changes into vapour at the atmospheric pressure.

(*v*) The amount of heat required to change 1 kg of a solid into a liquid state.

30. Give reasons for the following:

(*i*) Evaporation cools a liquid.

(*ii*) A desert cooler cools better on a hot dry day.

(*iii*) Solid carbon dioxide is known as dry ice.

(*iv*) Ice at 0°C is more effective in cooling than water at the same temperature.

(*v*) Steam causes more severe burns than boiling water.

What you have learnt

KEY TERMS

Diffusion	:	The intermixing of particles of two substances on their own.
Pressure of a gas	:	The force exerted by the gas molecules per unit area on the walls of the container.
Latent heat of fusion	:	The amount of heat energy required to convert 1kg of a solid into a liquid at atmospheric pressure without any change in temperature at its melting point.
Latent heat of vaporisation	:	The amount of heat energy required to convert 1kg of water into its vapour at atmospheric pressure without any change in temperature at its boiling point.
Sublimation	:	The process of change of a solid directly to its gaseous state without changing into liquid state or vice versa.
Liquefication	:	The process of conversion of a gas into liquid by increasing pressure or decreasing temperature.

Chapter Summary

- Matter occupies ***space*** and has ***mass.***
- Matter around us exists in ***three states*** : solid, liquid and gas.
- All matter consists of ***particles*** which may be atoms, molecules or ions.
- Solids have definite shape and definite volume, liquids have definite volume but no definite shape. Gases have neither definite shape nor definite volume.
- The intermolecular forces of attraction are maximum in solids, intermediate in liquids and minimum in gases.
- Intermolecular spaces and kinetic energy of particles are maximum in case of gases, intermediate in liquids and minimum is case of solids.
- Gases exert ***pressure*** due to bombardment of particles on the walls of the container.
- Rate of diffusion of gases is maximum among the three states of matter.
- The states of matter are ***interconvertible.*** These changes can be brought about by changing temperature and pressure.
- Change of solid state to liquid state is called **melting** or **fusion.**
- Change of liquid state to vapour state is called **vaporisation.**
- Change of solid state directly to gaseous state without going through liquid state is called ***sublimation.***
- Boiling is bulk phenomenon.
- The temperature at which a solid changes to a liquid is called ***melting point.***
- The temperature at which a liquid changes to vapour is called ***boiling point.***
- ***Melting point*** of ice is 273 K and ***boiling point*** of water is 373 K.
- Particles in steam at 373 K have more energy than water at the same temperature.
- The phenomenon of change of a liquid into gas at any temperature below its boiling point is called evaporation.
- Evaporation increases by (*i*) increase in surface area (*ii*) increase of temperature (*iii*) decrease in humidity and (*iv*) increase of wind speed.
- Evaporation causes cooling.

Some measurable quantities and their units

Quantity	Unit	Symbol
Mass	kilogram	kg
Length	meter	m
Temperature	kelvin	K
Weight / Force	newton	N
Volume	cubic metre	m^3
Density	kilogram / cubic metre	kg/m^3
Pressure	Pascal	Pa

Some Important Relations

1kg	=	1000 g
1m	=	100 cm
$1m^3$	=	10^6 cm^3 or 10^3 L (Litre)
10^3 cm^3	=	1L
K	=	273 + °C
°C	=	K – 273
1 atm	=	1.01×10^5 Pa

Knowledge Plus

Project/Activity

Time required : About 90 min.

Let us prepare a model to demonstrate the movement of particles in solids, liquids and gases.

Requirements: For making this model you need the following :

(*i*) a transparent jar

(*ii*) a big rubber balloon or a piece of stretchable rubber sheet.

(*iii*) a string and a tape.

(*iv*) a few chick-peas or black gram or dry green peas.

Model: Follow the following steps:

(*i*) Put seeds in the jar.

(*ii*) Sew the string to the centre of rubber sheet and put some tape to keep it tied perfectly.

(*iii*) Stretch and tie the rubber sheet on the mouth of the jar.

(*iv*) Now run your fingers up and down the string by first tugging at it slowly and then rapidly.

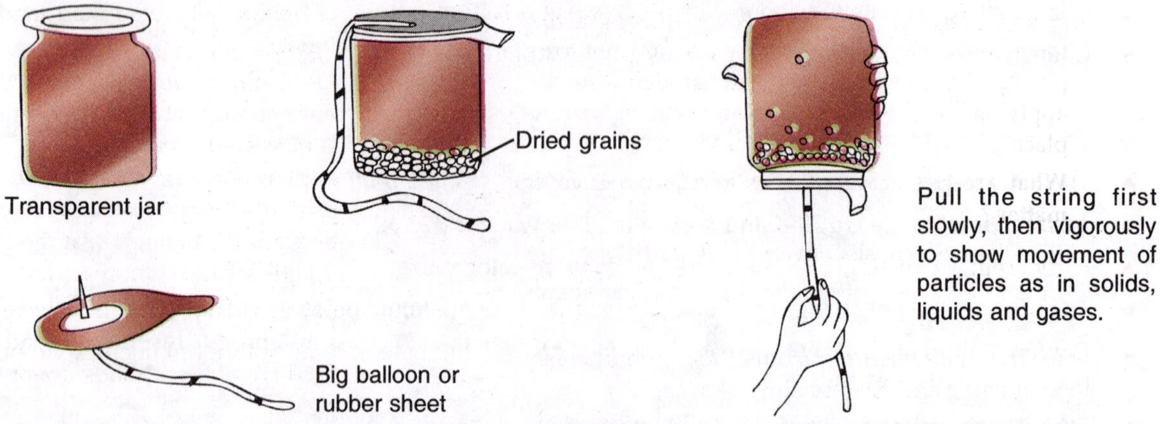

Fig.16. Demonstration of movement of particles on converting solid to liquid and liquid to gas.

Discussion

The model demonstrates that the particles of matter are not stationary but are constantly moving. In solids the particles move slowly (due to stronger forces of attraction), in liquids, they move little faster while in gases the particles move very rapidly (due to weakest forces of attraction). The movement of particles in solids, liquids and gases is observed by pulling the string first slowly and then vigorously.

NCERT File *with* Answers & Hints

In-Text *Questions*

1. Which of the following are matter ?
Chair, air, love, smell, hate, almonds, thought, cold-drink, smell of perfume.

Ans. Chair, air, almonds, cold drink and smell of perfume are matter.

2. Give reasons for the following observation :
The smell of hot sizzling food reaches you several metres away, but to get the smell from cold food you have to go close.

Ans. The smell of hot sizzling food reaches us more quickly as compared to smell of cold food. This is because rate of diffusion is faster at higher temperature than at lower temperature . The rate of diffusion of hot sizzling food is more and hence reaches you even several metres away. On the other hand ,rate of diffusion of cold food is less and therefore, you have to go quite close to it in order to get its smell.

3. A diver is able to cut through water in a swimming pool. Which property of matter does this observation show ?

Ans. The diver is able to cut through water in the swimming pool because matter is not continuous, but it is made up of particles which have vacant spaces between them. Moreover, the attractive forces between molecules of water are not very strong. The diver can easily cut through water by applying force to displace water and occupy its place.

4. What are the characteristics of the particles of matter ?

Ans. (*i*) All matter consist of very small particles.

(*ii*) The particles of matter have vacant spaces between them.

(*iii*) The particles of matter are continuously moving and possess kinetic energy .

(*iv*) The particles of matter attract each other with a force called intermolecular force of attraction. The intermolecular forces of attraction are maximum in solids and least in gases. Liquids have intermolecular forces in between solids and gases.

(*v*) Particles of matter mix with each other on their own and get into the spaces between particles of each other.

5. The mass per unit volume of a substance is called density (density = mass/volume). Arrange the following in order of increasing density— air, exhaust from chimneys, honey,water, chalk, cotton and iron.

Ans. The order of increasing density is : air < exhaust from chimney< cotton< water< honey < chalk < iron .

6. (*i*) Tabulate the differences in the characteristics of states of matter.

(*ii*) Comment upon the following: rigidity, compressibility, fluidity, filling a gas container, shape, kinetic energy and density.

Ans. (*i*) Please refer Text Table 1.

(*b*) (*i*) **Rigidity.** It is the property by virtue of which a substance can retain its shape when a force is applied to it. Solids have the property of rigidity, whereas liquids and gases are not rigid.

(*ii*) **Compressibility.** The particles of matter have spaces between them and they can be compressed (empty space is decreased) by appling force or pressure. Gases have high compressibility because of large empty spaces between the molecules of the gas. Solids and liquids are not compressed.

(*iii*) **Fluidity.** This is the tendency of a substance to flow. Liquids and gases possess fluidity, whereas solids donot flow, they are rigid.

(*iv*) **Filling a gas container.** Gases have negligible forces of attraction between their molecules and therefore, they move in all directions with very high velocities and fill the container.

(*v*) **Shape.** The definite geometrical arrangement of constituents of a substance determines its shape. Solids have definite shapes whereas liquids take the shape of the container in which they are placed. Gases also donot have any shape.

(*vi*) **Kinetic energy.** The energy possessed by the particles due to their motion. Molecules of gases possess maximum kinetic energy and those of solids possess least kinetic energy. The kinetic energy of substances decreases as: gases > liquids > solids.

(*vii*) **Density.** It is the mass of the substance per unit volume. The density in different states decreases as : solids > liquids > gases.

7. Give reasons

(*i*) A gas fills completely the vessel in which it is kept.

(*ii*) A gas exerts pressure on the walls of the container.

(*iii*) A wooden table should be called a solid.

(*iv*) We can easily move our hand in air but to do the same through a solid block of wood we need a karate expert.

Ans. (*a*) In gases, the particles are very loosely packed and the attractive forces between the particles are negligibly small. As a result, the particles of gases, move randomly in all directions and therefore, fill the vessels completely.

(*b*) The molecules of a gas are free to move randomly in all directions. During their motion, they collide with one another and also with the walls of the container. The constant bombartment of the molecules on the walls of the container exerts a steady force. The force acting per unit area on the walls of the container is called pressure. Thus, gases exert pressure.

(*c*) A wooden table is called a solid because it has a definite mass, volume and shape.

(*d*) In air, there is lot of empty space between the molecules and the forces between the particles are almost negligible. Hence we can move our hand in air. However, we cannot move our hand in a solid block because there are strong forces of attractions between particles in a solid and there is no empty space between them.

8. Liquids generally have lower density as compared to solids. But you must have observed that ice floats on water. Find out why.

Ans. In general, liquids have lower density than solids therefore, ice (solid form) is expected to be heavier than water (liquid state). However, ice has lower density than water because it has cage like structure. In this structure, a lot of vacant spaces are left when water molecules are linked in ice. The number of these vacant spaces are comparatively less in water and hence density of water is more than ice . Therefore, because of lower density of ice, it floats on water.

9. Convert the following temperatures to Celsius scale:

(a) 300 K **(b) 573 K**

Ans. (*a*) 300K = 300 – 273 = 27°C

(*b*) 573K = 573 – 273 = 300°C

10. What is the physical state of water at

(a) 250°C **(b) 100°C**

Ans. (*a*) Gaseous state

(*b*) Gaseous state

11. For any physical state, why does the temperature remains constant during the change of state ?

Ans. The temperature remains constant during the change of a state because the heat supplied during the change is used up in overcoming the intermolecular forces berween the particles of that state.

12. Suggest a method to liquefy atmospheric gases.

Ans. The atmospheric gases can be liquefied by cooling under pressure.

13. Why does a desert cooler cool better on a hot dry day ?

Ans. On a hot dry day, the humidity (amount of water vapour in air) is less and therefore, rate of evaporation is more. Since we know that evaporation causes cooling, therefore, as the rate of evaporation is more on a hot dry day, therefore, the desert cooler cools better.

14. How does the water kept in an earthen pot (matka) become cool during summer ?

Ans. Earthen pot has many small pores. Water kept in earthen pot comes out from the pores during the summer and it evaporate. Since evaporation causes cooling, therefore, water kept in earthen pot becomes cold.

15. Why does our palm feel cold when we put some acetone or petrol or perfume on it ?

Ans. As we put any of these on our palm, the particles of these substances absorb energy from the palm and evaporates. Therefore, it causes cooling and we feel sensation of cooling. Acetone, petrol or perfume are low boiling liquids.

16. Why are we able to sip hot tea or milk faster from a saucer rather than a cup ?

Ans. The surface area of hot tea or milk in a saucer is more than in a cup. Because of larger surface area, cooling will be more rapid in a saucer than in a cup. Hence we are able to sip hot tea or milk faster from a saucer rather than a cup.

17. What type of clothes should we wear in summer ?

Ans. We should wear white cotton clothes in summer . This is because cotton is a good absorber of water and therefore, it helps in absorbing sweat from our body. It also exposes it to the atmosphere for easy evaporation. The evaporation of this sweat cools our body. Therefore, our body feels cool.

Textbook *Exercises*

1. Convert the following temperatures to the Celsius scale.

(*a*) 300 K (*b*) 573K

Ans. (*a*) 300K = 300 – 273 = 27°C

(*b*) 573K = 573 – 273 = 300°C

2. Convert the following temperatures to the Kelvin scale.

(*a*) 25°C (*b*) 373°C

Ans. (*a*) 25°C = 273 + 25 = 298 K

(*b*) 373°C = 373 + 273 = 646 K

3. Give reason for the following observations.

(*i*) Naphthalene balls disappear with time without leaving any solid.

(*ii*) We can get the smell of perfume sitting several metres away.

Ans. (*a*) Naphthalene is volatile solid and has a tendency to sublime. Therefore, it changes into vapours completely which disappear into the air and no solid is left.

(*b*) This is because perfumes contain volatile solvent which carries pleasant smelling vapours. They diffuse quite fast and can reach to people sitting several metres away.

4. Arrange the following substances in increasing order of forces of attraction between the particles—water, sugar, oxygen.

Ans. The increasing order of intermolecular forces of attraction: Oxygen < Water < Sugar.

5. What is the physical state of water at

(*a*) 25°C (*b*) 0°C (*c*) 100°C

Ans. Physical state of water at

(*i*) 25°C is liquid

(*ii*) 0°C is solid

(*iii*) 100°C is vapour (or steam)

6. Give two reasons to justify-

(*a*) water at room temperature is a liquid.

(*b*) an iron almirah is a solid at room temperature

Ans. (*a*) (i) Water is liquid at room temperature because water has fixed volume but not fixed shape. It takes the shape of the container.

(*ii*) Water can flow from higher level to lower level.

(*b*) An almirah is a solid because

(*i*) It has a definite shape

(*ii*) It has a fixed volume

7. Why is ice at 273 K more effective in cooling than water at the same temperature ?

Ans. Ice at 273 K in more effective in cooling than water at 273 K because in ice, the molecules have lower energy as compared to particles in the liquid water at the same temperature. It requires latent heat of fusion for melting.

8. What produces more several burns, boiling water or steam ?

Ans. Steam produces more severe burns as compared to boiling water. This is because in steam, the molecules have higher kinetic energy than in boiling water because latent heat of vaporisation of steam is more than that of boiling liquid. Therefore, it produces more severe burns.

9. Name A, B, C, D, E and F in the following diagram showing change in its state :

Ans. A : Fusion

B : Vaporisation

C : Condensation

D : Solidification

E : Sublimation

F : Sublimation

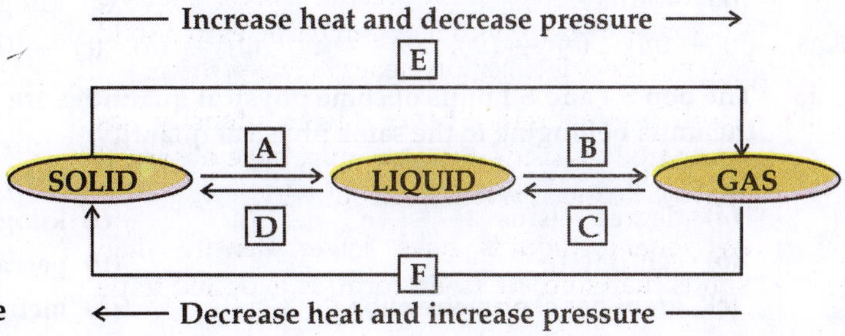

NCERT Exemplar Problems

Note: Multiple Choice Question (1–10) from Exemplar Problems are given in Revision Exercise, Page 40.

Short Answer Questions

11. A sample of water under study was found to boil at 102°C at normal temperature and pressure. Is the water pure? Will this water freeze at 0°C? Comment.

Ans. It is not pure because its boiling point is more than 100°C at normal temperature and pressure. It will freeze be low 0°C because of the presence of impurity.

12. A student heats a beaker containing ice and water. He measures the temperature of the content of the beaker as a function of time. Which of the following would correctly represent the result? Justify your choice.

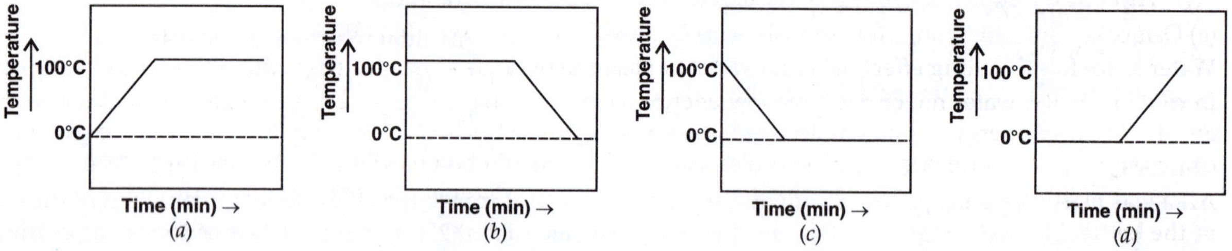

Ans. In the beginning, ice and water are in equilibrium and the temperature would be zero. When we heat the mixture, energy supplied is consumed in melting the ice and temperature does not change till all the ice melts because of latent heat of fusion. On further heating, the temperature of water would increase. Hence the correct option is (*d*).

13. Fill in the blanks:

(*a*) Evaporation of a liquid at room temperature leads to a __________ effect.

(*b*) At room temperature the fo rces of attraction between the particles of solid substances are __________ than those which exist in the gaseous state.

(*c*) The arrangement of particles is less ordered in the __________ state. However, there is no order in the __________ state.

(*d*) __________ is the change of gaseous state directly to solid state without going through the __________ state.

(*e*) The phenomenon of change of a liquid into the gaseous state at any temperature below its boiling point is called __________.

Ans. (*a*) cooling (*b*) stronger (*c*) liquid, gaseous (*d*) sublimation, liquid (*e*) evaporation.

14. Match the physical quantities given in column A to their S I units given in column B :

(A)	(B)
(*a*) Pressure	(*i*) cubic metre
(*b*) Temperature	(*ii*) kilogram
(*c*) Density	(*iii*) pascal
(*d*) Mass	(*iv*) kelvin
(*e*) Volume	(*v*) kilogram per cubic metre

Ans. (*a*) — (*iii*), (*b*) — (*iv*), (*c*) — (*v*), (*d*) — (*ii*), (*e*) — (*i*)

15. The non S I and S I units of some physical quantities are given in column A and column B respectively. Match the units belonging to the same physical quantity:

(A)	(B)
(*a*) degree celsius	(*i*) kilogram
(*b*) centimetre	(*ii*) pascal
(*c*) gram per centimetre cube	(*iii*) metre

(*d*) bar **(*iv*) kelvin**

(*e*) milligram **(*v*) kilogram per metre cube**

Ans. (*a*) — (*iv*), (*b*) — (*iii*), (*c*) — (*v*), (*d*) — (*ii*), (*e*) — (*i*)

16. 'Osmosis is a special kind of diffusion'. Comment.

Ans. Yes, osmosis is a special kind of diffusion. In both the phenomena, there is movement of particles. In diffusion there is movement of particles of solute and solvent from higher concentration of solute to lower concentration. However, in osmosis, only the movement of solvent occurs through a semi-permeable membrane which is permeable only to water molecules.

17. Classify the following into osmosis/diffusion

(*a*) Swelling up of a raisin on keeping in water.
(*b*) Spreading of virus on sneezing.
(*c*) Earthworm dying on coming in contact with common salt.
(*d*) Shrinking of grapes kept in thick sugar syrup.
(*e*) Preserving pickles in salt.
(*f*) Spreading of smell of cake being baked throughout the house.
(*g*) Aquatic animals using oxygen dissolved in water during respiration.

Ans. (*a*) Osmosis, (*b*) Diffusion, (*c*) Osmosis, (*d*) Osmosis, (*e*) Osmosis, (*f*) Diffusion, (*g*) Diffusion.

18. Water as ice has a cooling effect, whereas water as steam may cause severe burns. Explain these observations.

Ans. In case of ice, the water molecules have low energy whereas in the case of steam, the water molecules have high energy. The high energy of water molecules in steam is transferred as heat to our body and may cause burns. On the other hand, in case of ice, the water molecules take energy from our body and thus have a cooling effect.

19. Alka was making tea in a kettle. Suddenly she felt intense heat from the puff of steam gushing out of the spout of the kettle. She wondered whether the temperature of the steam was higher than that of the water boiling in the kettle. Comment.

Ans. The temperature of both boiling water and steam is 100°C. However, steam has more energy because of latent heat of vaporisation and therefore, steam gives intense heat.

20. A glass tumbler containing hot water is kept in the freezer compartment of a refrigerator (temperature < 0°C). If you could measure the temperature of the content of the tumbler, which of the following graphs would correctly represent the change in its temperature as a function of time.

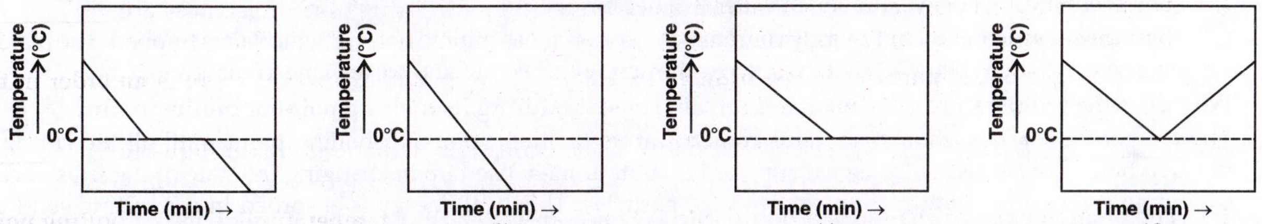

(*a*) (*b*) (*c*) (*d*)

Ans. The water will cool initially till it reaches 0°C, which is the freezing point of water. At this stage, the temperature will remain constant till whole of the water freezes. After this the temperature will decrease. Therefore, correct option is (*a*).

21. Look at figure and suggest in which of the vessels A,B, C or D the rate of evaporation will be the highest? Explain.

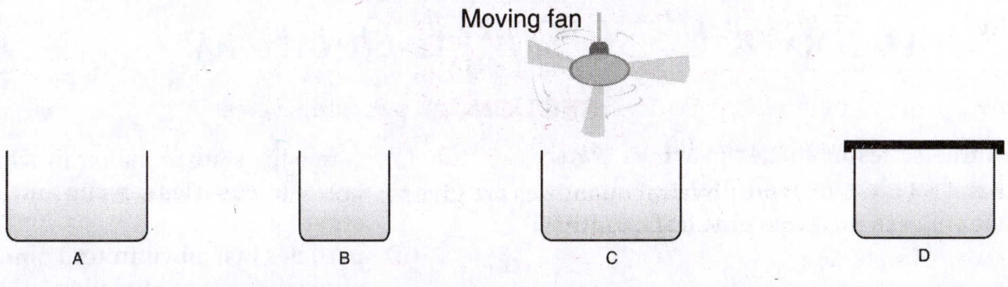

Ans. The rate of evaporation increases with increase in surface area as well as speed of air. Therefore, correct option is (*c*).

22. **(a) Conversion of solid to vapour is called sublimation. Name the term used to denote the conversion of vapour to solid.**

(b) Conversion of solid state to liquid state is called fusion; what is meant by latent heat of fusion?

Ans. (a) Sublimation

(b) Latent heat of fusion is the amount of heat required to convert 1 kg of solid into liquid at one atmosphere pressure at its melting point.

Long Answer Questions

23. **You are provided with a mixture of naphthalene and ammonium chloride by your teacher. Suggest an activity to separate them with well labelled diagram.**

Ans. Naphthalene and ammonium chloride are separated by the process of sublimation. *Refer Text.*

24. **(a) It is a hot summer day, Priyanshi and Ali are wearing cotton and nylon clothes respectively. Who do you think would be more comfortable and why?**

(b) You want to wear your favourite shirt to a party, but the problem is that it is still wet after a wash. What steps would you take to dry it faster? ***(2013-1014)***

Ans. (a) Priyanshi will be more comfortable because cotton clothes are good absorber of water than nylon. Therefore, cotton clothes help in absorption of sweat followed by evaporation which leads to cooling.

(b) The wet clothes can be dried by different methods such as :

(i) By spreading the shirt in air because evaporation increases with increase in surface area.

(ii) By spreading the shirt under fan in a room because increase in speed of wind increases evaporation.

(iii) By spreading the shirt under the sun or by warming the clothes because increase in temperature increases evaporation.

25. **Comment on the following statements:**

(a) Evaporation produces cooling.

(b) Rate of evaporation of an aqueous solution decreases with increase in humidity.

(c) Sponge though compressible is a solid.

Ans. (a) During evaporation, the high energy particles escape from the liquid surface. As a result particles having low energy are left behind. Therefore, evaporation causes cooling.

(b) Humidity is the amount of water vapour present in air. Air around us cannot hold more than a definite amount of water vapour at a given temperature. So, if the air is already rich in water vapour, it will not take up more water and therefore, rate of evaporation of water will decrease.

(c) Sponge is a solid but it can be easily compressed because it has minute holes in which air is trapped. The material is also not rigid. When we press the sponge, the air is expelled out and we are able to compress it.

26. **Why does the temperature of a substance remain constant during its melting point or boiling point?**

Ans. The temperature of a substance remains constant at its melting point and boiling point until all the substance melts or boils. This is because the heat supplied is continuously used up in changing the state of the substance by overcoming the forces of attraction between the particles. This heat energy is absorbed in converting solid into liquid at melting point as latent heat of fusion and liquid into gaseous state at its boiling point as latent heat of vaporisation and temperature remains constant.

PRACTICE QUESTIONS

Some Solved CBSE Sample Questions

SECTION-A

1. **Name the three states of matter in which water can exist. Are these interconvertible?** ***(CBSE 2011-12)***

Ans. The three states of water are :

(i) solid (ice)

(ii) liquid (water)

(iii) Gaseous (steam)

These are interconvertible.

2. **(a) Name the state of matter in which**

(i) layers of particles can slip and slide over each other

(ii) particles just move around randomly, because of weak force of attraction.

(b) List two ways by which a gas can be converted into a liquid.

(CBSE Sample Paper 2009-10, 2012-13)

Ans. (*a*) (*i*) liquid
(*ii*) gas
(*b*) A gas can be converted into a liquid by
(*i*) decreasing temperature
(*ii*) increasing pressure

3. Account for the following :
(*a*) The temperature of water remains constant during boiling.
(*b*) Evaporation is a surface phenomen.
(*c*) The spaces between the constituent particles are maximum in gases.
(CBSE Sample Paper 2009-10)

Ans. (*a*) The temperature of water during boiling remains constant. This is because the heat supplied is used up in changing the state from liquid water to water vapour by breaking the forces of attraction. As a result, there is no change in temperature till all the water evaporates.

(*b*) The particles on the surface gain energy from surrounding which increases their kinetic energy. As a result, the particles of energy higher than intermolecular forces of attraction leave the surface and become water vapour and go into the atmosphere. Thus, this is a surface phenomenon because the particles of a liquid present on the surface gain energy and leave the surface.

(*c*) The attractive forces between the constituent particles are weakest in gases. Therefore, the particles are very loosely packed and the intermolecular spaces between them are very large. Therefore, the spaces between the constituent particles are maximum in gases.

4. A gas jar containing air is inverted over another jar containing NO_2 gas which is brown in colour and heavier than air. After some time brown colour is seen in the inverted gas jar too. Identify the phenomenon associated with this observation.
(CBSE Sample Paper 2010-11)

Ans. Diffusion

5. (*a*) State one similarity and one difference between evaporation and boiling.
(*b*) List four factors which affect the rate of evaporation.
(*c*) Describe an activity to show that water vapour is present in air.

or

Distinguish solids, liquids and gases in a tabular form under the following characteristics.
(*i*) Rigidity
(*ii*) Compressibility
(*iii*) Inter-particle forces of attraction
(*iv*) Inter-particle spaces
(*v*) Kinetic energy of partilces
(CBSE Sample Paper 2010-11, 2012-13; 2014-15)

Ans. (*a*) Similarity : Liquid state changes into the gaseous state in both evaporation and boiling.

Difference :

Evaporation	Boiling
Evaporation can take place at all temperatures.	Boiling takes places at a fixed temperature.

(*b*) Four factors on which evaporation depends are :
(*i*) Surface area of the liquid exposed to atmosphere.
(*ii*) Temperature of the liquid
(*iii*) Wind velocity
(*iv*) Humidity.

(*c*) Take ice cold water or crushed ice in a dry tumbler. Allow it to stand undisturbed for some time in the atmosphere. You will observe that small drops of water appear on the outer surface of the tumbler. The water vapour present in air touches the cold surface of the tumbler. They lose their energy and get converted to water (liqid state). These water droplets appear outside the tumbler. This activity shows that water is present in the air.

or

Refer Text, Table 1.

6. 5 mL of water was taken in a china dish and in a test tube separately. These samples were placed under different conditions as given below:
(*i*) Both the samples were kept under fan.
(*ii*) Both the samples were kept inside a cupboard.
(*a*) State in which case evaporation will be faster? Give reasons to support your answer.
(*b*) How will the rate of evaporation change if the above activity is carried out on a rainy day? Justify your answer. ***(CBSE 2012-13)***

Ans. (*a*) Evaporation will be faster under a fan. This is because the movement of the air around the sample will increase, thereby increase the rate of evaporation. Therefore, evaporation will be faster under fan than in the cupboard where outside air will not come in contact with the sample.

(*b*) On a rainy day, there will be humidity in air. As a result, evaporation of water will be slow.

7. How will you justify that ice, water and steam are three states of matter and not different substances? ***(CBSE 2012-13)***

Ans. When ice is melted, water is produced and when water is heated steam is produced. Conversely, when steam is cooled, water is formed and when water is cooled further, ice is formed. Therefore, ice, water and steam are three states of matter which are interconvertible and not three different substances.

8. What happens when you open a bottle of perfume? ***(CBSE 2012-13)***

Ans. Particles of perfume diffuse into air and the smell of perfume can be felt even at a distance.

9. Archit dropped a crystal of potassium permanganate into two beakers A and B containing hot water and cold water respectively. After keeping the beakers undisturbed for some time, what did he observe and why? ***(CBSE 2012-13)***

Ans. Potassium permanganate crystals give purple colour in both beakers. In a beaker A containing hot water, the purple colour spreads more readily as compared to beaker B containing cold water. This is because diffusion is faster at higher temperature because kinetic energy of the particles increases with rise in temperature.

10. (*a*) Give reasons:

(*i*) Steam produces more severe burns than water.

(*ii*) We are able to sip hot tea faster from a saucer than a cup.

(*iii*) Water kept in earthen pot becomes cool during summer. ***(CBSE 2013-14)***

Ans. (*i*) Steam produces more severe burns as compared to boiling water. This is because in steam, the molecules have higher kinetic energy than in boiling water because latent heat of vaporisation of steam is more than that of boiling liquid. Therefore, it produces more severe burns.

(*ii*) The surface area of hot tea or milk in a saucer is more than in a cup. Because of larger surface area, cooling will be more rapid in a saucer than in a cup. Hence we are able to sip hot tea or milk faster from a saucer rather than a cup.

(*iii*) Earthen pot has many small pores. Water kept in earthen pot comes out from the pores during the summer and it evaporates. Since evaporation causes cooling, therefore, water kept in earthen pot becomes cold.

11. How does melting point of a solid indicate the strength of its intermolecular forces of attraction? ***(CBSE 2013-14)***

Ans. More stronger are the intermolecular forces of attraction between particles, more energy is required to break these forces. Hence, the substance which has higher melting point indicates that its particles are held strongly and hence strength of intermolecular forces of attraction is large.

12. List any two properties of liquids that are common to gases. ***(CBSE 2013-14)***

Ans. (*i*) Liquids do not have definite shape like gases. Both take the shape of the container in which these are kept.

(*ii*) Liquids have the property of diffusion like gases. However, liquids diffuse slower than gases.

13. Suppose you want to convert a gas into a liquid. Which two methods can you apply? ***(CBSE 2013-14)***

Ans. (*i*) By lowering the temperature of the gas or by cooling the gas.

(*ii*) By increasing the pressure or by compressing the gas.

14. Name the property of gases that helps aquatic plants and animals to survive in water. ***(CBSE 2014-15)***

Ans. **Diffusion:** The oxygen diffuses in water and is taken in by animals and plants for their survival.

15. (*a*) Explain the effect of temperature on the movement of particles of matter.

(*b*) Give reason why we get smell of hot sizzling food even when we are meters away from it? ***(CBSE 2014-15)***

Ans. (*i*) Increase of temperature increases the kinetic energy of the particles and, therefore, the movement of particles becomes fast.

(*ii*) The smell of hot sizzling food reaches us quickly as compared to smell of cold food. This is because rate of diffusion increases with increase in temperature.

16. Ravi added a small amount of common salt to water taken in a graduated cylinder. On dissolving, there was no detectable change in level of water. Explain, why is it so? ***(CBSE 2014-15)***

Ans. There will be no change in volume. This is because the particles of common salt will occupy interparticle empty spaces present in water.

17. A diver is able to cut through water in a swimming pool. Which property of matter does this observation show ? ***(CBSE 2014-15)***

Ans. The diver is able to cut through water in the swimming pool because matter is not continuous, but it is made up of particles which have vacant spaces between them. Moreover, the attractive forces between molecules of water are not very strong. The diver can easily cut through water by applying force to displace water and occupy its place.

18. Give reasons for the following :

(*i*) Naphthalene balls disappear with time without leaving any solid.

(*ii*) A gas fills the vessel completely. ***(CBSE 2015-16)***

Ans. (*i*) Naphthalene balls are converted from solid to gas by sublimation process. These balls keep on forming naphthalene vapours slowly which disappear into the air and finally no solid is left.

(*ii*) In gases, the particles are very loosely packed and the attractive forces between the particles are negligibly small. As a result, the particles of gases, move randomly in all directions and therefore, fill the vessels completely.

19. **(a) Define evaporation. Out of nylon and cotton clothes, which will be more comfortable during summer and why?**

(b) Is evaporation and boiling the same? If not, then why? ***(CBSE 2015-16)***

Ans. (*a*) The process of change of a liquid into its vapour is called evaporation.

During summer, cotton clothes will be more comfortable than nylon. So, during summer cotton clothes absorb more sweat, which on evaporation causes cooling effect to the body.

(*b*) Evaporation and boiling are not the same. This is because evaporation process takes place spontaneously at all temperatures but boiling takes place only at a definite temperature (called boiling point).

20. **Why does perspiration keep our body cool?** ***(CBSE 2015-16)***

Ans. On a hot summer day or after running or doing heavy exercise, the temperature of our body rises. Due to rise in temperature, we perspire and our body gives out sweat. When the sweat evaporates, it absorbs heat from our body. By losing heat our body feels cool.

21. **Explain :**

(*i*) Sponge though compressible is a solid.

(*ii*) Gases completely fill the vessel in which they are kept. ***(CBSE 2015-16)***

Ans. (*i*) Sponge is a solid but it can be easily compressed because it has minute holes in which air is trapped. The material is also not rigid. When we press the sponge, the air is expelled out and we are able to compress it.

(*ii*) In gases, the particles are very loosely packed and the attractive forces between the particles are negligibly small. As a result, the particles can move at random in all the directions and therefore can fill the vessel completely.

22. **Give one property of solid which liquid does not possess and property of liquid which solid does not possess.** ***(CBSE 2015-16)***

Ans. Solids have definite shape whereas liquids do not have definite shape.

Liquids have the property of fluidity whereas solids do not have fluidity.

23. **(a) When common salt is added to water, will there be any change in volume? Give reason.**

(b) Give any one similarity between three states of matter. ***(CBSE 2015-16)***

Ans. (*i*) There will be no change in volume. This is because the particles of common salt will occupy interparticle empty spaces present in water.

(*ii*) All the three states of matter consist of particles which have specific mass.

24. **Why is the rate of diffusion faster in gaseous state?** ***(CBSE 2015-16)***

Ans. In gases the particles are very loosely packed and the attractive forces between the particles are negligibly small. The particles have more kinetic energy and therefore have good tendency to intermix and hence rate of diffusion is more in gaseous state.

25. **State the physical state of water at the following temperatures:**

(*i*) 300K (*ii*) 225°C (*iii*) 225K ***(CBSE 2016-17)***

Ans. (*i*) liquid (*ii*) gaseous (*iii*) solid

26. **We feel cool after doing vigorous exercise. Why?** ***(CBSE 2016-17)***

Ans. When we do vigorous exercise, the temperature of our body rises. Due to rise in temperature, we perspire and our body gives out sweat. When the sweat evaporates, it absorbs heat from our body. By losing heat, our body feels cool.

SECTION–B (Based on Practical Skill)

Multiple Choice Questions (MCQs) (1 Mark Each)

1. Which one of the following is the correct set up for determining melting point of ice ?

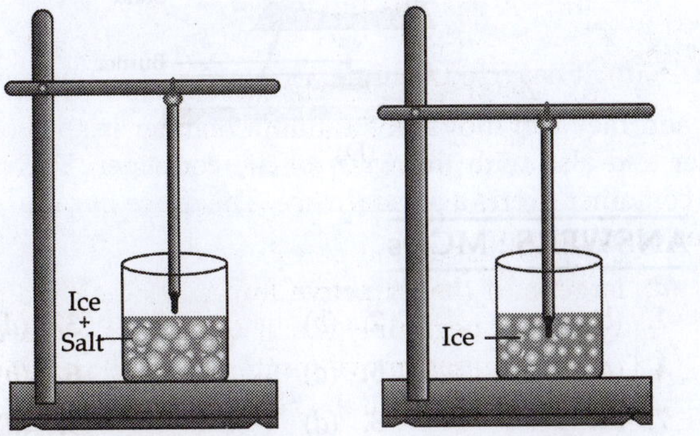

(a) (b)

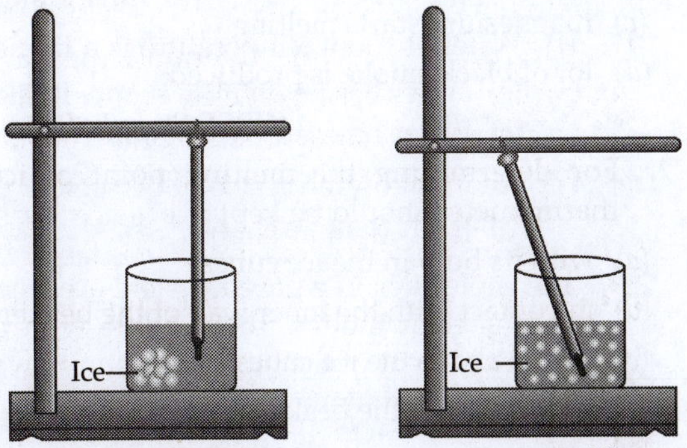

(c) (d)

2. On placing an iron nail in a copper sulphate solution, it is observed that :

(*a*) a soft and black coating is deposited on the iron nail.

(*b*) a reddish brown coating is deposited on the iron nail.

(*c*) a smooth and shiny coating is deposited on the iron nail.

(*d*) a grey and hard coating is deposited on the iron nail. ***(CBSE Sample Paper 2010)***

3. Rahul added 2 mL of barium chloride solution to 2 mL sodium sulphate solution in a test tube and observed that :

(*a*) a clear solution was obtained

(*b*) two solutions formed separate layers in the test tube

(*c*) the solution turned pink.

(*d*) a white solid settled at the bottom.

(CBSE Sample Paper 2010)

4. While determining the boiling point of water, the teacher suggested to add some pumice stone pieces to the hard glass test tube containing water. This was done to :

(*a*) avoid bumping

(*b*) avoid melting of hard glass test tube

(*c*) prevent unnecessary loss of heat energy

(*d*) spread the heat uniformly.

(CBSE Sample Paper 2010)

5. To determine the melting point of ice, a student immersed the thermometer bulb in crushed ice in a beaker and heated the beaker on a low flame. He would observe :

(*a*) an increase in temperature during melting of ice

(*b*) a decrease in temperature during melting of ice

(*c*) a decrease first and then an increase in temperature during melting of ice

(*d*) the temperature remains constant during melting of ice ***(CBSE Sample Paper 2010)***

6. A strip of magnesium metal is burnt in the flame. It is observed that :

(*a*) a yellow light appears

(*b*) a white dazzling light appears

(*c*) magnesium starts melting

(*d*) lot of black smoke is produced

(CBSE Sample Paper 2011)

7. For determining the melting point of ice, the thermometer should be kept :

(*a*) with its bulb in the ice cubes

(*b*) in contact with the inner wall of the beaker

(*c*) a little above the ice cubes

(*d*) in touch with the beaker from outside

(CBSE Sample Paper 2011)

8. A student takes some water in a beaker and heats it over a flame for determining its boiling point. He keeps on taking its temperature reading. He observes that the temperature of the water :

(*a*) keeps on increasing regularly

(*b*) keeps on increasing irregularly

(*c*) first increases slowly, then decreases rapidly and eventually becomes constant

(*d*) first increases gradually and then becomes constant ***(CBSE Sample Paper 2011)***

9. Out of A, B, C and D the correct set up of apparatus for sublimation is :

(*a*) A (*b*) B (*c*) C (*d*) D

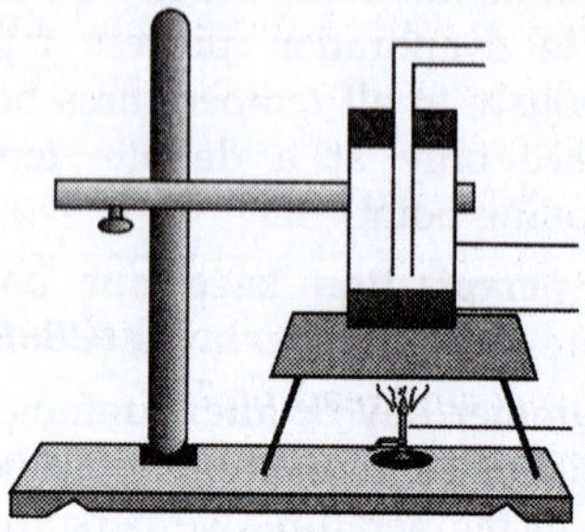

(A)

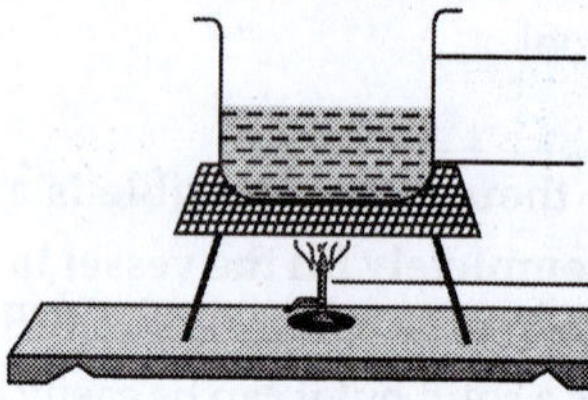

(B)

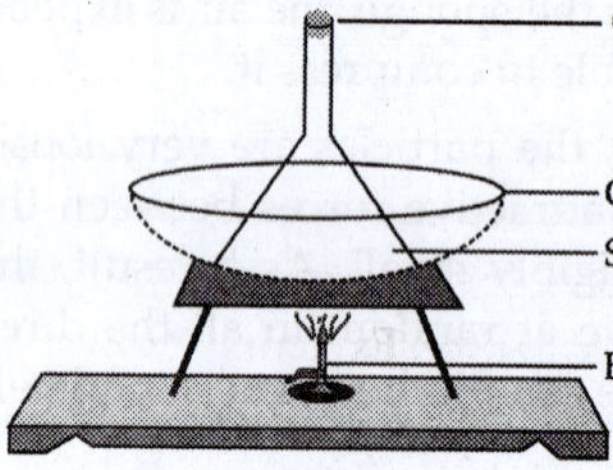

(C)

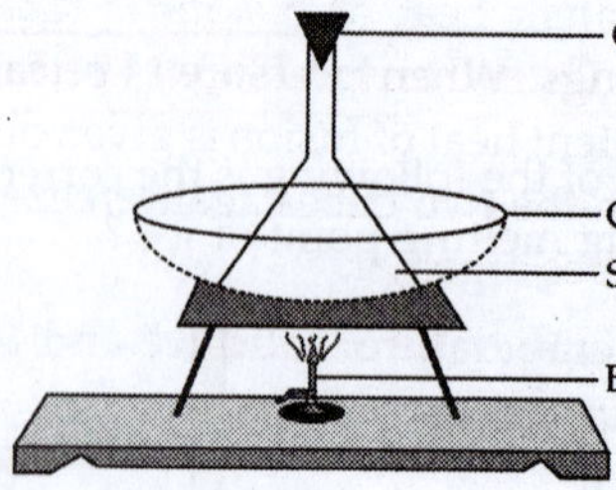

(D)

ANSWERS : MCQs

1. (*b*)	2. (*b*)	3. (*d*)
4. (*a*)	5. (*d*)	6. (*b*)
7. (*a*)	8. (*d*)	9. (*d*)

HOTS Higher Order Thinking Skill & Brain Twisting Questions with Answers

1. Ordinary water boils at 100°C. Can it be made to boil at 98°C or 103°C ?

Ans. It is possible. The boiling point of a liquid depends upon the pressure acting on it. Water boils at 100°C under 1 atmospheric pressure. If the pressure acting on water is less than 1 atmosphere, it will boil at temperature lower than 100°C. Conversely, if the pressure acting on water is more than 1 atmosphere, it will boil at temperature higher than 100°C. Hence, water can be made to boil at 98°C by reducing pressure on water less than one atmosphere or at 103°C by raising pressure above one atmosphere.

2. At what temperature, the Fahrenheit and Celsius scales have the same reading ?

Ans. The Celsius and Fahrenheit scales are related to each other as :

$$°F = \frac{9}{5}(°C) + 32$$

Let the temperature at which Celsius and Fahrenheit scales have same reading be x, then

$$\text{or} \quad x - \frac{9}{5}x = 32$$

$$\frac{5x - 9x}{5} = 32$$

$$-4x = 32 \times 5 = 160$$

$$\therefore \quad x = -\frac{160}{4} = -40°$$

Thus, $-40°C = -40°F$

3. Two cubes of ice are pressed hard between the palms. When the pressure is released, the two cubes join together. Explain.

Ans. When pressure is applied on ice cubes, the freezing point of ice decreases and, therefore, some of the ice in between two cubes melts. The energy required for melting (latent heat of fusion) is taken from the surroundings. When pressure is released, energy equal to latent heat of fusion is given out and water in between the two cubes again freezes to join the two ice cubes together.

4. At what temperature, solid ice and liquid water coexist ?

Ans. At the melting point of ice or freezing point of water solid ice and liquid water exist together.

5. Out of Celsius and Kelvin scale of temperature, which is considered better and why ?

Ans. Kelvin scale is regarded as better scale because in Celsius scale of temperature, we also come across negative value for temperature (e.g. –10°C, –50°C). But in Kelvin scale, the value is always positive and therefore, it is better.

6. When the forehead of a person is being sponged with cologne, he feels refreshed. Why ?

Ans. When the forehead of a person is sponged with a cologne, he feels refreshed. This is because this liquid contains a large proportion of alcohol which being more volatile, evaporates quickly. This results in soothing sensation and the person feels refreshed.

7. A student heats a beaker containing ice and water. He measures the temperature of the beaker as a function of time and draws the following graph.

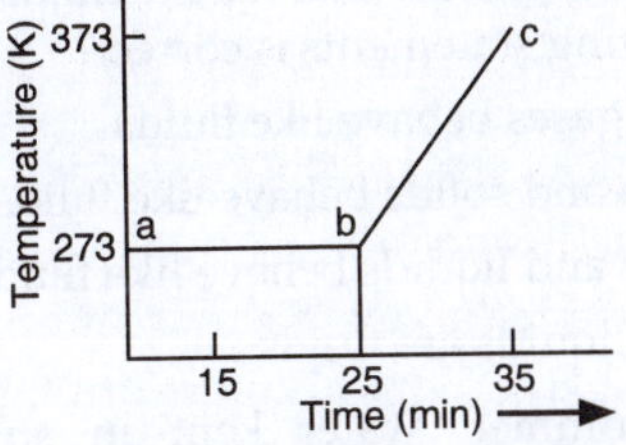

(i) What does the curve a b represent ?

(ii) What happens after 25 minutes ?

(iii) What does the curve b c represent ?

(iv) At what temperature and time ice melts ?

Ans. (i) The curve a b represents that ice and water are in equilibrium and temperature remains constant (273 K).

(ii) At 25 min, the ice gets completely converted to water and temperature of water increases on further heating.

(iii) The curve b c represents increasing temperature of water on heating.

(iv) Ice melts at 273 K after 25 minutes.

Revision Exercise

Answers and Hints on Page 45

OBJECTIVE QUESTIONS

A. Multiple Choice Questions

I. NCERT Exemplar Problems

1. Which one of the following sets of phenomena would increase on raising the temperature?
   (*a*) Diffusion, evaporation, compression of gases
   (*b*) Evaporation, compression of gases, solubility
   (*c*) Evaporation, diffusion, expansion of gases
   (*d*) Evaporation, solubility, diffusion, compression of gases
2. Seema visited a Natural Gas Compressing Unit and found that the gas can be liquefied under specific conditions of temperature and pressure. While sharing her experience with friends she got confused. Help her to identify the correct set of conditions
   (*a*) Low temperature, low pressure
   (*b*) High temperature, low pressure
   (*c*) Low temperature, high pressure
   (*d*) High temperature, high pressure
3. The property to flow is unique to fluids. Which one of the following statements is correct?
   (*a*) Only gases behave like fluids
   (*b*) Gases and solids behave like fluids
   (*c*) Gases and liquids behave like fluids
   (*d*) Only liquids are fluids
4. During summer, water kept in an earthen pot becomes cool because of the phenomenon of
   (*a*) diffusion (*b*) transpiration
   (*c*) osmosis (*d*) evaporation
5. A few substances are arranged in the increasing order of 'forces of attraction' between their particles. Which one of the following represents a correct arrangement?
   (*a*) Water, air, wind (*b*) Air, sugar, oil
   (*c*) Oxygen, water, sugar (*d*) Salt, juice, air
6. On converting 25°C, 38°C and 66°C to Kelvin scale, the correct sequence of temperature will be
   (*a*) 298 K, 311 K and 339 K
   (*b*) 298 K, 300 K and 338 K
   (*c*) 273 K, 278 K and 543 K
   (*d*) 298 K, 310 K and 338 K
7. Choose the correct statement of the following
   (*a*) conversion of solid into vapours without passing through the liquid state is called vaporisation.
   (*b*) conversion of vapours into solid without passing through the liquid state is called sublimation.
   (*c*) conversion of vapours into solid without passing through the liquid state is called freezing.
   (*d*) conversion of solid into liquid is called sublimation.
8. The boiling points of diethyl ether, acetone and n-butyl alcohol are 35°C, 56°C and 118°C respectively. Which one of the following correctly represents their boiling points in Kelvin scale?
   (*a*) 306 K, 329 K, 391 K (*b*) 308 K, 329 K, 392 K
   (*c*) 308 K, 329 K, 391 K (*d*) 329 K, 392 K, 308 K
9. Which condition out of the following will increase the evaporation of water?
   (*a*) Increase in temperature of water
   (*b*) Decrease in temperature of water
   (*c*) Less exposed surface area of water
   (*d*) Adding common salt to water
10. In which of the following conditions, the distance between the molecules of hydrogen gas would increase?
    (*i*) Increasing pressure on hydrogen contained in a closed container
    (*ii*) Some hydrogen gas leaking out of the container
    (*iii*) Increasing the volume of the container of hydrogen gas
    (*iv*) Adding more hydrogen gas to the container without increasing the volume of the container
    (*a*) (*i*) and (*iii*) (*b*) (*i*) and (*iv*)
    (*c*) (*ii*) and (*iii*) (*d*) (*ii*) and (*iv*)

II. Additional Questions

1. What is the correct term for the phase change from gas directly into solid?
   (*a*) Evaporation (*b*) Sublimation
   (*c*) Fusion (*d*) Condensation
2. When a crystal of copper sulphate is added to water in a beaker, water becomes blue. This is an example of
   (*a*) diffusion (*b*) evaporation
   (*c*) sublimation (*d*) effusion
3. When heat is supplied by a burner to boiling water, then the temperature of water during vaporisation
   (*a*) rises slowly
   (*b*) rises rapidly
   (*c*) first rises and then becomes constant
   (*d*) does not rise at all

4. A gas can be liquefied by
(*a*) lowering the temperature
(*b*) increasing the temperature
(*c*) increasing the pressure
(*d*) both by increasing the pressure and lowering the temperature

5. A liquid boils at 100°C. Its temperature can also be expressed as
(*a*) 87.5° F (*b*) 373 K (*c*) 173 K (*d*) 132° F

6. The three states of water; ice, water and steam can be arranged in the decreasing order of interparticle forces as
(*a*) ice < steam < water (*b*) water < steam < ice
(*c*) ice < water < steam (*d*) steam < water < ice

7. When water solidifies to ice, then heat is
(*a*) absorbed
(*b*) evolved
(*c*) may be evolved or absorbed
(*d*) no change in heat

8. Evaporation decreases by
(*a*) increase in temperature
(*b*) increase in humidity
(*c*) increase in wind speed
(*d*) increase in surface area

9. Which of the following state has maximum energy?
(*a*) ice (*b*) water
(*c*) steam (*d*) all have same energy

10. Which of the following is not matter?
(*a*) Cold drink (*b*) Cold
(*c*) Hot coffee (*d*) Air

11. The three states of matter are:
(*a*) melting point, boiling point and freezing point
(*b*) ice, liquid water and water vapour
(*c*) solid, liquid and gas
(*d*) sublimation, condensation and evaporation

12. Freezing involves the conversion of
(*a*) solid to liquid state (*b*) liquid to gaseous state
(*c*) liquid to solid state (*d*) solid to gaseous state

13. Which of the following is not a matter ?
(*a*) Chair (*b*) Air
(*c*) Smell (*d*) Cold drink.

14. 300 K temperature may be written in Celsius scale as
(*a*) 300°C (*b*) 127°C (*c*) 27°C (*d*) 573°C.

15. The physical state of water at 10°C is
(*a*) Solid (*b*) liquid
(*c*) gas (*d*) may be solid or liquid.

16. The substance which can readily sublime is
(*a*) Ammonium chloride (*b*) Sodium chloride
(*c*) Hydrochloric acid (*d*) Chlorine gas.

17. The large volumes of gases can be put into small volumes of cylinders because of their property known as
(*a*) Sublimation (*b*) Compressibility
(*c*) Evaporation (*d*) Solidification.

18. The temperature at which a liquid changes into gas is known as
(*a*) melting point (*b*) transition point
(*c*) boiling point (*d*) Kelvin point.

19. The boiling point of water at normal atmospheric pressure is
(*a*) 273 K (*b*) 373 K (*c*) 100 K (*d*) 0°C

20. Which of the following factor does not increase the rate of evaporation ?
(*a*) increase of temperature
(*b*) increase in wind speed
(*c*) increase in surface area
(*d*) increase in humidity

21. Which of the following is not correct regarding gases?
(*a*) Gases exert pressure
(*b*) Gases are more compressible than liquids
(*c*) Gases have very weak tendency to diffuse
(*d*) Gases have weak intermolecular forces of attraction.

22. In the sublimation process
(*a*) a solid changes directly to vapour state
(*b*) liquid changes to vapour state
(*c*) solid initially melts and then changes to vapour state
(*d*) vapour changes to the liquid state.

23. The standard room temperature is taken as
(*a*) 273 K (*b*) 0°C (*c*) 298 K (*d*) 373 K

24. Which of the following statements is not correct ?
(*a*) Steam produces more severe burns on the skin than the boiling water.
(*b*) Water at room temperature is a liquid.
(*c*) Ice at 273 K causes less cooling than water at the same temperature.
(*d*) We can sip hot tea from a saucer faster than from a cup.

25. Match the conversion in Column I with its term in Column II.

Column I	Column II
(P) Gas ⟶ Liquid	1. Evaporation
(Q) Solid ⟶ Liquid	2. Sublimation
(R) Solid ⟶ Gas	3. Condensation
(S) Liquid ⟶ Gas	4. Melting

(*a*) P–1, Q–3, R–2, S–4 (*b*) P–4, Q–3, R–1, S–2
(*c*) P–3, Q–4, R–2, S–1 (*d*) P–2, Q–4, R–1, S–3

26. Match the property (column I) with the state/states (column II).

Column I	Column II
(P) strongest interparticle forces of attraction	1. Liquid
(Q) easily compressible	2. Liquid and gas
(R) tendency to flow	3. Gas
(S) have fixed volume but no fixed shape	4. Solid

(*a*) P–4, Q–3, R–2, S–1 (*b*) P–4, Q–1, R–2, S–3
(*c*) P–4, Q–1, R–3, S–2 (*d*) P–3, Q–2, R–1, S–4

27. Match Column I and Column II

Column I	Column II
(P) changes directly into gaseous state	1. Latent heat
(Q) heat energy required to change state of a substance	2. Evaporation
(R) increases with increase in temperature	3. Plasma state
(S) consist of super energetic and super excited particles	4. Camphor

(*a*) P–3, Q–1, R–2, S–4 (*b*) P–4, Q–1, R–2, S–3
(*c*) P–2, Q–1, R–2, S–4 (*d*) P–4, Q–2, R–3, S–1

B. Assertion–Reason Type Questions

For the following questions, two statements are given-one labeled *Assertion* (A) and the other labeled *Reason* (R). Select the correct answer to these questions from the codes (*a*), (*b*), (*c*) and (*d*) as given below:

(*a*) *Both A and R are true and R is correct explanation of the assertion.*
(*b*) *Both A and R are true but R is not the correct explanation of the assertion*
(*c*) *A is true but R is false.*
(*d*) *A is false but R is true.*

1. **Assertion:** Solids donot diffuse in air.
Reason: The particles of solids are closely packed.
2. **Assertion:** The temperature of water remains constant during evaporation.
Reason: Liquid water on heating, changes to water vapour.
3. **Assertion:** Ice floats over water.
Reason: Liquids have lower density than solids.
4. **Assertion:** Evaporation is a surface phenomenon.
Reason: Particles of a liquid lose energy and leave the surface.
5. **Assertion:** Liquids diffuse more easily as compared to gases.
Reason: Intermolecular forces are more in liquids than gases.
6. **Assertion:** The rate of evaporation increases with increase in temperature.
Reason: Increase in temperature increases the kinetic energy of the particles.
7. **Assertion:** A gas fills the vessel completely.
Reason: The interparticles forces in gases are strongest.
8. **Assertion:** When common salt is added to water, there will be no change in volume.
Reason: Particles of common salt occupy inter particle spaces present in water.
9. **Assertion:** Naphthalene balls disappear with time without leaving any residue.
Reason: Naphthalene is a volatile solid.
10. **Assertion:** The particles in steam have more energy than water at the same temperature.
Reason: Latent heat of vaporization of water is 2.25×10^6 Jkg^{-1}.

C. Fill in the Blanks

1. With increase in surface area, evaporation ________.
2. The process of change of a solid directly into vapour state is called ________.
3. Solid carbon dioxide is called ________.
4. The condensation process is opposite to ________ process.
5. The force exerted by gas molecules per unit area on the walls of the container is called its ________.
6. Among the three states of matter ________ state is most compressible.
7. In liquid state, the intermolecular forces are ________ than solid state.
8. If the boiling point of a substance is above the room temperative, it exists as ________.
9. The temperature at which a liquid changes into gas/vapour is called ________.
10. Intermolecular space in solid is ________ than that of liquids.

D. Paragraph Based Questions

Answer the questions on the basis of your understanding of the following paragraph and the related studied concepts:

1. In nature, water keeps on changing its form. The heat of the sun evaporates the water on the surface of the earth into vapour. The evaporation of water takes place from oceans, rivers, lakes and ponds all the time. Sometimes, it is slow and sometimes, it is fast. The reverse process of evaporation is condensation, in which water vapour change into water by cooling. The formation of clouds, rain and water cycle is due to these two processes. Like evaporation, condensation also plays very important role in nature. Because of condensation, dew, fog, frost, hail, snow, etc., are formed under different conditions.

1(*a*) The conversion of liquid water to vapour is called evaporation. What is meant by latent heat of vaporisation?

1(*b*) Is condensation same as sublimation?

1(*c*) What is the boiling point of water at 1 atmospheric pressure on the Kelvin scale?

1(*d*) Does evaporation depend on the nature of the liquid?

2. A student heated a pure substance 'X' and obtained the following heat curve at 1 atmospheric pressure:

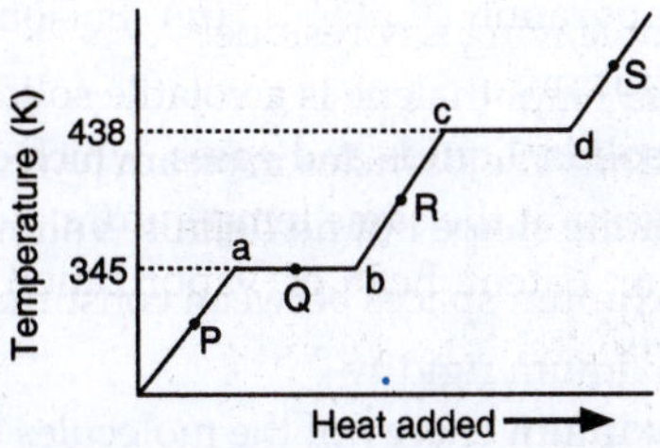

2(*a*) What is the freezing point of the substance in °C ?

2(*b*) What is the boiling point of the substance in K ?

2(*c*) What is the physical state of the substance at points P, Q, R and S ?

2(*d*) What does the line a b represent ?

Very Short Answer Questions

1. Name the physical state of matter which can be easily compressed.
2. Name a substance which sublimes.
3. Define evaporation.
4. Name the physical state of matter which is most rigid.
5. Give the characteristics of liquid.
6. Define (*i*) melting point and (*ii*) boiling point.
7. The boiling point of ethyl alcohol is 78.6°C. Explain it in Kelvin scale.
8. Which will have more density ice or steam?
9. In which physical state water exists at
   (*a*) 100°C (*b*) 0°C
10. Justify the statement "Sand is a solid".
11. At what temperature solid ice and liquid water coexist together?
12. Define latent heat of fusion.
13. Out of solids and liquids which will have greater movement of molecules.
14. Define sublimation.
15. What happens when you pour some acetone on your palm?
16. Will increase of surface area increase or decrease rate of evaporation?
17. What is fusion?
18. Write heat or cool on the arrows in the following :
    Solid state $\underset{(ii)}{\overset{(i)}{\rightleftarrows}}$ **Liquid state**
19. Will increase or decrease of pressure help to liquefy a gas?
20. Which of the following are matter :
    (*i*) Paper (*ii*) Ink (*iii*) Thought
    (*iv*) Pen (*v*) Smell.

Short Answer Questions

1. Define the following :
   (*i*) Latent heat of vaporisation
   (*ii*) Latent heat of fusion
   (*iii*) Sublimation
2. Compare the intermolecular forces between particles of a solid, a liquid and a gas.
3. Explain the following characteristics of gases :
   (*i*) Compressibility
   (*ii*) Gas pressure
   (*iii*) Diffusion
4. What is matter? Write three states of water in which it exists. Give two differences between these states.
5. Give reasons to justify
   (*i*) Wood is a solid.
   (*ii*) Water is a liquid at room temperature.
   (*iii*) A gas exerts pressure.
6. What is evaporation ? How will you show that evaporation causes cooling ?
7. Why do we see water droplets on the outer surface of a glass containing ice cold water ? Explain.
8. How do solids, liquids and gases differ in shape, volume and interparticle forces ?
9. Why do gases
   (*i*) exert pressure
   (*ii*) fill the containers completely in which placed
   (*iii*) get compressed
   Explain.
10. Convert the following :
    (*i*) 395 K to Celsius scale
    (*ii*) 27°C to Kelvin scale
    (*iii*) 1.01 x 10^5 Pa to atmosphere
11. Define the following :
    (*i*) boiling point
    (*ii*) evaporation
    (*iv*) latent heat of vaporisation
12. Give reasons for the following :
    (*a*) The smell of hot sizzling food reaches us several metres away but to get the smell from cold food you have to go close.
    (*b*) Naphthalene balls disappear without leaving any solid.
    (*c*) We can easily move our hand in air but to do the same through a solid block of wood or brick, we need a karate expert.
13. Compare the three states of matter in terms of
    (*i*) Compressibility
    (*ii*) Density
    (*iii*) Energy of molecules.
14. Explain the following :
    (*a*) Our palm feel cool when we put some acetone on it.

(*b*) We can sip hot tea or milk faster from a saucer rather than a cup.

(*c*) The smell of a perfume can be felt even at metres away.

15. Explain the following :

(*i*) Diffusion occurs more quickly in a gas than in a liquid.

(*ii*) Steam causes more severe burns than boiling water.

(*iii*) Rate of evaporation decreases with increase in humidity in the atmosphere.

Long Answer Questions

1. What is matter ? Explain the three states of matter on the basis of particulate nature of matter.

2. Explain the following :

(*i*) Gases exert pressure

(*ii*) Evaporation causes cooling

(*iii*) Solids can be converted to liquids

(*iv*) Gases diffuse rapidly

(*v*) Cotton clothes are comfortable in summer.

3. Define the following terms :

(*i*) Latent heat of fusion (*ii*) Sublimation

(*iii*) Evaporation (*iv*) Fusion

(*v*) Diffusion.

4. Out of solids, liquids and gases, which one has

(*i*) definite shape but no definite volume

(*ii*) maximum spaces between constituent particles

(*iii*) maximum rigidity

(*iv*) maximum energy of the molecules

(*v*) maximum compressibility.

5. Give one simple activity/experiment to show

(*i*) particles of matter are very very small

(*ii*) rate of diffusion in liquids increases with rise in temperature

(*iii*) Ammonium chloride sublimes.

6. (*a*) How will you justify that ice, water and steam are not different substaces but different states of the same substances ?

(*b*) Arrange these in increasing order of interparticle forces.

(*c*) Which of these states are regarded as fluids ?

7. What is evaporation? Discuss three factors on which evaporation depends.

Solution File

Answer & Solutions to Selected Questions

Practice Exercises

Practice Exercise 1A

1. (*i*), (*ii*), (*iii*), (*vi*), (*ix*), (*x*) **2.** Ice (solid), water (liquid), steam (gas) **3.** (*c*) < (*b*) < (*a*)

4. steam **5.** gaseous state **6.** solid state **7.** (*a*) gas (*b*) gas (*c*) gas (*d*) solid

8. (*a*) ice (*b*) steam (*c*) water **9.** (*i*) gas (*ii*) solid (*iii*) liquid **10.** gas phase

11. vibratory motion **12.** yes **13.** steam < water < ice **14.** gas

15. solid state **16.** Liquids are called fluids because they can flow and are not rigid.

17. (*i*) Water at room temperature is a liquid because

(*a*) Water has no definite shape. It takes the shape of the container.

(*b*) Water has definite volume.

(*ii*) An iron almirah is a solid because

(*a*) It has definite shape. (*b*) It has fixed volume.

19. The molecules in a gaseous state are free to move and they can move in a random manner in the container. During their motion, they collide with one another and also with the walls of the container. The constant bombardment of the molecules on the walls of the container exerts a steady force. This force per unit area on the walls of container is called pressure. Thus, gases exert pressure.

20. (*a*) more (*b*) rigid (*c*) less (*d*) larger (*e*) more

Practice Exercise 1B

1. (*i*) 50°C (*ii*) 327°C
2. (*i*) 400K (*ii*) 293K
3. (*a*) 99 (*b*) 355 (*c*) 746 (*d*) 296 (*e*) 1.01×10^5 (*f*) 2 (*g*) 2 (*h*) 1
4. (*i*) camphor (*ii*) Ammonium chloride
5. melting, evaporation
6. B
7. (*i*) solidification (*ii*) sublimation (*iii*) condensation (*iv*) sublimation
8. higher
9. A : 280 K B : 360 K C : 320 K
10. (*i*) heating (*ii*) cooling (*iii*) heating
11. (*i*) and (*iii*)
12. (*a*) evaporation (*b*) sublimation (*c*) condensation
13. (*a*) increases (*b*) decreases (*c*) increases (*d*) increases (*e*) decreases
14. (*a*) melting (*b*) evaporation (*c*) freezing (*d*) condensation
15. Liquid state
16. Condensation.
17. Kelvin scale is regarded as better scale because in celsius scale of temperature we also come across negative value for temperature (e.g. –20°C). But in Kelvin scale value is always positive and therefore, it is better.
18. At the melting point of ice i.e., 0°C.
19. Liquefied Petroleum Gas, Compressed Natural Gas.
20. more on a humid day.
21. Cotton clothes.
22. (*i*) increase of temperature (*ii*) increase of surface area.
23. K = °C + 273
24. Evaporation
25. (*i*) The amount of heat energy that is required to change 1 kg of a solid into liquid at atmospheric pressure without any change of temperature is called latent heat of fusion.
    (*ii*) The amount of heat energy that is required to change 1 kg of a liquid into vapour at atmospheric pressure without any change of temperature is called heat of vaporisaton.
26. (*a*) (*i*) Boiling point is the temperature at which a liquid changes into gas or vapour.
    (*ii*) Melting point is the temperature at which a solid melts to become a liquid.
    (*b*) When we heat the ice at its melting point, the heat is used up in changing the state by overcoming the intermolecular forces of attraction. Since the heat is absorbed by ice, there is no change in temperature.
27.

Evaporation	Boiling
1. Evaporation process takes place spontaneously at all temperatures.	Boiling takes place only at definite temperature (boiling point) at which the vapour pressure of the liquid is equal to the atmospheric pressure.
2. Evaporation takes place only at the surface of the liquid.	Boiling takes place even below the surface of the liquid in the form of bubbles.

28. (*a*) Latent heat is the amount of energy required to change the state of a substance.
    Latent heat is of two types:
    (*i*) Latent heat of fusion (*ii*) Latent heat of vaporisation
    (*b*) 3.35×10^5 J/kg
29. (*i*) Condensation (*ii*) Sublimation (*iii*) temperature (*iv*) boiling point (*v*) latent heat of fusion

Revision Exercise

OBJECTIVE QUESTIONS

A. Multiple Choice Questions

I. NCERT Exemplar Problems

1. (*c*) 2. (*c*)
3. (*c*) : Gases and liquids have tendency to flow and therefore behave as fluids.
4. (*d*) 5. (*c*)
6. (*a*) : Correct sequence : 273 + 25 = 298 K, 273 + 38 = 311 K, 273 + 66 = 339 K
7. (*b*)

8. (*c*) : 273 + 35 = 308 K, 273 + 56 = 329 K, 273 + 118 = 391 K.
9. (*a*)
10. (*c*) : By removing either hydrogen gas from the container or by increasing volume of the container, distance between the molecules increases.

II. Additional Questions

1. (*b*) sublimation involves direct change from solid to gas.
2. (*a*) 3. (*d*) 4. (*d*) 5. (*b*) 273 + 100 = 373 K
6. (*d*) 7. (*b*) 8. (*b*) 9. (*c*) 10. (*b*)
11. (*c*) solid, liquid and gas are three phases of all matter.
12. (*c*) 13. (*c*) Smell is not a matter.
14. (*c*) K = 273 + °C

∴ °C = K – 273 = 300 – 273 = 27°C

15. (*b*) 16. (*a*) 17. (*b*) 18. (*c*)
19. (*b*) The boiling point of water at normal atmospheric pressure is 100°C or 373 K.
20. (*d*) Increase in humidity decreases rate of evaporation.
21. (*c*) 22. (*a*)
23. (*b*) The standard room temperature is taken as 25°C or 298 K.
24. (*c*) 25. (*c*) 26. (*a*) 27. (*b*).

B. Assertion–Reason Type

1. (*a*)
2. (*b*) The temperature of water remains constant during evaporation because heat supplied is used up in changing the state from liquid water to water vapour by breaking the forces of attraction.
3. (*b*) Ice floats over water because ice has lower density than water.

In general, liquids have lower density than solids.

4. (*c*) Particles of liquid gain energy and leave the surface.
5. (*d*) Liquids diffuse less easily as compared to gases. Intermolecular forces are more in liquids than gases.
6. (*a*)
7. (*c*) The interparticle forces in gases are the weakest among the three states of matter.
8. (*a*)
9. (*b*) Naphthalene undergoes sublimation.
10. (*b*)

C. Fill in the Blanks

1. increases 2. sublimation
3. dry ice 4. evaporation
5. pressure 6. gaseous
7. weaker 8. liquid
9. boiling point 10. less

D. Paragraph Based Questions

1(*a*) Latent heat of vaporisation gives the amount of heat energy required to change 1 kg of liquid into its vapour at atmospheric pressure without any change in temperature at its boiling point.

1(*b*) No, condensation and sublimation are different.

1(*c*) 373 K

1(*d*) Evaporation depends on the nature of the liquid.

2(*a*) The freezing point of the substance is 72°C.

2(*b*) The boiling point of the substance is 438 K.

2(*c*) The physical states of the substance are : at P : solid, Q : solid and liquid, R : liquid, S : as gas.

2(*d*) Line a b represents that temperature remains constant during the conversion of solid into liquid.

Very Short Answer Questions

1. Gaseous 2. Camphor
4. Solid 7. 78.6 + 273 = 351.6 K
8. Ice 9. (*a*) vapour (*b*) Ice
11. At the melting point of ice (0°C)
13. liquids 16. Increase
18. (*i*) heat (*ii*) cool 19. increase
20. (*i*), (*ii*), (*iv*)

Short Answer Questions

10. (*a*) 122°C (*b*) 300 K (*c*) 1 atmosphere

Long Answer Questions

4. (*i*) Liquids (*ii*) Gases (*iii*) Solids (*iv*) Gases (*v*) Gases

Competition File

NTSE-SAT—Target: Scholastic Aptitude Test

1. Which of the following has highest intermolecular forces of attraction?

(*a*) liquid water (*b*) liquid ethyl alcohol
(*c*) gaseous CO_2 (*d*) solid CO_2.

(NTSE 2012-13)

2. When water solidifies to ice, then heat is

(*a*) absorbed (*b*) evolved
(*c*) heat may be evolved or absorbed
(*d*) no change in heat

3. The three states of matter can be arranged in the decreasing order of interparticle forces as
(*a*) solid > gas > liquid (*b*) liquid > gas > solid
(*c*) solid > liquid > gas (*d*) gas > liquid > solid
(NTSE 2013-14)

4. The freezing point of water is
(*a*) 273 K (*b*) 298 K (*c*) 373 K (*d*) 300 K

5. 1 atm is equal to
(*a*) 1 Pascal (*b*) 1.01×10^5 Pascal
(*c*) 1 mm Hg (*d*) 100 mm Hg

6. A solid melts at 52°C. Its temperature on Kelvin scale is
(*a*) 52 K (*b*) 325 K
(*c*) 352 K (*d*) 425 K *(NTSE 2014-15)*

7. A substance is said to be in the liquid state if under normal pressure its
(*a*) melting point is above the room temperature
(*b*) boiling point is below the room temperature
(*c*) melting point is below the room temperature
(*d*) boiling point is above the room temperature.

8. Which of the following statements explains why a gas fills the container in which it is kept?
(*i*) The particles in a gas are larger than those in a liquid.
(*ii*) The particles in a gas have very small attractive forces between them.
(*iii*) The particles in a gas are constantly moving very quickly.
(*a*) (*i*) only (*b*) (*ii*) only
(*c*) (*i*) and (*ii*) (*d*) (*ii*) and (*iii*)

9. When heat is supplied constantly by a gas burner with a small flame to melt ice, then the temperature of ice during melting.
(*a*) increases slowly to form water
(*b*) remains constant
(*c*) first remains constant and then decreases
(d) decreases very slowly. *(NTSE 2012-13)*

10. The conversion of a solid into vapours without passing through the liquid state is called
(*a*) sublimation (*b*) vaporisation
(*c*) fusion (*d*) liquefication
(NTSE 2013-14)

11. Latent heat of vaporisation of water is
(*a*) 18 kJ/kg (*b*) 22.5×10^2 kJ/kg
(*c*) 3.34×10^5 J/kg (*d*) Zero *(NTSE 2013-14)*

12. Which of the following does not undergo sublimation?
(*a*) Sodium chloride (*b*) Ammonium chloride
(*c*) Camphor (*d*) Iodine *(NTSE 2013-14)*

13. Ice melts at 0°C. This temperature is equivalent to
(*a*) 32°F (*b*) 0°F (*c*) 273°F (*d*) 66°F

14. The body temperature of a normal healthy person is 98.6°F. What is the temperature on the Celsius scale?
(*a*) 42°C (*b*) 28.6°C (*c*) 37°C (*d*) 48.2°C

15. When water solidifies to ice, then heat is
(*a*) absorbed (*b*) evolved
(*c*) no change
(*d*) may be evolved or absorbed

16. At the melting point temparature of ice,
(*a*) only ice is present
(*b*) only water is present
(*c*) both ice and water are present
(*d*) none of these is correct.

17. Dry ice is an example of .... process.
(*a*) evaporation (*b*) crystallisation
(*c*) sublimation (*d*) purification
(NTSE 2014-15)

18. The boiling point of a gas is – 80°C. This temperature is equivalent to
(*a*) –193 K (*b*) 193 K
(*c*) 353 K (*d*) –353 K.
(NTSE 2015-16)

19. The melting point of ice is ________.
(*a*) 273.15 K (*b*) 173.15 K
(*c*) 373.5 K (*d*) 100 K.
(NTSE 2018-19)

20. Physical state of water at 0°C is
(*a*) Solid (*b*) Liquid
(*c*) Gas (*d*) None of these
(NTSE 2018-19)

ANSWERS AND HINTS (NTSE) : SAT

1. (*d*) 2. (*b*) 3. (*c*) 4. (*a*) 5. (*b*)
6. (*b*) 273 + 52 = 325 K
7. (*c*) 8. (*d*) 9. (*b*) 10. (*a*) 11. (*b*) 12. (*a*)
13. (*a*)
14. (*c*) $°F = \frac{9}{5}(°C) + 32 \Rightarrow \frac{9}{5}(°C) = °F - 32$
$= 98.6 - 32 = 66.6 \Rightarrow °C = \frac{66.6 \times 5}{9} = 37°C$
15. (*b*) 16. (*c*) 17. (*c*)
18. (*b*) K = 273 + °C = 273 + (– 80) = 273 – 80 = 193 K
19. (*a*) 20. (*a*)

CHAPTER PRACTICE TEST

Time allowed : 1 Hour **Maximum Marks : 20**

1. Define sublimation 1
2. Answer questions 2(*a*) to 2(*d*) on the basis of the following observation and the related studied concepts:

   A student heats a beaker containing ice and water. He measures the temperature of the beaker as a function of time and draws the following graph.

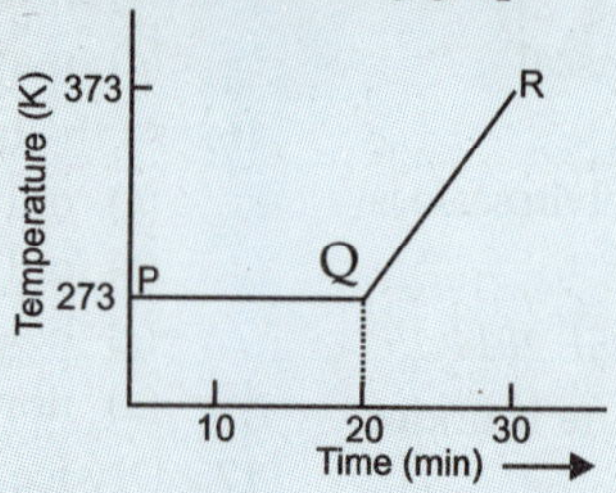

Answer the following questions :

2(*a*) At what temperature and time does ice melts? 1

2(*b*) What does the curve PQ represent? 1

2(*c*) Is evaporation and boiling the same? Give reasons. 1

2(*d*) State physical state of water at 373 K. 1

3. During summer, water kept in an earthen pot becomes cool because of the phenomenon of

   (*a*) sublimation (*b*) evaporation (*c*) diffusion (*d*) condensation 1
4. The three states of matter can be arranged in the decreasing order of interparticle forces as: 1

   (*a*) solid > liquid > gas (*b*) liquid > gas > solid

   (*c*) solid > gas > liquid (*d*) gas > liquid > solid
5. A solid melts at 72°C. Its temperature in Kelvin scale is 1

   (*a*) 355 K (*b*) 345 K (*c*) 172 K (*d*) 201 K
6. For the following questions two statements are given- one labeled *Assertion* (A) and the other labeled *Reason* (R). Select the correct answer to these questions from the codes (*a*), (*b*), (*c*) and (*d*) as given below:

   (*a*) Both A and R are true and R is correct explanation of the assertion

   (*b*) Both A and R are true and R is not the correct explanation of the assertion

   (*c*) A is true but R is false

   (*d*) A is false but R is true.

   Assertion : Liquids diffuse less easily as compared to gases. 1

   Reason : Interparticle forces in liquids are less than those in gases.
7. Explain the following :

   (*i*) A gas fills completely the vessel in which it is kept.

   (*ii*) Naphthalene balls disappear with time without leaving any solid.

   (*iii*) A desert cooler cools better on a hot dry day. 3
8. (*i*) What is evaporation? Name two factors on which it depends.

   (*ii*) Define latent heat of vaporisation. 3
9. (*a*) Enumerate the changes that take place inside the matter during the change of states.

   (*b*) When a solid melts, its temperature remains constant. Why ?

   (*c*) When sugar dissolves in water, the level of water does not rise appreciably. Why ? 5

❑❑❑

Chapter 2

Is Matter Around Us Pure ?

When we go to the market, we notice the word "pure" written on the packs of many items; on a packet of milk, ghee (butter), fruit juice, etc. For a common person, this means that there is no adulteration in these things and therefore, these are pure. However, according to scientists these may not be pure. According to scientists, **a pure substance means that it is a single substance**. For example, milk is not pure because it is not a single substance. Milk is actually a mixture of different substances such as water, fats, proteins etc.

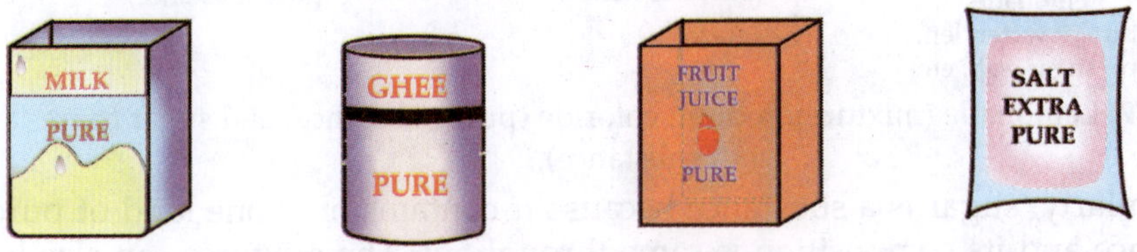

Fig. 1. Some consumable items in the market, marked 'pure'.

We sometimes say that air of this place is pure. This simply means that air at that place does not have pollution. Scientifically, air is not a pure substance because it is a mixture of several gases and water vapours.

According to scientists,

a pure substance consists of a single type of particles.

This means that all the constituting particles of a pure substance are the same in their chemical nature. Thus, ***a pure substance represents a single substance.***

As we look around, we can see that most of matter around us exist as mixtures of two or more pure substances or components. For example, sea water, minerals, air, soil etc. are all mixtures.

Thus, all the matter around us is of two types:

(*i*) pure substances and

(*ii*) mixtures.

PURE SUBSTANCES AND MIXTURES

Most of the materials that we come across in our daily life are mixtures. A mixture contains more than one kind of pure substances. A mixture may be solid, liquid or gas. For example, water from a pond or a river is a mixture of many salts, sand and clay particles. The water that we drink also contains very small amounts of various salts dissolved in

In this chapter

it. The air around us is a mixture of some gases such as oxygen, nitrogen, carbon dioxide, argon and water vapour. Some dust particles and smoke particles are also present in air. Many substances such as milk, jaggery (gur), sharbat drink, etc. which appear to contain only one type of substance are in fact mixtures. They contain different types of substances present in them. Thus,

mixture is made up of two or more pure substances.

The substances which make a mixture are called **constituents** or **components.** The components of a mixture retain their properties. The properties of a mixture are those of the substances of which mixture is made up. For example, lemonade (nimbu pani) is a mixture of water, lemon juice, sugar and salt. When we drink it, we get the sour taste of lemon, salty taste of salt and sweet taste of sugar. Moreover, since it contains water also, it quenches our thirst like water.

A mixture can be separated by physical methods into its two or more pure substances. For example, sodium chloride dissolved in water can be separated from water by the physical process of evaporation. However, sodium chloride is itself a substance and cannot be separated by any physical process into its chemical constituents.

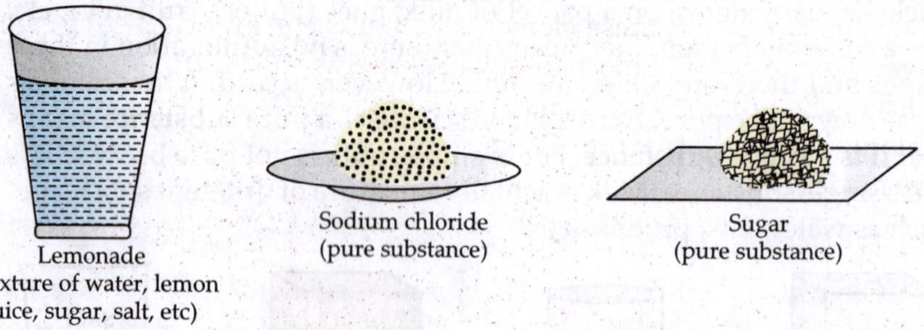

Fig. 2. Lemonade (mixture), sodium chloride (pure substance) and sugar (pure substance).

Similarly, sugar is a substance because it contains only one kind of pure substance and its composition is same throughout. The mixtures can also be obtained by mixing two or more pure substances without any chemical change in any proportion.

Let us learn more about pure substances and mixtures.

WHAT ARE THE TYPES OF PURE SUBSTANCES

On the basis of their chemical composition, the pure substances can be classified as:

(*i*) Elements (*ii*) Compounds

Elements

Robert Boyle was the first scientist to use the term element in 1661. He said that element could not be broken down into simpler substances. This definition of an element is still applicable. Antoine Laurent Lavoisier, a French chemist was the first to establish an experimentally useful definition of an element. According to him an **element** may be defined as :

A substance which can neither be broken down into simpler substances nor formed from two or more simpler substances by any known physical or chemical process.

For example, hydrogen is an element because it cannot be split up into two or more simpler substances by the usual methods of carrying out chemical reactions by applying heat, light and electricity. The common examples of elements are : hydrogen, oxygen, nitrogen, iron, gold, copper, mercury, sulphur, carbon, etc.

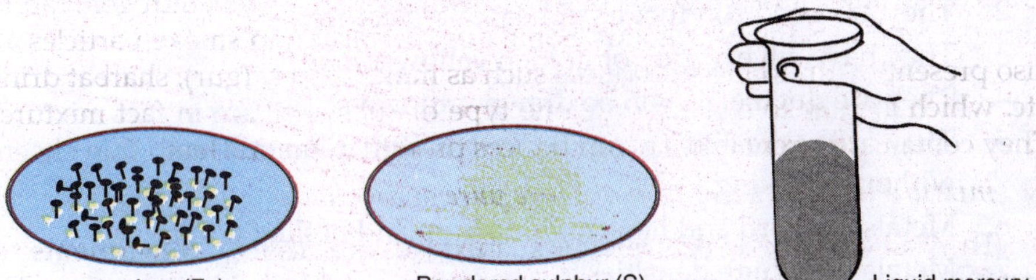

Fig. 3. Elements : Iron, sulphur and mercury.

An element cannot be split up into two or more simpler substances because it is **made up of only one kind of atoms.** Thus, we can also define an element as **the pure substance which is made up of only one kind of atoms.** For example, iron is an element and it is made up of only one kind of atoms called iron atoms. Similarly, element sulphur is made up of only sulphur atoms, the element mercury is made up of only mercury atoms and so on.

There are about 118 elements known at present. Out of these, about 92 have so far been found to occur naturally and the remaining have been prepared in the laboratories. All these elements do not occur in the crust of earth to the same proportion. The most abundant elements in the earth's crust are oxygen, silicon, aluminium, iron, calcium, sodium, potassium, magnesium, hydrogen, chlorine, carbon, etc. From these elements, all other substances on the earth are made. Thus,

the elements are regarded as the building blocks of the universe.

Oxygen and silicon are most common elements and they are the major constituents of sand, soil and rocks. Oxygen also occurs as free element in the atmosphere and in combination with hydrogen in water. The most common elements found in our body are oxygen, carbon, hydrogen, nitrogen, calcium, phosphorus, etc.

Elements may be **solids, liquids** and **gases**. Among all the known elements, only mercury (Hg) and bromine (Br) are liquids at room temperature; hydrogen (H), nitrogen (N), oxygen (O), fluorine (F), chlorine (Cl) and noble gases : Helium (He), neon (Ne), argon (Ar), krypton (Kr), xenon (Xe) etc. are gases while all other elements are solids.

Some common solid elements are carbon (C), sulphur (S), sodium (Na), potassium (K), calcium (Ca), barium (Ba), iron (Fe), copper (Cu), silver (Ag) etc. Thus,

Gaseous elements	:	H, N, O, F, Cl, and **Noble gases :** He, Ne, Ar, Kr, Xe, Rn
Liquid elements	:	Hg, Br
Solid elements	:	All other elements, *e.g.* C, S, Na, K, Ca, Ba, Fe, Ni, Co, Cu, Ag

Classification of Elements as Metals, Non metals and Metalloids

Elements may be simply divided as **metals, non-metals** and **metalloid**, depending upon their properties.

1. Metals

Metals usually show the following properties :

1. Metals have a lustre (shine) and can be polished.

MEMORISE

- Elements are regarded as the **building blocks of the universe.**
- **Nitrogen** is the most abundant element in the atmosphere.
- **Oxygen** is the most abundant element in the earth's crust.
- **Oxygen** and **silicon** are the main constituents of sand, soil and rocks.

MEMORISE

- There are about 118 elements known till today.
- 92 elements are natural and the remaining are man made.
- Most elements are solids.
- 11 elements are gaseous.
- **Mercury is the only metal** which is liquid at room temperature.
- **Bromine is the only non-metal** which is liquid at room temperature.
- Elements **gallium** and **cesium** can exist as liquid at a temperature above 30°C.

2. They are good conductors of heat and electricity.
3. They have silvery grey or golden yellow colour.
4. They are ductile, *i.e.* can be drawn into wires.
5. They are malleable, *i.e.* can be beaten with a hammer into thin sheets without breaking.
6. Metals are hard and have high melting and boiling points.
7. Metals have high densities.
8. Most of the metals are sonorous, i.e. they make a ringing sound when hit with an object.

The common examples of metals are sodium, potassium, zinc, copper, silver, gold, aluminium, iron, etc.

2. Non-metals

Non-metals usually show the following properties :

1. Non-metals are non-lustrous and cannot be polished.
2. They are poor conductors of heat and electricity.
3. They have variety of colours.
4. They are soft and brittle.
5. They are neither malleable nor ductile.
6. They are not sonorous.
7. Non-metals generally have low melting and boiling points.
8. They have low densities.

Examples of non-metals are hydrogen, oxygen, nitrogen, sulphur, iodine, carbon, bromine, phosphorus, etc.

About 80 percent of the elements are metals and the remaining 20 percent are non-metals. All the metals are solids except **mercury** which is a liquid. As we have learnt above, bromine is also liquid at room temperature but it is **non-metal.**

3. Metalloids

Some compounds have intermediate properties between those of metals and non-metals. They show some properties of metals and some properties of non-metals. These are called **metalloids.** The common examples of metalloids are boron (B), silicon (Si), germanium (Ge), arsenic (As), antimony (Sb) etc.

COMPOUNDS

A compound is a pure substance made up of two or more elements chemically combined with one another in a fixed proportion by mass.

It may be noted that a pure compound, whatever its source always contains definite or constant proportions of elements by mass. For example, H_2O is composed of two elements : hydrogen and oxygen. It may be noted that irrespective of its source, all samples of pure water contain these elements combined together in the ratio of 1 : 8 by mass. Similarly, carbon dioxide (CO_2) is a compound made up of two elements, carbon (C) and oxygen (O), chemically combined together in a fixed proportion of 3 : 8 by mass.

Common salt or sodium chloride (NaCl) is a compound made up of two elements sodium (Na) and chlorine (Cl) chemically combined together in a fixed proportion of 23 : 35.5 by mass.

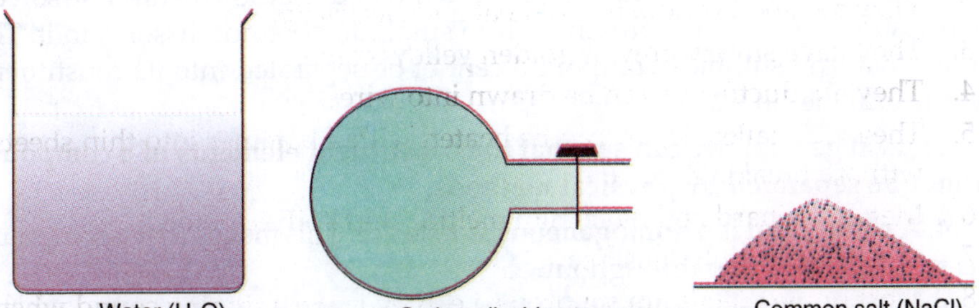

Fig. 4. Compounds : Water (H_2O), carbon dioxide (CO_2) and common salt (NaCl)

Other examples of compounds are ammonia (NH_3), sugar ($C_{12}H_{22}O_{11}$), sodium carbonate or washing soda (Na_2CO_3), chalk or limestone or calcium carbonate ($CaCO_3$), iron sulphide (FeS), hydrogen chloride (HCl), copper sulphate ($CuSO_4$), sulphur dioxide (SO_2) etc.

The compound can be formed by different chemical methods from their constituent elements. Alternately, it can also be decomposed into their constituent elements by different chemical methods.

For example, water is a compound made up of two elements, hydrogen and oxygen. It can be formed by the chemical combination of hydrogen and oxygen in a fixed proportion of 1:8 by mass.

$$\underbrace{\text{Hydrogen + Oxygen}}_{\text{Elements}} \rightleftharpoons \underbrace{\text{Water}}_{\text{Compound}}$$

[Atomic masses : H = 1, O = 16, so that in water, H_2O, $H_2 : O$ = 2:16 = 1:8]

Conversely, water can also be broken down into the elements, hydrogen and oxygen by passing electric current through it.

$$\text{Water} \rightleftharpoons \text{Hydrogen + Oxygen}$$

It may be noted that during decomposition, hydrogen and oxygen are also obtained in a fixed proportion of 1 : 8 by mass.

Thus, a chemical compound contains the same elements in a fixed proportion by mass.

The common examples of compounds are : Water, common salt and carbon dioxide.

Properties of Compounds

The main properties of compounds are given below :

1. A chemical compound consists of two or more elements combined together in a fixed proportion by mass. For example, water (H_2O) is a compound made up of two elements, hydrogen and oxygen combined together in a fixed ratio of 1 : 8 by mass.

2. The properties of a compound are entirely different from those of its constituent elements. Water is a compound made up of hydrogen and oxygen. But the properties of water are different from those of hydrogen and oxygen. Water is a liquid, while hydrogen and oxygen are gases.

Similarly, carbon dioxide is a compound of carbon and oxygen. Carbon is combustible and oxygen is supporter of combustion, but carbon dioxide has entirely different properties. It is neither combustible nor supporter of combustion. Instead, it helps in extinguishing fire.

3. The constituent elements of a compound cannot be separated by mechanical or physical methods. Iron sulphide is a compound of iron and sulphur. If we put a magnet close to the pieces of iron sulphide, iron present in iron sulphide does not get attracted towards the magnet. Further, sulphur

KEY NOTE

It is very interesting to note that only about 112 elements are known. But the number of compounds known is very large. This is not very strange. We know that there are only 26 letters of English alphabet (a, b, c,......x, y, z) but a large number of words can be framed out of these by different combinations of letters. In music also, there are only seven 'swaras' (*sa, re, ga, ma, pa, dha, ni*) but so many tunes can be created with the help of these. Similarly, innumerable compounds can also be prepared by the combinations of two or more kinds of elements.

dissolves in carbon disulphide solvent. But if we add carbon disulphide solvent to iron sulphide, sulphur present in iron sulphide does not dissolve in it. This shows that iron sulphide compound cannot be separated into its constituents by physical methods.

Thus in general, **we can say that the constituent elements of a compound cannot be separated by physical methods.**

4. A compound is a homogeneous substance. This means that a compound has same composition throughout.

For example, iron sulphide is a compound of iron and sulphur. If iron sulphide compound is seen through a magnifying glass or a microscope, no separate particles of iron and sulphur are seen. It appears to be same throughout.

5. A compound has a fixed melting point and boiling point.

For example, ice always melts at 0°C. Iron sulphide has a fixed melting point.

6. The formation of a compound occurs because of a chemical reaction and is accompanied by energy changes.

For example, iron sulphide compound is prepared by heating together iron filings and sulphur. When the reaction starts, a lot of heat and light are produced during the preparation of iron sulphide.

Thus, we can say that energy (in the form of heat, light, etc.) is generally either produced or absorbed during the preparation of a compound.

Since compounds are formed by the chemical combination of elements, they are also called **chemical compounds.**

MIXTURES

A mixture is a substance which consists of two or more pure substances (elements or compounds) mixed together in any proportion so that components do not lose their identity.

For example, air is a mixture of several gases and syrup is a mixture of sugar and water similarly, ghee, oil, milk, sea water, petrol, soil, soft drinks, lemonade, butter, cheese etc are mixtures.

Depending upon the nature of components which form the mixtures, we can have different types of mixtures.

TYPES OF MIXTURES

Mixtures are of two types :

(*i*) *Homogeneous mixtures* and (*ii*) *Heterogeneous mixtures*

(*i*) Homogeneous mixtures

A mixture is said to be homogeneous mixture if it has the same composition throughout the sample. A homogeneous mixture has no visible boundaries of separation between various constituents. For example, salt solution (sodium chloride dissolved in water), sugar solution (sugar dissolved in water), carbonated water (carbon dioxide dissolved in water), etc.

(*ii*) Heterogeneous mixtures

A mixture is said to be heterogeneous mixture if it consists of two or more parts (called phases) which have different compositions. It has visible boundaries of separation between the various constituents. For example, undissolved sugar (solid phase) in sugar solution (liquid phase), smoke (mixture of air and carbon particles), mixture of iron and sulphur, mixture of sand and water, mixture of sodium chloride and iron filings, salt and sulphur, oil and water, etc.

In our daily life, we usually deal with mixtures rather than pure substances. Sometimes, we can easily identify a mixture of substances by appearance. For example, when we shake powdered chalk in water, a milky liquid is formed. This is a mixture of water with the chalk particles suspended in it and can be easily identified with the naked eye. But if we see milk, it appears to be a homogeneous substance. However, if we observe milk with the help of a microscope, it appears as drops of fat suspended in a clear liquid. Thus, milk is also a heterogeneous mixture.

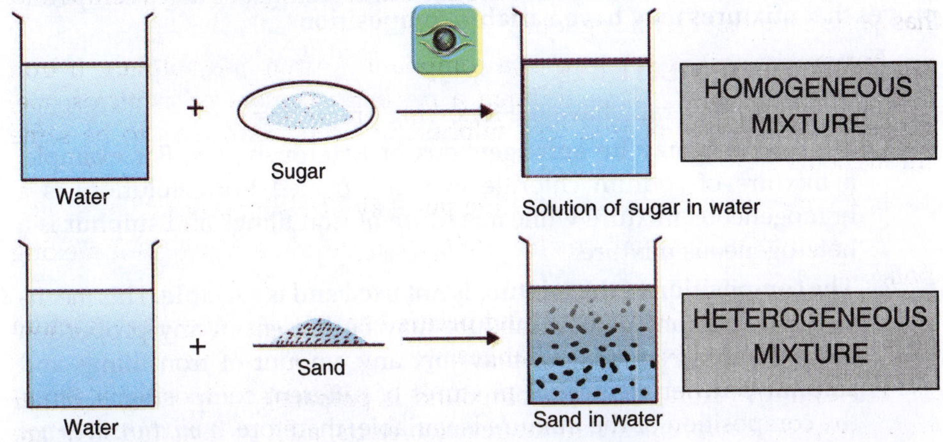

Fig. 5. Homogeneous and heterogeneous mixtures. Solution of sugar in water is a homogeneous mixture, while mixture of sand and water is a heterogeneous mixture.

Let us consider, a homogeneous mixture. When we shake sugar particles in water, a clear solution of sugar is obtained. The particles of sugar dissolved in water cannot be seen even with the help of a microscope. But the presence of sugar in the liquid can be easily detected if a drop of the solution is placed on a glass plate and allowed to dry. Sugar particles will remain on the glass as water evaporates.

Let us understand the homogeneous and heterogeneous nature of mixture with the help of the following activity.

Activity 1

To understand the concept of homogeneous and heterogeneous mixtures

1. Divide the class into four groups as A, B, C and D.
2. To group A, give a beaker containing 50 mL of water and one spatula full of copper sulphate powder.
3. To group B, give a beaker containing 50 mL of water and two spatula full of copper sulphate powder.
4. To group C, give one spatula full of copper sulphate powder and one spatula full of potassium permanganate (or common salt).
5. To group D, give one spatula full of copper sulphate and two spatula full of potassium permanganate (or common salt).
6. Ask these groups to mix the given components to form mixture.

What do you observe ?

All the four groups should compare their results and record their observations on uniformity in colour and texture. Discuss the observation.

On comparing the mixtures of groups A and B, it will be observed that both groups A and B have obtained mixtures which have uniform composition throughout. Both the groups have obtained a copper sulphate solution but their colours are different. The colour of copper sulphate solution of group B is darker. This shows that **mixture can have a variable composition**. Such mixtures are called **homogeneous mixtures.**

On comparing the mixtures of groups C and D, it will be observed that both groups C and D have also obtained mixtures. These contain physically distinct parts and have non-uniform compositions. Such mixtures are called **heterogeneous mixtures.** On comparing their colours, it is observed that though both the groups have obtained mixtures of copper sulphate and potassium permanganate but their compositions are different. This again proves that **mixtures may have variable compositions.**

PROPERTIES OF MIXTURES

The mixtures generally have the following properties:

1. **The mixture may be homogeneous or heterogeneous.** For example, a mixture of sodium chloride in water (called brine solution) is a homogeneous mixture while a mixture of iron filings and sulphur is a heterogeneous mixture.
2. **The composition of the mixture is not fixed and is variable.** This means that the components of a mixture may be present in any proportion by mass. For example, we may mix any amount of iron filings and sulphur powder to prepare mixtures of different compositions. Since the composition of the mixture is variable, therefore, *a mixture does not have a definite formula.*
3. **A mixture does not have a definite melting point or a boiling point.** Since the mixture does not have a definite composition or formula, therefore, it does not have a fixed melting point or a boiling point. For example, a mixture of iron filings and sulphur does not melt at a fixed temperature.
4. **The properties of a mixture are the properties of its components.** This means that a mixture shows the properties of all the components present in it. For example, a mixture of iron filings and sulphur shows the properties of both iron and sulphur. If dilute sulphuric acid is added to the mixture, iron reacts with dilute sulphuric acid and hydrogen gas is produced (which is odourless, colourless and combustible gas) and sulphur remains unchanged. This shows that the mixture of iron and sulphur shows the properties of iron. Now, if carbon disulphide is added to the mixture, sulphur dissolves in carbon disulphide leaving iron filings unchanged. This means that the mixture of iron filings and sulphur also shows the properties of sulphur. Hence, a mixture of iron filings and sulphur shows the properties of both its components *i.e.,* iron and sulphur.
5. **The formation of mixture is not accompanied by any change in heat.** During the formation of a mixture, the components do not react chemically. Therefore, no energy in the form of heat or light is evolved or absorbed when a mixture is formed. For example, when iron filings and sulphur are mixed to prepare the mixture, heat is neither absorbed nor evolved.
6. **The components of a mixture can be easily separated by ordinary physical methods.** The components of a mixture can be easily separated by simple methods such as filtration, evaporation, sublimation, distillation, extraction with solvents etc. For example, a mixture of sand and water can be separated by filtration. Similarly, a mixture of iron filings and sulphur can be separated by moving a magnet in the

mixture. Iron pieces will be attracted by the magnet leaving behind sulphur. Alternatively, if we shake the mixture of iron filings and sulphur with an organic solvent such as carbon disulphide (CS_2), sulphur will dissolve in CS_2 leaving behind iron filings. On filtration, iron is obtained as a residue on the filter paper. Sulphur is recovered from the filtrate by evaporating carbon disulphide.

DO YOU KNOW?

Mixture of Iron filings and sulphur

If we move a magnet in the mixture of iron filings and sulphur, the iron filings are attracted by the magnet and stick to the magnet and get separated from sulphur. Sulphur is not attracted by the magnet, so it is left behind. Thus, a mixture of iron filings and sulphur can be separated into its constituents by using a magnet.

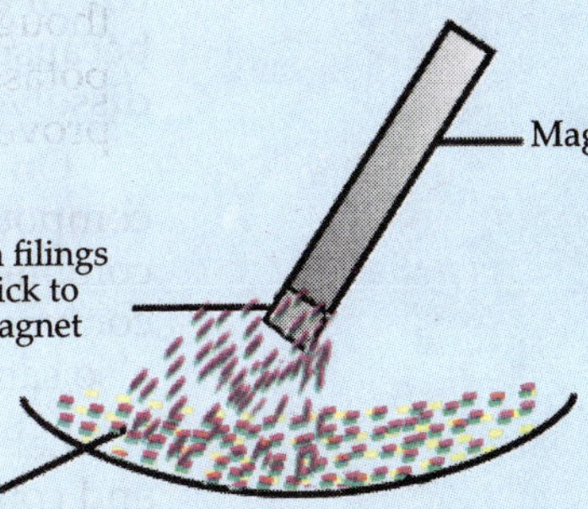

Differences between mixtures and compounds

To understand difference between a compound and mixture perform the following activity :

Activity 2

- **To understand the difference between mixtures and compounds**
  1. Divide the class into two groups A and B.
  2. Give 5 g of iron filings and 3 g of sulphur powder in a china dish to both the groups.
  3. Ask group A to mix and crush iron filings and sulphur powder together.
  4. Ask group B to mix and crush iron filings and sulphur powder. Heat this mixture strongly till red hot. Remove the flame and cool. Now perform the following experiments with both the products in steps 3 & 4.
     - (*i*) Check for magnetism in both the products obtained in steps 3 and 4 with the help of a magnet.
     - (*ii*) Add carbon disulphide to a part of products and stir well and filter.
     - (*iii*) Add dil H_2SO_4 or dil hydrochloric acid to the materials obtained.
     - (*iv*) Compare the colour and texture of the material obtained by both the groups.

What do you observe ?

Now answer the following questions :

- (*a*) **Perform all the steps above with both the elements, i.e. iron and sulphur separately. Check if any group has obtained the same results as that of the pure elements.**
- (*b*) **Did the material obtained by both the groups look same?**
- (*c*) **Can we separate the components of the materials obtained in both the groups?**
- (*d*) **On adding dilute sulphuric acid did both the groups obtain a gas?**
- (*e*) **Did the gas obtained in both the groups has same smell or different?**
- (*f*) **Which of the two groups get material which has magnetic properties?**

After studying the results, we will observe that the products obtained by the two groups are different and they show different properties. In group A, the mixture of iron filings and sulphur is obtained while in Group B a new compound is formed. So, Group A has carried out the activity involving a physical change, while Group B has carried out an activity involving a chemical change or a chemical reaction has taken place. A new compound has been formed in group B activity. This new compound has properties different as compared to combining elements iron and sulphur. Thus, we observe the following :

The mixture obtained in group-A is simply a mixture of two elements iron and sulphur. It shows all the properties of iron and sulphur. It has intermediate colour and texture between iron and sulphur. It will be attracted by the magnet because of the presence of iron. When we add carbon disulphide, sulphur will dissolve in it which can be removed by filtration.

On heating the two elements strongly we got a new substance called a compound. This substance has totally different properties as compared to the combining atoms. Moreover, it has been observed that the composition of the compound is same throughout. The colour and texture of the compound are also same throughout.

Let us sum up comparative characteristic differences between mixtures and compounds.

Mixtures	Compounds
1. In a mixture, the elements or compounds just mix together.	The elements combine or react to form compounds.
2. The components of a mixture may be present in any ratio. Its composition is variable.	The compounds contain two or more elements in a fixed ratio by mass. Its composition is always fixed.
3. There is no new substance formed.	A new substance is formed.
4. A mixture does not have a definite formula.	A compound has a definite formula.
5. A mixture may be homogeneous or heterogeneous.	A compound is always homogeneous.
6. No chemical reaction takes place and therefore, the formation of mixture is not accompanied by any energy change.	A chemical reaction takes place and therefore, the formation of a compound takes place with absorption or evolution of heat.
7. A mixture shows the properties of its constituents.	The properties of a compound are entirely different from those of its constituents.
8. A mixture can be separated into its constituents by physical methods (like filtration, evaporation, distillation, sublimation, mechanical separation, etc.)	A compound cannot be separated into its constituents by ordinary physical methods. These can be separated by chemical or electrochemical reactions.
9. A mixture does not have fixed melting point, boiling point, etc.	A compound has a fixed melting point, boiling point, etc.

Predicting whether a given substance is a compound or a mixture

On the basis of the points of differences, it can be easily decided whether the given substance is a compound or a mixture. Compounds are always homogeneous but mixtures may be homogeneous or heterogeneous. Therefore, the difference between a compound and a mixture cannot be easily predicted on the basis of homogeneous or heterogeneous nature of the substance.

In order to predict whether a given substance is a compound or a mixture, we should **remember** the following points :

1. If the substance can be separated into its constituents by physical methods, it is a **mixture.**

   On the other hand, if the substance cannot be separated into its constituents by physical methods, it is a **compound.** For example, iron-sulphur mixture is a mixture while iron sulphide is a compound.

2. If the substance shows the independent properties of its constituents, it is a **mixture.**

   On the other hand, if the substance shows entirely different properties from those of its constituents, it is a **compound.**

   For example, iron-sulphur mixture shows the properties of iron and sulphur (mixture) while iron sulphide shows properties different from iron and sulphur.

3. If the composition of the substance is variable, it is a **mixture.**
   On the other hand, if the composition of the substance is fixed, it is a **compound.**
   For example, iron-sulphur mixture can have any composition while iron sulphide always contains iron and sulphur in the proportion of 56 g of iron and 32 g of sulphur.
4. If no light or heat is given out or absorbed during the preparation of the substance, it is a **mixture.**
   If heat or light is given out or absorbed during the preparation of the substance, it is a **compound.**
   For example, during the preparation of iron-sulphur mixture, no change was observed except that the colour was a mixed colour of the colours of iron and sulphur. However, during the preparation of iron sulphide, large amount of heat was given out.
5. If the substance does not have a fixed melting point or boiling point, it is a **mixture.**
   On the other hand, if the substance has a fixed melting point or boiling point, it is a **compound.**
6. If the substance is heterogeneous, it is a **mixture.**
   On the other hand, if the substance is homogeneous, it may be a **compound** or a **mixture.**

Thus, we may summarize the nature of matter as :

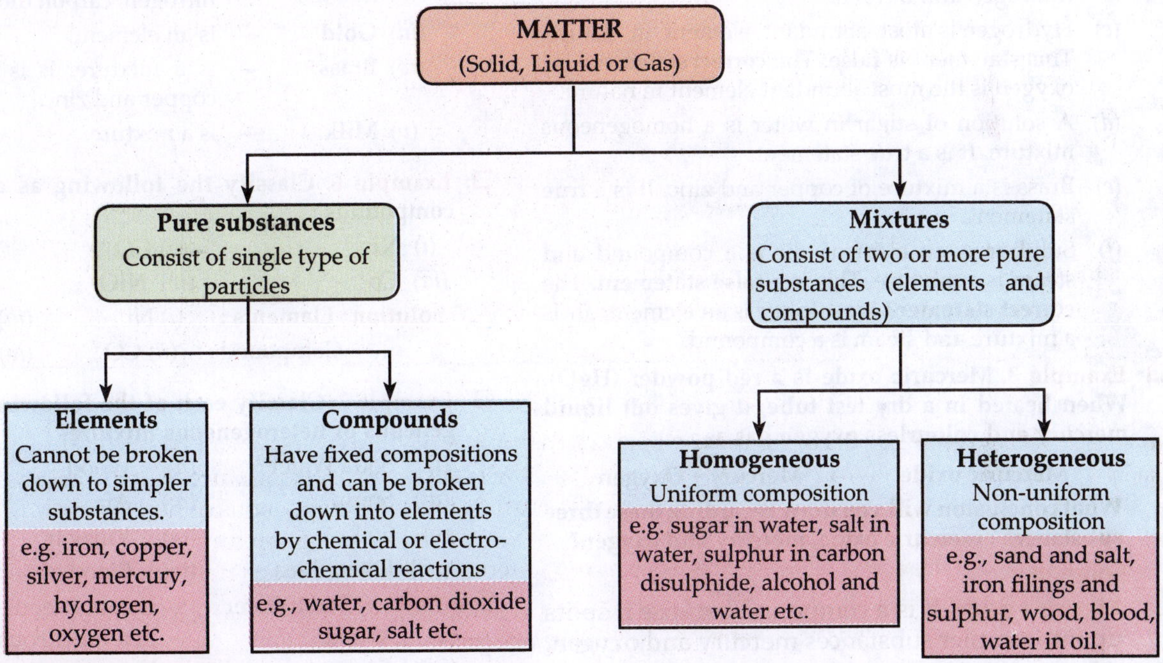

Solved Examples

❑ **Example 1. Classify the following substances as elements, compounds or mixtures :**

(*a*) iron (*b*) gun powder (*c*) soda water (*d*) gold (*e*) air (*f*) diamond (*g*) graphite (*h*) chalk (*i*) alcohol (*j*) common salt (*k*) brass.

Solution : The substances may be classified into elements, compounds or mixtures as given below :

(*a*) **iron** — element

(*b*) **gun powder** — mixture

(*c*) **soda water** — mixture

(*d*) **gold** — element

(*e*) **air** — mixture

(*f*) **diamond** — element

(*g*) **graphite** — element

(*h*) **chalk** compound

(*i*) **alcohol** — compound

(*j*) **common salt** — compound

(*k*) **brass** — mixture

Example 2. Which of the following statements are true? Correct the false statements :

(*a*) **Mercury, diamond and bromine are elements.**

(*b*) **Sugar is a compound which contains elements carbon, hydrogen, nitrogen and oxygen.**

(*c*) **Hydrogen is the most abundant element in nature.**

(*d*) **A solution of a sugar in water is a homogeneous mixture.**

(*e*) **Brass is a mixture of two elements copper and zinc.**

(*f*) **Sulphur is an element, air is a compound and steam is a mixture.**

Solution : (*a*) Mercury, diamond and bromine are elements. This is a **true** statement.

(*b*) Sugar is a compound which contains elements carbon, hydrogen, nitrogen and oxygen. This is a **false** statement because sugar does not contain nitrogen. The **true statement** is : Sugar is a compound which contains elements carbon, hydrogen and oxygen.

(*c*) Hydrogen is most abundant element in nature. This statement is **false.** The **correct statement** is : oxygen is the most abundant element in nature.

(*d*) A solution of sugar in water is a homogeneous mixture. It is a **true** statement.

(*e*) Brass is a mixture of copper and zinc. It is a **true** statement.

(*f*) Sulphur is an element, air is a compound and steam is a mixture. This is a **false statement.** The **correct statement** is : sulphur is an element, air is a mixture and steam is a compound.

Example 3. Mercuric oxide is a red powder (HgO). When heated in a dry test tube, it gives out liquid mercury and colourless oxygen gas as :

$$\text{Mercuric oxide} \longrightarrow \text{Mercury + Oxygen}$$

What conclusion will you draw regarding these three substances : mercuric oxide, mercury and oxygen?

Solution :

Mercuric oxide. It is a compound because it splits up into simpler substances mercury and oxygen.

Mercury. It is an element because it cannot be further decomposed into simpler substances.

Oxygen. It is also an element because it cannot be further decomposed into simpler substances.

Example 4. Give reasons to justify that water is a compound and not a mixture.

Solution : Water is a compound. This can be justified by the following reasons :

(*i*) Water cannot be separated into its constituents, hydrogen and oxygen by simple physical methods such as filtration, evaporation, distillation, etc.

(*ii*) The composition of water is fixed. It contains hydrogen and oxygen combined together in a fixed proportion of 1:8 by mass. Therefore, it has a definite composition and is a compound. It has a definite formula H_2O.

(*iii*) Water has properties entirely different from those of its constituents, hydrogen and oxygen. For example, water is a liquid whereas hydrogen and oxygen are gases. Similarly, water does not burn whereas hydrogen burns; water does not support combustion whereas oxygen supports combustion.

(*iv*) Heat and light are given out when water is formed from its elements, hydrogen and oxygen.

(*v*) Water has fixed boiling point of 100°C under standard atmospheric pressure.

The above facts support that water is a compound.

Example 5. Classify the following into elements, compounds and mixtures :

(*i*) **Marble** (*ii*) **Air**
(*iii*) **Gold** (*iv*) **Brass** (*v*) **Milk**

Solution :

(*i*) **Marble**	—	is a compound ($CaCO_3$)
(*ii*) **Air**	—	is a mixture containing oxygen, nitrogen, carbon dioxide, etc.
(*iii*) **Gold**	—	is an element.
(*iv*) **Brass**	—	is a mixture. It is an alloy of copper and zinc.
(*v*) **Milk**	—	is a mixture.

Example 6. Classify the following as elements or compounds :

(*i*) **Ni** (*ii*) **CO**
(*iii*) **Co** (*iv*) **NiO**

Solution : Elements : (*i*) Ni (*iii*) Co
Compounds : (*ii*) CO (*iv*) NiO

Example 7. Classify each of the following as homogeneous or heterogeneous mixtures :

(*i*) Soda Water	(*ii*) Wood
(*iii*) Snow	(*iv*) Air
(*v*) Soil	(*vi*) Vinegar
(*vii*) Filtered tea	(*viii*) Blood

Solution :

(*i*) Soda Water	– homogeneous
(*ii*) Wood	– heterogeneous
(*iii*) Snow	– heterogeneous
(*iv*) Air	– homogeneous
(*v*) Soil	– heterogeneous
(*vi*) Vinegar	– homogeneous
(*vii*) Filtered tea	– homogeneous
(*viii*) Blood	– heterogeneous

Example 8. Hydrogen is a combustible gas and oxygen is a supporter of combustion. Water contains both hydrogen and oxygen but it is used to existinguish fire. Explain.

Solution : Hydrogen and oxygen are elements and have their characteristic properties. But water is a compound of hydrogen and oxygen combined together in a fixed ratio of 1:8 by mass. The properties of a compound are entirely different from those of its constituent atoms from which it is formed. Therefore, water has different properties than hydrogen and oxygen.

Example 9. Is steam an element, a compound or a mixture?

Solution : Steam is a compound (H_2O).

Practice Exercise 2A

Answers and Hints on Page 59

1. Which of the following are substances according to scientific meaning ?
   (*i*) Wood (*ii*) Mercury
   (*iii*) Chalk (*iv*) Sodium chloride
   (*v*) Milk (*vi*) Air
   (*vii*) Lead (*viii*) Butter
2. Classify the following substances into elements, compounds and mixtures :
   (*i*) air (*ii*) common salt
   (*iii*) iron filings (*iv*) marble
   (*v*) oxygen (*vi*) milk
   (*vii*) zinc (*viii*) bronze
   (*ix*) sand (*x*) water.
3. Sulphur is an element, ice is a compound and smoke is a mixture. Is the statement correct or incorrect ?
4. Fill in the blanks :
   (*i*) Air is a ....
   (*ii*) Marble is a ....
   (*iii*) Blood is a .... mixture.
5. Give two examples of elements which exist as (*a*) solid (*b*) liquid and (*c*) gas, under normal conditions.
6. Classify the following as homogeneous or heterogeneous mixtures :
   (*a*) sugar solution (*b*) milk
   (*c*) blood (*d*) iron-sulphur.
7. Which of the following are elements?
   (*i*) Tungsten (*ii*) Steam
   (*iii*) Glucose (*iv*) Argon
   (*v*) Manganese.
8. Select compound, mixture and element from the following :
   Common salt, sugar syrup, washing soda, gypsum, cement, mercury, gallium, sugar, graphite.
9. Classify the following into element, compound and mixture :
   Coal, methane, carbon dioxide, sugar solution, granite, aluminium, graphite, hydrogen peroxide, blood, soil and sugar.
10. State one property in which a solution of sugar in water resembles a mixture of sugar and sand and one property in which it differs from it.
11. Pick out the odd one from amongst the following which does not belong to the set :
    Hydrogen, steam, graphite, gold.
12. Pick out the odd one from amongst the following which does not belong to the set :
    Milk, honey, coal, brass, common salt.
13. Correct the statement :
    Water always contains H and O in the ratio of 1:16 by mass.
14. Two chemical substances A and B combine to form a product C which contains both A and B :
    $$A + B \longrightarrow C$$
    A has fixed composition and can be broken down into simpler substances by simple chemical reactions but B cannot. Which of the following statements concerning A, B and C are correct?
    (*i*) A and B are compounds
    (*ii*) A and B are elements
    (*iii*) A is a compound and B in an element
    (*iv*) C is a compound
    (*v*) C has fixed composition
    (*vi*) A and C are compounds
15. Match the item of Column I with those of Column II.

Column I	Column II.
(A) Iron	(*i*) Heterogeneous mixture
(B) Iron sulphide	(*ii*) Soluble in CS_2
(C) Sulphur	(*iii*) Homogeneous mixture
(D) Mixture of iron and sulphur	(*iv*) Compound
(E) Brass	(*v*) Element

16. Classify the following substances as mixtures: homogeneous or heterogeneous or pure substances, elements or compounds :
    (*i*) sugar dissolved in water
    (*ii*) sea water
    (*iii*) rust
    (*iv*) sugar
    (*v*) mercury in a thermometer
    (*vi*) steel
    (*vii*) soda water
    (*viii*) sand and water

17. Choose the homogeneous mixture out of the following :

(*a*) ink (*b*) milk

(*c*) brass (*d*) muddy water

18. In the boxes below different atoms are represented by ● and o.

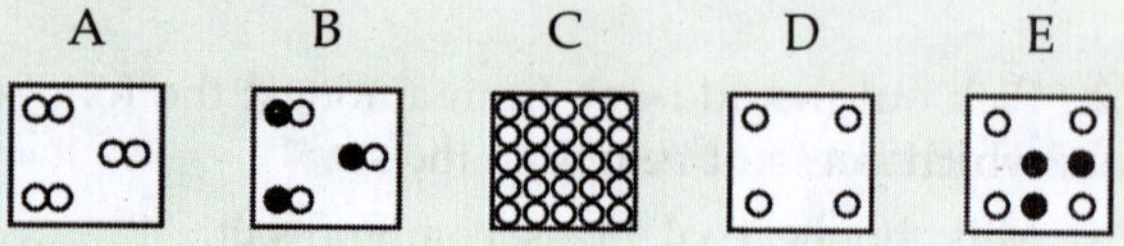

Match the letter on the box to the following descriptions :

(*a*) a solid

(*b*) a gaseous compound

(*c*) a diatomic gas

(*d*) a pure gas made up of single atoms

(*e*) a mixture of gases.

19. Give two reasons for supporting that

(*i*) sugar is a pure substance and not a mixture

(*ii*) brass is a mixture and not a compound

(*iii*) water is a compound and not a mixture

20. Name a

(*i*) metal which is liquid at room temperature

(*ii*) non-metal which is liquid at room temperature

(*iii*) an element which can show the properties of metals and non-metals

WHAT IS A SOLUTION?

A solution is a homogeneous mixture of two or more substances.

We come across many types of solutions in our daily life. The lemonade, *sharbat*, soda water, coke, pepsi, etc. are all examples of solution. At particle level, there is homogeneity. For example, a lemonade has same taste throughout. This shows that the particles of sugar or salt are evenly distributed in solution. The substances making up the solution are called **components** of the solution. A solution is generally made up of two components:

(*i*) *solvent* (*ii*) *solute*.

Solvent. ***A component which is present in large amount*** **is called solvent.**
Solute. ***The component which is present in lesser amount*** **is called solute.**

Thus, a solute is a substance which dissolves and the solvent is a substance in which dissolution takes place. For example, if a crystal of sugar is dropped into a beaker of water, it dissolves to form a solution. In this case, sugar is solute and water is solvent. Thus,

$$\underset{\text{(Solute)}}{\text{Sugar}} + \underset{\text{(Solvent)}}{\text{Water}} \longrightarrow \text{Solution of sugar in water}$$

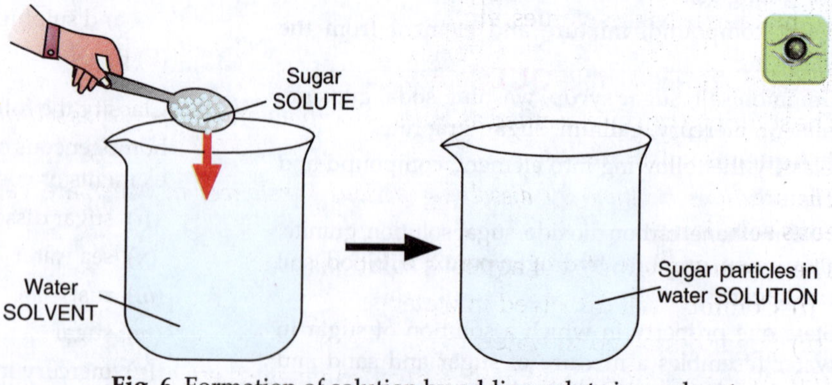

Fig. 6. Formation of solution by adding solute in a solvent.

These solutions are also called **true solutions** because the particles of solutions have very small size (less than 10^{-9} m or 1nm or 10^{-7} cm).

We come across various types of solutions in our daily life. It may be noted that most of the common solutions contain solid solutes and liquid solvents. For example, sugar dissolved in water to prepare ***sharbat***. However, the solutes may be even liquids or gases. All these are called ***liquid solutions***. Mixture of miscible liquids (alcohol in water) is a common example of liquid in liquid solutions and CO_2 dissolved in water is a common example of gas in liquid solutions.

In addition to liquid solutions, we can have examples of solutions in which solid or gas acts as solvent.

Some common examples of different types of solutions are :

(*i*) A solution of sugar and water is a **solid in liquid solution**. In this solution, sugar is a solute and water is a solvent.

(*ii*) A solution of iodine and ethyl alcohol known as 'tincture of iodine'. In this solution, iodine (solid) is a solute and alcohol (liquid) is a solvent.

(*iii*) Vinegar which is used as preservative and is also added in chinese foods is an example of **liquid in liquid solution**. It has acetic acid dissolved in water.

(*iv*) Aerated drinks like soda water, coke, etc. are **gas in liquid solutions**. These contain carbon dioxide (CO_2) as solute dissolved in water (liquid) as solvent.

The above four types of solutions are also called **liquid solutions.**

(*v*) Air is mixture of **gas in gas solution**. It is a homogeneous mixture of mainly two components: oxygen (20%) and nitrogen (78%). The other gases are present in very small quantities. This is an example of **gaseous solution**.

(*vi*) Mixtures of silver and gold and copper and gold are common examples of **solid in solid solution**. An important alloy, brass containing approximately 70% copper and approximately 30% zinc contains zinc as solute and copper as solvent.

Metal alloys. Alloys are homogeneous mixtures of two or more metals. These cannot be separated into their components by physical methods. However, these are considered as mixtures because these show the properties of its constituents and can have variable composition. For example:

(*i*) Brass is a mixture of approximately 70% copper and 30% zinc.

(*ii*) Stainless steel which we use for utensils is a mixture of iron, chromium and nickel.

(*iii*) Bronze is a mixture of copper and tin and it is also commonly used for making utensils, statues, etc.

AQUEOUS AND NON-AQUEOUS SOLUTIONS

The solutions can be classified as *aqueous solutions* and *non-aqueous solutions*.

1. Aqueous solutions

The solutions obtained by dissolving various substances in water are called **aqueous solutions.**

The common examples of aqueous solutions are :

(*i*) Common salt dissolved in water

(*ii*) Sugar dissolved in water

(*iii*) Acetic acid dissolved in water (called vinegar) etc.

2. Non-aqueous solutions

The solutions obtained by dissolving a substance in liquids other than water are called **non-aqueous solutions.** The common non-aqueous solvents are alcohol, carbon disulphide, carbon tetrachloride, acetone, benzene, etc. Examples of non-aqueous solutions are :

(*i*) Iodine dissolved in carbon tetrachloride

(*ii*) Sulphur dissolved in carbon disulphide

(*iii*) Bromine dissolved in chloroform

(*iv*) Sugar dissolved in alcohol, etc.

Properties of Solutions

The important properties of solution are :

1. A solution is **homogeneous in nature**. It may be noted that in a solution, there is homogeneity at micro level. For example, in sugar solution, sugar and water molecules mix with each other so uniformly that if we take 1 mL of solution from any part of the solution, it will have the same sweetness and concentration. In other words, it will have the same number of sugar and water molecules per unit volume.
2. The size of the particles of solution is less than 10^{-9} m (called 1 nm). Therefore, they cannot be seen with naked eye.
3. The particles of the solution cannot be seen even with the help of a microscope.
4. The particles of the solution easily pass through a filter paper. Therefore, they cannot be separated by the process of filtration.
5. The solute particles in solution do not settle on keeping, *i.e.*, a solution is stable.
6. Because of very small size, they donot scatter a beam of light passing through the solution. So, the path of light is not visible in a solution.

Advantages of Preparing a Solution

We know that in a solution, solute and solvent are present in the form of molecules or ions. When two reacting solid substances come in contact, the reaction is very slow and sometimes not even visible. However, when their solutions are mixed, the reaction take place very fast. This is because of close mixing of two reacting substances at molecular level.

The use of solutions of substances have many advantages in industries, medicines and laboratories. Many medicines dissolved in suitable non-aqueous solvents such as alcohol are given to patients. Saline glucose solution (which is a homogeneous mixture of various salts and glucose in water) is administered to a person suffering from dehydration. Large varieties of solvents are used in industries to dissolve different types of substances.

CONCENTRATION OF A SOLUTION

In activity 1, we observed that groups A and B obtained different shades of solution. This indicates that these two solutions contained different relative proportion of solute (copper sulphate) and solvent (water). The relative proportion of solute and solvent may be varied to any extent. Depending upon the amount of solute present in a given solution, we can call the solution as dilute, concentrated or a saturated solution. Dilute and concentrated are relative terms. For example in activity 1, solution obtained by group A is dilute as compared to that obtained by group B.

Expressing concentration of a solution

There are many ways of expressing concentration of a solution. The simplest method of expressing concentration of a solution is the amount of solute present in a given amount (mass or volume) of solution.

$$\text{Concentration} = \frac{\text{Amount of solute}}{\text{Amount of solution}}$$

It may also be expressed as the amount of solute dissolved in a given amount (mass or volume) of solvent.

$$\text{Concentration} = \frac{\text{Amount of solute}}{\text{Amount of solvent}}$$

There are two common ways :

1. Mass percentage

The simplest way of expressing concentration of solution is mass percentage of solution. It gives mass of solute per 100 mass unit of solution. This may be expressed as :

$$\text{Mass \% of solute} = \frac{\text{Mass of solute}}{\text{Mass of solution}} \times 100$$

The mass of solution is equal to mass of solute plus the mass of solvent.

Mass of solution = Mass of solute + Mass of solvent

In other words, *the concentration may be defined as the mass of solute in grams present in 100g of the solution.* For example, a 10% of solution of glucose ($C_6H_{12}O_6$) means that 10 g of glucose is dissolved in 100 g of solution. In other words, this means that 10 g of glucose is added to 90 g of water. Similarly, if 25 g of sucrose is dissolved in 200 g of solution, then

$$\text{Mass \% of sucrose} = \frac{25}{200} \times 100 = 12.5\%$$

It may be noted that *unless otherwise specified, per cent means per cent by mass and water as solvent.*

2. Volume percentage

If a solution is prepared by dissolving a liquid solute in a liquid solvent, then concentration may also be expressed as *volume percentage* of solute or *percentage by volume*. This means the volume of solute in millilitres present in 100 millilitres of the solution.

$$\text{Concentration of solute in volume percent} = \frac{\text{Volume of solute}}{\text{Volume of solution}} \times 100$$

For example, a 20 percent of alcohol means that 20 mL of alcohol are present in 100 mL of solution. In other words, 20 mL of alcohol are added to 80 mL of water (so that total volume becomes 100 mL).

Solved Examples

❑ **Example 10. A given solution contains 40 g of sugar in 320 g of water. Calculate the concentration of solution.**

Solution : Mass of sugar = 40 g

Mass of water = 320 g

Mass of solution = Mass of solute + Mass of solvent

= 40 + 320 = 360 g

Mass percentage of solution

$$= \frac{\text{Mass of sugar}}{\text{Mass of solution}} \times 100$$

$$= \frac{40}{360} \times 100$$

= **11.1%**

❑ **Example 11. A solution contains 30 g of common salt dissolved in 350 g of water. Calculate the concentration of solution.**

Solution : Mass of solute (common salt) = 30g

Mass of solvent (water) = 350g

Mass of solution = Mass of solute + Mass of solvent

= 30 + 350 = 380 g

Concentration of solution = $\frac{\text{Mass of solute}}{\text{Volume of solution}} \times 100$

= $\frac{30}{380} \times 100$

= **7.89% by mass**

❑ **Example 12. If 55 g of salt are present in 550 g of solution, what is the concentration of the solution?**

Solution : Mass of solute = 55 g

Mass of solution = 550 g

Concentration of solution = $\frac{\text{Mass of solute}}{\text{Mass of solution}} \times 100$

= $\frac{55}{550} \times 100$

= **10%**

❑ **Example 13. A solution contains 25 g of sugar in 100 g of water. Calculate the concentration of this solution.**

Solution : Mass of sugar (solute)

= 25 g

Mass of solution = Mass of solute + Mass of solvent

= 25 + 100 = 125 g

Concentration of solution = $\frac{\text{Mass of solute}}{\text{Mass of solution}} \times 100$

= $\frac{25}{125} \times 100$

= **20%**

❑ **Example 14. A solution contains 50 mL of ethyl alcohol mixed with 150 mL of water. Calculate the concentration of solution.**

Solution : Volume of solute (alcohol)

= 50 mL

Volume of solvent (water) = 150 mL

Volume of solution = Vol. of solute + Vol. of solvent

= 50 + 150 = 200 mL

Concentration of solution = $\frac{\text{Vol. of solute}}{\text{Vol. of solution}} \times 100$

= $\frac{50}{200} \times 100$

= **25% by volume**

❑ **Example 15. A solution of sugar in water is 5% by mass. How much sugar is present in 250 g of the solution?**

Solution : Concentration of solution

= 5% by mass

Mass of solution = 250 g

Mass concentration = $\frac{\text{Mass of solute}}{\text{Volume of solution}} \times 100$

5 = $\frac{\text{Mass of solute}}{250} \times 100$

∴ Mass of solute (sugar) = $\frac{5 \times 250}{100}$

= **12.5 g**

❑ **Example 16. Calculate the mass by volume percentage of 20% solution by mass of sulphuric acid (density = 1.10 g mL⁻¹).**

Solution : 20% solution of sulphuric acid by mass means that 20g of sulphuric acid is present in 100 g of solution.

Mass of H_2SO_4 dissolved = 20 g

Mass of solution = 100 g

Density of the solution = 1.10 g mL^{-1}

Volume of solution = $\frac{\text{Mass}}{\text{Density}}$

= $\frac{100 \text{ g}}{1.10 \text{ g mL}^{-1}} = 90.9 \text{ mL}$

∴ Mass by volume percentage of the solution

= $\frac{\text{Mass of solute}}{\text{Volume of solution}} \times 100$

= $\frac{20}{90.9} \times 100 = 22.0\%$

Saturated and Unsaturated Solutions

Suppose one spoon of sugar is added to about 200 ml of water in a beaker at 25°C. On stirring, the sugar dissolves and disappears. If one more spoon of sugar is added to this solution, it also dissolves. In this way, we can dissolve different amounts of same solute (sugar) in same quantity of solvent. Therefore, we can prepare solutions of different concentrations of a substance. A particular solution may contain less amount of the dissolved solute whereas another solution may contain a larger amount of the solute. Depending upon the amount of solute present, solutions may be classified as :

(*i*) *Unsaturated solution,*

(*ii*) *Saturated solution*

The concept of saturated solution or unsaturated solution can be examined by the following activity:

Activity 3

To understand the solubility of different substances in a solvent

1. Take approximately 50 mL of water in two beakers A and B.
2. Add common salt in beaker A and sugar (or barium chloride) in beaker B slowly with continuous stirring. On stirring the salt dissolves. Go on adding more and more salt and sugar (or barium chloride) in respective beakers with constant stirring.
3. Keep a close watch at the bottom of the beaker to see whether the solute (salt, sugar or barium chloride) is getting dissolved or not.
4. Note the stage when no more solute dissolves.
5. Now heat the contents of the beaker and raise the temperature by 10°C.
6. Start adding more solute in warm water.

Now answer the following questions :

(a) What is your observation?

(*b*) Is the amount of solute that can be dissolved in water at a given temperature is same?

(*c*) What is the effect of warming the solution?

It is observed that, a stage (step 4) is reached at which no more solute dissolves. This means that at any particular temperature, at this stage a solution has dissolved as much solute as it is capable of dissolving. The solution is said to be **saturated** at that temperature. In other words,

a solution in which no more solute can be dissolved at a given temperature is called **saturated solution.**

Thus, the saturated solution corresponds to the maximum amount of solute that can be dissolved at a particular temperature.

The amount of solute that can be dissolved in a solution is different for salt and sugar or barium chloride.

On the other hand, **a solution in which the amount of solute is less than the saturation level** is called **unsaturated solution**. In other words, in an unsaturated solution, more quantity of solute can be dissolved at a given temperature.

Sometimes, a solution may contain more amount of solute than the saturation concentration. If a solution contains more amount of solute than the saturation level, it is called **super saturated solution.**

Thus, we can conclude

Saturated solution	⇒	Amount of solute equal to saturation level.
Unsaturated solution	⇒	Amount of solute less than saturation level.
Super saturated solution	⇒	Amount of solute more than saturation level.

Solubility

The amount of solute required to prepare a saturated solution in a given quantity of solvent at a given temperature is called the solubility of the solute. It is generally referred to solubility for 100 g of the solvent. Thus,

the amount of solute which can be dissolved in 100 g of solvent at a given temperature is called its **solubility**.

Different substances have different solubility in water. For example, the solubility of sodium chloride (NaCl) in water is 36 g at 20°C and that of copper sulphate ($CuSO_4$) is 21 g at 20°C. This means that we can dissolve maximum of 36 g of NaCl in 100 g of water at 20°C but we can dissolve only 21 g of $CuSO_4$ in 100 g of water at 20°C.

The solubility of solids in liquids generally increases with rise in temperature (except in few cases) and decreases with decrease in temperature. For example, solubility of potassium chloride and potassium nitrate increases with increase in temperature as shown below:

Temperature	10°	20°	40°	60°	80°
Potassium chloride (KCl)	35	35	40	46	54
Potassium nitrate (KNO_3)	21	32	62	106	167

Solved Examples

Example 17. 21 g of sodium chloride dissolves in 60 g of water at 20°C to form a saturated solution. What is the solubility of sodium chloride at 20°C ?

Solution : Solubility is the amount of solute dissolved in 100 g of the solvent. Therefore,

60 g of water dissolves = 21 g of sodium chloride

100 g of water will dissolve $= \frac{21}{60} \times 100$

$= 35$ g

∴ Solubility of sodium chloride at 20°C = 35 g/100g

Example 18. What mass of potassium nitrate (KNO_3) would be needed to form a saturated solution in 250 g of water at 293 K ? Given that the solubility of the salt is 32 g/100 g at this temperature.

Solution : Mass of KNO_3 in 100 g of water = 32 g

Mass of KNO_3 in 250 g of water in saturated solution

$= \frac{32}{100} \times 250 = 80$ g

WHAT IS A SUSPENSION?

Suspension is a heterogeneous mixture in which the solute particles do not dissolve but remain suspended throughout the bulk of the solvent.

Therefore, the suspensions contain small insoluble particles of the solute spread throughout the solvent. The common example of suspension is muddy water which is a suspension of soil particles in water. Some other examples of suspensions are chalk water, paints, smoke in the air. Sparingly soluble salts such as barium sulphate ($BaSO_4$) dipersed in water is also an example of suspension. The particle size of the solute particles is greater than 10^{-7} m or 10^{-5} cm (or 100 nm). These particles may or may not be visible to naked eye but are visible under microscope.

Properties of Suspensions

The main properties of suspensions are :

1. Suspension is a heterogeneous mixture.
2. The particles of suspensions are bigger than 10^{-7}m or 100 nm (10^{-5} cm) in diameter.
3. The particles of suspensions can be easily seen. They may or may not be visible by naked eye. But they are visible under microscope.
4. The particles of suspension scatter a beam of light passing through it and make its path visible.
5. The particles of suspension settle down when left undisturbed. Therefore, a suspension is unstable.
6. The suspension can be separated from the mixture by the process of filtration.

WHAT IS A COLLOIDAL SOLUTION ?

A colloidal solution is a solution in which the size of the solute particles is intermediate between those in true solutions and suspensions.

In other words, the particles of colloidal solution are bigger than particles of true solution but smaller than the particles of suspensions. The common examples of colloidal solutions are milk, gum solution, blood, milk cream, ink, soap solution, etc. The mixtures obtained by groups E and F are colloids. The size of the particles is between 10^{-7}m and 10^{-9}m (100 nm and 1 nm).

Due to relatively small size of particles as compared to a suspension, the mixture appears to be homogeneous. But actually, a colloidal solution is a heterogeneous mixture. It consists of two phases :

(i) dispersed phase and

(ii) dispersion medium

Dispersed phase. *It is the component which is present in small proportion and consists of particles of colloidal dimensions* **(10^{-9}m to 10^{-7}m).**

Dispersion medium. *It is the component which is present in excess and acts as a medium in which colloidal particles are dispersed.*

For example, in a colloidal solution of sulphur in water, sulphur particles constitute dispersed phase and water acts as dispersion medium.

It may be noted that dispersed phase is like a solute and dispersion medium is like a solvent in solution. Thus, the particles of the dispersed phase are distributed in the dispersion medium. The two phases, dispersed phase and dispersion medium may be solid, liquid or a gas. Depending on the physical state of dispersed phase and dispersion medium, different types of colloidal solutions are possible.

Table 1. Types of Colloidal Solutions

Dispersion medium	Dispersed phase	Type	Examples
Gas	Liquid	aerosol	Mist, fog, cloud
Gas	Solid	aerosol	Smoke, dust, storm, automobile exhaust
Liquid	Gas	foam	Shaving cream, soda water
Liquid	Liquid	emulsion	Milk, medicine, face cream
Liquid	Solid	sol	Paints, mud, gold sol
Solid	Gas	foam	Pumice stone, foam rubber, sponge
Solid	Liquid	gel	Jelly, Cheese, butter, curd
Solid	Solid	solid sol	Alloys, gem stone, glass

The three types of solutions *i.e.,* true solutions, suspension and colloids may be classified on the basis of the particle size as shown in Fig. 7.

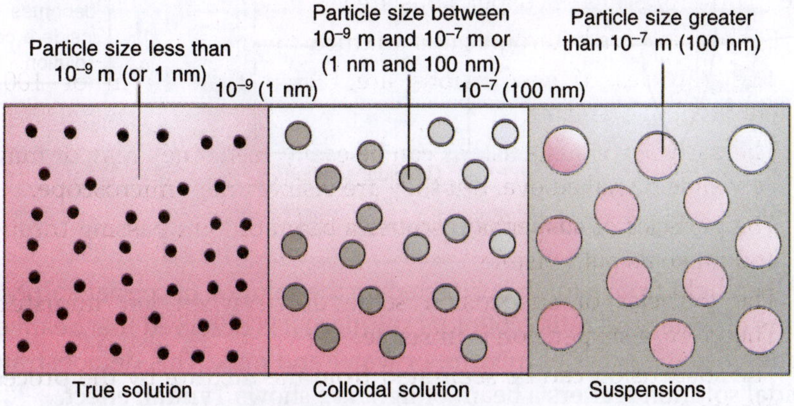

Fig. 7. Three types of solutions.

MEMORISE

Particle size and type of solution

True solution : Less than 10^{-9}m

Colloidal solution : between 10^{-9}m and 10^{-7}m or 1nm and 100 nm

Suspensions : more than 10^{-7}m (100 nm)

Size of particles increases as : True solution < Colloidal solution < Suspensions

- 10^{-9} m = 1 nanometer written as 1 nm

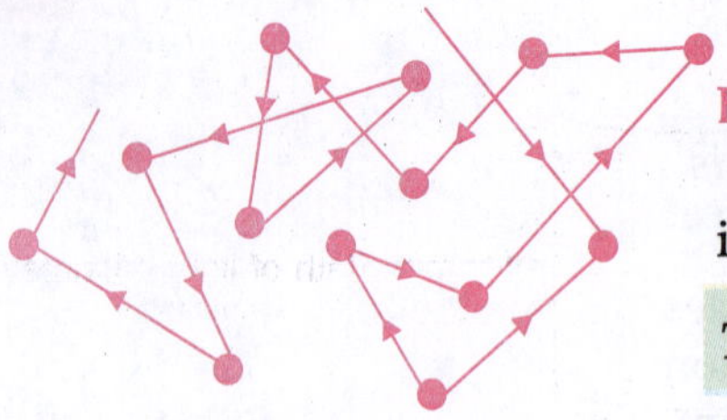

Fig. 8. Brownian movement of colloidal particles.

The colloids show the following characteristics :

Brownian movement of colloids

The colloidal particles are moving at random in a zig-zag motion in all directions.

The zig-zag motion of colloidal particles is called ***Brownian movement.***

This is shown in Fig. 8. *The Brownian movement is caused by the collision of the colloidal particles with the molecules of the dispersion medium.*

Tyndall effect of colloids

The size of colloidal particles are too small to be seen by naked eye. However, they exhibit a property known as **Tyndall effect**. When a strong beam of light is passed through a true solution in a beaker, in dark room, the path of the light does not become visible. However, if the same beam of light is passed through the colloidal solution, placed in the same room, the path of the light becomes visible when seen from a direction at right angle to that of the incident beam. This effect can also be observed when a fine beam of light falls in a room through a small hole in the window.

This phenomenon was studied for the first time by Tyndall and therefore, it is called **Tyndall effect.** This effect is due to scattering of light by colloidal particles. The particles in the true solutions are too small in size to cause any scattering. Therefore, Tyndall effects is not observed in true solutions.

The phenomenon of scattering of light by colloidal particles as a result of which the path of the beam becomes visible is called **Tyndall effect.**

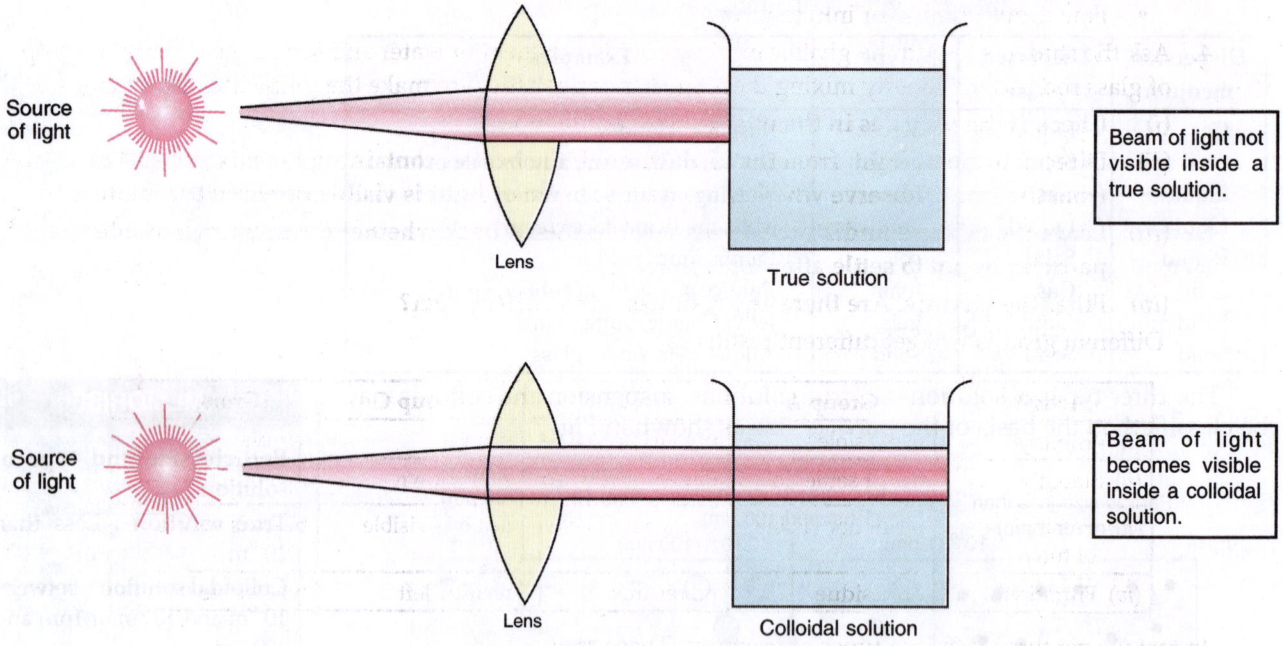

Fig. 9. Tyndall effect.

When light from a torch is directed on the solution of copper sulphate and mixture of water and milk (colloidal solution) it is observed that beam of light becomes visible in case of mixture of water and milk. This demonstrates that colloidal solution scatters a beam of light *i.e.*, shows Tyndall effect.

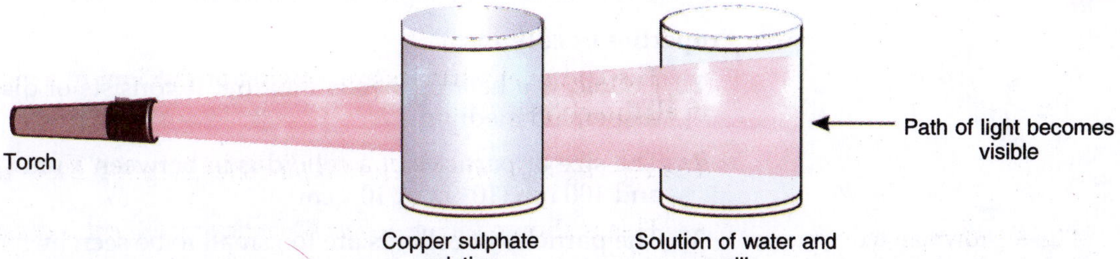

Fig. 10. Light directed on a solution of copper sulphate and a mixture of water and milk.

Tyndall effect can also be observed when sunlight passes a dense forest. In the forest, fog contains tiny droplets of water which act as particles of colloid dispersed in air.

To understand the difference between a true solution, suspension and colloid perform the following activity :

Activity 4

To understand the difference between solutions, suspensions and colloidal solutions

1. Divide the class into four groups and label them as A, B, C and D.
2. Give each group 2 beakers, a torch, a glass rod, funnel and filter paper.
3. Distribute the following samples to each group:
   - Four crystals of copper sulphate to group A
   - One spatula full of copper sulphate to group B
   - Chalk powder (or wheat flour) to group C and
   - Few drops of milk (or ink) to group D.
4. Ask the students to add the given samples provided to them in water and stir properly with the help of glass rod. After properly mixing these substances, ask them to make the following observations.
   (i) **Check if the particles in the mixture are visible or not?**
   (ii) **Direct a beam of light from the torch through the beaker containing the mixture and observe from the front. Observe whether the path of beam of light is visible or not in the mixture?**
   (iii) **Leave the mixture undisturbed for a few minutes. Check whether the mixture is stable or the particles began to settle after some time.**
   (iv) **Filter the mixture. Are there any residues on the filter paper?**

   Different groups will get different results as :

Activity	Group A	Group B	Group C	Group D
(i) Visibility	not visible	not visible	visible	visible
(ii) Stability	donot settle down	donot settle down	settle down	do not settle down
(iii) Passing beam of torch	beam not visible	beam not visible	beam is visible	beam is visible
(iv) Filtration	no residue	no residue	residue left	no residue

In fact we get three different types of mixtures. These are :

Group A and B have got a **solution** (also called true solution)

Group C has got a **suspension**.

Group D has got a **colloidal solution**

However, the intensity of the blue colour of solution obtained by group A is lower than that of the solution obtained by group B. This is because the amount of copper sulphate in solution of group B is more than that of solution of group A. Thus, the intensity of colour depends upon the amount of substance dissolved.

Let us sum up the properties of colloids.

Properties of colloids

1. Colloid is a heterogeneous mixture. It consists of dispersed phase and dispersion medium.
2. The size of particles of a colloid is in between 1 nm (10^{-9} m or 10^{-7} cm) and 100 nm (10^{-7}m or 10^{-5} cm).
3. The particles of colloids are too small to be seen by naked eyes.
4. The particles of colloid are big enough to scatter a beam of light passing through it and make its path visible. Thus, they show Tyndall effect.
5. A colloid is quite stable. Its particles donot settle down when left undisturbed.
6. The particles of colloidal solution cannot be seperated from mixture by the process of filtration. However, they can be separated by a special technique known as centrifugation.

Let us sum up the comparison of true solution, colloid and suspension.

Property	True solution	Colloid	Suspension
1. Nature	Homogeneous	Heterogeneous	Heterogeneous
2. Particle size	Less than 10^{-9} m	Between 10^{-9} m to 10^{-7} m	More than 10^{-7} m
3. Appearance	Clear and transparent	Generally transparent	Opaque
4. Filterability through filter paper	Pass through filter paper	Pass through filter paper	Cannot pass through filter paper
5. Settling of particles	Do not settle	Settle only on centrifugation	Settle under gravity
6. Visibility	Not visible	Visible only under ultra-microscope	Particles are generally visible
7. Tyndall effect	Do not show	Show	Show

Solved Examples

Example 19. Arrange true solutions, colloids and suspensions in the

(*i*) decreasing order of stability

(*ii*) increasing order of particle size

Solution : (*i*) **Decreasing order of stability:**

true solutions > colloids > suspensions

(*ii*) **Increasing order of particle size**

true solutions < colloids < suspensions

Example 20. Which of true solutions, colloids, suspensions donot show Tyndall effect?

Solution : True solutions

Example 21. What is the name of colloidal sol containing:

(*i*) Liquid as dispersed phase and gas as dispersion medium.

(*ii*) Gas as dispersed phase and liquid as dispersion medium.

(*iii*) Liquid as dispersed phase and solid as dispersion medium

Solution : (*i*) Aerosol

(*ii*) Foam

(*iii*) Gel

Practice Exercise 2B

Answers and Hints on Page 60

1. How much water should be added to 10 g of common salt to obtain 10% salt solution?
2. Pick out the colloid from the following :
   Salt solution, sugar solution, muddy water, milk
3. Which of the following is not an aerosol?
   (*i*) Smoke (*ii*) Clouds
   (*iii*) Shaving cream (*iv*) Mist
4. A solution contains 18 g of sugar mixed with 72 g of water. Calculate the concentration of this solution.
5. Choose the correct answer :
   20% alcohol solution means :
   (*i*) 20 mL of alcohol and 80 mL of water.
   (*ii*) 20 mL of alcohol and 100 mL of water.
6. Fill in the blanks :
   (*i*) Vinegar is a __________ solution and milk is a __________ solution.
   (*ii*) The size of solute particles in a colloid is between __________ and __________ m.
7. Which of the following will show Tyndall effect ?
   (*i*) Common salt solution
   (*ii*) Copper sulphate solution
   (*iii*) Milk
8. Arrange true solution, suspension and colloid in the decreasing order of size of the particles.
9. Give one example each of :
   (*i*) aerosol and sol
   (*ii*) solution
10. Which of the following shows Tyndall effect ?
    Salt solution or starch solution
11. X, Y and Z are three solutions. X is solution of sodium chloride in water, Y is gelatin solution and Z is solution of $BaSO_4$ in water. Which of these has smallest size of particles ?
12. How would you prepare a saturated solution of sodium chloride in water at 30°C? What will happen if this solution is
    (*i*) cooled to 10°C
    (*ii*) heated to 40°C
13. Define the following giving one example of each:
    (*i*) emulsion
    (*ii*) sol
    (*iii*) aerosol
14. Give one example each of
    (*i*) aqueous solution (*ii*) non-aqueous solution
15. What are colloidal solutions ? Give one example of the following types of colloids :
    (*i*) Liquid dispersed in gas
    (*ii*) Gas dispersed in liquid
    (*iii*) Liquid dispersed in solid
    (*iv*) Liquid dispersed in liquid
    (*v*) Solid dispersed in gas
16. What volume of ethyl alcohol and water must be mixed together to prepare 300 mL of 60 % by volume of alcohol in water ?
17. What mass of potassium sulphate (K_2SO_4) would be needed to prepare a saturated solution in 250 g of water at 60°C ? The solubility of potassium sulphate in water is 16 g at 60°C.
18. A solution contains 25 g of sugar in 250 g of water. Calculate its concentration.
19. Write two properties each of a solution, suspension and a colloid with respect to stability and filterability.
    (*CBSE Sample Paper 2010*)
20. Complete the table for characteristics of suspension, colloidal solution and solution.

Property	Suspension	Colloidal solution	Solution
(*a*) Particle size	> 100 nm	....	....
(*b*) Nature	....	Heterogeneous	....
(*c*) Tyndall effect	....	....	does not show
(*d*) Separation by ordinary filter paper	....	Not possible	....
(*e*) Brownian movement	May show	....	....

SEPARATING THE COMPONENTS OF A MIXTURE

We have learnt that most of the naturally occurring substances are not chemically pure. We use some of these as such in our daily life. In many materials, we have to separate the useful components from the unwanted components before we can use them. Different methods are used to get individual components from the mixtures. The separation of components of a mixture is necessary to get pure and useful components.

The heterogeneous mixtures can be readily separated into their respective components by simple physical methods such as *hand picking, sieving, sedimentation, decantation, filtration, etc* which we use in our day-to-day life. Sometimes, special techniques are to be used for separation of components of mixtures.

You have already learnt some simple methods of separation of mixtures in your earlier classes.

Let us learn some more methods of separation of components of mixtures by performing activities.

1. How to obtain coloured component (dye) from blue or black ink ?

The coloured component (dye) can be obtained from blue/black ink by the process of evaporation.

To learn about the method let us perform a simple activity.

Activity 5

To separate the components of a mixture by evaporation

1. Take a beaker, a watch glass which can rest on the mouth of beaker, a burner and some blue ink.
2. Fill half the beaker with water.
3. Place watch glass on the mouth of the beaker.
4. Put a few drops of ink on the watch glass.
5. Now start heating the beaker. It may be noted that we should not heat ink directly. Therefore, this arrangement is needed. You will observe that evaporation is taking place from the watch glass.
6. Continue heating till evaporation goes on and stop when you donot see any further change on the watch glass.
7. Observe the changes carefully and make records.

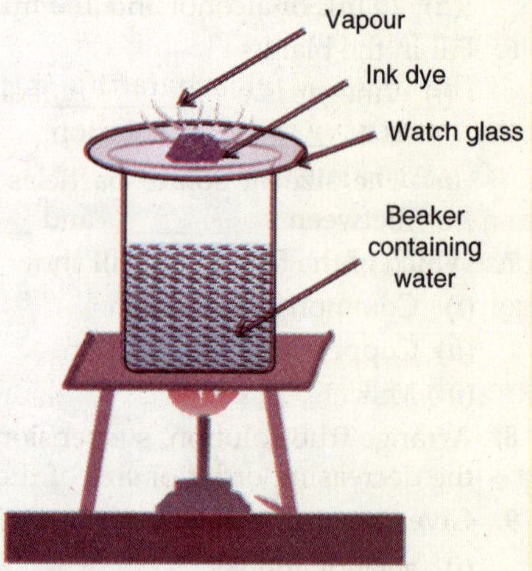

Fig. 11. Separating blue ink.

Now answer the following questions.

(*a*) **What has evaporated from the watch glass?**

(*b*) **Is there a residue left on the watch glass?**

(*c*) **What do you conclude, is ink a single substance or is it a mixture ?**

We observe that ink is a mixture of a dye in water. The dye remains on the watch glass whereas water evaporates. This process of separating any substance from its solution by removing water is called **evaporation.** This method can be used to separate the **non-volatile component (solute) from its volatile component (solvent).**

This process is used on a large scale to obtain common salt from sea water or lake water containing common salt. Sea water is collected in open, shallow beds at high tide. The shallow beds are also called *lagoons*. In the hot sun, water evaporates and salt is left behind. The salt is then collected in heaps and packed.

2. How to separate cream from milk?

Cream from milk can by obtained by the process of centrifugation.

Nowadays, we get different varieties of milk such as full cream milk, tonned milk, double tonned milk etc. packed in poly packs or tetra packs.

These varieties of milk contain different amount of milk fat. We generally require cream for different purposes. This can be obtained from milk. The method can be learnt by the following activity:

Activity 6

To separate cream from milk by centrifugation

1. Take some full cream milk in a test tube.
2. Centrifuge the cream using a centrifugal machine for 2–3 minutes. If centrifugal machine is not available you can do it with the help of a churner used in the kitchen. For this take milk in a jug and churn with a churner for 4–5 minutes.

What do you observe on churning or centrifuging the milk ?

We observe that before churning or centrifuging, the solid fat particles were uniformly mixed all through the liquid. After centrifuging, the lighter cream has collected at the top and milk without cream has remained below. Cream can be separated from the milk.

This **method of separating the solid particles suspended in liquid is** called **centrifugation.**

Centrifugation : This is a method for separating the particles suspended in a liquid. Sometimes, the solid particles in a liquid are too small and readily pass through a filter paper. These solid particles can be separated with the help of a machine known as centrifugal machine. The machine can be rotated at very high speed. The principle of this process is that the denser particles are forced to the bottom and the lighter particles stay at the top when spun rapidly. So in the suspension of particles suspended in a liquid, the heavier particles settle down at the bottom of test tubes. This method of separation finds its importance when

(*i*) the test tubes are rotated at a very high speed.

(*ii*) one material is heavier than the other.

Applications of centrifugation

The process of centrifuging finds many applications in our day-to-day life. Some of these are :

1. The process of centrifuging is used in dairies and homes to separate butter from cream. For this cream is centrifuged and the butter being lighter floats at the top. It is easily removed. In homes, this method of separation is made use in a **mixture-grinder** commonly called **mixi.** It is a very useful kitchen appliance.
2. It is used in washing machines to squeeze out water from wet clothes.
3. It is extremely used in diagnostic laboratories for different tests of bloods and urine.
4. It is used in chemical laboratories and industries for separating suspended materials from liquids.

3. How to separate a mixture of two immiscible liquids?

The immiscible liquids can be separated by a separating funnel.

A separating funnel is shown in Fig.12 ahead.

Let us learn this method for separating mustard oil in water by performing the following activity :

Activity 7

To understand the separation of two immiscible liquids using a separating funnel.

1. Take the mixture of mustard oil (or kerosene oil) in water.
2. Pour the mixture in the separating funnel.
3. Allow it to stand undisturbed for sometime till separate layers of oil and water are formed.

   What do you observe ?

   You will observe that

   (*i*) Mustard oil forms the upper layer

   (*ii*) Water forms the lower layer.
4. Open the stop cork of the separating funnel and pour the lower layer carefully in a beaker.
5. Close the stop cork as the oil reaches down and is left behind in the separating funnel.

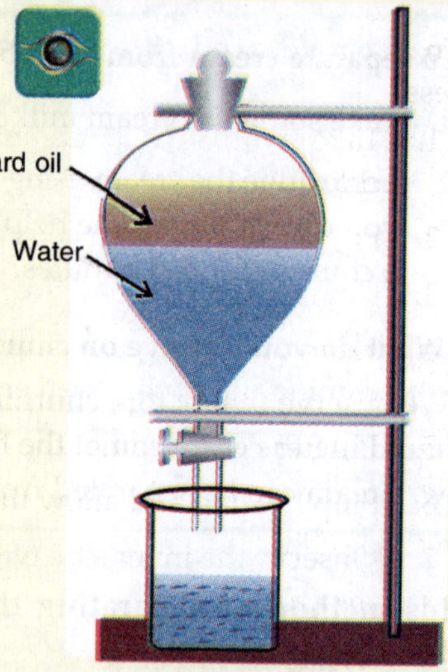

Fig. 12. Use of a separating funnel.

So we have learnt that when the two liquids are immiscible, they can be easily separated with the help of a separating funnel. The principle of the method is that immiscible liquids separate out in layers depending on their densities. However, it may be noted that a small amount of the mixture remains unseparated.

Applications of the method

This method is used

(*i*) to separate a mixture of oil and water.

(*ii*) to separate some organic compounds present in aqueous solution.

(*iii*) for the extraction of iron during its metallurgy. The lighter slag is removed from the top by this method to leave the molten iron at the bottom of the furnace.

KEY NOTE

A mixture of more than two immiscible liquids can also be separated with a separating funnel. For example, when a mixture of water, benzene and mercury is put in a separating funnel, it separates into three layers. Mercury is the heaviest liquid (maximum density) and forms the bottom layer, water forms the middle layer and benzene being the lightest (least density) forms the top layer. On opening the stop cock, mercury will come out first, followed by water and then benzene.

4. How to separate a mixture of common salt and ammonium chloride?

A mixture of common salt and ammonium chloride can be separated by the process of sublimation.

We have learnt in the previous chapter that most of the solids first change into liquids and then into their gaseous states. However, some liquids on heating change directly to their gaseous states without changing into liquids. This process in which a solid changes directly into gaseous state without changing into its liquid state is called **sublimation**. Some common examples of solids which sublime are **ammonium chloride, camphor, nepthalene, anthracene, benzoic acid, etc.**

Thus, to separate the mixtures which contain a sublimable volatile component from a non sublimable impurity, the process of sublimation is used. For example, a mixture of common salt and camphor can be separated by this method as illustrated by the following activity :

Activity 8

To separate a mixture of two solids by sublimation process.

1. Take a mixture of common salt and ammonium chloride.
2. Put the mixture in a china dish.
3. Cover the mixture with an inverted glass funnel.
4. Heat the china dish slowly till white fumes start coming out of the open end of the inverted funnel.
5. Plug the open end of the funnel with cotton.
6. Stop heating and allow the funnel to cool.
7. Observe the inner side of funnel and the contents in the china dish.

What do you observe ?

You will observe that ammonium chloride has deposited on the walls of the funnel. This is because ammonium chloride changed from solid to its vapour form directly without changing into its liquid form.

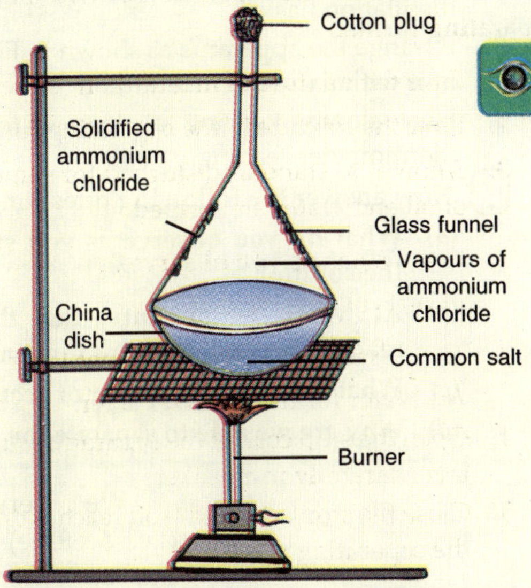

Fig. 13. Use of sublimation to separate a mixture of ammonium chloride and common salt.

It has cooled down on the inner sides of the funnel. The common salt is left in the china dish.

So, ***sublimation process can be used for separating those substances which sublime on heating.***

5. How to separate a mixture of two miscible liquids?

A mixture of miscible liquids can be separated by the process of distillation.

Two miscible liquids can be separated by a process known as **distillation.** In this process, the liquid is heated to its boiling point so that it is converted into vapours. On cooling the vapours, pure liquid is obtained and collected separately. The apparatus used for the process is shown in Fig. 14. It consists of a flask known as distillation flask having a side tube connected to a condenser. The mixture to be separated is taken in this flask. The flask is gently heated on a water bath or even directly. The liquid having lower boiling point will vapourize first and when it passes through the condenser, the vapours get condensed in the liquid form. Water is passed through the condenser which cools the vapours. In this way, whole of the component having low boiling point is collected in the receiver and the other component having high boiling point remains in the flask.

Let us learn about the method by performing an activity to separate acetone and water from their solution.

Activity 9

To understand the separation of two miscible liquids using distillation

1. Take the solution of acetone and water in a distillation flask.
2. Arrange the apparatus as shown in Fig. 14 and fit it with a thermometer.
3. Heat slowly keeping a close watch at the thermometer reading.

Now answer the following questions :

(a) **What do you observe as you start heating the solution?**

(b) **At what temperature the thermometer reading became constant for sometime?**

(c) **What is the boiling point of acetone?**

(d) **Why are we able to separate the two components?**

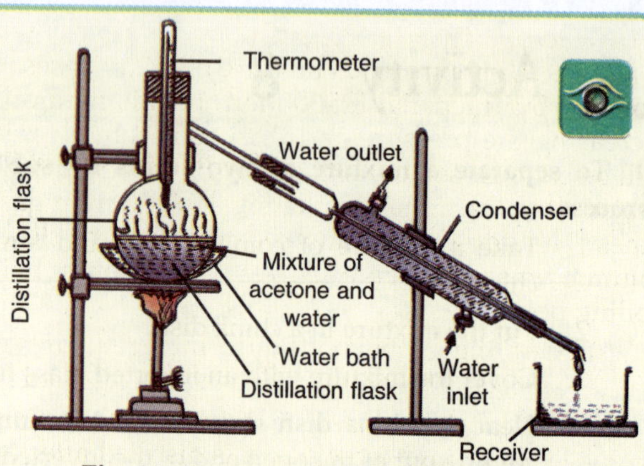

Fig. 14. Apparatus for simple distillation for separation of two miscible liquids.

We observe that when we start heating, the vapours of low boiling liquid (i.e., acetone) are formed first and start rising. As the vapours pass through the condenser, they get cooled and are collected in the receiver. The reading of thermometer becomes constant at 56°C. This represents the boiling point of acetone. After sometime, no more vapours of alcohol are formed. We observe that water is left behind in the distillation flask. This method is called distillation. It is used for the separation of the liquids whose boiling points are sufficiently different.

Applications of simple distillation.

This method of distillation is used for

(*i*) separation of two miscible liquids that boil without decomposition and have sufficient difference (more than 25 K) in their boiling points.

(*ii*) separation of volatile liquids from non-volatile impurities.

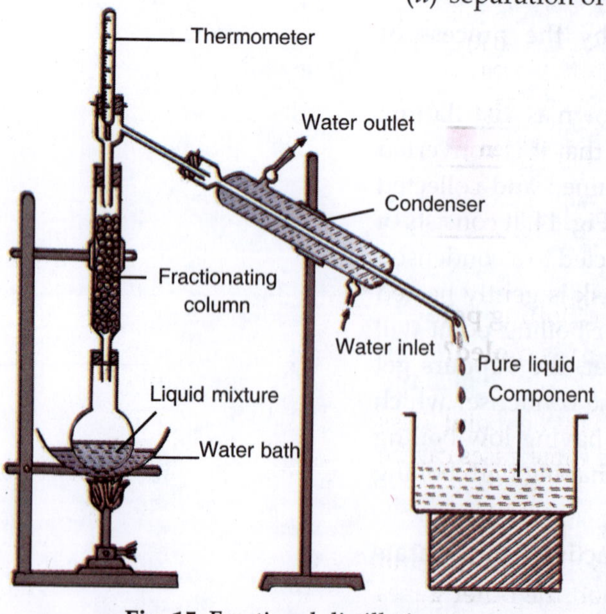

Fig. 15. Fractional distillation.

This method has been used for the separation of mixtures of

(*a*) ether (b.p. 308K) and toluene (b.p. 384K)

(*b*) benzene (b.p. 353K) and aniline b.p. (457K)

(*c*) hexane (b.p. 342K) and toluene (b.p. 384K)

Fractional distillation

If the difference in the boiling points of two miscible liquids of the mixture is less than 25°, then the process of simple distillation cannot be used. This is because the vapours of both the liquids will be formed simultaneously (because they have close boiling points) and the distillate will also contain both of these. To solve the problem, the distillation is carried out by using fractionating columns. The method used is called **fractional distillation.** In this method, some obstructions are provided to the passage of vapours. This is shown in Fig. 15. The fractionating column is a tube packed with glass beads. These beads provide surface for vapours to cool and condense.

The fractional distillation method can be used to separate acetone (b.p = 56°C) and methyl alcohol (b.p = 65°C).

One of the technical application of fractional distillation is to separate different fractions of crude oil in petroleum industry.

6. How to obtain gases from air?

Air is a homogeneous mixture of many gases. The gases can be separated from air by fractional distillation. In this method, the air is compressed by increasing the pressure and then cooled by decreasing the temperature. Air will be compressed to form liquid air called **liquefied air**. Then liquefied air is subjected to fractional distillation and different gases are collected at different times. The liquid air is allowed to warm up slowly in fractional distillation column, where gases are separated at different heights depending upon their boiling points.

(*i*) The boiling point of liquid nitrogen (present in the air) is the lowest (–196°C). Therefore, nitrogen gets distilled first of all.

(*ii*) Liquid argon (present in the air) has a slightly higher boiling point (–186°C) and therefore, it is distilled after nitrogen.

(*iii*) Liquid oxygen (present in liquid air) has higher point (–183°C) after argon. Therefore, it is distilled after argon and so on.

The flow sheet diagram for the method is shown below :

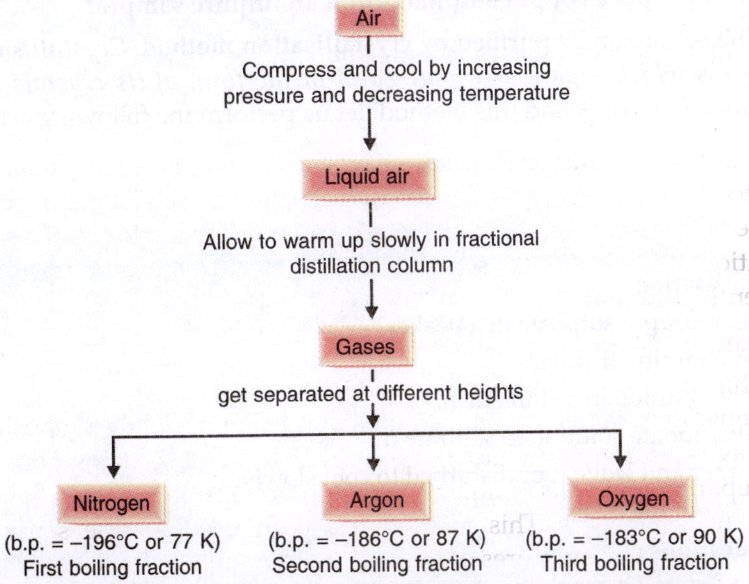

The boiling points of three common gases obtained from air are.

Gas	Oxygen	Argon	Nitrogen
Boiling point (°C)	–183	–186	–196
% air by volume	20.9	0.9	78.1

Answer the following questions :

(*i*) Arrange the gases in the increasing order of boiling point.

(*ii*) Which gas forms the liquid first when the air is cooled?

(*iii*) Which gas boils up first when air boils?

From the table, it is clear that oxygen has higher boiling point (less negative) than argon which is less than nitrogen. So, these three gases can be arranged in the increasing order of boiling point as :

Nitrogen < Argon < Oxygen

When we cool the air, oxygen will be cooled first. On heating liquid air, nitrogen will boil up first. To get oxygen from air all the other gases present must be separated.

A diagram showing separation of components of air is given in Fig. 16.

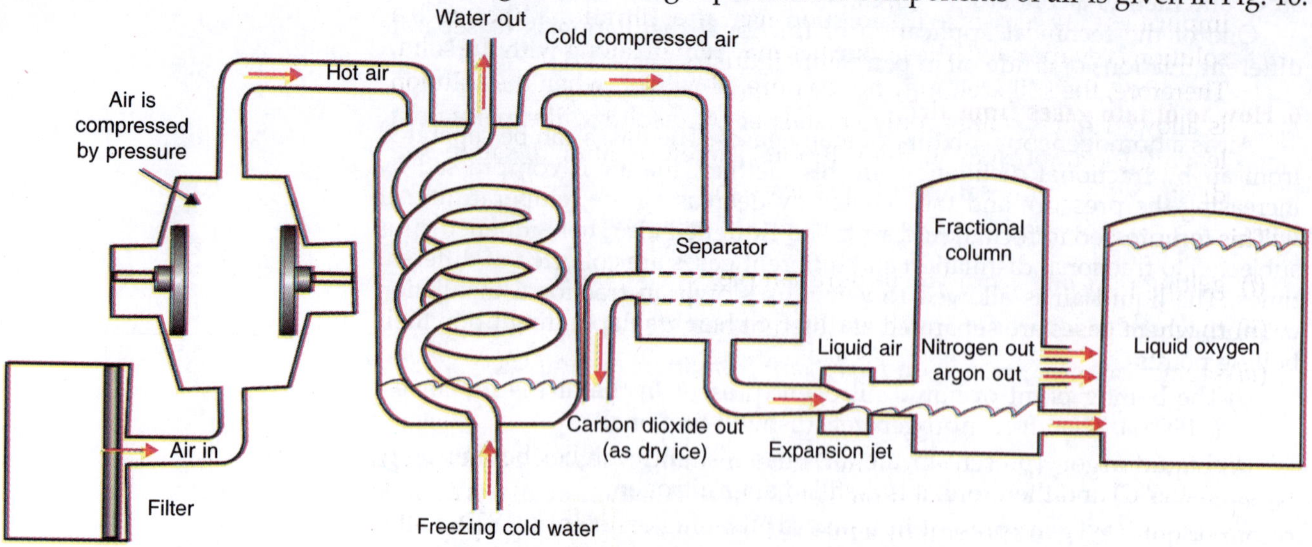

Fig. 16. Separation of components of air.

7. How to get pure copper sulphate from an impure sample?

The solids can be purified by **crystallisation method.** ***Crystallisation is a process which separates a pure solid in the form of its crystals from a solution.*** To understand this method, let us perform the following activity :

Activity 10

To understand the process of crystallisation

1. Take about 5 g of impure sample of copper sulphate in a beaker.
2. Dissolve the sample in minimum quantity of water.
3. Filter the impurities and collect the solution in a china dish.
4. Evaporate water from the copper sulphate solution to saturate it.
5. Cover the solution with a filter paper and leave it undisturbed to cool slowly.
6. You will obtain the crystals of sugar in the dish.

Now answer the following questions :

(*a*) What do you observe in china dish?

(*b*) How will you separate the crystals from the liquid in the china dish?

(*c*) Why is heating of solution required?

We observe that crystals of pure copper sulphate are formed in the china dish. The crystals can be separated from the liquid by filtration. You must have noticed that the solution is heated to saturate the solution. This process is called **crystallisation.** It may be defined as a **process which separates a pure solid in the form of its crystals from a solution.**

The crystallisation technique is better than simple evaporation technique because of the following reasons :

(*i*) During evaporation, the solution is heated to dryness. During heating some solids may decompose or some solids like sugar may get charred. There is no such problem in crystallisation.

(*ii*) In both evaporation and crystallisation, the solution of the impure solid is prepared in water or any other solvent. This solution is then filtered to remove insoluble or suspended impurities. However, some soluble impurities may remain in the solution even after filtration. When such a solution is evaporated, the impurities may remain along with the solid. Therefore, the solid left may not be pure. However, when the solution is allowed to crystallise, only crystals of pure solid will separate out leaving the impurities in the solution. Therefore, after filtration and drying we get pure sample of the substance.

This technique has been used for

(*i*) getting pure sugar from an impure sample.

(*ii*) the purification of salt which we get from sea water.

(*iii*) separation of crystals of alum (*phitkari*) from impure samples.

8. Is the dye in the blue/black ink a single colour?

As we have learnt that dye (coloured substance) from blue or black ink can be separated from ink by evaporation. Let us check whether the dye is a single colour or not. This can be learnt by a method known as **chromatography**. This is a special method to separate small amounts of dissolved solids. Let us learn this technique by performing the following activity :

Activity 11

To understand the process of chromatography

Take a strip of filter paper, a gas jar or tall glass or beaker and water soluble ink. For this check the solubility of ink in water by taking a small amount of ink and add water.

Perform the following activity :

1. Draw a line with a pencil approximately 3 cm above the lower edge.
2. Put a small drop of ink in the centre of line with the help of a thin capillary tube or an ink pen. Dry it.
3. Lower the filter paper till the line into the jar or tall glass or test tube containing water as shown in Fig.17
4. Leave it undisturbed for sometime.

What do you observe? Now answer the following questions :

(*a*) What do you observe on the filter paper as time passes ?

(*b*) Do you obtain different colours?

(*c*) Can you think why this happens?

We observe that as time passes, water seeps up the paper carrying the dye with it. As the water rises on the filter paper, it takes along with it the dye particles. After sometime we get different spots on the filter paper. This shows that the dye is not a single colour. The ink that we use has water as the solvent and dye is soluble in it. The dye is usually a mixture of two or more colours. The coloured component which is more soluble in water rises faster

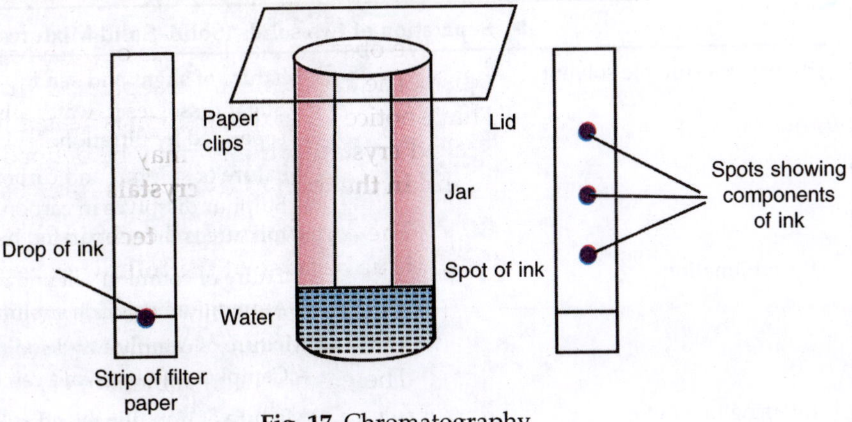

Fig. 17. Chromatography

and in this way different colours get separated. The different components form their spots at different places. This process of separation of components is called **chromatography.** The name comes from *Greek word, kroma* meaning *colour* because this technique was first of all used for the separation of colours. Chromatography has been used for separation of those solutes which dissolve in the same solvent. This has also been used to identify unknown substances. With the advancement of technology newer techniques of chromatography have been developed.

Applications of Chromatography

The main applications of chromatography is to separate

(*i*) colours in a dye. (*ii*) pigments from natural colours
(*iii*) amino acids. (*iv*) sugar from urine sample
(*v*) drugs from blood

So, this technique is finding use in science laboratories and hospitals.

Thus, according to the nature of the mixtures, different techniques can be selected to get a pure substance. It may be noted that with the advancement of technology, many more methods of separation techniques have been developed. The discussion of more methods is beyond the scope of present book. In cities, we get drinking water supplied from water works. A simple flow diagram of a typical water works is shown in Fig. 18. Carefully observe the diagram and learn the processes involved to get the supply of drinking water to your home from water works and discuss in your class.

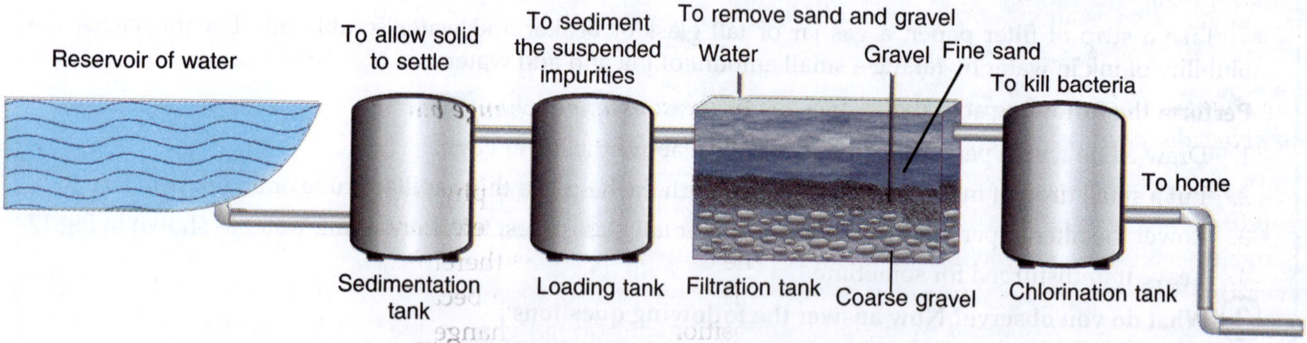

Fig. 18. Purification of water in water works.

Let us sum up the main separation techniques which are commonly used. These are summarized below :

Separation Method	Example
▶ **Separation of two solids (Solid–Solid Mixtures)**	
• By using a suitable solvent	❑ Mixture of sugar and sand – Sugar dissolves in water while sand is insoluble. The mixture is then separated by filtration. ❑ Mixture of sulphur and carbon – Sulphur dissolves in carbon disulphide while carbon does not. The mixture is then separated by filtration.
• By sublimation	❑ Mixture of common salt and ammonium chloride – Ammonium chloride sublimes and can be collected as sublimate. ❑ Mixture of camphor and sodium chloride – Camphor sublimes and can be collected as sublimate.
• By using magnet	❑ Mixture of iron filings and sulphur – Iron filings are attracted by the magnet while sulphur is not.

▶ Separation of a solid and a liquid (Solid–Liquid Mixtures)	
• By filtration (insoluble solid in a liquid)	❑ Mixture of chalk (insoluble) and water ❑ Mixture of sand (insoluble) and water
• By centrifugation (suspended particles from a liquid)	❑ Cream from milk
• By evaporation (solid dissolved in water or other solvent)	❑ Dye from ink ❑ Common salt dissolved in water
• By crystallisation	❑ Pure copper sulphate from impure sample
• By chromatography	❑ Separate dyes in black ink
• By distillation	❑ Mixture of common salt and water
▶ Separation of liquid and a liquid (Liquid-Liquid Mixtures)	
• By distillation (two miscible liquids having b.p. difference more than 25 °C)	❑ Mixture of acetone and water
• By fractional distillation (two miscible liquids having b.p. difference less than 25 °C)	❑ Mixture of acetone and methyl alcohol

PHYSICAL AND CHEMICAL CHANGES

You have learnt about physical and chemical changes in your previous classes. Let us recall about these.

Physical change

The changes in which the physical properties of the substances change but no new substances are formed **are called** ***physical changes.***

Physical change is a purely temporary change in which only the physical properties of the substances such as colour, volume, shape, state, etc may change. It can be easily reversed by changing the conditions and is therefore, **reversible** in nature. Transformation of states is a physical change because these changes occur without a change in composition and do not change the chemical nature of the substance. Although ice, water and water vapour appear to be different and show different physical properties, yet they are chemically same. The common examples of physical changes are:

(*i*) Conversion of water into steam or ice are physical changes.

(*ii*) Dissolution of sugar in water is also a physical change. In solution, sugar and water retain their identity. Water can be evaporated from the sugar solution and sugar can be recovered.

(*iii*) Conversion of a piece of iron into a magnet.

(*iv*) Heating of iron ball to redness which on cooling comes to its original conditions.

(*v*) Glowing of electric bulb.

(*vi*) Breaking a piece of wood into smaller pieces.

(*vii*) Dissolution of sugar in water because the properties of both sugar and water donot change.

(*viii*) Boiling of water.

Chemical change

The changes in which new substances are formed* are called *chemical changes.

In chemical change one or more kinds of matter are transformed into a new kind of matter or several kinds of matter. It is a **permanent change** and cannot be easily reversed. A chemical change is also called a **chemical reaction**. For example,

(*i*) When iron is exposed to oxygen (present in air and water), it rusts. Rusting is due to the formation of a new substance, iron oxide (rust).

(*ii*) When magnesium ribbon is burnt in oxygen, it forms magnesium oxide.

(*iii*) Burning of candle to give carbon dioxide and water is also chemical change.

(*iv*) Reaction of zinc metal with hydrochloric acid.

(*v*) Formation of iron sulphide from iron and sulphur.

(*vi*) Electrolysis of water.

Differences between physical and chemical changes

The main points of distinction between physical and chemical changes are summarised below :

Physical change	Chemical change
1. A physical change brings about changes only in the physical properties of the substance such as physical state, shape, size, etc.	1. A chemical change brings about changes in chemical properties of the substance.
2. No new substance is formed in a physical change.	2. New substances are formed during the chemical change.
3. It is a temporary change.	3. It is a permanent change.
4. Physical change can be easily reversed.	4. Chemical change cannot be reversed.
5. There is no change in chemical composition of the substance.	5. There is always a change in the chemical composition of the substance.
6. During a physical change, energy change may or may not be observed.	6. During a chemical change, energy change (evolution or absorption of heat, light, etc) always occurs.

Solved Examples

❑ Example 22. **Name the method used to separate a mixture of**

(*i*) ammonium chloride and sodium chloride
(*ii*) salt and water
(*iii*) alcohol and water

Solution : (*i*) sublimation
(*ii*) evaporation
(*iii*) distillation

❑ Example 23. **Name the two main steps used for separation of gases from air.**

Solution : (*i*) Liquefication by compressing and cooling
(*ii*) Fractional distillation

❑ Example 24. **Classify the following as a chemical or physical change :**

(*i*) Melting of butter in a pan.
(*ii*) Cutting of grass.
(*iii*) An almirah gets rusted.
(*iv*) Water boils to form steam.
(*v*) Electric current is passed through water and it is broken down into hydrogen and oxygen
(*vi*) Dissolving salt in water.

Solution :

(*i*) Melting of butter in a pan. — Physical change
(*ii*) Cutting of grass — Physical change
(*iii*) An almirah gets rusted — Chemical change
(*iv*) Water boils to form steam — Physical change
(*v*) Electric current is passed through water and it is broken down into hydrogen and oxygen. — Chemical change
(*vi*) Dissolving salt in water — Physical change.

Practice Exercise 2C

Answers and Hints on Page 61

1. Name the property of one of the constituents which can be used to separate a mixture of
   (i) Iron filings and sulphur
   (ii) Ammonium chloride and camphor
   (iii) Sulphur and carbon
   (iv) Common salt dissolved in water
2. Name the process
   (i) to recover dye from black ink
   (ii) to get cream from milk
   (iii) to separate a mixture of water and acetone
   (iv) to separate a mixture of salt and iodine
3. Outline the method with the help of flow sheet to separate a mixture of sand, ammonium chloride, iron filings and sulphur.
4. Select the chemical changes from the following:
   (i) Digestion of food
   (ii) Boiling of water
   (iii) Cooking of food
   (iv) Tarnishing of silver spoon
   (v) Sublimation of iodine
   (vi) Electrolysis of water
   (vii) Melting of butter in a pan
   (viii) Burning of wood
5. How will you separate
   (i) Impure sample of common salt containing some chalk.
   (ii) a mixture of sodium chloride, ammonium chloride and sand.
6. Name the separation techniques to separate the mixtures of
   (i) immiscible mixture of liquids
   (ii) miscible mixture of liquids
   (iii) solution of solid in a liquid
7. Name one mixture each of the following which can be separated by
   (i) fractional distillation
   (ii) distillation
   (iii) using separating funnel
   (iv) sublimation
   (v) centrifugation
8. Which of the following statements are true?
   (a) Burning of candle is a physical change as well as chemical change.
   (b) Tea leaves from tea can be separated by evaporation.
   (c) Sodium chloride from its solution in water can be separated by filtration.
   (d) Mercury and water can be separated by using a separating funnel.
   (f) Iron filings and sulphur can be separated by heating.
   (g) Milk is churned to separate cream from it.
   (h) Corrosion of copper is a physical change.
9. Draw a neat and labelled diagram of
   (i) Fractional distillation
   (ii) Sublimation process
10. Explain the process of fractional distillation of air with the help of labelled flow sheet diagram.
11. Choose from the list given below the most suitable method for each of the following separations :

Distillation	Crystallization
Chromatography	Evaporation
Separating funnel	Sublimation

   (a) To separate a mixture of common salt and ammonium chloride.
   (b) To separate mustard oil in water.
   (c) To separate a mixture of alcohol and water.
   (d) To get pure sugar from impure sample.
   (e) To check whether a dye is a single colour or not.
12. Three gases present in air have the following boiling points :

Gas	X	Y	Z
Boiling point	– 196°C	– 186°C	– 183°C

   (a) Arrange these gases in the increasing order of their boiling points.
   (b) Which gas forms the liquid first when the air is cooled.
   (c) Which gas will boil first ?
13. Write 'P' for physical change and 'C' for chemical change in the following :
   (a) Dissolving salt in water
   (b) Freezing of water
   (c) Rusting of iron
   (d) Frying an egg
   (e) Heating ice to form water
   (f) Digestion of food

What you have learnt

KEY TERMS

Solution : a homogeneous mixture of two or more substances.

Suspension : a heterogenous mixture which contains small insoluble particles of solute spread throughout the solvent without dissolving in it.

True solution : a solution whose particles are of very small size (less than 10^{-9} m).

Colloidal solution : a solution in which the size of particles is intermediate between those in true solution and suspension (i.e., between 10^{-9} m to 10^{-7} m).

Brownian movement : the zig-zag motion of colloidal particles.

Tyndall effect : the phenomenon of scattering of light by colloidal particles as a result of which the path of the beam becomes visible.

Physical change : the change in which the physical properties of a substance change but no new substance is formed.

Chemical change : the change in which a new substance is formed.

Chapter Summary

- A substance is a kind of matter which cannot be separated into other kinds of matter by any physical process.
- Scientifically something is pure means that it is a single substance.
- The pure substances can be elements or compounds.
- Element is the basic form of matter that cannot be broken down into simpler substances by ordinary chemical methods.
- A compound is a pure substance made up of two or more elements chemically combined in a fixed proportion by mass.
- A mixture is a substance containing two or more substances (elements or compounds) in any proportion.
- Properties of a compound are different from its constituent elements whereas a mixture shows the properties of its constituting elements or compounds.
- A mixture contains more than one substance, elements or compounds.
- A solution is a homogeneous mixture of two or more than two substances.
- In a solution, a component present in excess is called **solvent** and the component present in lesser amount is called **solute.**
- The concentration of solution is expressed as the amount of solute, as percentage of mass or volume of solution.
- A suspension is a heterogeneous mixture containing solid particles suspended in a liquid. The size of the particle is about 100 nm.
- Colloids are heterogeneous mixtures having particle size between 1 nm to 100 nm.
- In colloids, the solute particles are called the dispersed phase and the solvent in which they are distributed throughout is called the dispersion medium.
- Colloids show Brownian movement and Tyndall effect.
- Mixture can be separated into pure substances by using appropriate separation techniques.

NCERT File with Answers & Hints

In-Text Questions

1. **What is meant by a pure substance ?**

Ans. A pure substance consists of a single type of particles. In a pure substance, all the constituent particles are the same in their chemical nature. For example, sodium chloride is a pure substance because it represents only one kind of matter and its composition is the same throughout.

2. **List the points of differences between homogeneous and heterogeneous mixtures.**

Ans.

Homogeneous mixtures	Heterogeneous mixtures
1. They have uniform composition throughout.	They donot have uniform composition throughout.
2. They donot have physically distinct parts.	They have physically distinct parts. They have visible boundaries of separation between its various parts.
3. They have same properties throughout the bulk.	They donot have same properties throughout the bulk.

3. **Differentiate between homogeneous and heterogeneous mixtures with examples .**

Ans. For differences refer Q. 2.

Homogeneous mixtures : Sodium chloride dissolved in water, ethyl alcohol dissolved in water

Heterogeneous mixtures : Air, gun powder, mixture of chalk in water.

4. **How are sol, solution and suspension different from each other ?**

Ans.

	Sol	True solution	Suspension
(*i*) Nature	Heterogeneous	Homogeneous	Heterogeneous
(*ii*) Particle size	between 1 to 100 nm	less than 1 nm	more than 100 nm
(*iii*) Visibility	Particles can be seen only under electron microscope	Particles cannot be seen	Particles can be seen with naked eye
(*iv*) Appearance	Generally clear and transparent	Clear and transparent	opaque
(*v*) Diffusion	Diffuse slowly	Diffuse rapidly	Donot diffuse
(*vi*) Tyndall effect	Show	Donot show	May or may not show

5. **To make a saturated solution, 36g of sodium chloride is dissolved in 100 g of water at 293 K. Find its concentration at this temperature.**

Ans. Its concentration is 36% by mass at 293 K.

6. **How will you separate a mixture containing kerosene and petrol (difference in their boiling points is more than 25°C), which are miscible with each other ?**

Ans. Since the mixture contains two liquids which are miscible with each other and have a boiling point difference of more than 25°C, these can be separated by simple distillation method (discussed in Text).

7. **Name the technique to separate**

(*i*) **butter from curd.** (*ii*) **salt from sea-water.**

(*iii*) **camphor from salt.**

Ans. (*i*) Centrifugation (*ii*) Evaporation

(*iii*) Sublimation

8. What type of mixtures are separated by the technique of crystallisation ?

Ans. The crystallisation technique is used to separate a mixture of those two components in which one dissolves in a given solvent but the other remains insoluble. The component which gets dissolved in the solvent can be separated after crystallisation.

9. Classify the following as chemical or physical changes :

(*i*) cutting of trees (*ii*) Melting of butter in a pan (*iii*) Rusting of almirah

(*iv*) boiling of water to form steam

(*v*) passing of electric current through water and the water breaking down into hydrogen and oxygen gases

(*vi*) dissolving common salt in water

(*vii*) making a fruit salad with raw fruits and

(*viii*) burning of paper and wood.

Ans. (*i*) Physical change (*ii*) Physical change (*iii*) Chemical change
(*iv*) Physical change (*v*) Chemical change (*vi*) Physical change
(*vii*) Physical change (*viii*) Chemical change.

Textbook Exercises

1. Which separation techniques will you apply for the separation of the following?

(*a*) Sodium chloride from its solution in water.

(*b*) Ammonium chloride from a mixture containing sodium chloride and ammonium chloride.

(*c*) Small pieces of metal in the engine oil of a car.

(*d*) Different pigments from an extract of flower petals.

(*e*) Butter from curd.

(*f*) Oil from water.

(*g*) Tea leaves from tea.

(*h*) Iron pins from sand.

(*i*) Wheat grains from husk.

(*j*) Fine mud particles suspended in water.

Ans. (*a*) Evaporation
(*b*) Sublimation
(*c*) Filtration
(*d*) Chromatography
(*e*) Centrifugation
(*f*) Separating Funnel
(*g*) Filtration
(*h*) Magnetic separation
(*i*) Gravity separation or winnowing
(*j*) Filtration

2. Write the steps you would use for making tea. Use the words solution, solvent, solute, dissolve, soluble, insoluble, filtrate and residue.

Ans. Take 100 mL of water which acts as **solvent.** Boil water on a gas stove. Add one teaspoon of sugar which acts as **solute.** Sugar gets **dissolved** in water and forms a **solution.** Now add about half a teaspoon of tea leaves which are insoluble in water. Boil the contents for 4 to 5 minutes and add half a cup of milk and allow it to boil again for 2–3 minutes. **Filter** the tea with the help of a sieve. Tea leaves will be left as **residue** while tea will be obtained as **filtrate.**

3. Pragya tested the solubility of three different substances at different temperatures and collected the data as given below (results are given in the following table, as grams of substances dissolved in 100 grams of water to form a saturated solution).

	Temperature in K				
Substance dissolved	**283**	**293**	**313**	**333**	**353**
Potassium nitrate	21	32	62	106	167
Sodium chloride	36	36	36	37	37
Potassium chloride	35	35	40	46	54
Ammonium chloride	24	37	41	55	66

(a) What mass of potassium nitrate would be needed to produce a saturated solution of potassium nitrate in 50 grams of water at 313 K ?

(b) Pragya makes a saturated solution of potassium chloride in water at 353 K and leaves the solution to cool at room temperature. What would she observe as the solution cools ? Explain.

(c) Find the solubility of each salt at 293 K. Which salt has the highest solubility at this temperature ?

(d) What is the effect of change of temperature on the solubility of a salt ?

Ans. (a) Solubility of potassium nitrate at 313 K = 62g/100g of water

100g of water contains potassium nitrate = 62g

50 g of water will contain potassium nitrate

$$= \frac{62}{100} \times 50 = 31\text{g}$$

∴ 31g of potassium nitrate would be needed to produce a saturated solution of potassium nitrate in 50g of water at 313 K

(b) On cooling the saturated solution of potassium chloride in water at 353 K to room temperature, crystals of potassium chloride will be formed.

(c) Solubility of different salts in 100g water at 293 K is :

Potassium nitrate : 32g,

Sodium chloride : 36g

Potassium chloride : 35g,

Ammonium chloride : 37g

Ammonium chloride has the highest solubility.

(d) The solubility of salts increases with increase in temperature.

4. **Explain the following by giving examples:**

(a) saturated solution

(b) pure substance

(c) colloid

(d) suspension

Ans. **(a) Saturated solution.** A solution in which no more solute can be dissolved in a given amount of solvent at a particular temperature is called **saturated solution.** For example, if we dissolve 40g sodium chloride in 100g of water at 293K, it will form a saturated solution because the solubility of sodium chloride at 293K is 36g per 100g of water.

(b) **Pure substance.** A substance made up of only one kind of atoms or molecules is called a pure substance. A pure substance has the same colour, taste and texture at a given temperature and pressure. A pure substance also has a fixed melting and boiling point at a constant pressure. For example, hydrogen gas, sodium chloride, water.

(c) **Colloid.** A substance is said to be a colloid if its particles size lies between 1 to 100 nm. A colloidal solution is a heterogeneous and consists of two phases i.e., dispersed phase (colloidal particles) and dispersion medium in which colloidal particles are suspended. For example, colloidal solution of sulphur or starch, milk etc.

(d) **Suspension.** It is a heterogeneous mixture in which the particles of the solute donot dissolve but remain suspended throughout the bulk of the solvent. The size of the suspension particles is more than 10^{-7}m. For example, chalk powder in water is a suspension.

5. **Classify each of the following as a homogeneous or heterogeneous mixture.**

Soda water, wood, air, soil, vinegar, filtered tea.

Ans.

Soda water	:	Homogeneous mixture
Wood	:	Heterogeneous mixture
Air	:	Homogeneous mixture
Vinegar	:	Homogeneous mixture
Filtered tea	:	Homogeneous mixture

6. **How would you confirm that a colourless liquid given to you is pure water ?**

Ans. Determine the boiling point of the given liquid. If its boiling point is 100°C at atmospheric pressure, then it is pure water because water has boiling point of 100°C.

7. **Which of the following materials falls in the category of a "pure substance" ?**

(a) Ice **(b) Milk**
(c) Iron **(d) Hydrochloric acid**
(e) Calcium oxide **(f) Mercury**
(g) Brick **(h) Wood**
(i) Air.

Ans. (a) Ice (c) iron
(d) hydrochloric acid
(f) mercury are pure substances.

8. **Identify the solutions among the following mixtures.**

(a) Soil **(b) Sea water**
(c) Air **(d) Coal**
(e) Soda water.

Ans. (b) Sea water
(e) Soda water are solutions.

9. Which of the following will show "Tyndall effect"?

(a) Salt solution

(b) Milk

(c) Copper sulphate solution

(d) Starch solution.

Ans. (b) Milk and (d) Starch show Tyndall effect because these are colloidal solutions.

10. Classify the following into elements, compounds and mixtures :

(a) Sodium	**(b) Soil**
(c) Sugar solution	**(d) Silver**
(e) Calcium carbonate	
(f) Tin	**(g) Silicon**
(h) Coal	**(i) Air**
(j) Soap	**(k) Methane**
(l) Carbon dioxide	**(m) Blood**

Ans.

(a)	Sodium	– element
(b)	Soil	– mixture
(c)	Sugar solution	– mixture
(d)	silver	– element
(e)	Calcium carbonate	– compound
(f)	Tin	– element
(g)	Silicon	– element
(h)	Coal	– mixture
(i)	Air	– mixture
(j)	Soap	– mixture
(k)	Methane	– compound
(l)	Carbon dioxide	– compound
(m)	Blood	– Mixture

11. Which of the following are chemical changes?

(a) Growth of a plant

(b) Rusting of iron

(c) Mixing of iron filings and sand

(d) Cooking of food

(e) Digestion of food

(f) Freezing of water

(g) Burning of a candle.

Ans. (a), (b) (d), (e) and (g) are chemical changes.

NCERT Exemplar Problems

Note: Multiple Choice Question (1-9) from Exemplar Problems are given in Revision Exercise, Page 54

Short Answer Questions

10. Suggest separation technique(s) one would need to employ to separate the following mixtures:

(a) Mercury and water

(b) Potassium chloride and ammonium chloride

(c) Common salt, water and sand

(d) Kerosene oil, water and salt

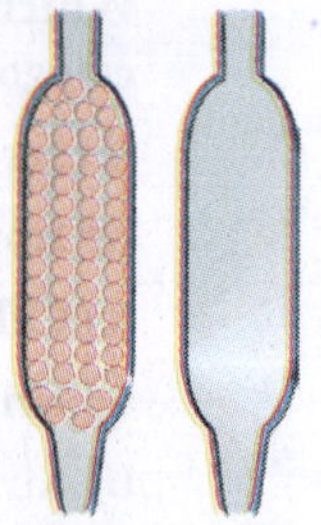

(a) (b)

Ans. (a) Separation with the separating funnel.

(b) Sublimation

(c) Filtration followed by evaporation

(d) Separation by using separating funnel to separate kerosene oil and then distillation.

11. Which of the tubes in the given figures (a) and (b) will be more effective as a condenser in the distillation apparatus?

Ans. Tube (a) because the presence of beads in it provides a larger surface area for cooling.

12. Salt can be recovered from its solution by evaporation. Suggest some other technique for the same?

Ans. Crystallization.

13. The 'sea-water' can be classified as a homogeneous as well as heterogeneous mixture. Comment.

Ans. Sea water can be regarded as homogeneous at the places where it contains only mixture of salts and water. On the other hand, it can be regarded as heterogeneous at places where it contains salts, mud and many other suspended impurities.

14. While diluting a solution of salt in water, a student by mistake added acetone (boiling point 56°C). What technique can be employed to get back the acetone? Justify your choice.

Ans. Acetone can be separated by distillation because it is more volatile and it will separate out first.

15. What would you observe when

(a) a saturated solution of potassium chloride prepared at 60°C is allowed to cool to room temperature.

(*b*) an aqueous sugar solution is heated to dryness.

(*c*) a mixture of iron filings and sulphur powder is heated strongly.

Ans. (*a*) a solid potassium chloride will separate out.

(*b*) Initially water will be left in the container. On further heating sugar will get charred.

(*c*) When a mixture of iron filings and sulphur are heated, iron sulphide will be formed.

16. Explain why particles of a colloidal solution do not settle down when left undisturbed, while in the case of a suspension they do.

Ans. The particles of colloids are constantly moving in all directions and therefore, their particles donot settle down when left undisturbed. On the other hand, the particle sizes in a suspension are larger than those in colloidal solution and donot have random movement. Moreover, the molecular interaction in a suspension are not strong enough to keep the particles suspended. Therefore, the particles settle down.

17. Smoke and fog both are aerosols. In what way are they different?

Ans. Both smoke and fog have gas as the dispersion medium. The difference is that the dispersed phase in smoke is solid while that in fog is liquid.

18. Classify the following as physical or chemical properties

(*a*) The composition of a sample of steel is: 98% iron, 1.5% carbon and 0.5% other elements.

(*b*) Zinc dissolves in hydrochloric acid with the evolution of hydrogen gas.

(*c*) Metallic sodium is soft enough to be cut with a knife.

(*d*) Most metal oxides form alkalis on interacting with water.

Ans. (*a*) Physical property

(*b*) Chemical property

(*c*) Physical property

(*d*) Chemical property

19. The teacher instructed three students 'A', 'B' and 'C' respectively to prepare a 50% (mass by volume) solution of sodium hydroxide (NaOH). 'A' dissolved 50g of NaOH in 100 mL of water, 'B' dissolved 50g of NaOH in 100g of water while 'C' dissolved 50g of NaOH in water to make 100 mL of solution.

Which one of them has made the desired solution and why?

Ans. C has made the desired solution.

$$\text{Mass \% by volume} = \frac{\text{Mass of solute}}{\text{Volume of solution}} \times 100$$

$$= \frac{50}{100} \times 100$$

= 50% mass by volume.

20. Name the process associated with the following:

(*a*) Dry ice is kept at room temperature and at one atmospheric pressure.

(*b*) A drop of ink placed on the surface of water contained in a glass spreads throughout the water.

(*c*) A potassium permanganate crystal is in a beaker and water is poured into the beaker with stirring.

(*d*) An acetone bottle is left open and the bottle becomes empty.

(*e*) Milk is churned to separate cream from it.

(*f*) Settling of sand when a mixture of sand and water is left undisturbed for some time.

(*g*) Fine beam of light entering through a small hole in a dark room, illuminates the particles in its paths.

Ans. (*a*) Sublimation

(*b*) Diffusion

(*c*) Dissolution and diffusion

(*d*) Evaporation and diffusion

(*e*) Centrifugation

(*f*) Sedimentation

(*g*) Scattering of light known as Tyndall effect.

21. You are given two samples of water labelled as 'A' and 'B'. Sample 'A' boils at 100°C and sample 'B' boils at 102°C. Which sample of water will not freeze at 0°C? Comment.

Ans. Sample A boils at 100°C and therefore, it is pure water. It will also freeze at 0°C. But sample B is not pure and it will not freeze at 0°C.

22. What are the favourable qualities given to gold when it is alloyed with copper or silver for the purpose of making ornaments?

Ans. Pure gold is soft as compared to gold alloyed with copper or silver. Thus, when gold is alloyed with copper or silver, its strength increases.

23. An element is sonorous and highly ductile. Under which category would you classify this element? What other characteristics do you expect the element to possess?

Ans. It is a metal. The other characteristics of this are lustre, malleability and ductility, heat conductivity and electrical conductivity.

24. Give an example each for the mixture having the following characteristics. Suggest a suitable method to separate the components of these mixtures

(*a*) A volatile and a non-volatile component.

(*b*) Two volatile components with appreciable difference in boiling points.

(*c*) Two immiscible liquids.

(*d*) One of the components changes directly from solid to gaseous state.

(*e*) Two or more coloured constituents soluble in some solvent.

Ans. (*a*) Evaporation or distillation

(*b*) Distillation

(*c*) Separation by separating funnel.

(*d*) Sublimation

(*e*) Chromatography.

25. Fill in the blanks

(*a*) A colloid is a _______ mixture and its components can be separated by the technique known as _______.

(*b*) Ice, water and water vapour look different and display different _______ properties but they are _______ the same.

(*c*) A mixture of chloroform and water taken in a separating funnel is mixed and left undisturbed for some time. The upper layer in the separating funnel will be of _______ and the lower layer will be that of _______.

(*d*) A mixture of two or more miscible liquids, for which the difference in the boiling points is less than 25 K can be separated by the process called _______.

(*e*) When light is passed through water containing a few drops of milk, it shows a bluish tinge. This is due to the _______ of light by milk and the phenomenon is called _______. This indicates that milk is a _______ solution.

Ans. (*a*) heterogeneous, centrifugation

(*b*) physical, chemically

(*c*) water, chloroform

(*d*) fractional distillation

(*e*) scattering, Tyndall effect, colloidal.

26. Sucrose (sugar) crystals obtained from sugarcane and beetroot are mixed together. Will it be a pure substance or a mixture? Give reasons for the same.

Ans. It is a pure substance because the chemical composition of sugar crystals is the same irrespective of its source.

27. Give some examples of Tyndall effect observed in your surroundings?

Ans. Tyndall effect is observed when light passes through a heterogeneous mixture. For example when sunlight passes through the canopy of a dense forest Tyndall effect is observed.

28. Can we separate alcohol dissolved in water by using a separating funnel? If yes, then describe the procedure. If not, explain.

Ans. No, water and alcohol cannot be separated by a separating funnel. This is because the two liquids are completely miscible. These can be separated by fractional distillation.

29. On heating calcium carbonate gets converted into calcium oxide and carbon dioxide.

(*a*) Is this a physical or a chemical change?

(*b*) Can you prepare one acidic and one basic solution by using the products formed in the above process? If so, write the chemical equation involved.

Ans. (*a*) It is a chemical change.

(*b*) Acidic and basic solutions can be prepared by dissolving the products of above process in water as :

The products of the above process are carbon dioxide and calcium oxide

$$CaCO_3 \xrightarrow{\text{Heat}} CaO + CO_2$$

Calcium oxide dissolves in water to give basic solution

$$CaO + H_2O \longrightarrow Ca(OH)_2 \text{ (basic solution)}$$

Carbon dioxide dissolves in water to give acidic solution.

$$CO_2 + H_2O \longrightarrow H_2CO_3 \text{ (acidic solution)}$$

30. Non-metals are usually poor conductors of heat and electricity. They are non-lustrous, non-sonorous, non-malleable and are coloured.

(*a*) Name a lustrous non-metal.

(*b*) Name a non-metal which exists as a liquid at room temperature.

(*c*) The allotropic form of a non-metal is a good conductor of electricity. Name the allotrope.

(*d*) Name a non-metal which is known to form the largest number of compounds.

(*e*) Name a non-metal other than carbon which shows allotropy.

(f) Name a non-metal which is required for combustion.

Ans. (a) Iodine (b) Bromine
(c) Graphite (d) Carbon
(e) Sulphur (f) Oxygen

31. Classify the substances given in following figure into elements and compounds

Ans. Elements : Cu, Zn, F_2, O_2, Hg, Diamond (C)
Compounds : $CaCO_3$, H_2O.

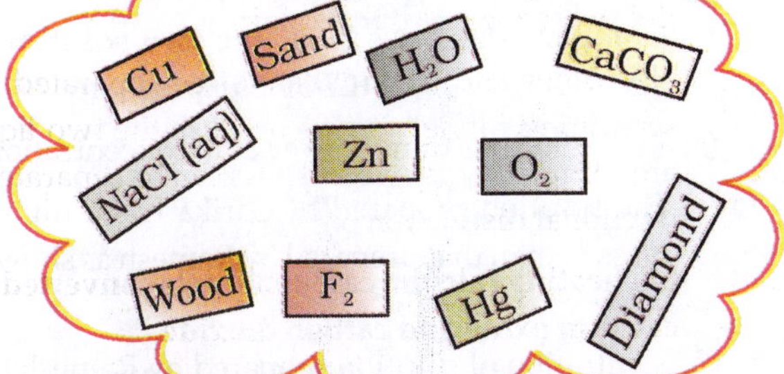

32. Which of the following are not compounds?
(a) Chlorine gas
(b) Potassium chloride
(c) Iron
(d) Iron sulphide
(e) Aluminium
(f) Iodine
(g) Carbon
(h) Carbon monoxide
(i) Sulphur powder

Ans. The following are not the compounds :
Chlorine gas, iron, aluminium, iodine, carbon, sulphur powder.

Long Answer Questions

33. Fractional distillation is suitable for separation of miscible liquids with a boiling point difference of about 25 K or less. What part of fractional distillation apparatus makes it efficient and possess an advantage over a simple distillation process? Explain using a diagram.

Ans. The main part of fractional distillation which provides advantage over simple distillation is fractionating column. The fractionating column packed with glass beads provides a surface for the vapours to collide and lose energy so that these can get quickly condensed and hence distilled.

The length of the column also increases the efficiency. For details and figure refer Text.

34. (a) Under which category of mixtures will you classify alloys and why?
(b) A solution is always a liquid. Comment.
(c) Can a solution be heterogeneous?

Ans. (a) Homogeneous mixtures because they have uniform composition throughout the alloys.

(b) No, solid solutions and gaseous solutions are also possible. Examples are brass (solid solution) and air (gaseous solution).

(c) No, solution cannot be heterogeneous. It is a homogeneous mixture of two or more substances.

35. Iron filings and sulphur were mixed together and divided into two parts, 'A' and 'B'. Part 'A' was heated strongly while Part 'B' was not heated. Dilute hydrochloric acid was added to both the Parts and evolution of gas was seen in both the cases. How will you identify the gases evolved?

Ans. **Part A** in which iron and sulphur are heated

$$Fe(s) + S(s) \xrightarrow{\text{Heat}} FeS(s)$$

$$FeS(s) + 2HCl(aq) \longrightarrow FeCl_2 + H_2S$$

In Part A, H_2S gas is evolved.

Part B in which iron and sulphur are not heated. It will contain a mixture of iron filings and sulphur. When dil HCl is added to it, hydrogen gas will be evolved.

$$Fe(s) + S(s) \longrightarrow \text{Mixture of Fe and S}$$

$$Fe(s) + S(s) + 2HCl(aq) \longrightarrow FeCl_2 + H_2(g)$$

Sulphur remains unreacted.

H_2S gas has a foul smell and on passing through lead acetate solution, it turns the solution black. Hydrogen gas burns with a pop sound.

36. A child wanted to separate the mixture of dyes constituting a sample of ink. He marked a line by the ink on the filter paper and placed the filter paper in a glass containing water as shown in figure. The filter paper was removed when the water moved near the top of the filter paper.

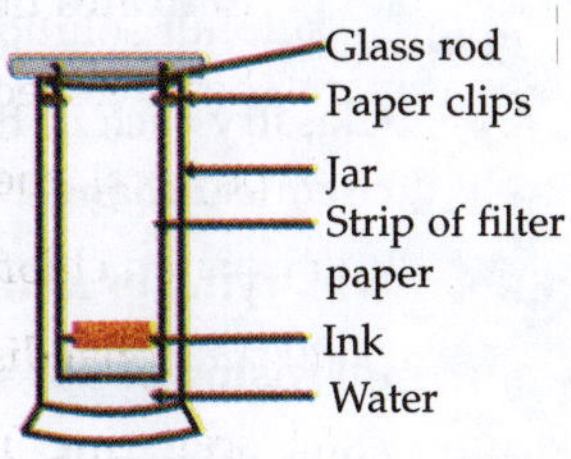

(i) What would you expect to see, if the ink contains three different coloured components?

(ii) Name the technique used by the child.

(iii) Suggest one more application of this technique.

Ans. In this experiment

(i) three different bands will be observed.

(ii) the technique is known as chromatography.

(iii) to separate the pigments present in chlorophyll.

For details refer Text.

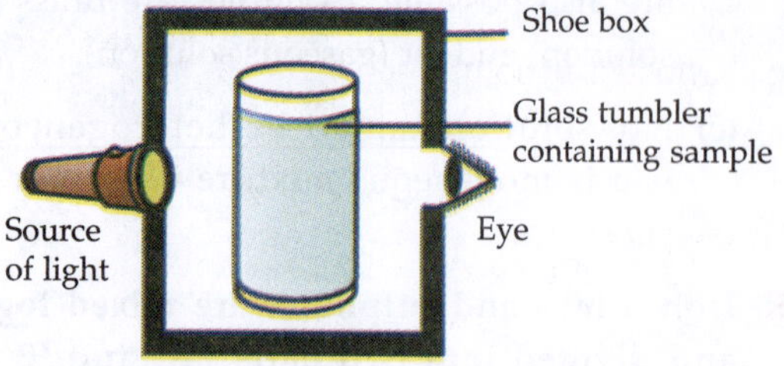

37. **A group of students took an old shoe box and covered it with a black paper from all sides. They fixed a source of light (a torch) at one end of the box by making a hole in it and made another hole on the other side to view the light. They placed a milk sample contained in a beaker/tumbler in the box as shown in the adjacent figure. They were amazed to see that milk taken in the tumbler was illuminated. They tried the same activity by taking a salt solution but found that light simply passed through it?**

(a) Explain why the milk sample was illuminated. Name the phenomenon involved.

(b) Same results were not observed with a salt solution. Explain.

(c) Can you suggest two more solutions which would show the same effect as shown by the milk solution? ***(CBSE Sample Paper 2010)***

Ans. (a) Milk is a colloidal solution and shows scattering of light known as Tyndall effect.

(b) Salt solution is a true solution and does not scatter light *i.e.*, no Tyndall effect.

(c) The two solutions showing Tyndall effect are (i) sulphur solution (ii) detergent solution.

38. **Classify each of the following, as a physical or a chemical change. Give reasons.**

(a) Drying of a shirt in the sun.

(b) Rising of hot air over a radiator.

(c) Burning of kerosene in a lantern.

(d) Change in the colour of black tea on adding lemon juice to it.

(e) Churning of milk cream to get butter.

Ans. (a) Physical change (b) Physical change

(c) Chemical change (d) Chemical change

(e) Physical change

For details, refer Text.

39. **During an experiment the students were asked to prepare a 10% (Mass/Mass) solution of sugar in water. Ramesh dissolved 10g of sugar in 100g of water while Sarika prepared it by dissolving 10g of sugar in water to make 100g of the solution.**

(a) Are the two solutions of the same concentration

(b) Compare the mass % of the two solutions. ***(CBSE Sample Paper 2010)***

Ans. (a) Two solutions donot have same concentration.

(b) The solution prepared by Sarika has a higher mass % than that prepared by Ramesh as shown below :

Concentration of solution prepared by Ramesh:

Mass % of solute =

$$\frac{\text{Mass of solute}}{\text{Mass of solute + Mass of solvent}} \times 100 =$$

$$\frac{10}{10+100} \times 100 = \frac{10}{110} \times 100 = 9.09\%$$

Concentration of solution prepared by Sarika:

$$\text{Mass \% of solute} = \frac{10}{100} \times 100 = 10\%$$

40. **You are provided with a mixture containing sand, iron filings, ammonium chloride and sodium chloride. Describe the procedures you would use to separate these constituents from the mixture?**

Ans. The mixture can be separated by the following steps :

Step 1. Separate iron filings with the help of a magnet, iron filings will be attracted by the magnet.

Step 2. Sublime the remaining mixture. On sublimation ammonium chloride will be separated.

Step 3. Add water to the remaining mixture, stir the contents and filter. Sand will be separated and sodium chloride will go into the filtrate.

Step 4. Evaporate the filtrate to dryness. The residue will be sodium chloride.

41. **Arun has prepared 0.01% (by mass) solution of sodium chloride in water. Which of the following correctly represents the composition of the solutions?**

(a) 1.00 g of NaCl + 100g of water

(b) 0.11g of NaCl + 100g of water

(c) 0.01 g of NaCl + 99.99g of water

(d) 0.10 g of NaCl + 99.90g of water

Ans. Mass % of solute =

$$\frac{\text{Mass of solute}}{\text{Mass of solute + Mass of solvent}} \times 100$$

(a) $\frac{1.0}{1+100} \times 100 = 0.99\%$

(b) $\frac{0.11}{0.11+100} \times 100 = 0.1098\%$

(c) $\frac{0.01}{0.01+100} \times 100 = 0.001\%$

(d) $\frac{0.10}{0.10+99.99} \times 100 = 0.01\%$

(d) represents correct composition.

42. Calculate the mass of sodium sulphate required to prepare its 20% (mass percent) solution in 100g of water?

Ans. Let the mass of sodium sulphate required = x g

Mass of solution = $(x + 100)$ g

$$\text{Mass \% of solute} = \frac{\text{Mass of solute}}{\text{Mass of solution}} \times 100$$

$$20 = \frac{x}{x+100} \times 100$$

$$20x + 2000 = 100x$$

or $80x = 2000$

$$x = \frac{2000}{80} = 25\text{g}$$

PRACTICE QUESTIONS

Some Solved CBSE Sample Questions

SECTION–A

1. Rama tested the solubility of four substances at different temperatures and found in grams, of each substance dissolved in 100 g of water to form a saturated solution.

S. No.	Substance dissolved (in grams)	Temperature (K)		
		293 K	313 K	333 K
(i)	Ammonium chloride	37 g	41 g	55 g
(ii)	Potassium chloride	35 g	40 g	46 g
(iii)	Sodium chloride	36 g	36 g	37 g
(iv)	Potassium nitrate	32 g	62 g	106 g

(i) Which substance is least soluble in water at 293 K ?

(ii) Which substance shows maximum change in its solubility when temperature is raised from 293 K to 313 K ?

(iii) Find the amount of ammonium chloride that will separate out when 55 g of its solution at 333 K is cooled to 293 K ?

(iv) What is the effect of change of temperature on the solubility of a salt ?

(v) What mass of sodium chloride would be needed to make a saturated solution in 10 g of water at 293 K ?

(CBSE Sample Paper 2010)

Or

With the help of labeled diagram, describe an activity to separate a mixture containing ammonium chloride, sodium chloride and sand. ***(CBSE Sample Paper 2010)***

Ans. (i) Potassium nitrate

(ii) Potassium nitrate

(iii) Amount of NH_4Cl soluble at 333 K = 55 g

Amount of NH_4Cl soluble at 293 K = 37 g

Amount of NH_4Cl that will separate on cooling the solution from 333 K to 293 K = 55 g – 37 g = 18 g

(iv) Solubility of a salt increases with increase in temperature.

(v) Amount of sodium chloride needed for making saturated solution in 100 g of water = 36 g

Amount of sodium chloride needed for making saturated solution in 10 g of water

$= \frac{36}{100} \times 10 = 3.6\text{g}$

Or

Crush the mixture of ammonium chloride, sodium chloride and sand and put it in a china dish. Put an inverted funnel over the china dish (as shown in Fig. 13, page 78). Now heat the mixture slowly. Ammonium chloride will deposit on the walls of the funnel. This is because ammonium chloride changed from solid to its vapour form directly on heating. It gets cooled on the inner sides of funnel. The sodium chloride and sand are left in the china dish. Now add water to the remaining mixture and stir it well. Filter it. Sand will be collected as a residue on the filtrate. Evaporate the filtrate to dryness. Common salt will be collected as residue.

2. (a) Distinguish among true solution, suspension and colloid in a tabular form under the following heads.
(i) Stability (ii) Filterability (iii) Type of mixture
(b) What is meant by concentration of a solution? How will you prepare a 10% solution of glucose in water?

(CBSE Sample Paper 2011)

Ans. (a)

Property	Solution	Suspension	Colloid
1. Stability	Stable *i.e.,* the particles donot settle down on standing.	Not stable i.e., the particles settle down on standing.	Stable i.e., the particles donot settle down on standing.
2. Filterability	Passes through filter paper because the particle size is very small.	Donot pass through the filter paper because the particles are of large size.	Passes through the filter paper because the particle size is very small.
3. Type of mixture	Homogeneous.	Heterogeneous	Heterogeneous but appears to be homogeneous

(b) Concentration of a solution is the amount of the solute present in a given amount (mass or volume) of the solution or the solvent.

To prepare 10% solution of glucose dissolve 10 g of glucose in 90 g of water so that the total solution becomes 100 g.

3. Distinguish between homogeneous and heterogeneous mixture. Classify the following mixtures as homogeneous and heterogeneous.
(i) Tincture of iodine
(ii) Smoke
(iii) Brass
(iv) Sugar solution

(CBSE Sample Paper 2011)

Ans. Refer NCERT In-Text Questions, Q. 2.
(i) Homogeneous
(ii) Heterogeneous
(iii) Homogeneous
(iv) Homogeneous

4. (a) Draw a neat and labelled diagram of the apparatus used to separate components of blue-black ink. Name the process and state the principle involved.
(b) Identify the physical and chemical changes from the following :
(i) Burning of magnesium in air.
(ii) Tarnishing of silver spoon.
(iii) Sublimation of iodine.
(iv) Electrolysis of water.

(CBSE Sample Paper 2011)

Ans. (a) *Refer Text, group Activity 11.*
Process : Chromatography
Principle : The coloured component which is more soluble in water rises faster and in this way, the colour of different dyes present in the blue black ink get separated.
(b) (i) Chemical change
(ii) Chemical change
(iii) Physical change
(iv) Chemical change

5. Which of the two will scatter light : soap solution or salt solution? *(CBSE 2012-13)*

Ans. Soap solution.

6. Give an example for each of the following:
(i) Solid – liquid homogeneous mixture
(ii) Gas – gas homogeneous mixture
(iii) Liquid – liquid homogeneous mixture

(CBSE 2013-14)

Ans. (i) Mixture of sugar in water
(ii) Air is a mixture of number of gases
(iii) Emulsion of oil and water

7. What is distillation ? List two conditions essential for using this method of separation of components of a mixture ? *(CBSE 2013-14)*

Ans. Distillation is a process which involves conversion of a liquid into vapours by heating to its boiling temperature and then condensation of the vapours by cooling process.
Essential conditions

(*i*) The difference in the boiling points of two liquids of the mixture should not be less than 25K.

(*ii*) Liquids should boil without decomposition.

8. What volume of ethyl alcohol and water must be mixed together to prepare 250 mL of 50% by volume of alcohol in water ? (*CBSE 2013-14*)

Ans. Let the volume of ethyl alcohol to be added = x mL

Volume percentage

$$= \frac{\text{Volume of ethyl alcohol}}{\text{Volume of solution}} \times 100$$

$$50 = \frac{x}{250} \times 100$$

$$\therefore \quad x = \frac{250 \times 50}{100} = 125 \text{ mL}$$

9. Why is crystallisation better than evaporation technique ? (*CBSE 2013-14*)

Ans. The crystallisation technique is better than simple evaporation technique because of the following reasons:

(*i*) Some solids decompose or some solids like sugar may get charred on heating to dryness during evaporation. There is no such problem in crystallisation.

(*ii*) Some soluble impurities do not get removed in the process of evaporation. But such impurities get removed during crystallisation.

10. Name the method used to obtain pure copper sulphate from an impure sample. (*CBSE 2013-14*)

Ans. Crystallisation

11. The teacher instructed three students A, B and C to prepare 50% (mass by volume) solution of sodium hydroxide (NaOH). 'A' dissolved 50 g of NaOH in 100 mL of water, B dissolved 50 g of NaOH in 100 g of water and C dissolved 50 g of NaOH in water to make 100 mL of solution. Which one of them has made the desired solution? (*CBSE 2013-14*)

Ans. 'C' has made the desired solution.

Mass by volume %

$$= \frac{\text{Mass of solute}}{\text{Volume of solution}} \times 100$$

$$= \frac{50}{100} \times 100 = 50\% \text{ mass by volume.}$$

12. You are given a mixture containing sand, iron filings, naphthalene and sodium chloride. Describe the procedure you would use to separate these constituents from the mixture. (*CBSE 2014-15*)

Ans. The mixture can be separated by the following method:

(*i*) Move the magnet in the mixture. Iron filings will cling to the magnet and get separated. We are then left with sand, naphthalene and sodium chloride.

(*ii*) Heat the mixture to sublime. Naphthalene will be separated by this sublimation method and we are left with sand and sodium chloride.

(*iii*) Add water to the mixture and filter. Sand will remain on the filter paper and get separated. The filtrate will contain sodium chloride.

(*iv*) Evaporate the filtrate to dryness. This will give us sodium chloride.

13. A mixture containing two liquids visibly separated, is placed in a separating funnel. Answer the following:

(*i*) What type of liquids form the mixture?

(*ii*) Which of the liquid will form lower layer ?

(*iii*) What is the principle behind this method of separation ? (*CBSE 2014-15*)

Ans. (*i*) Immiscible liquids.

(*ii*) Liquid of higher density

(*iii*) Immiscible liquids separate out in layers depending on their densities.

14. (*a*) Name a technique to separate a mixture of two or more miscible liquids for which difference in boiling points is less than 25 K.

(*b*) What type of column is used in the above technique and why? (*CBSE 2014-15*)

Ans. (*i*) Fractional distillation.

(*ii*) A fractionating column in used which is a glass tube packed with glass beads and is placed in between the distillation flask and the condenser.

Fractionating column provides larger surface for vapours to cool and condense repeatedly.

15. Air is considered to be a mixture and not a compound ? Justify. (*CBSE 2015-16*)

Ans. Air is a homogeneaus mixture of different gases which can be separated by suitable methods. Therefore, air is a mixture and not a compound.

16. Compare suspension and colloidal solution on the basis of (*a*) type of mixture (*b*) particle size (*c*) scattering of light and (*d*) stability. (*CBSE 2015-16*)

Ans. (*a*) Suspension is heterogeneous solution. Colloidal solution is also heterogeneous but appears to be homogeneous.

(*b*) The particle size of suspension is larger than that of colloidal solution. In colloidal solution, the particle size ranges between 10^{-9} m to 10^{-7} m, whereas in suspensions the particle size is larger than 10^{-7} m.

(*c*) Colloidal solution has capacity to scatter the path of light when made to pass through it. Suspension is also capable to do so because of its particles are of large size.

(*d*) A suspension is less stable than a colloidal solution.

17. Why is the path of light not visible in a solution when a beam of light is passed through it? ***(CBSE 2015-16)***

Ans. This is because the size of solute particles is very small and they do not scatter light and hence they do not show Tyndall effect.

18. When is a solution said to be saturated? How can you change an unsaturated solution to a saturated solution without adding any more solute to it? ***(CBSE 2014-15)***

Ans. A solution is said to be saturated if it has maximum amount of solute dissolved in a given amount of solvent at a given temperature.

By heating the unsaturated solution, it can be converted into a saturated solution.

19. Name the appropriate method used to separate the following:

(*i*) Nitrogen from air

(*ii*) Dye from blue ink

(*iii*) Butter from cream

(*iv*) Ammonium chloride from common salt. ***(CBSE 2015-16)***

Ans. (*i*) Fractional distillation

(*ii*) Chromatography

(*iii*) Centrifugation

(*iv*) Sublimation

20. (*a*) How can you say that sugar is a pure substance whereas milk is not?

(*b*) Which of the following materials fall in the category of a pure substance?

(*i*) Ice **(*ii*) Iron**

(*iii*) Wood **(*iv*) Brick**

(CBSE 2015-16)

Ans. (*a*) Sugar is a pure substance because it contains only sugar ($C_{12}H_{22}O_{11}$) molecules which have fixed composition of C, H and O while milk is a mixture of fats suspended in liquid and hence is not a pure substance.

(*b*) Ice (*ii*) Iron

21. (*a*) Illustrate with an example that physical and chemical changes can take place together.

(*b*) Which of the following are chemical changes:

(*i*) Mixing of iron filing and sand

(*ii*) Growth of plant

(*iii*) Rusting of iron

(*iv*) Freezing of water ***(CBSE 2015-16)***

Ans. (*a*) Burning candle is an example where both physical and chemical changes are occurring together. The burning of wax is a chemical change and simultaneously it is melting also which is a physical change.

(*b*) Chemical changes are :

(*i*) Growth of plant and (*iii*) rusting of iron

SECTION–B (Based on Practical Skill)

I. Multiple Choice Questions (MCQs) (1 Mark Each)

1. Rama heated a mixture of iron filings and sulphur in a hard glass test tube for sometime till a grey-black product was formed. She cooled the test tube and then added 2 mL carbon-disulphide in it and shook the contents of the test tube. The observation made by her was likely to be as shown below :

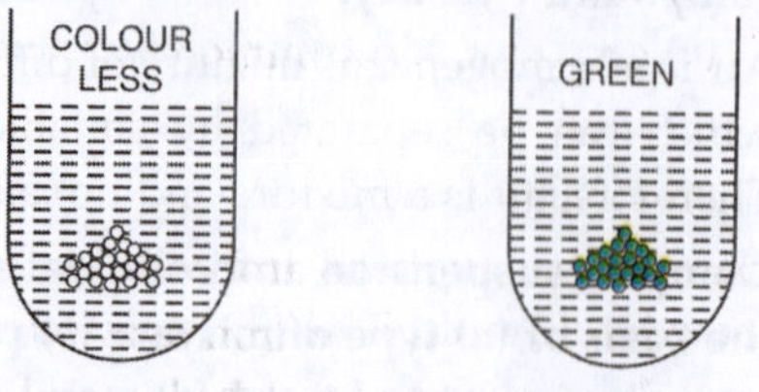

I II

(*a*) I (*b*) II

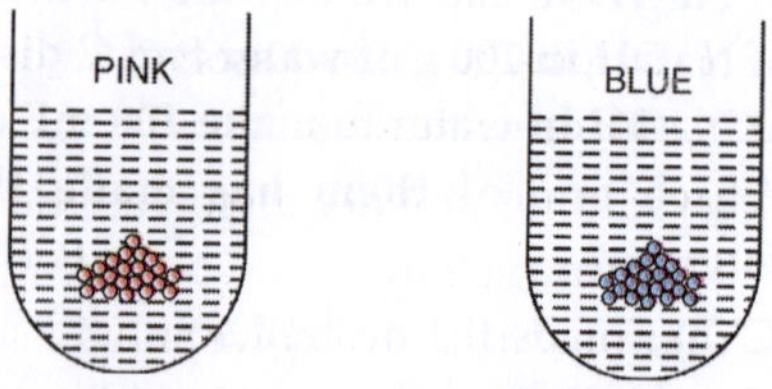

III IV

(*c*) III (*d*) IV

(CBSE Sample Paper 2010)

2. To separate a mixture of sand, common salt, camphor and iron filings, Dhoni added water to the mixture in a test tube and shook it well. He found that one component dissolved in water. It was :

(*a*) Sand (*b*) Iron filings

(*c*) Camphor (*d*) Common salt

(CBSE Sample Paper 2010)

3. The sequence of steps taken for separating a mixture of ammonium chloride, sand and common salt is:

    (*a*) sublimation, adding water, filteration, evaporation.

    (*b*) evaporation, adding water, filteration, sublimation.

    (*c*) Filteration, evaporation, sublimation, adding water.

    (*d*) Evaporation, sublimation, adding water, filteration. ***(CBSE Sample Paper 2010)***

4. Four students prepared mixtures in water by taking sugar, sand, chalk powder and starch respectively, in four different test tubes. After stirring, the mixture that appeared clear and transparent was that of :

    (*a*) starch and water

    (*b*) chalk powder and water

    (*c*) sand and water

    (*d*) sugar and water

    (CBSE Sample Paper 2010)

5. Rohit mixed starch with water, boiled the mixture well and stirred it. He observed that:

    (*a*) starch floats on the surface of water

    (*b*) starch settles down at the bottom

    (*c*) starch forms a translucent mixture

    (*d*) starch forms a transparent mixture

    (CBSE Sample Paper 2011)

6. You are provided with a mixture of iron filing and sulphur powder. When you add carbon-disulphide to the mixture, you would observe:

    (*a*) iron particles dissolve and the solution turns black

    (*b*) sulpur powder dissolves and the solution turns colourless

    (*c*) sulphur powder dissolves and the solution turns yellow

    (*d*) iron particles dissolve and the solution turns grey

    (CBSE Sample Paper 2011)

7. The colour of sodium chloride and ammonium chloride respectively is :

    (*a*) yellow and white (*b*) white and yellow

    (*c*) both are white (*d*) grey and yellow

    (CBSE Sample Paper 2011)

8. In the laboratory, carbon disulphide is used as a solvent to separate a mixture of iron filings and sulphur powder. What precaution has to be taken with carbon disulphide?

    (*a*) Keep away from water

    (*b*) Keep away from flame

    (*c*) Keep away from air

    (*d*) Keep away from iron-sulphide

    (CBSE Sample Paper 2011)

9. In an experiment to separate the components of a mixture of sand, common salt and ammonium chloride, the component which will be removed by filtration is :

    (*a*) sand (*b*) common salt

    (*c*) ammonium chloride (*d*) none of these

    (CBSE Sample Paper 2011)

10. The correct procedure for heating a mixture of iron filings and sulphur powder is:

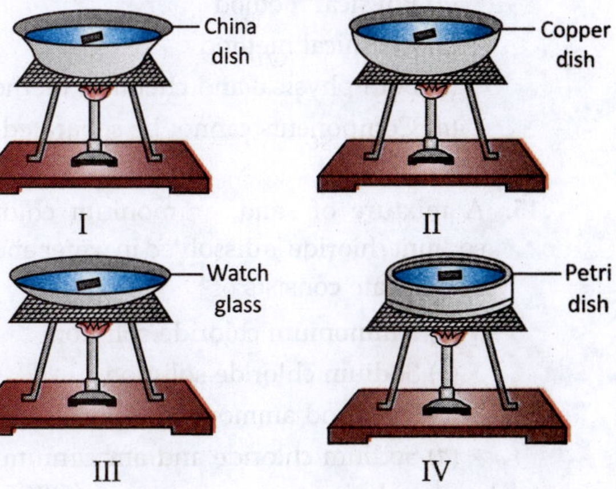

    (*a*) (I) (*b*) (II) (*c*) (III) (*d*) (IV)

    (CBSE 2012-13)

11. Sulphur powder dissolves carbon disulphide to form yellow coloured solution but solid sulphur reappears by :

    (*a*) evaporation of carbon disulphide

    (*b*) sublimation of sulphur

    (*c*) cooling the solution

    (*d*) distillation ***(CBSE 2013-14)***

12. While separating the components of a mixture of sand, camphor and common salt, Mohan added water to the mixture in a breaker and stirred it well. He observed that component that has dissolved in water is :

    (*a*) camphor

    (*b*) camphor and common salt

    (*c*) sand

    (*d*) common salt. ***(CBSE 2013-14)***

13. Sample 'A' contains iron filings and sulphur powder, Sample 'B' is iron sulphide. Sample 'A' and 'B' are taken on a watch glass and a bar magent is rolled over both. You will observe that :

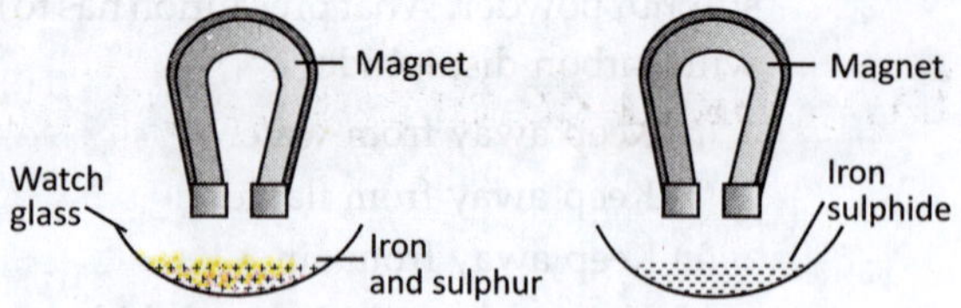

(*a*) sample 'A' as a whole clings to magnet

(*b*) only iron from 'A' clings to magnet

(*c*) Iron in both samples A and B clings to the magnet.

(*d*) Iron sulphide clings to the magnet.

(CBSE 2014-15)

14. In a china dish, 7g iron filings and 4g sulphur powder are mixed properly. Suggest a method to separate the individual constituents from its mixture.

(*a*) Physical method

(*b*) Chemical method

(*c*) Both physical and chemical method

(*d*) Components cannot be separated.

(CBSE 2013-14)

15. A mixture of sand, ammonium chloride and sodium chloride is dissolved in water and filtered. The filtrate consists of :

(*a*) Ammonium chloride solution

(*b*) Sodium chloride solution

(*c*) Sand and ammonium chloride solution

(*d*) Sodium chloride and ammonium chloride solution. ***(CBSE 2013-14)***

16. To separate a mixture of iron filings, sulphur powder and iron sulphide, which sequence of methods should be used ?

(*a*) Magnet, dissolve in CS_2, filter, evaporation.

(*b*) Magnet, dissolve in water, filter, evaporation

(*c*) Dissolve in water, filter, crystallize, decant.

(*d*) Magnet, filter, decant, crystallize.

(CBSE 2014-15)

17. A mixture contains iodine, ammonium chloride and sand. Only iodine and ammonium chloride sublime. Only iodine dissolves in carbon tetrachloride. How will you separate the three components ? Sequence of steps will be :

(*a*) By sublimation, addition of CCl_4

(*b*) Addition of CCl_4, filtration, sublimation

(*c*) Sublimation, addition of H_2O, filtration.

(*d*) Evaporation, distillation, crystallization.

(CBSE 2013-14)

18. A mixture of ammonium chloride and sodium chloride is heated in the apparatus as shown below :

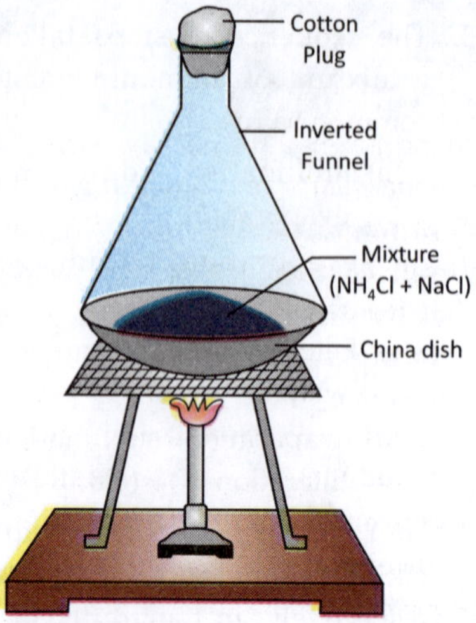

After the experiment, ammonium chloride will be obtained in the

(*a*) china dish (*b*) inverted funnel

(*c*) at both the place (*d*) No where

(CBSE 2014-15)

19. Mixture of common salt and water can be separated completely by the process of :

(*a*) evaporation

(*b*) distillation

(*c*) filtration

(*d*) dissolving in more water. ***(CBSE 2014-15)***

20. A mixture containing iron filings and sulphur powder is spread on the white paper and a magnet is rolled in it. The particles which cling to the magnet are :

(*a*) Sulphur

(*b*) Iron particles

(*c*) Iron sulphide

(*d*) Mixture of iron and sulphur.

(CBSE 2015-16)

ANSWERS AND HINTS : MCQs

1. (*a*); **2.** (*d*) : Common salt dissolves in water

3. (*a*); **4.** (*a*); **5.** (*c*); **6.** (*c*); **7.** (*c*);

8. (*b*); **9.** (*a*); **10.** (*a*); **11.** (*a*); **12.** (*d*);

13. (*b*) : Iron is attracted by the magnet

14. (*a*); **15.** (*d*); **16.** (*a*); **17.** (*b*);

18. (*b*) : A white sublimate of ammonium chloride will be deposited inside the inverted funnel.

19. (*a*); **20.** (*b*).

HOTS Higher Order Thinking Skill & Brain Twisting Questions with Answers

1. During an experiment the students were asked to prepare 20% (mass/mass) solution of common salt in water. Prashant dissolved 20 g of common salt in 100g of water and Sangeeta prepared it by dissolving 20 g of common salt in water to make 100g of the solution. Another student Rashmi could not get enough common salt and dissolved only 5g in 20g of water. Which of the three students prepared the solutions of required concentration ?

Ans. Let us calculate the concentrations of the solutions prepared by Prashant, Sangeeta and Rashmi from the relation,

Mass % of common salt

$$= \frac{\textbf{Mass of common salt}}{\textbf{Mass of common salt + Mass of water}} \times 100$$

(*i*) Solution prepared by Prashant

$$\text{Concentration} = \frac{20}{20+100} \times 100$$

$$= \frac{20}{20+100} \times 100 = 16.76\%$$

(*ii*) Solution prepared by Sangeeta

$$\text{Concentration} = \frac{20}{100} \times 100 = 20\%$$

(*iii*) Solution prepared by Rashmi

$$\text{Concentration} = \frac{5}{5+20} \times 100 = 20\%$$

Sangeeta and Rashmi prepared solutions of required concentration.

2. Madhu prepared a saturated solution of potassium chloride and sodium chloride in water separately in beakers A and B respectively at 40°C. She left the solutions to cool at room temperature. What would she observe as the solutions cool ? What will happen to solution in beaker B if she heats it to 80°C.

Ans. On cooling the saturated solution of potassium chloride and sodium chloride in water at 40°C to room temperature crystals of KCl and NaCl will be formed in beakers A and B respectively.

When she heats the solution of sodium chloride in beaker B, solubility will increase and more of NaCl can be dissolved to prepare saturated solution.

3. Give an example of each of the following :

(*a*) Liquid-liquid homogeneous mixture

(*b*) Solid-solid homogeneous mixture

(*c*) Liquid-gas heterogeneous mixture

(*d*) Liquid-liquid heterogeneous mixture

(*e*) Solid-solid heterogeneous mixture

(*f*) Solid-liquid homogeneous mixture

(*g*) Solid-liquid heterogeneous mixture

Ans. (*a*) Water-alcohol solution

(*b*) Brass

(*c*) Fog

(*d*) Milk

(*e*) Coloured gemstones

(*f*) Sugar dissolved in water

(*g*) Muddy water.

4. Can physical and chemical changes occur together? Explain.

Ans. In some cases physical and chemical changes occur together. For example, burning candle is an example of physical and chemical changes occurring together. The solid wax present in the candle first changes into liquid state and then into the vapour state. Both these changes are physical changes. The wax vapours then combine with oxygen of the air to form a mixture of carbon dioxide and water. This involves a chemical change. The unburnt wax vapours again change first to the liquid state and then to the solid state. This interconversion of states is also a physical change. Thus, burning of candle involves both physical and chemical changes.

5. Ramanjit studied the properties of three solutions A, B and C as reported the following observations:

Solution A

(*i*) Homogeneous

(*ii*) Transparent

(*iii*) Filtration not possible

(*iv*) Do not Settle under gravity

Solution B

Heterogeneous

Transparent

Filtration not possible

Settle on centrifugation

Solution C

Heterogeneous

Opaque

Filtration possible

Settle under gravity

Label these solutions as colloid, true solutions and suspension.

Ans. Solution A : True solution

Solution B : Colloidal solution

Solution C : Suspension

6. Both sugar and common salt are soluble in water. Suggest a method to separate a mixture of sugar and salt ?

Ans. Since both sugar and common salt are soluble in water therefore, water cannot be used to separate sugar from salt. The mixture can be separated by using hot ethyl alcohol. In ethyl alcohol, sugar dissolves but salt remains insoluble. The hot solution is filtered through Buchner funnel when salt remains as residue on the filter paper of the Buchner funnel while sugar goes into the filtrate. Evaporation of filtrate gives sugar as residue.

7. Water contains 88.9% oxygen and 11.1% hydrogen. It is often used for extinguishing fire. Can a mixture containing H_2 and O_2 in the same ratio by mass be used for extinguishing fire ? Explain.

Ans. The properties of a compound are totally different from the elements from which these are formed. Therefore, water, a compound of hydrogen and oxygen extinguishes fire. In contrast, hydrogen is a combustible gas while oxygen is a supporter of combustion. When H_2 and O_2 are mixed together in the same ratio by mass, they donot form water and, therefore, these do not show the properties of water and hence cannot extinguish fire.

Revision Exercise

Answers and Hints on Page 61

OBJECTIVE QUESTIONS

A. Multiple Choice Questions

I. NCERT Exemplar Problems

1. Which of the following statements are true for pure substances?
   (*i*) Pure substances contain only one kind of particles
   (*ii*) Pure substances may be compounds or mixtures
   (*iii*) Pure substances have the same composition throughout
   (*iv*) Pure substances can be exemplified by all elements other than nickel
   (*a*) (*i*) and (*ii*) (*b*) (*i*) and (*iii*)
   (*c*) (*iii*) and (*iv*) (*d*) (*ii*) and (*iii*)
2. Rusting of an article made up of iron is called
   (*a*) corrosion and it is a physical as well as chemical change
   (*b*) dissolution and it is a physical change
   (*c*) corrosion and it is a chemical change
   (*d*) dissolution and it is a chemical change
3. A mixture of sulphur and carbon disulphide is
   (*a*) heterogeneous and shows Tyndall effect
   (*b*) homogeneous and shows Tyndall effect
   (*c*) heterogeneous and does not show Tyndall effect
   (*d*) homogeneous and does not show Tyndall effect
4. Tincture of iodine has antiseptic properties. This solution is made by dissolving
   (*a*) iodine in potassium iodide
   (*b*) iodine in vaseline (*c*) iodine in water
   (*d*) iodine in alcohol
5. Which of the following are homogeneous in nature?
   (*i*) ice (*ii*) wood (*iii*) soil (*iv*) air
   (*a*) (*i*) and (*iii*) (*b*) (*ii*) and (*iv*)
   (*c*) (*i*) and (*iv*) (*d*) (*iii*) and (*iv*)
6. Which of the following are physical changes?
   (*i*) Melting of iron metal
   (*ii*) Rusting of iron
   (*iii*) Bending of an iron rod
   (*iv*) Drawing a wire of iron metal
   (*a*) (*i*), (*ii*) and (*iii*) (*b*) (*i*), (*ii*) and (*iv*)
   (*c*) (*i*), (*iii*) and (*iv*) (*d*) (*ii*), (*iii*) and (*iv*)
7. Which of the following are chemical changes?
   (*i*) Decaying of wood
   (*ii*) Burning of wood
   (*iii*) Sawing of wood
   (*iv*) Hammering of a nail into a piece of wood
   (*a*) (*i*) and (*ii*) (*b*) (*ii*) and (*iii*)
   (*c*) (*iii*) and (*iv*) (*d*) (*i*) and (*iv*)
8. Two substances, A and B were made to react to form a third substance, A_2B according to the following reaction:
   $2A + B \rightarrow A_2B$
   Which of the following statements concerning this reaction are incorrect?
   (*i*) The product A_2B shows the properties of substances A and B

(*ii*) The product will always have a fixed composition

(*iii*) The product so formed cannot be classified as a compound

(*iv*) The product so formed is an element

(*a*) (*i*), (*ii*) and (*iii*) (*b*) (*ii*), (*iii*) and (*iv*)

(*c*) (*i*), (*iii*) and (*iv*) (*d*) (*ii*), (*iii*) and (*iv*)

9. Two chemical species X and Y combine together to a product P which contains both X and Y

$X + Y \rightarrow P$

X and Y cannot be broken down into simpler substances by simple chemical reactions. Which of the following concerning the species X, Y and P are correct?

(*i*) P is a compound

(*ii*) X and Y are compounds

(*iii*) X and Y are elements

(*iv*) P has a fixed composition

(*a*) (*i*), (*ii*) and (*iii*) (*b*) (*i*), (*ii*) and (*iv*)

(*c*) (*ii*), (*iii*) and (*iv*) (*d*) (*i*), (*iii*) and (*iv*)

II. Additional Questions

1. A chemical compound which can be used to separate a mixture of carbon powder and sulphur powder successfully is

(*a*) carbon dioxide

(*b*) hydrochloric acid

(*c*) carbon disulphide

(*d*) hydrogen sulphide

2. Naphthalene can be separated from sand by

(*a*) sublimation (*b*) distillation

(*c*) centrifugation (*d*) evaporation

3. Which of the following is not a chemical change ?

(*a*) ripening of apple

(*b*) corrosion of photo frame

(*c*) burning of wood

(*d*) sublimation of naphthalene

4. Which of the following is a suspension ?

(*a*) sugar solution (*b*) milk

(*c*) milk of magnesia (*d*) sugar

5. Which of the following is a pure substance in the liquid from ?

(*a*) Milk (*b*) sugar solution

(*c*) mercury (*d*) germanium

6. Which of the following is not a mixture ?

(*a*) air (*b*) petrol

(*c*) milk (*d*) steam

7. How can we recover pure sugar from sugar solution ?

(*a*) by distillation

(*b*) by filtration

(*c*) by crystallisation

(*d*) by evaporation to dryness

8. The dye present in fountain pen ink can be separated by the technique of

(*a*) fractional distillation

(*b*) chromatography

(*c*) centrifugation

(*d*) crystallisation

9. Milk of magnesia is a

(*a*) true solution

(*b*) suspension

(*c*) colloid

(*d*) homogeneous mixture

10. Which of the following is not a compound?

(*a*) common salt (*b*) water

(*c*) iron filings (*d*) copper sulphate.

11. Which of the following pairs does not contain both elements?

(*a*) carbon, silicon (*b*) helium, nitrogen

(*c*) bronze, zinc (*d*) copper, silver.

12. Which of the following is not a mixture?

(*a*) Soil (*b*) Air

(*c*) Steam (*d*) Milk

13. Which of the following is not a physical change?

(*a*) freezing of water

(*b*) mixing of iron filings and sulphur

(*c*) cooking of food

(*d*) evaporation of alcohol

14. Odd one among the following which does not belong to the set is

(*a*) graphite (*b*) gold

(*c*) germanium (*d*) ice

15. Which of the following is not a chemical change?

(*a*) electrolysis of water

(*b*) boiling of water

(*c*) digestion of food

(*d*) burning of magnesium ribbon in oxygen to form magnesium oxide.

16. The size of colloidal solution is in the range of

(*a*) 1 – 100 nm (*b*) 100 – 1000 nm

(*c*) 10^{-5} m – 10^{-7} m (*d*) 10^{7} – 10^{9} m

17. Which of the following is a liquid metal?

(*a*) Copper (*b*) Mercury

(*c*) Bromine (*d*) Silver

18. Brass contains
(*a*) Gold and copper
(*b*) Copper and zinc
(*c*) Zinc and silver
(*d*) Copper and silver

19. Which of the following is not a pure substance?
(*a*) Mercury (*b*) Sugar
(*c*) blood (*d*) salt

20. The correct order which describes the true solution, colloidal solution and suspension in the order of their increasing stability is
(*a*) suspension < colloidal solution < true solution
(*b*) colloidal solution < true solution < suspension
(*c*) true solution < colloidal solution < suspension
(*d*) colloidal solution < suspension < true solution

21. In which of the following the dispersion medium is liquid?
(*a*) Emulsion (*b*) Gel
(*c*) Aerosol (*d*) Alloy

22. Which of the following solutions have concentration more than 10%.
(*i*) 10 g of ethyl alcohol mixed with 100 g of water
(*ii*) 5 g of ethyl alcohol mixed with 40 g of water
(*iii*) 1 g of ethyl alcohol mixed with 25 g of water
(*iv*) 10 g of ethyl alcohol mixed with 85 g of water
(*a*) (*i*), (*ii*) and (*iii*) (*b*) (*i*), (*ii*) and (*iv*)
(*c*) (*ii*) and (*iv*) (*d*) (*ii*) and (*iii*)

23. The incorrect statement is
(*a*) Two immiscible liquids can be separated by separating funnel.
(*b*) Mixture of gases in air can be separated by fractional distillation.
(*c*) Cream can be separated from milk by centrifugation.
(*d*) Mixture of sodium chloride and ammonium chloride can be separated by sedimentation method.

24. Match the method of separation in Column I with example in Column II.

Column I	Column II
(P) Distillation	1. Mixture of sand and water
(Q) Centrifugation	2. Mixture of common salt and water
(R) Filtration	3. Dyes in black ink
(S) Chromatography	4. Cream from milk

(*a*) P–2, Q–1, R–3, S–4 (*b*) P–4, Q–2, R–1, S–3
(*c*) P–2, Q–4, R–1, S–3 (*d*) P–1, Q–4, R–2, S–3

25. Match the mixture in Column I with technique used for separation in Column II

Column I	Column II
(P) Common salt and ammonium chloride	1. Using separating funnel
(Q) Mustard oil in water	2. Distillation
(R) Ink	3. Sublimation
(S) Mixture of acetone and water	4. Evaporation

(*a*) P–3, Q–1, R–4, S–2 (*b*) P–1, Q–3, R–4, S–2
(*c*) P–3, Q–2, R–4, S–1 (*d*) P–3, Q–4, R–1, S–2

26. Match the colloidal solution in Column I with its type in Column II

Column I	Column II
(P) Fog	1. Liquid in liquid
(Q) Shaving cream	2. Liquid in gas
(R) Cheese	3. Gas in liquid
(S) Milk	4. Liquid in solid

(*a*) P–2, Q–4, R–1, S–3 (*b*) P–2, Q–3, R–4, S–1
(*c*) P–2, Q–1, R–4, S–3 (*d*) P–1, Q–4, R–3, S–2

27. Match Column I with Column II

Column I	Column II
(P) zig-zag motion of colloidal particles	1. Suspensions
(Q) scattering of light by colloidal particles	2. Brownian movement
(R) homogeneous solution with particles size less than 10^{-9} m.	3. True solution
(S) heterogeneous solution with particle size more than 10^{-9} m.	4. Tyndall effect

(*a*) P–2, Q–4, R–1, S–3 (*b*) P–2, Q–4, R–3, S–1
(*c*) P–1, Q–4, R–3, S–2 (*d*) P–2, Q–1, R–3, S–4

B. Assertion – Reason Type Questions

For the following questions, two statements are given- one labeled *Assertion* (A) and the other labeled *Reason* (R). Select the correct answer to these questions from the codes (*a*), (*b*), (*c*) and (*d*) as given below:

(*a*) *Both A and R are true and R is correct explanation of the assertion.*
(*b*) *Both A and R are true but R is not the correct explanation of the assertion*
(*c*) *A is true but R is false.*
(*d*) *A is false but R is true.*

1. Assertion: Air is considered to be a mixture.
Reason: A mixture is said to be homogeneous if it has same composition throughout the sample.

2. Assertion: Mercury, bromine and diamond are elements.
Reason: All these are solids.

3. **Assertion:** Pure substances have fixed melting points.
Reason: The properties of a compound are similar to those of its components.
4. **Assertion:** A colloidal solution is a homogeneous mixture.
Reason: The particle size of colloidal solution is more than that of a true solution.
5. **Assertion:** A mixture of camphor and ammonium chloride cannot be separated by sublimation.
Reason: Camphor on heating sublimes but ammonium chloride does not.
6. **Assertion:** The zigzag motion of colloidal particles is called Brownian movement.
Reason: Colloidal particles are not visible.
7. **Assertion:** Impure benzoic acid can be purified by sublimation.
Reason: Benzoic acid sublimes on heating.
8. **Assertion:** A mixture of sand and iron filings can be separated by using a magnet.
Reason: Iron filings and sand form heterogeneous mixture.
9. **Assertion:** Melting of butter in a pan is a physical change.
Reason: Physical change is a permanent change.
10. **Assertion:** Mixture of acetone and methyl alcohol can be separated by fractional distillation.
Reason: The difference in their boiling points is very large.

C. Fill in the Blanks

1. Digestion of food is a __________ change.
2. Different pigments from an extract of flower petals can be separated by ________ technique.
3. Oil and water are separated by ________.
4. Fractional distillation technique is used for separating two liquids having boiling point difference ________ than 25°C.
5. The zig zag motion of colloidal particles is called ________.
6. Suspension is ________ mixture.
7. In general, solubility of solids in liquids ________ with rise in temperature.
8. Butter is a colloidal solution in which liquid is dispersed in ________.
9. The most abundant element in the atmosphere is ________.
10. A component which is present in large amount in a solution is called ________.

D. Paragraph Based Questions

1. Answers questions 1(*a*) – 1(*d*) on the basis of your understanding of the following paragraph and the related studied concepts.

Most of the substances that we come across in our daily life are mixtures of two or more than two pure substances. These may be true solutions, suspensions or colloids. We adopt different methods to get individual components from these mixtures. Two immiscible liquids can be easily separated with the help of separating funnel while miscible liquids can be separated by distillation. In some cases, the process of simple distillation cannot be used and we use fractional distillation method. One of the technical application of fractional distillation is to separate different fractions of crude oil in petroleum industry.

1(*a*) A mixture of two miscible liquids whose boiling points differ by less than 25 K can be separated by the process called ....

1(*b*) How will you separate a mixture of water and kerosene ?

1(*c*) Which out of true solution, suspension and colloid is/are stable ?

1(*d*) Name the technique used to separate pigments from natural colours.

2. **A student tested the solubility of five substances at different temperatures. He noted the amount of each substance dissolved in 100 g of water to form a saturated solution at a particular temperature and reported the following data :**

Substance dissolved	Temperature		
	20°C	35°C	50°C
A	18.6	21.4	23.8
B	20.0	25.0	35.0
C	8.2	7.9	7.6
D	36.2	40.6	45.4
E	32.0	62.0	106.0

2(*a*) Which substance is least soluble and which substance is most soluble in water at 20°C ?

2(*b*) What is the concentration of solution B at 35°C ?

2(*c*) Find the amount of E that will separate out when 106.0 g of its solution at 50°C is cooled to 20°C.

2(*d*) Do all solutions show the same effect of temperature on the solubility of a salt ?

Very Short Answer Questions

1. Define a mixture. Is its composition fixed or variable.
2. What is a substance?
3. Name a method to check the purity of a liquid.
4. Is sugar in water solution homogeneous or heterogeneous mixture?

5. Give one example each of a homogeneous and a heterogeneous mixture.
6. Choose the compound from the following substances :
   Air, Steam, Graphite, Diamond.
7. Which elements does steam contain?
8. Which of the two will scatter light, soap solution or sugar solution?
9. A solution contains 30 g of sugar dissolved in 370 g of water. What is the concentration of sugar solution?
10. A 10% salt solution means that:
    (a) 10 g of salt is present in 100 g of water.
    (b) 10 g of salt is present in 90 g of water.
    Choose the correct answer.
11. Give one example of a solid solution.
12. What are the terms : saturated solution and unsaturated solution?
13. Define colloidal solution.
14. Is colloidal solution homogeneous or heterogeneous?
15. Name the dispersed phase and dispersion medium in
    (i) Jelly (ii) Smoke
16. Name the process by which the coloured components can be obtained from blue ink?
17. Name the process used to separate a mixture of salt and ammonium chloride.
18. Name the method used to separate two miscible liquids.
19. Which of the following is a chemical change?
    (i) Melting of butter in a pan
    (ii) An almirah getting rusted
    (iii) Water boiling to steam
20. Which of the two is a good conductor of heat and electricity :
    Sodium or chlorine
21. Name two elements which are liquid at room temperature.
22. When we heat iron filings and sulphur till red hot, do we get compound or mixture?
23. What happens when we bring a magnet near a compound formed from iron filings and sulphur?
24. Which of the following is a substance according to scientific meaning :
    air, water, smoke, fog
25. Name the solution which show Tyndall effect.

Short Answer Questions

1. What do you understand by
   (i) Saturated solution
   (ii) Unsaturated solution
   (iii) Concentration of solution
2. Give the differences between homogeneous and heterogeneous mixture.
3. Explain the method to separate
   (i) cream from milk.
   (ii) a mixture of comman salt and ammonium chloride.
4. Write a brief note on :
   (i) Tyndall effect
   (ii) Solubility.
   (iii) Brownian movement
5. Name the technique used to separate
   (a) butter from curd
   (b) Salt from sea water.
   (c) kerosene and water
6. (i) What type of mixtures are separated by the technique of crystallization? Explain one.
   (ii) How will you justify that rusting of iron is a chemical change?
7. (i) When a beam of light is passed through a solution of substance A dissolved in water, the path of light could be seen. Predict the nature of the solution.
   (ii) Two miscible liquids A and B are present in a solution. The boiling point of A is 52°C and that of B is 86°C. Suggest a method to separate them.
   (iii) Sodium chloride contains two elements still it is a pure substance. How will you justify this ?
8. What is a solution? Give its three properties.
9. What is a suspension? Give its three properties.
10. How can we obtain coloured component from blue/black ink? Explain.
11. Discuss the method to separate a mixture of
    (i) two miscible liquids
    (ii) two immiscible liquids.
12. Explain the method to obtain gases from air.
13. How is water purified and supplied for drinking purposes? Explain.
14. What are physical and chemical changes? Give two examples of each.
15. Define two types of pure substances. Give three examples of each.
16. How will you separate a mixture containing kerosene and petrol, both of which are miscible with each other.
17. What do you understand by physical change

and chemical change? Classify the following as physical or chemical changes :

(*i*) Dissolving salt in water

(*ii*) Electric current is passed through water and it is broken down into hydrogen and oxygen

(*iii*) Evaporation of alcohol

(*iv*) Digestion of food

18. Define element, compound and mixture. Give two examples of each.

19. Give five differences between compounds and mixtures.

20. Classify the following into element, compound and mixture :

(*i*) Coal, (*ii*) methane, (*iii*) copper, (*iv*) carbon dioxide, (*v*) steam, (*vi*) honey, (*vii*) granite, (*viii*) blood, (*ix*) sugar, (*x*) germanium.

21. Define the terms ; solution, suspension and colloid. Make a comparison of size of their particles.

22. Write the steps you would use for making tea. Use the words : Solution, solvent, solute, dissolve, soluble, insoluble, filtration and residue.

23. Explain the following giving examples :

(*a*) Saturated solution

(*b*) Colloid

(*c*) Suspension.

Long Answer Questions

1. What separation techniques will you apply for the separation of the following :

(*i*) Sodium chloride from its solution in water.

(*ii*) Ammonium chloride from a white powder containing sodium chloride and ammonium chloride.

(*iii*) Small pieces of metal from the engine oil of a car.

(*iv*) Benzene from a mixture of benzene and methyl benzene.

(*v*) The different pigments from an extract of flower petals.

2. Suggest a method to separate the following :

(*a*) Butter from curd.

(*b*) Oil from water.

(*c*) Tea leaves from tea.

(*d*) Iron pins from sand.

(*e*) Wheat grains from husk.

3. What are solution, colloids and suspensions? How do these differ? Give two characteristics of each.

4. Explain the following terms used for separation of mixtures :

(*a*) Filtration (*b*) Crystallisation

(*c*) Evaporation (*d*) Sublimation

(*e*) Centrifugation

5. Explain the differences between :

(*i*) Compound and mixture

(*ii*) Homogeneous and heterogeneous mixture

(*iii*) Colloid and solution

(*iv*) Physical and chemical change

6. Define element, compound and mixture. Give two differences between homogeneous and heterogeneous mixtures. Identify each of the following substance as mixture, compound or element :

(*i*) Sugar (*ii*) mercury

(*iii*) tea (*iv*) sulphur

(*v*) milk (*vi*) silver

(*vii*) table salt (*viii*) wood

(*ix*) smoke (*x*) boron.

7. Define the following terms :

(*i*) Dispersed phase

(*ii*) Dispersion medium

(*iii*) Saturated solution

(*iv*) Brownian movement

(*v*) Solvent

Solution File

Answer & Solutions to Selected Questions

Practice Exercises

Practice Exercise 2A

1. (*ii*) Mercury (*iv*) Sodium chloride (*vii*) Lead

2. (*i*) mixture (*ii*) compound (*iii*) element (*iv*) compound (*v*) element
(*vi*) mixture (*vii*) element (*viii*) mixture (*ix*) mixture (*x*) compound.

3. Correct.

4. (*i*) mixture (*ii*) compound (*iii*) heterogeneous.
5. (*a*) Sodium, Carbon (*b*) Mercury, Bromine (*c*) Hydrogen, Oxygen.
6. (*a*) homogeneous (*b*) heterogeneous (*c*) heterogeneous (*d*) heterogeneous.
7. (*i*) Tungsten (*iv*) Argon (*v*) Manganese.
8. *Compounds* : Common salt, washing soda, gypsum, sugar.
   Mixtures : Sugar syrup, cement.
   Elements : Mercury, gallium, graphite.
9. Coal – mixture, methane – compound, sugar solution – mixture, granite – mixture, aluminium – element, graphite – element, hydrogen peroxide – compound, blood – mixture, soil – mixture, sugar – compound.
11. Steam
12. Common salt
13. Water always contains H and O in the ratio of 1:8 by mass.
14. (*iii*), (*iv*), (*v*), (*vi*)
15. (A)–(*v*), (B)–(*iv*), (C)–(*iii*), (D)–(*i*), (E)–(*ii*)
16. (*i*) mixture: homogeneous
    (*ii*) mixture : homogeneous
    (*iii*) pure substance : compound
    (*iv*) pure substance : compound
    (*v*) pure substance : element
    (*vi*) mixture : homogeneous
    (*vii*) mixture : homogeneous
    (*viii*) mixture : heterogeneous
17. Brass
18. (a)–(C), (b)–(B), (c)–(A), (d)–(D), (e)–(E)
20. (*i*) mercury (*ii*) bromime (*iii*) gallium

Practice Exercise 2B

1. 90 g
2. milk
3. (*iii*)
4. 20%
5. (*i*)
6. (*i*) true, colloidal (*ii*) 10^{-7}, 10^{-9}
7. Milk
8. Suspension > Colloid > True solution
9. (*i*) Aerosol : Smoke, Sol : Milk of magnesia
   (*ii*) Solution : Sugar dissolved in water
10. Starch solution
11. 'X'
12. (*i*) Sodium chloride will separate out
    (*ii*) more of sodium chloride may be dissolved
14. (*i*) Common salt dissolved in water
    (*ii*) Iodine dissolved in carbon tetrachloride
15. (*i*) fog (*ii*) soda water (*iii*) butter (*iv*) face cream (*v*) smoke
16. Let volume of ethyl alcohol be x mL

$$\text{Volume percentage} = \frac{\text{Volume of ethyl alcohol}}{\text{Volume of solution}}$$

$$60 = \frac{x}{300} \times 100$$

$$\therefore \quad x = 180 \text{ mL}$$

17. Mass of K_2SO_4 in 100 g of water = 16 g

    Mass of K_2SO_4 in 250 g of water in saturated solution = $\frac{16}{100} \times 250 = 40$ g

18. Mass of solution = 250 + 25 = 275 g

    Concentration of sugar = $\frac{25}{275} \times 100 = 9.09$ %

19.

Property	Solution	Suspension	Colloid
Stability	Stable	Unstable	Stable
Filterability	Cannot be filtered	Can be filtered	Cannot be filtered

20. (*a*) 1 to 100 nm, < 1 nm (*b*) Heterogeneous, Homogeneous
(*c*) shows, shows (*d*) Possible, not possible
(*e*) shows (*f*) may or may not show

Practice Exercise 2C

1. (*i*) Iron filings are attracted by the magnet (*ii*) Camphor undergoes sublimation
(*iii*) Sulphur is soluble in carbon disulphide (*iv*) Water can be evaporated
2. (*i*) evaporation (*ii*) centrifugation (*iii*) distillation (*iv*) sublimation
4. (*i*), (*iii*), (*iv*), (*vi*), (*viii*)
6. (*i*) Separating funnel
(*ii*) Distillation and fractional distillation
(*iii*) Evaporation, centrifugation, distillation
7. (*i*) alcohol and water
(*ii*) acetone and water
(*iii*) oil and water
(*iv*) Ammonium chloride and sodium chloride
(*v*) cream from milk
8. (*a*), (*d*), (*e*), (*g*)
11. (*a*) sublimation (*b*) separating funnel (*c*) distillation (*d*) crystallization (*e*) chromatography
12. (*a*) X < Y < Z (*b*) Z (*c*) X
13. (*a*) P (*b*) P (*c*) C (*d*) C (*e*) P (*f*) C

Revision Exercise

OBJECTIVE QUESTIONS

A. Multiple Choice Questions

I. NCERT Exemplar Problems

1. (*b*); 2. (*c*); 3. (*d*); 4. (*d*); 5. (*c*); 6. (*c*);
7. (*a*); 8. (*c*); 9. (*d*).

II. Additional Questions

1. (*c*) 2. (*a*) 3. (*d*) 4. (*c*) 5. (*c*)
6. (*d*) 7. (*c*) 8. (*b*) 9. (*b*) 10. (*c*)
11. (*c*) Bronze is not an element, it is a mixture.
12. (*c*) Steam is a compound.
13. (*c*)
14. (*d*) Ice is a compound while all others are element.
15. (*b*) 16. (*a*) 17. (*b*) 18. (*b*) 19. (*c*)
20. (*a*) 21. (*a*)
22. (*c*) (*i*) $\frac{10}{110}\times 100 = 9.09\%$

(*ii*) $\frac{5}{45}\times 100 = 11.11\%$

(*iii*) $\frac{1}{26}\times 100 = 3.85\%$

(*iv*) $\frac{10}{95}\times 100 = 10.53\%$

(*ii*) and (*iv*) have concentration more than 10%

23. (*d*) Mixture of sodium chloride and ammonium chloride can be separated by sublimation process.
24. (*c*) 25. (*a*) 26. (*b*) 27. (*b*)

B. Assertion–Reason Type

1. (*b*)
2. (*c*) Mercury (liquid), bromine (gas), diamond (solid).
3. (*c*) The properties of compounds are different from those of its components.
4. (*d*) A colloidal solution is heterogeneous. The particle size of colloidal solution is more than that of a true solution.
5. (*c*) A mixture of camphor and ammonium chloride cannot be separated by sublimation.
Both camphor and ammonium chloride sublime.
6. (*c*) The zig zag motion of colloidal particles is called Brownian movement.
Colloidal particles are visible.

7. (*a*) 8. (*b*)

9. (*c*) Melting of butter in a pan is a physical change. Chemical change is a permanent change.

10. (*c*) The difference in boiling points of acetone and methyl alcohol is very less.

C. Fill in the Blanks

1. chemical
2. chromatography
3. separating funnel
4. less
5. Brownian movement
6. heterogeneous
7. increases
8. solid
9. nitrogen
10. solvent

D. Paragraph Based Questions

1(*a*) fractional distillation

1(*b*) by using a separating funnel

1(*c*) True solution and colloid are stable.

1(*d*) Chromatography

2(*a*) C, D

2(*b*) Mass of B = 25 g

Mass of solution = 100 + 25 = 125 g

Concentration of solution = $\frac{25}{125} \times 100 = 20\%$

2(*c*) Amount of substance E soluble at 50°C = 106.0 g

Amount of substance E soluble at 20°C = 32.0 g

Amount of substance E that will separate out on cooling from 50°C to 20°C = 106.0 – 32.0 = 74.0 g

2(*d*) No, solubility of substances A, B, D and E increases with increase in temperature while solubility of C decreases with increase in temperature.

Very Short Answer Questions

1. variable composition
3. determination of boiling point
4. homogeneous
5. homogeneous : salt in water ; heterogeneous - salt and sulphur
6. Steam
7. Hydrogen, oxygen
8. soap solution
9. 7.5%
10. (*b*) solution
11. Brass containing copper and zinc
15. (*i*) liquid, solid
    (*ii*) solid, gas
16. evaporation
17. Sublimation
18. distillation
19. (*ii*)
20. sodium
21. bromine, mercury
22. compound
23. Magnet is not attracted
24. water
25. colloids

Short Answer Questions

7(*i*). colloid

(*ii*) by simple distillation

(*iii*). sodium chloride is a compound

17. (*i*) physical (*ii*) chemical
    (*iii*) physical (*iv*) chemical

20. Elements are : (*iii*), (*x*)
    Compounds are : (*ii*), (*iv*), (*v*), (*ix*)
    Mixtures are : (*i*), (*vi*), (*vii*), (*viii*)

Competition File

NTSE-SAT—Target: Scholastic Aptitude Test

1. Which of the following solution does not show Tyndall effect?
   (*a*) Milk (*b*) Starch solution
   (*c*) Ink (*d*) Sugar solution
   (*NTSE 2014–15*)

2. Ammonium chloride shows the property of
   (*a*) Boiling (*b*) Sublimation
   (*c*) Freezing (*d*) Cooling
   (*NTSE 2013–14*)

3. Which of the following is not a suspension?
   (*a*) Aluminium paint (*b*) Dust storm
   (*c*) Muddy water (*d*) Milk
   (*NTSE 2014–15*)

4. A liquid with soluble impurities is purified by
   (*a*) Crystallisation (*b*) Filtration
   (*c*) Sublimation (*d*) Distillation
   (*NTSE 2013–14*)

5. Gases can be obtained from air by the process of
   (*a*) fractional distillation (*b*) condensation
   (*c*) crystallisation (*d*) evaporation

6. Which method cannot be used for separating solution of solid in liquid ?
   (*a*) distillation
   (*b*) separating funnel
   (*c*) crystallisation
   (*d*) evaporation

7. Brownian movement is due to
(a) convection currents
(b) heat changes in the liquid state
(c) impact of molecules of dispersion medium on colloidal particles
(d) attractive forces between the particles of dispersed phase and dispersion medium.

8. The first boiling fraction in the fractional distillation of liquefied air is
(a) argon (b) nitrogen
(c) oxygen (d) hydrogen

9. The dyes present in the fountain pen ink can be separated by the technique
(a) Fractional distillation
(b) Centrifugation
(c) Crystallisation
(d) Chromatography (NTSE 2014–15)

10. Which of the following does not show Tyndall effect ?
(a) Starch solution (b) Milk
(c) Soap solution (d) Sugar solution
(NTSE 2012–13)

11. Which of the following are chemical changes :
(i) cutting of trees
(ii) burning of paper
(iii) boiling of water to form steam
(iv) rusting of iron almirah
(a) (i) and (ii) (b) (i) and (iii)
(c) (ii) and (iv) (d) (ii) and (iii)

12. The main characteristics of colloidal solution are
(i) it shows Tyndall effect
(ii) its size is between 10 to 100 nm
(iii) heterogeneous
(iv) generally clear and transparent
(a) (i), (ii) and (iii) (b) (i) and (iii)
(c) (i), (ii) and (iii) (d) (i), (iii) and (iv)

13. Which of the following are pure substances?
(i) Soda water (ii) Blood
(iii) Liquid mercury (iv) Chalk
(a) (i), (iii), (iv) (b) (iii) and (iv)
(c) (i) and (iv) (d) (iv) only

14. Which of the following are elements?
(i) Diamond (ii) Liquid mercury
(iii) Milk (iv) Glucose
(a) (i) and (ii) (b) (i), (ii) and (iv)
(c) (ii) and (iii) (d) (i), (ii) and (iii)

15. Which of the following are physical changes ?
(i) Rusting of iron metal
(ii) Melting of iron metal
(iii) Reacting iron metal with steam
(iv) Drawing of wire of iron metal
(a) (i), (iii) (b) (ii), (iii), (iv)
(c) (ii), (iv) (d) (ii) and (iii)

16. Which of the following is suspension ?
(a) Milk
(b) Milk of magnesia
(c) Sugar solution
(d) Vinegar

17. A mixture of naphthalene and sodium chloride can be separated by
(a) Filteration (b) Distillation
(c) Crystallisation (d) Sublimation
(NTSE 2014–15)

18. The method for separation of mixture of common salt and ammonium chloride is
(a) Fractional distillation (b) Sublimation
(c) Chromatography (d) Crystallisation.
(NTSE 2017–18)

19. Solution is
(a) Homogeneous mixture
(b) Heterogeneous mixture
(c) Colloidal
(d) All of the above (NTSE 2018–19)

20. Components present in air can be separated by
(a) Fractional distillation (b) Evaporation
(c) Boiling (d) None
(NTSE 2018–19)

ANSWERS AND HINTS (NTSE) : SAT

1. (d) 2. (b) 3. (d) 4. (d) 5. (a)
6. (b) 7. (c) 8. (b) 9. (d)
10. (d) Sugar solution does not show Tyndall effect.
11. (c) 12. (d) 13. (b) 14. (a) 15. (c):
16. (b) Milk of magnesia is a suspension.
17. (d) 18. (b) 19. (a) 20. (a)

TEST YOURSELF

CHAPTER PRACTICE TEST

Time allowed : 1 Hour **Maximum Marks : 20**

1. Which of the two : soap solution or sugar solution scatter light? 1

2. Which of the following is a suspension?

(*a*) Milk (*b*) Milk of magnesia (*c*) Mercury (*d*) Sugar solution 1

3. A mixture of common salt and ammonium chloride can be separated by

(*a*) Crystallisation (*b*) Chromatography (*c*) Sublimation (*d*) Fractional distillation 1

4. Which of the following solution has concentration less than 15%?

(*i*) 25 g of sugar is dissolved in 100 g of water

(*ii*) 15 g of sugar is dissolved in 100 g of water

(*iii*) 30 g of sugar is dissolved in 250 g of water

(*iv*) 55 g of sugar is dissolved in 500 g of water

(*a*) (*i*), (*iii*), (*iv*) (*b*) (*ii*), (*iii*), (*iv*) (*c*) (*i*), (*iv*) (*d*) (*ii*), (*iv*) 1

5. Which of the following is/are compounds?

(*i*) Mercury (*ii*) Steam (*iii*) Air (*iv*) Alcohol

(*a*) (*i*), (*iv*) (*b*) (*ii*), (*iv*) (*c*) (*ii*), (*iii*) (*d*) (*iv*) only 1

6. For the following questions two statements are given- one labeled *Assertion* (A) and the other labeled *Reason* (R). Select the correct answer to these questions from the codes (*a*), (*b*), (*c*) and (*d*) as given below:

(*a*) Both A and R are true and R is correct explanation of the assertion

(*b*) Both A and R are true and R is not the correct explanation of the assertion

(*c*) A is true but R is false

(*d*) A is false but R is true.

Assertion : During fractional distillation of liquefied air, nitrogen gets distilled first of all components.

Reason : The boiling point of nitrogen is the lowest. 1

7. Which separation technique is used for the separation of the following:

(*i*) Butter from curd

(*ii*) Oil from water

(*iii*) Sodium chloride from its solution in water 3

8. What is meant by crystallisation ? How is copper sulphate purified from its impure sample by this method? Explain the procedure. 3

9. Distinguish between homogeneous and heterogeneous mixtures. Classify the following as homogeneous and heterogeneous mixtures :

(*i*) Smoke (*ii*) Tincture of iodine (*iii*) Brass (*iv*) Sugar solution 3

10. (*a*) What are colloids ? Give two examples.

(*b*) Why do colloids show Tyndall effect ?

(*c*) Compare the following properties of true solution, colloid and suspension

(*i*) Stability (*ii*) Size of particles (*iii*) Filterability 5

Chapter 3

Atoms and Molecules

In the previous chapters, we have learnt that all matter is made up of elements from which all forms of matter can be built. The elements also combine to form compounds. Many questions come to our mind such as :

How do elements combine to form compounds ?

Can we divide the pure form of matter (elements and compounds) further and find the smallest particles of matter ?

These questions have been a puzzle for scientists and philosophers for many years.

HISTORICAL ACCOUNT OF DIVISIBILITY OF MATTER

The ancient Greeks have always wondered as what would happen if we keep on breaking matter into smaller and smaller particles. Is there any point at which we would have to stop after which the particle cannot be further broken. Idea of divisibility of matter was also considered long back in India around 500 BC. The Indian philosopher Maharshi Kanad postulated that if we go on dividing matter (*padarth*) we shall get smaller and smaller particles. Ultimately, we will get the smallest particles, which cannot be devided further. He named these ultimate particles as **"parmanu"**. Another Indian philosopher Pakudha Katyayama also supported the view that these smallest particles normally exist in a combined form which gives us various forms of matter.

Around the same period the ancient Greek philosophers like Leucippus, Democritus and Epicurus (in sixth century BC) suggested that sub division of matter is possible. If we go on dividing the matter a stage will come when particles cannot be further divided. They called these indivisible particles as **atoms**. The word atom comes from a Greek word meaning *something which cannot be split i.e., indivisible*. However, the ancient theories, proposed by Kanad and Greek philosophers were based on philosophical thinking and not on experimental work. By the end of eighteenth century, scientists understood the differences between elements and compounds. They started finding how and why elements combine and what happens when elements combine. The major credit goes to Antoine Lavoisier who laid the foundation of chemical sciences by establishing two laws of chemical combination.

In this chapter

LAWS OF CHEMICAL COMBINATION

In the seventeenth century, the scientists were trying to find out methods for converting one substance into another. During the studies of the chemical changes, they made certain generalisations. These generalisations are known as ***laws of chemical combination.*** The following two laws of chemical combination were given after much experimentation by Lavoisier and Proust.

1. Law of conservation of mass

This law deals with the relation between the mass of the reactants and the products during the chemical changes. It was stated by a French chemist, **A. Lavoisier** in 1774.

The **law of conservation of mass** states that

> *during any chemical change, the total mass of the products is equal to the total mass of the reactants.*

In other words, the law of conservation of mass means that ***mass can neither be created nor destroyed during any chemical combination.*** This law is also known as law of ***indestructibility of matter.*** From a large number of experiments, it was concluded that although substances may undergo chemical changes, the total mass of the products of the reaction is exactly equal to the total mass of the reactants. For example, 12 g carbon combines with 32 g of oxygen to form 44 g of carbon dioxide :

$$\underset{12\ g}{C} + \underset{32\ g}{O_2} \longrightarrow \underset{44\ g}{CO_2}$$

Activity 1

To understand the law of conservation of mass

Collect the following apparatus and chemicals:

- Weighing balance, conical flask, small ignition tube, thread, cork to fit the flask
- Barium chloride and sodium sulphate

(*i*) Prepare separately about 5% solution of barium chloride and sodium sulphate in water.
(*ii*) Take a small amount of barium chloride solution in the conical flask.
(*iii*) Put some sodium sulphate solution in the ignition tube. Hang the ignition tube in the flask carefully by holding from the free end of the thread tied to its neck. Fix the rubber cork in the mouth of the conical flask so that it holds the thread firmly as shown in Fig. 1(*a*).
(*iv*) The mouth of the ignition tube should remain above the liquid level in the flask so that the two solutions (in the flask and the ignition tube) donot get mixed.
(*v*) Weigh the flask with the contents carefully.
(*vi*) Now tilt and swirl the flask so that the solutions get mixed.
(*vii*) Weigh the flask again.

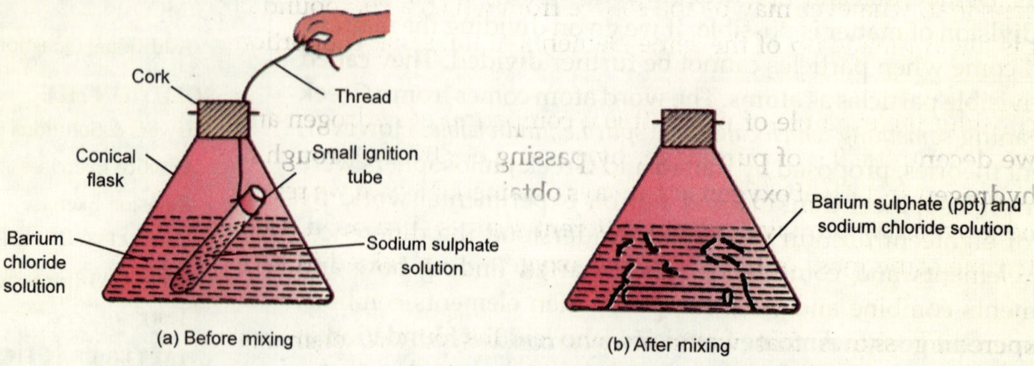

Fig. 1. Reaction between barium chloride and sodium sulphate.

Note the following observations

(i) What happens in the flask ?

(ii) Do you think a chemical reaction has taken place?

(iii) Why should we put a cork on the mouth of the flask?

(iv) Does the mass of the flask change?

We observe that a white precipitate is formed which shows that a reaction takes place between barium chloride and sodium sulphate. The white precipitate is of barium sulphate.

When we weigh the flask again with its contents, the weight will be found to be same as before and after the experiment. This shows that the mass remains same after the reaction.

This supports the law of conservation of mass.

The chemical reaction taking place in the above experiment can be written as:

Barium chloride + Sodium sulphate ⟶ Barium sulphate + Sodium chloride
(Solution) (Solution) (White precipitate) (Solution)

From the above experiment, we may say that:

Mass of barium chloride (solution) + Sodium sulphate (solution) =
Mass of barium sulphate (precipitate) + Sodium chloride (solution)

Note: The above experiment may also be carried out by taking the following solutions:

(i) Copper sulphate solution and sodium carbonate solution

(ii) Lead nitrate solution and sodium chloride solution

(iii) Silver nitrate solution and hydrochloric acid solution

2. Law of constant proportions

Lavoisier and other scientists observed that many compounds were composed of two or more elements and each compound had the same elements in the same proportions irrespective of the fact from where the compound came or who prepared it. This led to the **law of constant proportions** which is also known as the **law of definite proportions.** It was given by J. Proust in 1799.

This law states that

a pure chemical compound is always made up of the same elements combined together in a fixed (or definite) proportions by mass.

This law is also known as **the law of definite proportions.**

This means that, whatever may be the source from which a compound is obtained, it is always made up of the same elements in the same proportion by mass.

Let us consider the example of water. It is a compound of hydrogen and oxygen. If we decompose 9 g of pure water by passing electricity through it, then 1 g of hydrogen and 8 g of oxygen are always obtained. Now, if we repeat the experiment by taking pure water from different sources (like pond, well, river, sea etc.) the same mass of hydrogen and oxygen are obtained in each case.

This experiment shows that water always consists of two elements, hydrogen and oxygen and these elements are combined together in the same proportion of 1:8 by parts.

REMEMBER

Law of Conservation of Mass. During any physical or chemical change, total mass of products is equal to total mass of the reactants.

Law of Constant Composition. A pure chemical compound always contains same elements combined together in a fixed or definite proportions by mass.

Similarly, carbon dioxide can be prepared by a number of methods as given below :

(*i*) Carbon dioxide can be prepared by burning coal.

(*ii*) Carbon dioxide can be prepared by the action of dilute hydrochloric acid on the marble pieces.

(*iii*) Carbon dioxide can be prepared by heating limestone (calcium carbonate).

It has been observed that each sample of carbon dioxide (obtained by above methods) contains carbon and oxygen in the ratio of 3:8 by mass. This means that carbon dioxide always contains two elements, carbon and oxygen and these are combined together in the ratio of 3:8 by mass. In other words, 3 g of carbon will always combine with 8 g of oxygen to form carbon dioxide or 6 g of carbon will combine with 16 g of oxygen or 1 g of carbon will combine with 8/3 g of oxygen and so on.

Similarly, in ammonia (NH_3), nitrogen and hydrogen, are always present regardless of the method or the source from which it is obtained in the ratio of 14 : 3 by mass.

Solved Examples

Example 1. In a reaction 5.3 g of sodium carbonate were reacted with 6 g of ethanoic acid solution. The products were 2.2 g of carbon dioxide, 0.9 g of water and 8.2 g of sodium ethanoate solution. Show that these observations are in agreement with law of conservation of mass. ***(NCERT)***

Solution : The reaction is

Sodium carbonate + Ethanoic acid solution ⟶ Sodium ethanoate solution + Carbon dioxide + Water

Mass of reactants = Mass of sodium carbonate + Mass of ethanoic acid solution

= 5.3 + 6.0

= 11.3 g

Mass of products = Sodium ethanoate + Carbon dioxide + Water

= 8.2 + 2.2 + 0.9

= 11.3 g

Since mass of reactants is same as the mass of products, this illustrates the law of conservation of mass.

Example 2. Silver nitrate reacts with sodium chloride to form sodium nitrate and silver chloride according to the reaction :

Silver nitrate + Sodium chloride ⟶ Silver chloride + Sodium nitrate

It is found that 3.40 g of silver nitrate combines with 1.5 g of sodium chloride and 2.8 g of silver chlorideis precipitated. Applying law of mass action to calculate the mass of sodium nitrate formed.

Solution : The reaction is

Silver nitrate +	Sodium chloride ⟶	Silver chloride +	Sodium nitrate
3.40 g	1.50 g	2.80 g	x

According to law of mass action, the total mass of the products is equal to the total mass of the reactants.

Mass of reactants = 3.40 + 1.50 = 4.90 g

Mass of products = 2.80 + x

∴ 2.80 + x = 4.90 g

or x = 4.90 – 2.80 = 2.10 g

∴ Mass of sodium nitrate formed = **2.10 g.**

Example 3. Calcium carbonate on heating decomposes to give calcium oxide and carbon dioxide. When 10g of calcium carbonate is decomposed completely, it formed 5.6g of calcium oxide and 4.4 g of carbon dioxide. Show that the data is in agreement with the law of conservation of mass.

Solution : The chemical reaction is

$$\text{Calcium carbonate} \xrightarrow{\text{Heat}} \text{Calcium oxide + Carbon dioxide}$$

Mass of reactants = Mass of calcium carbonate = 10 g

Mass of products = Mass of calcium oxide + Mass of carbon dioxide

= 5.6 + 4.4 = 10.0

Since the mass of products is equal to the mass of reactants, the data is in agreement with the law of conservation of mass.

Example 4. With the help of law of mass action, predict the values of x, y and z in the following reaction :

	A	+ B	⟶ C	+ D
(*i*)	1.0 g	2.5 g	1.5 g	x
(*ii*)	y	5.0 g	3.0 g	4.0 g
(*iii*)	1.5 g	3.8 g	z	3.0 g

Solution : According to law of mass action, the total mass of reactants is equal to the total mass of the products. Therefore, the values of x, y and z can be easily calculated :

(*i*) Mass of reactants $= 1.0 + 2.5 = 3.5$ g

Mass of products $= 1.5 + x = (1.5 + x)$ g

$\therefore$ $3.5 \text{ g} = 1.5 + x$

or $x = 3.5 - 1.5 = $ **2.0 g.**

(*ii*) Mass of reactants $= y + 5.0$

Mass of products $= 3.0 + 4.0 = 7.0$ g.

$\therefore$ $y + 5.0 = 7.0$

or $y = 7.0 - 5.0 = $ **2.0 g.**

(*iii*) Mass of reactants $= 1.5 + 3.8 = 5.3$ g

Mass of products $= z + 3.0$

$\therefore$ $5.3 \text{ g} = z + 3.0$

or $z = 5.3 - 3.0 = $ **2.3 g.**

❑ **Example 5. In an experiment, 2.192g of copper oxide was obtained from 1.751g of copper. In another experiment, 1.824g of copper oxide on reduction gave 1.457g of copper. Show that the given data illustrates the law of constant proportions.**

Solution : In the first experiment,

Mass of copper = 1.751g

Mass of copper oxide = 2.192g

Mass of oxygen = 2.192–1.751 = 0.441g

$$\text{\% of copper in copper oxide} = \frac{1.751}{2.192} \times 100 = 79.9\%$$

$$\text{\% of oxygen in copper oxide} = \frac{0.441}{2.192} \times 100 = 20.1\%$$

In the second experiment,

Mass of copper = 1.457g

Mass of copper oxide = 1.824

Mass of oxygen = 1.824 – 1.457 = 0.367

$$\text{\% of copper in copper oxide} = \frac{1.457}{1.824} \times 100 = 79.9\%$$

$$\text{\% of oxygen in copper oxide} = \frac{0.367}{1.824} \times 100 = 20.1\%$$

Thus, copper oxide in the two experiments contains same elements, copper and oxygen in the same proportion by mass. Therefore, the given data illustrates the law of constant proportions.

❑ **Example 6. Hydrogen and oxygen combine in the ratio of 1 : 8 by mass to form water. What weight of oxygen gas would be required to completely react with 3 g of hydrogen gas.**

Solution : Ratio in which hydrogen and oxygen combine = 1 : 8

1 g of hydrogen combines with oxygen = 8 g

$\therefore$ 3 g of hydrogen will combine with oxygen = 8 × 3 = **24 g.**

❑ **Example 7. A 0.24g of a sample of compound of boron and oxygen was found on analysis to contain 0.096g of boron and 0.144g of oxygen. Calculate the percentage composition of the compound by mass.**

Solution : Mass of compound = 0.24g

Mass of boron in the compound = 0.096g

Mass of oxygen in the compound = 0.144g

Percentage of boron =

$$\frac{\text{Mass of boron in compound}}{\text{Mass of compound}} \times 100$$

$$= \frac{0.096}{0.24} \times 100 = 40\%$$

Percentage of oxygen =

$$\frac{\text{Mass of oxygen in compound}}{\text{Mass of compound}} \times 100$$

$$= \frac{0.144}{0.24} \times 100 = 60\%$$

DALTON'S ATOMIC THEORY

The scientists started thinking to give appropriate explanation to the laws of combinations. Guided by the laws of chemical combinations and other facts, John Dalton provided the basic theory about the nature of matter. He took the name atoms for the smallest particle of matter as given by the Greek. Based on the laws of chemical combination, he proposed a model of an atom known as **Dalton's atomic theory.**

The main postulates of the Dalton's atomic theory are :

1. All matter is made up of very small particles. These small particles are called **atoms.**
2. Atoms cannot be further broken down. They are tiny, indivisible and indestructible ultimate particles.
3. Atoms can neither be created nor destroyed in a chemical reaction.
4. All the atoms of a given element are identical in all respects having the same mass, size and chemical properties.
5. Atoms of different elements are different and have different mass, size and chemical properties.

6. During chemical combination, atoms of different elements combine in a simple whole number ratio to form compounds.
7. The relative number and kinds of atoms are constant in a given compound.
8. Atoms of same element can combine in more than one ratio to form more than one compound. For example, hydrogen and oxygen combine to give water and hydrogen peroxide. In water, two atoms of hydrogen combine with one atom of oxygen while in hydrogen peroxide, two atoms of hydrogen combine with two atoms of oxygen.

Thus, the Dalton's atomic theory gave the **concept of atom** as the smallest particle of matter.

ATOM : AN ULTIMATE PARTICLE OF MATTER

What is an Atom?

According to Dalton, an atom is something that cannot be divided further. This is the ultimate particle of an element that maintains its chemical identity throughout all chemical and physical changes. Thus, the atoms are the building blocks of all matter.

How big are atoms ?

The atoms are very small. In fact they are smaller than anything we can imagine or campare with. More than millions of atoms when stacked one on top of the other would make a layer barely as thick as the sheet of this paper. The size of an atom is expressed as atomic radius. It is generally measured in nanometres. The nanometres are related to metres as

$$1 \text{ nm} = 10^{-9} \text{ m or} = \frac{1}{10^9} \text{m}$$
$$\text{or } 1 \text{ m} = 10^9 \text{ nm}$$

The relative sizes of atoms and molecules as compared to other common species are given below :

Species	Atom of hydrogen	Molecule of water	Molecule of hemoglobin	Grain of sand	Ant	Watermelon
Approx. atomic radius (in m)	10^{-10}	10^{-9}	10^{-8}	10^{-4}	10^{-2}	10^{-1}

We might think that if atoms are so insignificant in size then why should we care about them. In fact, we cannot ignore atoms because our entire world is made up of atoms. We may not be able to see them because they are extremely small. But atoms are there and are constantly affecting us whatever we do.

Modern technology has made it possible to take photographs of atoms. It can be done with the help of sophisticated instrument called **Scanning Tunneling Microscope** (STM). It was developed in 1981. It can produce the image of the surfaces of elements which show the individual atoms. An image of surface of silicon constructed with STM has been shown in Fig. 2. In this image, the silicon atoms are shown to be arranged in a regular pattern.

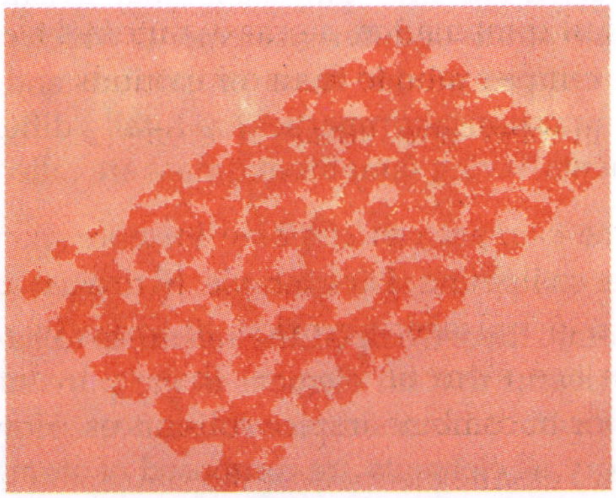

Fig. 2. An image of the surface of silicon constructed with scanning tunneling microscope (STM).

Explanation of Laws of Chemical Combination by Dalton's Atomic Theory

Dalton's atomic theory provided a simple explanation for the laws of chemical combination.

1. Explanation for the law of conservation of mass

According to Dalton's atomic theory, matter is made up of atoms and atoms can neither be created nor destroyed during any physical or chemical change. This means that the number of various types of atoms in the products of a chemical reaction is the same as the number of all these atoms in the reactants. A chemical reaction only involves rearrangement of atoms to form the products. Since the same number of atoms are present in products as those in the reactants, therefore, there will be no change in mass. Hence, the total mass of products is equal to the total mass of reactants. Thus, the law of conservation of mass is supported by Dalton's atomic theory.

2. Explanation of Law of Constant proportions

According to one of the postulates of Dalton's atomic theory, the relative number and kind of atoms in a given compound is fixed. Since the kind of atoms in a compound is fixed, this means that a compound is always made up of the same elements. Moreover, the number of atoms in different elements in the compound is fixed and all the atoms of a given element are identical in mass, this means that a compound will always have the same elements combined together in the same proportion by mass. This is law of constant proportions and hence the law is supported by Dalton's atomic theory.

Drawbacks of Daltons atomic theory

Dalton's atomic theory gave a powerful initiative to scientists in the begining of 19th century. But later work by scientists about the nature of atom pointed out some limitations of this theory.

The main limitations of Dalton's atomic theory are:

(*i*) Atoms have been found to be made of still smaller subatomic particles — electron, proton and neutron. Therefore, atom is no longer indivisable.

(*ii*) Atoms of the same element may have different masses. For example, there are two different types of chlorine atoms having atomic mass 35 and 37, though their chemical properties are same. Such atoms of the same element having different atomic masses are called **isotopes** (discussed later).

(*iii*) Atoms of different elements may be similar in one or more respects. There are certain atoms of different elements which possess same atomic masses. For example, atomic mass of calcium and argon is same (40 a.m.u). but their chemical properties are totally different. Such atoms of different elements having same atomic mass are called **isobars** (discussed later).

Dalton's atomic theory and the terms, elements and compounds

The Dalton's atomic theory helped the scientists to have a mental picture of matter. We have learnt that an element is the pure substance which can neither be broken nor built from simpler substances. However, according to Dalton's atomic theory all elements are composed of atoms. Thus,

an element is a pure substance which is made up of only one kind of atoms.

Thus, the ultimate particle of an element is an atom. To understand this, consider a piece of an element say gold. If we break this into smaller and smaller pieces, it will become so small that we will not be able to see it without a microscope. If we keep on breaking this particle, we will ultimately reach a stage when this particle cannot be further broken. This ultimate particle of an element is called an atom. Thus,

an atom is the smallest particle of an element which may or may not have independent existence.

Atoms of most of the elements are very reactive and take part in chemical combinations. For example,

hydrogen is composed of atoms of hydrogen, oxygen is composed of atoms of oxygen, copper and silver are composed of atoms of copper and silver respectively. There are about 118 elements known and obviously there are 118 different types of atoms. The atoms of certain elements, such as hydrogen, chlorine, nitrogen, oxygen etc., do not have independent existence. On the other hand, atoms of certain elements such as helium, neon, argon etc., have independent existence.

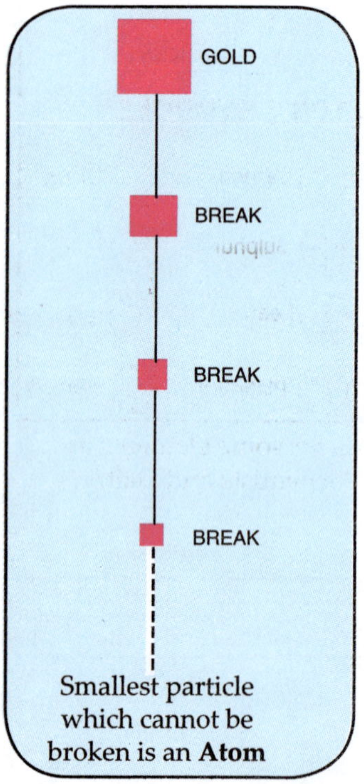

Smallest particle which cannot be broken is an **Atom**

Just as the ultimate particle of an element is atom, the ultimate particle of a compound is called a **molecule.** Molecules are formed by the combination of atoms of the same or different elements and are capable of independent existence. For example, water molecule is made up of hydrogen and oxygen atoms, carbon dioxide is made up of carbon and oxygen atoms. Thus,

molecule is the smallest particle of a substance (element or compound) which is capable of independent existence under ordinary conditions and shows all the properties of that substance.

Thus, a molecule contains two or more atoms. For example, a molecule of water contains two atoms of hydrogen and one atom of oxygen. It is represented by H_2O. Similarly, a molecule of carbon dioxide contains one atom of carbon and two atoms of oxygen. It is represented as CO_2. The properties of a substance are the properties of its molecules.

Dalton's atomic theory and difference between an element and a compound

Dalton's atomic theory helps us to clearly understand the difference between an element and a compound. As already studied, an element has one type of atoms, which are alike in all respects but different from those of other elements. Fig. 3 shows atoms of two different elements A and B. All atoms of A are identical but different from atoms of B.

Now, a molecule is formed by the combination of different atoms. For example, Fig. 3(*c*) shows a compound having molecules AB_2 in which one atom of A combines with two atoms of B (compounds are formed by the combination of atoms in a fixed ratio).

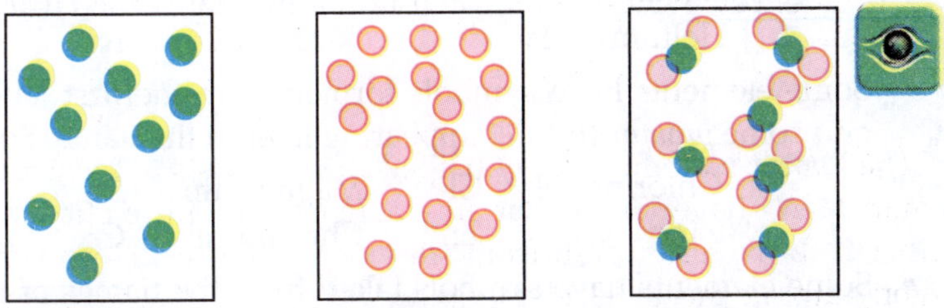

(a) Atoms of A (b) Atoms of B (c) Molecules of compound AB_2

Fig. 3. Representation of (a) atoms of element A, (b) atoms of element B, (c) molecules of a compound AB_2, in which one atom of A combines with two atoms of B (in definite ratio).

MODERN DAY SYMBOLS OF ATOMS OF THE ELEMENTS

The names of some elements are very ancient. They were generally named from the name of the place where they were found for the first time. For example the name copper is derived from **Cyprus**, where the element was once mined. Some names were taken from the specific colour of the element. For example, the word *gold* is derived from the old English word meaning *"yellow"*. Some names describe a characteristic property. For example, chlorine is a yellow green gas and its name is derived from the Greek word meaning *"yellow green"*. Some elements are named by the name of their discoverers or to honour some people or places. For example, Americium, Einsteinium, Nobelium, Cerium, etc.

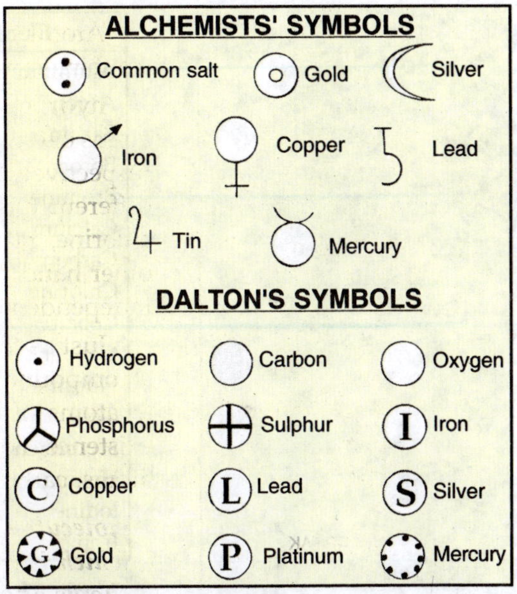

Fig. 4. Symbols for some elements as proposed by Alchemists and Dalton.

Chemists have a useful system that saves writing out the full names of the elements. They represented elements with chemical symbols.

Thus, a **symbol** is **the shorthand representation of an element.**

Dalton was the first scientist to use the symbols for elements in a specific sense. The symbols for some elements as proposed by Dalton are given in Fig. 4. When he used a symbol for an element he also meant a definite quantity of that element *i.e.*, one atom of that element.

Dalton's symbols of elements were difficult to draw and inconvenient to use. These are only of historical importance. Berzilius suggested that the symbols of elements be made from one or two letters of the name of the element. **Some guidelines for writing the symbols of the elements** are given below:

- The first letter of the name of the element represents its symbol. For example,

Boron	B	Nitrogen	N
Carbon	C	Oxygen	O
Hydrogen	H	Sulphur	S

- Some elements are represented by two letters. The necessity of adding another letter arises because there are number of elements whose names begin with the same letter. For example, barium, bromine, boron and bismuth begin with the letter 'b'. Therefore, names of these elements are represented by two letters. The first letter of the symbol is capital and the second letter is small. For example, Aluminium is represented as Al and not AL. Similarly,

Cobalt	Co	Calcium	Ca
Helium	He	Nickel	Ni

- Some elements have symbols formed from the first letter of the name and some *prominent letter* appearing later in the name. For example,

Chlorine	Cl	Magnesium	Mg
Zinc	Zn	Chromium	Cr

- Some elements have symbols taken from the names of the elements in Latin, German or Greek language. For example:
  Iron has symbol Fe from its Latin name *ferrum*
  Sodium has symbol Na from its Latin name *natrium*
  Potassium has symbol K from its Latin name *kalium*
  Silver has symbol Ag from its Latin name *argentum*

  Now the International Union of Pure and Applied Chemistry known as **IUPAC**, approves names of elements.

  Thus, we see that each element has a name and a unique chemical symbol. The symbols of some common elements are given in Table 1.

Table 1. Names and symbols of some common elements.

Element	Symbol	Element	Symbol
Aluminium	Al	Lead	Pb
Argon	Ar	Magnesium	Mg
Barium	Ba	Manganese	Mn
Boron	B	Neon	Ne
Bromine	Br	Nitrogen	N
Calcium	Ca	Nickel	Ni
Carbon	C	Oxygen	O
Chlorine	Cl	Platinum	Pt
Cobalt	Co	Potassium	K
Copper	Cu	Silicon	Si
Fluorine	F	Silver	Ag
Gold	Au	Sodium	Na
Hydrogen	H	Sulphur	S
Helium	He	Tin	Sn
Iodine	I	Uranium	U
Iron	Fe	Zinc	Zn

Note. There is no need to memorise all the symbols at one go. With the passage of time and repeated usage, you will automatically be able to remember these symbols.

ATOMIC MASSES

The most remarkable concept which Dalton's atomic theory proposed was atomic mass. Each element has a characteristic atomic mass. This theory could explain the law of constant proportions on the basis of atomic masses so successfully that the scientists were prompted to measure the atomic masses of atoms. However, the atoms are extremely small particles and it is very difficult to determine their actual masses. For example, mass of one atom of hydrogen has been found to be 0.000000000000000000000000167 g $= 1.67 \times 10^{-24}$ g. Obviously, such a small mass cannot be determined even with the help of a very sensitive balance. To overcome, this problem, the atomic masses are expressed as *relative masses i.e.,* with reference to mass of a standard atom.

In fact, this was done on the basis of chemical combinations of elements to form compounds. For example, a compound is formed between carbon and oxygen. 3.0 g of carbon were combined with 4.0 g of oxygen. This means that oxygen contributed $\frac{4}{3}$ times as much mass towards the formation of compound (CO) as the carbon. If the substance is made up of molecules, each containing one atom of carbon and one atom of oxygen, then each oxygen atom must weigh $\frac{4}{3}$ times as much as one carbon atom. Suppose, we define atomic mass unit as equal to one carbon atom and assign carbon an atomic mass of 1.0 a.m.u., then oxygen would have atomic mass of $\frac{4}{3}$ or 1.33 a.m.u. However, it is more convenient to have these numbers as whole numbers (or as near to whole numbers). To solve the problem, scientists thought of different atomic mass units with passage of time.

Initially, scientists decided to choose **hydrogen atom** as the standard substance because it is the lightest of all the atoms known. Its atomic mass was taken as 1 a.m.u. Later on **oxygen** was fixed as standard because it is more reactive than hydrogen. The **atomic mass of an element is taken as the number of times an atom of it is heavier than $\frac{1}{16}$ th of an atom of oxygen.** This method was considered relevant because :

(*i*) oxygen reacted with a large number of elements and formed compounds.

(*ii*) this atomic mass unit gave masses of elements as whole numbers.

However, later on it was observed that all atoms of oxygen do not have same mass because naturally occurring oxygen was later found to be composed of a mixture of atoms of slightly different masses. These were called **isotopes** (discussed later).

In 1961, the International Union of Chemists selected the stable isotope of carbon (carbon-12) as the standard for comparing the atomic and molecular masses of elements and compounds. The atomic mass of the standard, the isotope carbon-12 of carbon is chosen to be 12. Thus, **atomic mass** may be defined as :

the average relative mass of an atom of the element as compared to an atom of carbon (carbon-12) taken as 12.

In other words, atomic mass expresses the number of times an atom of the element is heavier than a carbon atom taken as 12 or $\frac{1}{12}$ th of the mass of carbon atom. Therefore,

$$\text{Atomic mass} = \frac{\text{Mass of an atom}}{\frac{1}{12}\text{th mass of a carbon atom (carbon - 12)}}$$

This scale of relative masses of atoms is called **atomic mass unit scale** and is abbreviated as a.m.u. Now, IUPAC has recommended a new symbol 'u' (unified mass) in place of a.m.u. The quantity of mass equal to $\frac{1}{12}$ th of the mass of an atom of carbon (carbon-12) is called **atomic mass unit.**

Table 2. Atomic masses of some common elements.

Element	Symbol	At. mass
Aluminium	Al	27
Arsenic	As	74.9
Argon	Ar	39.9
Antimony	Sb	122
Barium	Ba	137.3
Boron	B	10.8
Bromine	Br	79.9
Cadmium	Cd	112.4
Cesium	Cs	132.9
Calcium	Ca	40.1
Carbon	C	12
Chlorine	Cl	35.5
Chromium	Cr	52
Cobalt	Co	58.9
Copper	Cu	63.5
Fluorine	F	19
Gold	Au	197.0
Helium	He	4.0
Hydrogen	H	1.008
Iodine	I	126.9
Iron	Fe	55.8
Lead	Pb	207.2
Lithium	Li	6.9
Magnesium	Mg	24.3
Manganese	Mn	54.9
Mercury	Hg	200.6
Neon	Ne	20.1
Nickel	Ni	58.7
Nitrogen	N	14.0
Oxygen	O	16.0
Phosphorus	P	31
Platinum	Pt	195.1
Potassium	K	39.1
Radon	Rn	222
Scandium	Sc	44.9
Silicon	Si	28.1
Selenium	Se	79
Silver	Ag	107.9
Sodium	Na	23
Sulphur	S	32
Tin	Sn	118.7
Titanium	Ti	47.9
Tungsten	W	183.8
Uranium	U	238
Vanadium	V	50.9
Xenon	Xe	131.1
Zinc	Zn	65.4

Note. The atomic masses in the table are approximate. The exact values of all the elements are given in the beginning of the book. For calculations, these approximate values can be used.

Atomic mass unit = $\frac{1}{12}$ th the mass of a carbon-12 atom.

Hence, 1 atom of hydrogen has $\frac{1}{12}$ th the mass of standard carbon-12, so its atomic mass is 1 a.m.u. Similarly, it is observed that an atom of oxygen is 16 times heavier than $\frac{1}{12}$ th of the mass of carbon atom (1 a.m.u.), therefore, its atomic mass is 16 u.

The atomic masses of some common elements are given in Table 2.

DO YOU KNOW?

Concept of Average Atomic Mass

It may be noted that the word average has been used in the above definition. This is because most of the elements occur in nature as mixtures of atoms having different atomic masses. These different atoms of the same element having different atomic masses are called **isotopes**. Therefore, the average atomic mass of different types (isotopes) of the same element is taken as atomic mass. For example, chlorine occurs in nature in the form of two types of atoms (isotopes) with atomic mass 35 and 37 in the ratio of 3:1 respectively. Therefore, average atomic mass of chlorine is taken as:

$$\text{Average atomic mass of chlorine} = \frac{35\times3+37\times1}{3+1} = 35.5$$

Thus, we say that on an average, an atom of chlorine is 35.5 times heavier than 1/12th of the mass of carbon atom (C^{12}).

Mass of 1 amu !

1 amu is $\frac{1}{12}$ th of the mass of carbon -12 atom.

It has been found by experiments that the mass of carbon-12 atom is 1.9926×10^{-23}g.

$$\therefore \quad 1\text{ amu} = \frac{1.9926\times10^{-23}\text{g}}{12} = \mathbf{1.6605\times10^{-24}g}$$

HOW DO ATOMS OCCUR ?

Atoms of most elements do not occur independently. They aggregate (join together) in different ways to form matter that we are able to see, feel, or touch. The atoms may combine to form neutral molecules or charged ions which further form compounds. For example, atoms join together to form neutral molecules which may exist as elements or molecular compounds. The atoms may also form charged species called **ions** which form compounds known as **ionic compounds**. These basic types of aggregation of atoms is shown in Fig. 5.

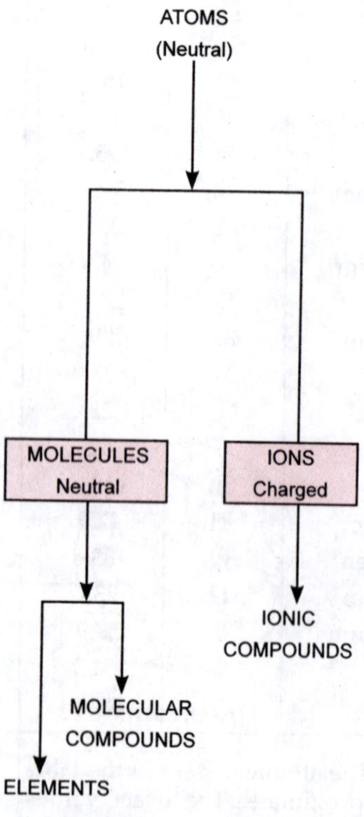

Fig. 5. Aggregation of atoms in different ways.

MOLECULE

What is a Molecule?

As we have learnt a **molecule is the smallest particle of a substance (element or compound) which is capable of independent existence and shows all the properties of that substance.** A molecule may be regarded as a group of two or more atoms that are chemically bonded together. The atoms in a molecule are tightly connected by attractive forces.

Atoms of same or different elements can join together to form molecules.

Molecules of Elements

Many elements like helium (He), neon (Ne) argon (Ar), sodium (Na), iron (Fe), etc can be easily represented by their symbols because they contain single atom.

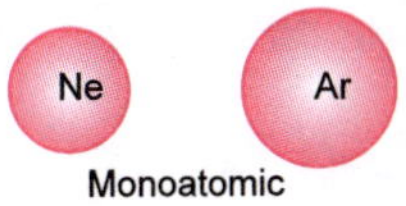

Monoatomic

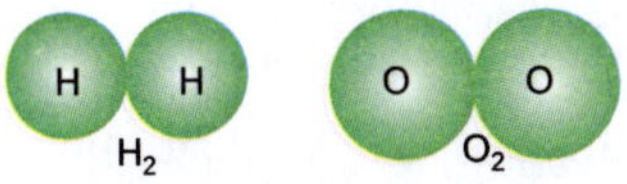

(Diatomic)

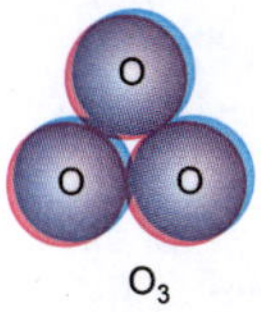

O_3
(Triatomic)

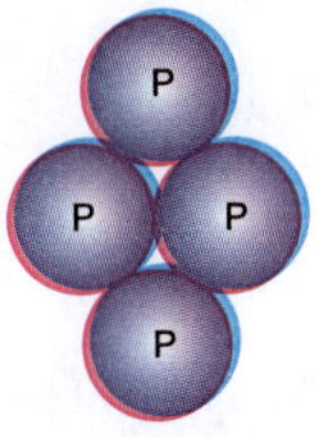

P_4
(Tetra-atomic)

However, some elements especially non-metals donot exist as single atoms. For example, oxygen exists as diatomic, consisting of two atoms. Therefore, it is written as O_2. Similarly, hydrogen gas consists of two atoms of hydrogen, written as H_2, chlorine gas consists of two atoms of chlorine written as Cl_2. **The number of atoms in a molecule of an element** is called **atomicity.**

For example, noble gases such as helium, neon, argon, etc have only one atom each in their molecules such as He, Ne, Ar, etc. Therefore, their **atomicity is one** and called **monoatomic.**

Hydrogen and nitrogen has two atoms in their molecules and therefore, have **atomicity two** and are called **diatomic molecules.**

Ozone has three oxygen atoms in its molecule and is represented as O_3. Therefore, its **atomicity is three** and is called **triatomic molecule.**

Similarly, phosphorus has four atoms and sulphur has 8 atoms in their molecules. These are represented as P_4 and S_8 respectively and their atomicities are 4 and 8. These are also called **tetra-atomic** or **octa-atomic (or polyatomic** *meaning* **many)** molecules respectively.

The atomicity of some common elements are given below :

Table 3. Atomicity of some common elements.

Type of Element	Name	Symbol	Atomicity
Non-metal	Helium	He	Monoatomic
	Argon	Ar	Monoatomic
	Neon	Ne	Monoatomic
	Hydrogen	H_2	Diatomic
	Chlorine	Cl_2	Diatomic
	Nitrogen	N_2	Diatomic
	Oxygen	O_2	Diatomic
	Phosphorus	P_4	Tetratomic
	Sulphur	S_8	Polyatomic
Metals	Sodium	Na	All monoatomic
	Iron	Fe	
	Aluminium	Al	
	Copper	Cu	

DO YOU KNOW?

Some elements donot have simple molecular structure but consists of a very large number of atoms bonded together. These elements may be represented by their atomic symbols. For example, a recently discovered form of carbon called **buck minster fullerence** has the molecular formula C_{60}. Its structure is a prefect sphere and looks like a soccer ball. Therefore, it is popularly known as **bucky ball.**

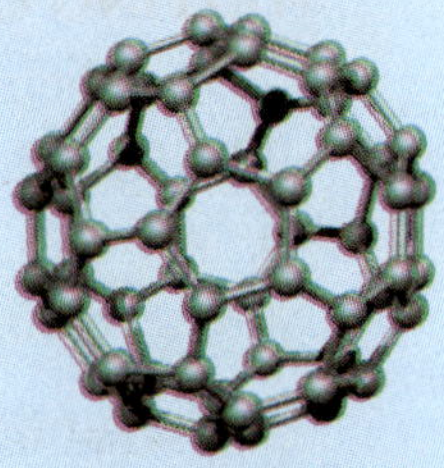
Fullerene molecule (C_{60})

Represented as soccer ball

Molecules of Compounds

Atoms of different elements may join together in definite proportion to form molecules of compounds. For example, as already studied hydrogen and oxygen always combine in the ratio of 1:8 to form water. Similarly, carbon dioxide is a comound whose molecules consist of carbon and oxygen atoms. The molecules of some compounds are given in Table 4.

Table 4. Molecules of some compounds.

Compound	Combining elements	Formula	Ratio by mass
Water	Hydrogen and oxygen	H_2O	1 : 8
Ammonia	Nitrogen and hydrogen	NH_3	14 : 3
Carbon dioxide	Carbon and oxygen	CO_2	3 : 8
Sulphur dioxide	Sulphur and oxygen	SO_2	1 : 1

ION

What is an Ion?

Compounds containing only non-metals consist of molecules. For example, hydrogen and oxygen in water, nitrogen and hydrogen in ammonia and carbon and oxygen in carbon dioxide exist as molecules. However, in some compounds the smallest particles are charged species instead of neutral molecules. An **ion is a charged particle having negative or positive charge.** The compounds containing metal and non-metals consist of ions. For example, sodium chloride (common salt) consists of sodium and chloride ions. These compounds are called **ionic compounds**. For example, sodium chloride has positively charged sodium ions (Na^+) and negatively charged chloride ions (Cl^-). These ions may consist of a single charged atom or a group of atoms that have a charge on them. **A group of atoms carrying a charge on them are** called **polyatomic ions.** For example,

Sodium ion (Na^+), calcium ion (Ca^{2+}) exist as single charged ions while ammonium ion having formula NH_4^+ exist as polyatomic ion.

In ionic compounds also the constituting elements are present in a fixed ratio by mass. This is given below in Table 5.

Table 5. Some ionic compounds.

Ionic compound	Constituting elements	Ratio by mass
Calcium oxide	Calcium and oxygen	5 : 2
Magnesium sulphide	Magnesium and sulphur	3 : 4
Sodium chloride	Sodium and chlorine	23 : 35.5

Thus, the formula of an ionic compound gives the simplest whole number ratio of ions present in it.

WRITING CHEMICAL FORMULAE

The chemical formulae of different compounds can by written easily by knowing the chemical symbols of the constituting atoms and the combining capacity of the elements.

The combining capacity (*or power*) *of an element* **is** *known* as its **valency.**

The fundamental reason for a particular atom having a particular valency or combining capacity will be understood in next chapter of Atomic Structure.

The valency of an atom may be used to find out how many atoms of one element will combine with other to form a chemical formula.

The valency of an atom of the element can be thought of as hands and arms of that atom. As we know, human beings have two hands while an octopus has eight hands. If one octopus has to catch hold of a few people in such a manner that all the eight arms of octopus and two arms of all the humans are locked, how many humans do you think the octopus can hold? It can hold four humans.

Now represent humans with H and octopus with O, then we write the formula for this combination as OH_4. The subscript 4 indicates the number of humans held by the octopus.

It may be noted that besides atoms and ions having a valency sometimes groups of atoms behave as if they have a valency of their own. These are also called polyatomic ions.

The ions can be of two types :

(*i*) **Positively charged ions** and

(*ii*) **Negatively charged ions.**

The *positive ions* are also called **cations.** The *negative ions* are also called **anions.** For example, sodium chloride (NaCl) consists of positive sodium (Na^+) ion and negative chloride (Cl^-) ion.

The positive and negative ions may broadly be classified into two types :

(*i*) Simple or monoatomic ions, and

(*ii*) Compound or polyatomic ions.

(*i*) A **simple** or monoatomic ion contains only one atom. For example :

Sodium	: Na^+	Potassium	: K^+
Chloride	: Cl^-	Sulphide	: S^{2-}

(*ii*) A **compound ion** contains atoms of more than one atom and behaves as a single unit. These are also known as **polyatomic ions.** For example,

Ammonium	: NH_4^+	Sulphate	: SO_4^{2-}
Carbonate	: CO_3^{2-}	Nitrate	: NO_3^-

It may be noted that we generally find polyatomic ions under negative charge. Some common monoatomic ions are given in Tables 6 and 7 and polyatomic ions are given in Table 8.

Table 6. Some common monoatomic ions (positively charged)

+1 Charge	+2 Charge	+3 Charge	+4 Charge
Hydrogen H^+	Barium Ba^{2+}	Aluminium Al^{3+}	Lead (IV)
Sodium Na^+	Calcium Ca^{2+}	iron (III) or	or plumbic Pb^{4+}
Potassium K^+	Copper (II) or	Ferric Fe^{3+}	Platinum Pt^{4+}
Copper (I) or	cupric Cu^{2+}	Chromium Cr^{3+}	
cuprous Cu^+	Mercuric Hg^{2+}	Bismuth Bi^{3+}	
Mercurous Hg^+	Cobalt Co^{2+}		
Silver Ag^+	Nickel Ni^{2+}		
	Iron (II) or		
	ferrous Fe^{2+}		
	Magnesium Mg^{2+}		
	Manganese Mn^{2+}		
	Zinc Zn^{2+}		
	Lead (II) or		
	Plumbous Pb^{2+}		

It may be noted that some metals like copper, mercury, iron, tin etc. form two types of ions having different charges or valencies. In these cases, Roman numerals in brackets are used to show their valencies. Alternatively, *–ous* is written after the name for lower valency and *–ic* is written after the name for higher valency.

For example, copper metal (Cu) forms two types of ions, Cu^+ and Cu^{2+}. The Cu^+ ion having 1 unit positive charge is written as copper (I) or it is written as cuprous ion (*–ous* after the name). Cu^{2+} ion having 2 unit positive charge is written as copper (II) or cupric ion (*–ic* after the name). Thus, Cu^+ indicates valency of 1+ and is written as copper (I) ion or cuprous ion and Cu^{2+} indicates valency of 2+ and is written as copper (II) ion or cupric ion.

Similarly,

Mercury (Hg) forms two ions, Hg^+ (valency 1+) and Hg^{2+} (valency 2+). These are named as :

Hg^+ : Mercury (I) ion or mercurous ion

Hg^{2+} : Mercury (II) ion or mercuric ion

Iron (Fe) forms two ions, Fe^{2+} (valency 2+) and Fe^{3+} (valency 3+). These are named as :

Fe^{2+} : Iron (II) ion or ferrous ion

Fe^{3+} : Iron (III) ion or ferric ion

Lead (Pb) forms two ions, Pb^{2+} (valency 2+) and Pb^{4+} (valency 4+). These are named as :

Pb^{2+} : Lead (II) ion or plumbous ion

Pb^{4+} : Lead (IV) ion or plumbic ion.

Table 7. Some common monoatomic ions (negatively charged)

–1 Charge	–2 Charge	– 3 Charge
Fluoride F^- Chloride Cl^- Bromide Br^- Iodide I^- Hydride H^-	Sulphide S^{2-} Oxide O^{2-}	Phosphide P^{3-} Nitride N^{3-}

The compound ions or polyatomic ions containing more than one elements are given in Table 8.

Table 8. Some common polyatomic ions

Positively charged		Negatively charged	
+1 Charge	**– 1 Charge**	**– 2 Charge**	**– 3 Charge**
Ammonium NH_4^+	Hydroxide OH^- Bicarbonate HCO_3^- Nitrate NO_3^- Acetate CH_3COO^-	Carbonate CO_3^{2-} Sulphite SO_3^{2-} Sulphate SO_4^{2-} Chromate CrO_4^{2-} Dichromate $Cr_2O_7^{2-}$	Phosphate PO_4^{3-} Phosphite PO_3^{3-} Borate BO_3^{3-} Phosphide P^{3-} Nitride N^{3-}

Rules for Writing a Chemical Formula

The following general rules should be followed while, writing a chemical formula :

1. ***The valencies or charges of the ion must balance.*** For example, carbon has a valency 4. Therefore, it will combine with four atoms of an element, like hydrogen which has a valency of 1. Thus, the formula of methane having one carbon atom is CH_4.
2. ***When a compound consists of a metal and a non-metal, the symbol of the metal is written on the left hand side and that of the non-metal is written on the right hand side.*** For example,

Sodium chloride : NaCl, Calcium oxide : CaO,

Iron sulphide : FeS, Copper oxide : CuO

Here sodium, calcium, iron and copper are metals and so are written on the left hand side while chlorine, oxygen and sulphur are non-metals and therefore, are written on the right hand side.

3. *In compounds with polyatomic ions, the ion is enclosed in a bracket before writing the number to indicate the ratio.* For example,

Calcium bicarbonate : $Ca(HCO_3)_2$, Ammonium sulphate : $(NH_4)_2SO_4$

Chemical formula for molecular compounds

Compounds which donot have constituting ions are molecular compounds.

We can write the chemical formula for molecular compounds in a simple way as shown below :

(*i*) Write the symbols of the elements which form the compound.

(*ii*) Write the valencies of the atoms below their symbols.

(*iii*) If there is a common factor between the valencies of the combining atoms, the valencies are divided by the common factor.

(*iv*) Cross over the valencies of the combining atoms *i.e.,* shift the valency numerals crosswise to the lower right corner of the symbols. Thus, we write the valency of second atom with first atom (as a subscript) and the valency of first atom with the second atom (as a subscript). For example,

(*i*) **Formula of hydrogen chloride.** The elements present are hydrogen (H) having valency 1 and chlorine (Cl) having valency 1.

Symbol H Cl

Valency 1 1

Formula : HCl

(*ii*) **Formula of hydrogen sulphide.** It contains element hydrogen (H) with valency 1 and sulphur (S) with valency 2.

H S

1 2

Formula : H_2S

(*iii*) **Formula of water.** The elements present are hydrogen (H) having valency 1 and oxygen (O) having valency 2.

H O

1 2

Formula : H_2O

(*iv*) **Formula of ammonia.** The elements present are hydrogen (H) having valency 1 and nitrogen (N) having valency 3.

N H

3 1

Formula : NH_3

(*v*) **Formula of carbon dioxide.** The elements present are carbon (C) having valency 4 and oxygen (O) having valency 2.

C O

4 2

or 2 1

Formula : CO_2

(Dividing by common factor 2)

In this case, there is a common factor 2 between the valencies of C and O. Therefore, the valencies are divided by 2 and the formula is CO_2 and not C_2O_4.

(*vi*) **Formula of methane.** The elements present are carbon (C) having valency 4 and hydrogen (H) having valency 1.

C H

4 1

Formula : CH_4

(*vii*) **Formula of carbon tetrachloride.** The elements present are carbon (C) having valency 4 and chlorine (Cl) having valency 1.

C ↖ ↗ Cl

4 ✕ 1   Formula : CCl_4

Writing the Formula of Ionic Compound

The knowledge of valencies of various radicals helps us to write the formulae of chemical compounds. The total positive charge on positive ions (cations) is equal to the total negative charge on negative ions (anions) in a molecule. Therefore, in writing the formula of a compound, the positive and negative ions are adjusted in such a way that the total number of positive charges of positive ions (cations) becomes equal to the total number of negative charges of negative ions (anions). For example, let us try to write the formula of magnesium chloride. Magnesium chloride is made up of two ions : magnesium ion (Mg^{2+}) and chloride ion (Cl^-). We write the symbol of cation (Mg^{2+}) first followed by the symbol of anion (Cl^-) as

Mg^{2+} Cl^-

We find that magnesium ion has 2 unit of positive charge whereas chloride ion has one unit of negative charge. Since the positive and negative charges are to be made equal, we change the number of Cl^- ions to two. This means that one Mg^{2+} ion will react with $2Cl^-$ ions so that the charges become equal (+2 = –2). Thus, the formula of magnesium chloride is $MgCl_2$. It may be noted that the charges on the ions are not indicated in the formula.

There is another simple method for writing the formulae of ionic compounds. In this method, the valencies (or positive or negative charges) of the ions can be 'crossed over' to give subscripts. The purpose of crossing over of charges is to find the number of ions required to equalise the number of positive and negative charges. For example, we first write the symbols of magnesium ion and chloride ion. Below the symbol of magnesium ion we write the charge +2 and below chloride ion we write the charge –1 as shown below :

Ions	Mg^{2+}	Cl^-	Mg ↖ ↗ Cl	= $MgCl_2$ formula
Charge	2+	1–	+2 ✕ –1	

Cross over charges

We now cross over the charges of magnesium and chloride ions. The cross over charges are written as subscripts with the ions (without positive or negative charges). So we get the formula $MgCl_2$ for magnesium chloride.

Thus, in magnesium chloride, there are two chloride (Cl^-) ions for each magnesium (Mg^{2+}) ion. The positive and negative charges are balanced and overall structure is neutral.

We can check the charge balance as follows :

$Mg^{2+} = 2$ $2\ Cl^- = 2$

The steps involved in writing the formula of a compound are summarized below :

Step 1. *Write the symbols of formulae of the ions of the compound side by side with positive ion on the left hand side and negative ion on right hand side.*

Step 2. *Enclose the polyatomic ion (containing atoms of more than one element, e.g.,* CO_3^{2-}, NH_4^+, SO_4^{2-} *etc.) in a bracket.*

Step 3. *Write the charge of each ion below its symbol.*

Step 4. *Reduce the charge numerals to a simple ratio by dividing with a common factor, if any.*

Step 5. *Cross over the charges i.e., shift the charge numerals crosswise to the lower right corner of the ions.*

Do not write the charges positive or negative of the ions.

Let us apply the above steps in order to write formula of **barium nitrate.** It contain Ba^{2+} and NO_3^- ions.

Step 1. Writing the formulae of the ions :

Ba NO_3

Step 2. Enclose the compound radical nitrate in bracket.

Ba (NO_3)

Step 3. Write the charges of both the ions :

Ba (NO_3)

2+ 1–

Step 4. Not applicable, because ratio is already simple.

Step 5. Cross over the charges.

Ba NO_3

2+ 1–

Thus, the formula of barium nitrate is $Ba(NO_3)_2$

(Generally the subscript 1 is not written)

We can check the charge balance as :

$Ba^{2+} = +2$

and $2(NO_3^-) = -2$

Let us write the formulae of more compounds.

Aluminium oxide

Symbol Al O

Charges 3+ 2–

Formula Al_2O_3

Calcium oxide

Symbol Ca O

Charges 2+ 2–

or 1+ 1–

Formula CaO

(The valencies are written in simple ratio so, the formula is not Ca_2O_2)

Calcium hydroxide

Symbol Ca OH

Charges 2+ 1–

Formula $Ca(OH)_2$

(We use bracket when we have two or more atoms of the same ion *i.e.,* polyatomic ion so the formula is not $CaOH_2$).

Sodium carbonate

Symbol Na CO_3

Charges 1+ 2–

Formula Na_2CO_3

(Bracket is not needed if there is only one polyatomic ion)

Sodium nitrate

Symbol Na NO_3

Charges 1+ 1–

Formula $NaNO_3$

Ammonium sulphate

Symbol NH_4 SO_4

Charges 1+ 2–

Formula $(NH_4)_2SO_4$

Aluminium sulphate

Al SO_4

3+ 2–

$Al_2(SO_4)_3$

Barium carbonate

Ba (CO_3)

2+ 2–

or 1– 1–

$BaCO_3$

(valency numerals are reduced to simple numbers)

Potassium carbonate

K (CO_3)

1+ 2–

K_2CO_3

Magnesium hydroxide

Mg (OH)

2+ 1–

$Mg(OH)_2$

Calcium chloride

Ca Cl

2+ 1–

$CaCl_2$

Sodium phosphate

Na PO_4

1+ 3–

Na_3PO_4

Ammonium chloride

NH_4 Cl

1+ 1–

NH_4Cl

Barium sulphide

Ba S

2+ 2–

or 1+ 1–

BaS

Calcium carbonate

Ca CO_3

2+ 2–

or 1+ 1–

$CaCO_3$

(Bracket is not needed if there is only one polyatomic ion)

In a simple and quick way, one the chemical formula may be written as:

- Write the ions with their valencies or charges
- Cross over the numerals of the valencies or charges (reducing the numerals to simple ratio, if needed). For example,

Aluminium oxide	:	Al^{3+} O^{2-}	$\Rightarrow Al_2O_3$
Barium chloride	:	Ba^{2+} Cl^{2-}	$\Rightarrow BaCl_2$
Lead carbonate	:	Pb^{2+} CO_3^{2-}	$\Rightarrow PbCO_3$ (dividing by 2)
Aluminium sulphate	:	Al^{3+} SO_4^{2-}	$\Rightarrow Al_2(SO_4)_3$

Some more examples are :

Magnesium bicarbonate	:	$Mg^{2+}(HCO_3)^-$	$Mg(HCO_3)_2$
Silver nitrate	:	$Ag^+(NO_3)^-$	$AgNO_3$
Lead phosphate	:	$Pb^{2+}(PO_4)^{3-}$	$Pb_3(PO_4)_2$
Magnesium nitrate	:	$Mg^{2+}(NO_3)^-$	$Mg(NO_3)_2$
Barium sulphate	:	$Ba^{2+}(SO_4)^{2-}$	$BaSO_4$
Chromium sulphate	:	$Cr^{3+}(SO_4)^{2-}$	$Cr_2(SO_4)_3$
Potassium nitrate	:	$K^+(NO_3)^-$	KNO_3
Sodium sulphide	:	Na^+S^{2-}	Na_2S
Ammonium carbonate	:	$(NH_4^+)(CO_3)^{2-}$	$(NH_4)_2CO_3$
Potassium iodide	:	K^+I^-	KI
Silver sulphide	:	$Ag^+ S^{2-}$	Ag_2S
Calcium carbonate	:	$Ca^{2+}(CO_3)^{2-}$	$CaCO_3$

Solved Examples

Example 8. Write the chemical formulae of the following compounds :

(a) aluminium oxide **(b) aluminium chloride**

(c) hydrogen sulphide **(d) Calcium hydroxide**

Solution : (a) Aluminium oxide :

Al O

3+ 2–

Formula : Al_2O_3

(b) Aluminium chloride

Al Cl

3+ 1–

Formula : $AlCl_3$

(c) Hydrogen sulphide

H S

1+ 2–

Formula : H_2S

(*d*) Calcium hydroxide

Ca ⟵ ⟶ OH

2+ 1–

Formula : $Ca(OH)_2$

Example 9. Write the chemical formulae for the following :

(*i*) Silver oxide (*ii*) Copper (II) sulphide

(*iii*) Iron (II) bromide (*iv*) Calcium fluoride

Solution : (*i*) Silver oxide : $Ag^+ O^{2-} = Ag_2O$

(*ii*) Copper (II) sulphide : $Cu^{2+} S^{2-} = CuS$

(*iii*) Iron (II) bromide : $Fe^{2+} Br^- = FeBr_2$

(*iv*) Calcium fluoride : $Ca^{2+} F^- = CaF_2$.

Example 10. Write down the names of compounds represented by the following formulae :

(*i*) $Al_2(SO_4)_3$ (*ii*) $MgCl_2$ (*iii*) K_2SO_4

(*iv*) KNO_3 (*v*) $CaCO_3$

Solution :

(*i*) $Al_2(SO_4)_3$: Aluminium sulphate

(*ii*) $MgCl_2$: Magnesium chloride

(*iii*) K_2SO_4 : Potassium sulphate

(*iv*) KNO_3 : Potassium nitrate

(v) $CaCO_3$: Calcium carbonate

Example 11. An element X shows a variable valency of 3 and 5. Write the formulae of two oxides of this element.

Solution : Formula of oxide of element X when its valency is 3.

Symbol X ⟵ ⟶ O

Valency 3 2

Formula : X_2O_3

Formula of oxide of element X when its valency is 5.

Symbol X ⟵ ⟶ O

Valency 5 2

Formula : X_2O_5

Example 12. An element E forms an oxide with formula E_2O_3.

(*a*) State the valency of E.

(*b*) Write the formula of its

(*i*) chloride (*ii*) sulphate (*iii*) phosphate

Solution :(*a*) In E_2O_3,

Valency of one O atom = 2

Valency of three O atom = 2 × 3 = 6

∴ In E_2O_3, the valencies of 2E atoms should be equal to the total valencies of O i.e., 6.

Valency of 2E atoms = 6

Valency of one E atom = 6/2 = 3

(*b*) (*i*) Formula of chloride

E ⟵ ⟶ Cl

3 1

Formula : ECl_3

(*ii*) Formula of sulphate

E ⟵ ⟶ SO_4

3 2

Formula : $E_2(SO_4)_3$

(*iii*) Formula of phosphate

E ⟵ ⟶ PO_4

3 3

Formula : EPO_4

Example 13. Predict which of the following are correct or wrong. Correct the wrong formula :

(*a*) Magnesium nitrate : $Mg(NO_3)_2$

(*b*) Barium carbonate : $Ba(CO_3)_2$

(*c*) Silver sulphide : AgS

(*d*) Potassium sulphate : K_2SO_4

Solution :

(*a*) Magnesium nitrate

Mg ⟵ ⟶ (NO_3)

2+ 1–

Formula : $Mg(NO_3)_2$

It is correct.

(*b*) Barium carbonate

Ba ⟵ ⟶ CO_3

2+ 2–

or 1+ 1–

$BaCO_3$

So the given formula is wrong. It should be $BaCO_3$.

(*c*) Silver sulphide

Ag ⟵ ⟶ S

1+ 2–

Formula Ag_2S

The given formula is wrong.

It should be Ag_2S.

(*d*) Potassium sulphate

K ⟵ ⟶ SO_4

1+ 2 –

Formula K_2SO_4

The given formula is correct.

NAMING BINARY MOLECULAR COMPOUNDS

For naming a binary molecular compound, we first write the name of the element, whose symbol appears on the left hand side of the molecular formula of the compound. The name of the other element is changed to end in – *ide* and is written on the right. For example,

HCl is named as hydrogen chloride (chlorine changes to chloride).

When there are more than one elements of an element in a compound, their number is indicated by attaching a Greek numeral prefix (prefix is a word used before a name). For example, the prefix *mono* is used for 1, *di* for 2, *tri* for

Table 10. Some common binary molecular compounds

Formula	Name
H_2O	Water
CO	Carbon monoxide
CO_2	Carbon dioxide
NO	Nitrogen monoxide
NO_2	Nitrogen dioxide
N_2O_5	Dinitrogen pentoxide
NH_3	Ammonia
CH_4	Methane
SO_2	Sulphur dioxide
SO_3	Sulphur trioxide
CCl_4	Carbon tetrachloride
N_2O_4	Dinitrogen tetroxide

3, *tetra* for 4, *penta* for 5, *hexa* for 6, etc. It may be noted that – *o* or –*a* at the end of a prefix is dropped if it is followed by another vowel (i.e. *a, e, i, o, u*). For example, mono-oxide is written as monoxide (*o* is dropped), penta-oxide is written as pentoxide (*a* is dropped) etc. For example,

(*i*) CO is named as carbon monoxide (here the prefix *mono* means 1 oxygen atom).

(*ii*) CO_2 is named as carbon dioxide (here the prefix *di* means 2 oxygen atoms).

The use of numeral prefixes is shown below :

Table 9. Use of numeral prefixes

No. of atoms	Prefix	Formula	Name
1	Mono	CO	Carbon monoxide
2	Di	CO_2	Carbon dioxide
3	Tri	PCl_3	Phosphorus trichloride
4	Tetra	CCl_4	Carbon tetrachloride
5	Penta	PCl_5	Phosphorus pentachloride

It may be noted that the prefixes are needed in naming binary compounds in which the same two non-metallic elements can form many different compounds. For example, the two elements namely nitrogen and oxygen can form six different compounds. These are named as :

NO : Nitrogen monoxide
NO_2 : Nitrogen dioxide
N_2O : Dinitrogen monoxide
N_2O_3 : Dinitrogen trioxide
N_2O_4 : Dinitrogen tetroxide (*a* of tetra is not written because it is followed by vowel–*o*).
N_2O_5 : Dinitrogen pentoxide (*a* of penta is not written because it is followed by vowel–*o*).

Therefore, it is very necessary to use prefixes in naming such compounds.

When hydrogen is the first element in the formula no prefixes is added before hydrogen irrespective of the number. For example, the compound H_2S is named as hydrogen sulphide and not as dihydrogen sulphide. It may be noted that some binary molecular compounds are named by their common names. For example,

H_2O is water though it is hydrogen monoxide
NH_3 is ammonia though it is nitrogen trihydride.
CH_4 is methane though it is carbon tetrahydride.

The names of some common binary molecular compounds are given in Table 10.

Practice Exercise 3A

Answers and Hints on Page 62

1. Silver nitrate reacts with sodium chloride to form sodium nitrate and silver chloride. It is found that 6.8 g of silver nitrate reacts with 2.4 g of sodium chloride and forms 3.4 g of sodium nitrate. Applying law of conservation of mass, calculate the weight of silver chloride formed.
2. When 4.2g of sodium bicarbonate, $NaHCO_3$ is added to a solution of acetic acid (CH_3COOH) weighing 10.0g, it is observed that 2.2g of CO_2 is released to the atmosphere. The residue left is found to weigh 12.0g. Show that the observations are in agreement with the law of conservation of mass.
3. 1.2 g of copper powder on heating gave 6.0 g of copper oxide. In another experiment copper oxide contained 20% oxygen. Show that these results illustrate the law of constant composition.

4. 2.0g of a metal burnt in oxygen gave 3.2 of its oxide. 1.42g of the same metal heated in steam gave 2.27g of its oxide. Which law is shown by this data?
5. Write the formula and names of the compounds formed between :
   (*i*) Potassium and carbonate ions
   (*ii*) Sodium and sulphide ions
   (*iii*) Ammonium and phosphate ions
6. Write the formulae of the following molecular compounds :
   (*i*) Sulphur trioxide
   (*ii*) Dinitrogen trioxide
   (*iii*) Ammonia
   (*iv*) Carbon tetrachloride
7. Write the formulae of the following compounds :
   (*i*) Copper carbonate
   (*ii*) Calcium phosphate
   (*iii*) Ammonium carbonate
   (*iv*) Barium sulphate
8. Write the names of the following compounds
   (*i*) $Cr_2(SO_4)_2$ (*ii*) K_2SO_4
   (*iii*) $Mg(NO_3)_2$ (*iv*) NiS
9. Pick up the correct formulae :
   (*i*) Ag_2S (*ii*) $Cr(NO_3)_2$
   (*iii*) K_2PO_4 (*iv*) Na_2SO_4
   (*v*) CdI_2 (*vi*) $(NH_4)_2 PO_4$
   (*vii*) Ag_2CO_3
10. Write the formulae of the compounds formed by :
   (*i*) Cr^{3+} and F^- (*ii*) Hg^{2+} and S^{2-}
   (*iii*) Pb^{2+} and $(PO_4)^{3-}$
11. The formula of carbonate of a metal M is M_2CO_3. What will be the formula of its (*i*) chloride and (*ii*) sulphate ?
12. An element Z has a valency of 4. Write the formula for its
   (*i*) chloride (*ii*) sulphate
   (*iii*) oxide (*iv*) carbonate
   (*v*) nitrate.
13. If calcium salt of anion has formula Ca_3X_2, what is the valency of X ? Write the formula of (*i*) sodium salt of X and (*ii*) aluminium salt of X.
14. What is the valency of nitrogen in Mg_3N_2?
15. Iron forms two ions, Fe^{2+} and Fe^{3+}. Write the formulae of two oxides formed by these ions.
16. Mercury forms two ions, Hg^+ and Hg^{2+}. Write the formulae of two nitrates formed by these ions.
17. An element X forms oxide XO. Write the formulae of its chloride and carbonate.
18. Copper forms two ions Cu^+ and Cu^{2+}. Write the formulae of two chlorides formed by these ions.
19. Write the valency of cations in the following compounds :
   (*i*) Mercuric chloride
   (*ii*) Copper (II) sulphate
   (*iii*) Ferric sulphate
   (*iv*) Ferrous chloride.
20. Point out the mistakes in the following and correct them:
   (*i*) $baCl_2$ (*ii*) $AL(NO_3)_3$
   (*iii*) $PB (MNO_4)_2$ (*iv*) $NaCl_2$
   (*v*) $CUSO_4$ (*vi*) $Mg_2(SO_4)_3$
   (*vii*) $CaNO_3$ (*viii*) Ag S
21. Predict which of the formulae are not correct for the given compounds : Correct the wrong ones.
   (*a*) Silver phosphate : $Ag_3(PO_4)_2$
   (*b*) Bismuth carbonate : $Bi_2(CO_3)_3$
   (*c*) Silver oxide : Ag_2O
   (*d*) Aluminium sulphate : $Al_3(SO_4)_2$
   (*e*) Silver sulphide : AgS
   (*f*) Cadmium iodide : CdI_3
   (*g*) Ammonium nitrate : NH_4NO_3
22. Make corrections to symbols and formulae.
   (*a*) Zn PO_4 (*b*) AL
   (*c*) NI (*d*) $Bi_3(PO_4)_2$
   (*e*) AgS (*f*) $NH_4(HCO_3)_2$
   (*g*) CA (*h*) CaCl
   (*i*) Ca_2O
23. What observations of the scientists led to the formulation of the law of constant composition?
24. Complete the following table:

Formula	Chemical name
(*i*) $(NH_4)_2 CO_3$	....
(*ii*)	Ferric sulphate
(*iii*)	Aluminium sulphate
(*iv*) $KMnO_4$	....
(*v*)	Magnesium phosphate

25. Consider the following chemical formulae:
   NH_4Cl, $Ca(ClO_3)_2$, $AlPO_4$, $Al_2(SO_4)_3$, Mg_3N_2, $NaHSO_3$
   Which formula represent the following:
   (*i*) a chlorate
   (*ii*) cation and anion have three valency
   (*iii*) a nitride
   (*iv*) cation and anion have one valency
   (*v*) a bisulphite
   (*vi*) cation has three valency and anion has two valency.

MOLECULAR MASS AND MOLE CONCEPT

Molecular Mass

Just like atoms, the actual masses of molecules are very small and cannot be measured by actual weighing. Like atomic masses, the molecular masses are also expressed relative to stable isotope of carbon (carbon- 12) taken as 12 u. Thus, **molecular mass** of a substance may be defined as :

the relative mass of its molecule as compared to the mass of an atom of carbon (carbon-12) taken as 12.

In other words, molecular mass expresses as to how many times a molecule of a substance is heavier than $\frac{1}{12}$ th of the mass of an atom of carbon (carbon-12).

Thus,

$$\text{Molecular mass} = \frac{\text{Mass of a molecule}}{\frac{1}{12}\text{th mass of a carbon atom (carbon - 12)}}$$

For example, a molecule of water is 18 times heavier than $\frac{1}{12}$ th of the mass of carbon atom. Therefore, the molecular mass of water is 18 u. Similarly, a molecule of CO_2 is 44 times heavier than $\frac{1}{12}$ th of the mass of a carbon atom. Therefore, its molecular mass is 44 u.

Calculation of molecular mass from atomic masses

We know that the molecules are made up of two or more atoms of different elements. Therefore, the molecular mass may be calculated as the **sum of the atomic masses of all the atoms in a molecule of that substance.** For example, ammonia has the formula, NH_3. It consists of one atom of N and three atoms of H. The atomic mass of N and H are 14.0 and 1 respectively. Therefore, the molecular mass of NH_3 is

Molecular mass of NH_3 = Atomic mass of N + 3 × Atomic mass of H

$= 14 + 3 \times 1 = 17$ u

Similarly, sulphuric acid has the formula H_2SO_4. It consists of two H, one S and four O atoms. The atomic masses of H, S and O are 1, 32 and 16 respectively. Therefore, the molecular mass of H_2SO_4 is :

Molecular mass of H_2SO_4= (2 × at. mass of H) + (1 × at. mass of S) + (4 × at. mass of O)

$= (2 \times 1) + (1 \times 32) + (4 \times 16) = 98$ u

The molecular masses of some other common molecules are :

Nitric acid, HNO_3 = H + N + 3O

= $1 + 14 + 3 \times 16 = 63$ u

Sulphur dioxide, SO_2 = S + 2O

= $32 + 2 \times 16 = 64$ u

Glucose, $C_6H_{12}O_6$ = 6C + 12H + 6O

= $12 \times 6 + 12 \times 1 + 6 \times 16 = 180$ u

Urea, NH_2CONH_2 or CN_2H_4O = C + 2N + 4H + O

= $12 + 2 \times 14 + 4 \times 1 + 16 = 60$ u

Sugar, $C_{12}H_{22}O_{11}$ = 12C + 22H + 11O

= $12 \times 12 + 22 \times 1 + 11 \times 16$

= 342 u

Molecular masses of some common molecules are given in Table 11.

Table 11. Molecular masses of some common substances

Name	Formula	Molecular mass (u.)
Hydrogen	H_2	2.0
Oxygen	O_2	32.0
Nitrogen	N_2	28.0
Chlorine	Cl_2	71.0
Phosphorus	P_4	124.0
Methane	CH_4	16.0
Carbon monoxide	CO	28.0
Carbon dioxide	CO_2	44.0
Water	H_2O	18.0
Ammonia	NH_3	17.0
Sulphur dioxide	SO_2	64.0
Nitrogen dioxide	NO_2	46.0
Methyl alcohol	CH_3OH	32.0
Ethyl alcohol	C_2H_5OH	46.0
Benzene	C_6H_6	78.0
Glucose	$C_6H_{12}O_6$	180
Sugar	$C_{12}H_{22}O_{11}$	342
Methane	CH_4	16
Ethane	C_2H_6	30
Ethylene	C_2H_4	28

FORMULA UNIT MASS

Some compounds containing ions (called ionic compounds) donot contain discrete molecules. In these compounds we call formula unit which gives the simple ratio between various atoms present in the compound. For these we use the term formula unit mass instead of molecular mass.

Formula unit mass** of a substance is **the sum of atomic masses of all atoms in a formula unit of the compound.

Formula unit mass is calculated in the same manner as we calculate the molecular mass. For example, sodium chloride has a formula unit NaCl. Its formula unit mass can be calculated as

Formula unit mass of NaCl = Atomic mass of Na + Atomic mass of Cl
= 23 + 35.5
= 58.5 u

Similarly, formula unit mass of $CaCl_2$ can be calculated as
Formula unit mass = Atomic mass of Ca + 2 × Atomic mass of Cl
= 40 + 2 × 35.5
= 111 u

REMEMBER

The average relative mass of an atom of the element as compared to an atom of carbon (carbon - 12) taken as 12 is **Atomic Mass** of the element.

The quantity of mass equal to $\frac{1}{12}$ th of the mass of an atom of carbon is **ATOMIC MASS UNIT** (1u)

Mass of 1 u = 1.66×10^{-24} g.

Molecular Mass of a substance is the relative mass of its molecules as compared to the mass of an atom of carbon taken as 12.

Molecular Mass = Sum of atomic masses of all the atoms in a molecule.

Formula Unit Mass = Sum of atomic masses of all the atoms represented by the formula of the compound.

Solved Examples

Example 14. Calculate the molecular masses of the following molecules :

(*i*) Chlorine (Cl_2) (*ii*) Chloroform ($CHCl_3$) (*iii*) Methane (CH_4) (*iv*) Water (H_2O) (*v*) Carbon dioxide (CO_2).

Atomic masses are : C = 12, H = 1, Cl = 35.5, S = 32, O = 16.

Solution : Molecular masses can be calculated by adding atomic masses of all the atoms present in one molecule.

(*i*) **Chlorine (Cl_2)** = 2 × at. mass of Cl = 2 × 35.5 = 71 u

(*ii*) **Chloroform ($CHCl_3$)** = at. mass of C + at. mass of H + 3 × at. mass of Cl
= 12 + 1 + 3 × 35.5
= 119.5 u

(*iii*) **Methane (CH_4)** = at. mass of C + 4 × at. mass of H = 12 + 4 × 1
= 16 u

(*iv*) **Water (H_2O)** = 2 × at. mass of H + at. mass of O = 2 × 1 + 16 = 18 u

(*v*) **Carbon dioxide (CO_2)** = at. mass of C + 2 × at. mass of O = 12 + 2 × 16 = 44 u

Example 15. Calculate the formula unit mass of the following

(*i*) ZnO (*ii*) Na_2O (*iii*) K_2CO_3

Atomic masses are : Zn = 65 u, Na = 23 u, K = 39 u, C = 32 u, O = 16 u, S = 32 u

Solution : (*i*) ZnO

Formula unit mass = Atomic mass of Zn + Atomic mass of O
= 65 + 16
= **81 u**

(*ii*) Na_2O

Formula unit mass = 2 × (atomic mass of Na) + Atomic mass of O
= 2 × 23 + 16
= **62 u**

(*iii*) K_2CO_3

Formula unit mass = 2 × atomic mass of K + atomic mass of C + 3 × atomic mass of O
= 2 × 39 + 12 + 3 × 16
= 78 + 12 + 48
= **138 u**

Example 16. Calculate the molecular mass of the following substances

(*a*) Ethyne, C_2H_2 (*b*) Sulphur molecule, S_8 (*c*) Phosphorus molecule, P_4 (*d*) Hydrochloric acid, HCl (e) Nitric acid, HNO_3

Solution : (*i*) Ethyne, C_2H_2

Molecular mass = 2 (atomic mass of C) + 2 (atomic mass of H)
= 2 × 12 + 2 × 1
= **26 u**

(*ii*) Sulphur molecule, S_8

Molecular mass = 8 × atomic mass of S
= 8 × 32 = **256 u**

(*iii*) Phosphorus molecule, P_4

Molecular mass = 4 × atomic mass of P
= 4 × 31 = **124 u**

(*iv*) Hydrochloric acid, HCl

Molecular mass = atomic mass of H + atomic mass of Cl
= 1 + 35.5 = **36.5 u**

(*v*) Nitric acid, HNO_3

Molecular mass = atomic mass of H + atomic mass of N + 3(atomic mass of O)
= 1 + 14 + 3 × 16 = **63 u**

Example 17. Calculate the molecular mass of the following :

(*i*) PCl_5 (*ii*) NH_3 (*iii*) CH_2Cl_2 (*iv*) H_2O_2

Atomic masses : P = 31, Cl = 35.5, N = 14, H = 1, O = 16, S = 32.

Solution : (*i*) PCl_5

Molecular mass = Atomic mass of P + 5 (Atomic mass of Cl)
= 31 + 5 × 35.5 = 208.5 u

(*ii*) NH_3

Molecular mass = Atomic mass of N + 3 (Atomic mass of H)
= 14 + 3 (1) = **17 u**

(*iii*) CH_2Cl_2

Molecular mass = Atomic mass of C + 2 × Atomic mass of H + 2 × Atomic mass of Cl
= 12 + 2 × 1 + 2 × 35.5 = **85 u**

(*iv*) H_2O_2

Molecular mass = 2 × Atomic mass of H + 2 × Atomic mass of O
= 2 × 1 + 2 × 16 = **34 u**

Example 18. The molecular formula of caffeine is $C_8H_{10}N_4O_2$. What is its molecular mass?

Solution : Molecular mass is the sum of the atomic masses of various atoms present.

Molecular mass of $C_8H_{10}N_4O_2$ = 8 × at. mass of C + 10 × at. mass of H + 4 × at. mass of N + 2 × at. mass of O

$= 8 \times 12 + 10 \times 1 + 4 \times 14 + 2 \times 16 =$ **194 u.**

Example 19. The mass of one atom of carbon (carbon-12) has been found to be 1.993 × 10^{-23} g. Calculate the mass of 1 u.

Solution : We know that

$$1\text{ u} = \frac{1}{12} \text{ of the mass of carbon atom}$$

$$\text{Mass of carbon atom} = 1.993 \times 10^{-23}\text{ g}$$

$$1\text{ u} = \frac{1.993 \times 10^{-23}\text{ g}}{12}$$

$$= 1.66 \times 10^{-24}\text{ g}$$

$$1\text{ u} = \mathbf{1.66 \times 10^{-24}\text{ g}}$$

GRAM ATOMIC MASS AND GRAM MOLECULAR MASS

Gram atomic mass

Gram atomic mass is the amount of an element whose mass in grams is numerically equal to its atomic mass. In simple words, *atomic mass of an element expressed in grams is the gram atomic mass.* For example,

Atomic mass of hydrogen = 1u
Gram atomic mass of hydrogen = 1g
Atomic mass of oxygen = 16u
Gram atomic mass of oxygen = 16g

Atomic mass of an element is expressed in amu or 'u' and, therefore, to convert atomic mass into gram atomic mass simply replace atomic mass unit (u) by gram (g).

Gram atomic mass is also called **gram atom.**

Gram molecular mass

Gram molecular mass is the amount of a substance whose mass in grams is numerically equal to its molecular mass. In simple words, *molecular mass expressed in grams is the gram molecular mass.* Thus, to convert molecular mass of a substance into gram molecular mass simply replace the units amu (u) to gram (g). For example,

Molecular mass of H_2 = 2u
Gram molecular mass of H_2 = 2g
Molecular mass of O_2 = 32u
Gram molecular mass of O_2 = 32g
Molecular mass of H_2O = 18u
Gram molecular mass of H_2O = 18g
Molecular mass of CO_2 = 44u
Gram molecular mass of CO_2 = 44g

Gram molecular mass is also called **gram molecule**

MOLE CONCEPT

We have learnt that according to law of definite proportions, in a chemical reaction definite number of atoms or molecules of one substance react with a definite number of atoms or molecules of another substance to form a compound. For example, consider the reaction :

$$2H_2 + O_2 \longrightarrow 2H_2O$$

In this reaction, two molecules of hydrogen combine with one molecule of oxygen to form two molecules of water. But how to just pick 2 molecules of hydrogen and one molecule of oxygen ? This is very difficult as such because atoms and molecules are very very small. To overcome this problem, a new term known as **mole** was introduced.

Quite commonly we use the unit dozen to count 12 articles irrespective of their nature. For example, one dozen books means 12 books, one dozen oranges means 12 oranges and one dozen pencils means 12 pencils and so on.

Similarly, 1 gross means 144 articles. For example, 1 gross pencils means 144 pencils. In a similar way, the chemists use the unit mole for counting atoms, molecules or ions.

A mole represents 6.022×10^{23} particles.

Thus,

1 mole (of anything) $= 6.022 \times 10^{23}$ in number

For example,

1 mole of atoms $= 6.022 \times 10^{23}$ atoms

1 mole of molecules $= 6.022 \times 10^{23}$ molecules

1 mole of ions $= 6.022 \times 10^{23}$ ions

Thus, the number of particles present in 1 mole of any substance is fixed *i.e.*, 6.022×10^{23} . This number is also called **Avogadro constant** or **Avogadro number**. It is represented by N_0. This is an experimentally obtained value and is named in honour of the Italian scientist **Amadeo Avogadro.**

MOLE IN TERMS OF MASS

Besides being related to a number, a mole has one more advantage over a dozen or a gross. This advantage is that **mass of 1 mole of a particular substance is also fixed.**

Mole and gram atomic mass

The mass of 1 mole of a substance is equal to its relative atomic or molecular mass in grams (g). Now atomic mass of an element gives us the mass of one atom of that element in atomic mass units (u). To get the molar mass *i.e.* mass of 1 mole of that element we have to take the same numerical value but change the units from 'u' to 'g'. Molar mass of atoms is also known as **gram atomic mass.** For example,

Atomic mass of hydrogen = 1 u

Gram atomic mass of hydrogen = 1 g

Now 1 gram atomic mass of hydrogen or 1 g of hydrogen has 1 mole atoms i.e. 6.022×10^{23} atoms of hydrogen.

Similarly,

Atomic mass of oxygen = 16 u

∴ Gram atomic mass of oxygen = 16 g

or 16 u oxygen has only 1 atom of oxygen

16 g oxygen has 1 mole atoms *i.e.* 6.022×10^{23} atoms of oxygen

Thus,

1 mole of atoms of an element = Gram atomic mass of element or **Molar mass of element**

$= 6.022 \times 10^{23}$ atoms of element

The mass of 1 mole of atoms of some elements are given in Table 12

Table 12. Mass of 1 mole of atoms

Element	Mass	Contains
Carbon	12 g (1 gram atomic mass of C)	6.022×10^{23} C atoms or 1 mole of C atoms
Iron	55.8 g (1 gram atomic mass of Fe)	6.022×10^{23} Fe atoms or 1 mole of Fe atoms
Hydrogen	1 g (1 gram atomic mass of H)	6.022×10^{23} H atoms or 1 mole of H atoms
Oxygen	16 g (1 gram atomic mass of O)	6.022×10^{23} O atoms or 1 mole of O atoms

One mole of these elements are also shown in Fig. 6.

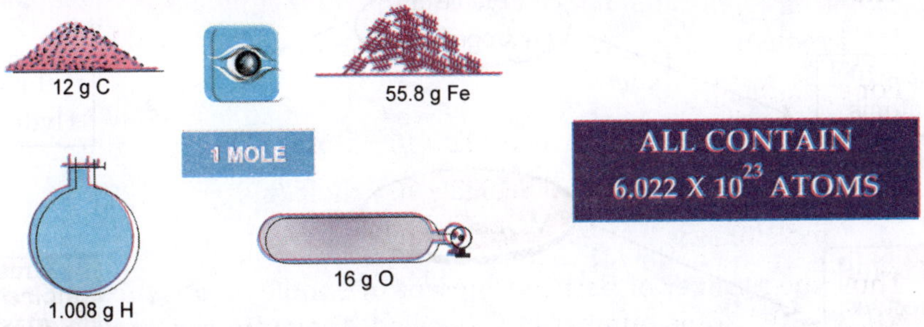

Fig. 6. Representation of 1 mole of some common elements.

Mole and molar mass

To find the gram molecular mass or molar mass of a molecule we keep the numerical value same as the molecular mass but simply change units from u to g. For example, as we have already calculated,

Molecular mass of H_2O = 18 u

Gram molecular mass of H_2O = 18 g

But gram molecular mass *i.e.*, 18 g contain 6.022×10^{23} molecules of H_2O

Thus,

18 u water has only 1 molecule of water

18 g water has 1 mole molecules of water *i.e.* 6.022×10^{23} molecules of water

Similarly,

Molecular mass of CO_2 = 44 u

Molar mass of CO_2 = 44 g

Molecular mass of SO_2 = 64 u

Molar mass of SO_2 = 64 g

Thus,

1 mole molecules of a substance = Gram molecular mass of substance or Molar mass of substance

= 6.022×10^{23} molecules of substance

The mass of one mole of molecules of some common molecules are shown in Fig. 7.

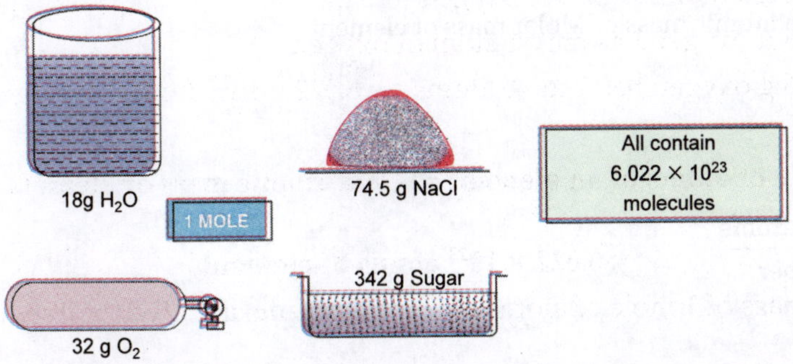

Fig. 7. Representation of one mole of some substances.

SUM UP

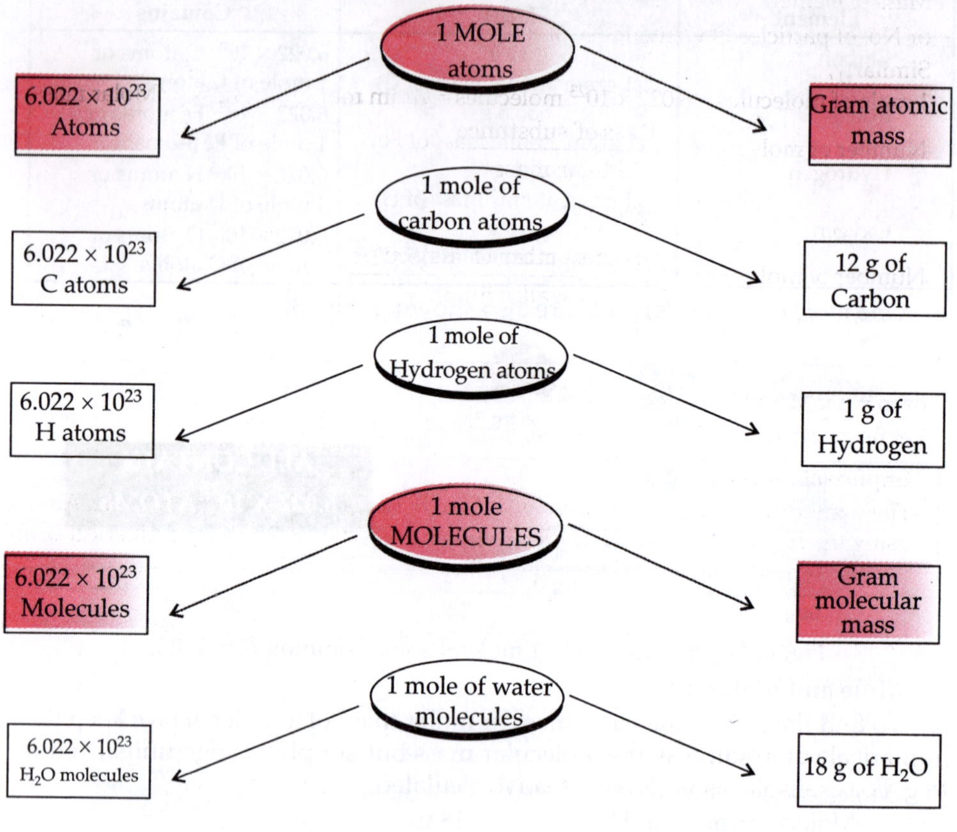

Fig. 8. Relationship between mole, Avogadro number and mass.

Thus, to count the atoms or molecules during reactions, mass can be related to number with the help of mole.

1 Mole = 6.022×10^{23} number = Relative mass in g

Thus, a mole is the chemist's counting unit.

REMEMBER

While doing numerical problems of mole concept, the following relations should be remembered :

Key for Symbols

No. of moles = n

Given mass = m

Molar mass = M

Given number of particles = N

Avogadro number of particles = N_0

Key Formulae

1 mole of atoms = 6.022×10^{23} atoms = Gram atomic mass or Molar mass of element

$$\text{Number of moles} = \frac{\text{Mass of element}}{\text{Molar mass}}$$

$$n = \frac{m}{M}$$

$$\text{Number of moles} = \frac{\text{Given number of atoms}}{\text{Avogadro number}}$$

$$n = \frac{N}{N_0}$$

These relations can be interchanged as

Mass of element, $m = n \times M$

or No. of particles of element, $N = n \times N_0$

Similarly,

1 mole of molecules = 6.022×10^{23} molecules = Gram molecular mass or Molar mass

$$\text{Number of moles} = \frac{\text{Mass of substance}}{\text{Molar mass}}$$

$$n = \frac{m}{M}$$

$$\text{Number of moles} = \frac{\text{Given number of molecules}}{\text{Avogadro number}}$$

$$n = \frac{N}{N_0}$$

or $m = n \times M$ and $N = n \times N_0$

Let us apply these formulae to solve numerical problems.

Important Note

The numerical problems can be solved directly by using the above formulae. Alternatively, these can be solved by using the main relations and applying unitary method. Most of the numerical problems in the chapter are solved by this method because it is easy and no cramming of the formulae is needed.

A. Calculation of Moles of a substance (element or compound)

We have learnt that

1 Mole of an element = Gram atomic mass

1 Mole of a compound = Gram molecular mass or Molar mass

Moles can be calculated from mass by using these relations.

Solved Examples

Example 20. **An ornament of silver contains 20 g of silver. Calculate the moles of silver present (atomic mass of silver = 108 u)**

Solution : We know that

1 mole of silver atoms = Gram atomic mass of silver = 108g

Now, 108g of silver = 1 mole of silver

$$20\text{g of silver} = \frac{1}{108} \times 20 = \mathbf{0.185\ mole}$$

Note: The above problem can also be solved by applying the relation:

$$\text{Moles of atoms, } n = \frac{\text{Mass of element in grams}}{\text{Gram atomic mass}}$$

$$\therefore n = \mathbf{0.185\ mole}$$

Example 21. **How many moles of CO_2 are present in 51.2 g of it ?**

(atomic masses, C = 12 u, O = 16 u)

Solution : Molecular mass of $CO_2 = 12 + 2 + 16 = 44$ u

We know that,

1 mol of CO_2 = Gram molecular mass of CO_2 = 44g

Now, 44g of CO_2 = 1 mole of CO_2

$$51.2\text{g of } CO_2 = \frac{1}{44} \times 51.2$$

$$= \mathbf{1.16\ mole}$$

Example 22. **Calculate the number of moles of 52 g of He. (atomic mass of He = 4 u)**

Solution : We know that

1 mole of He = Gram atomic mass of He = 4g

Now, 4 g of He = 1 mole of He

$$52\text{ g of He} = \frac{1}{4} \times 52$$

$$= \mathbf{13\ mole}$$

Example 23. **Calculate the mass of**

***(i)* 0.5 moles of N_2 gas**

***(ii)* 0.5 moles of N atoms**

Solution : ***(i)* 0.5 moles of N_2 gas**

Molecular mass of $N_2 = 2 \times 14 = 28$u

1 mole of N_2 = Gram molecular mass of N_2 = 28g

Now, 1 mole of N_2 = 28g

0.5 mole of $N_2 = 28 \times 0.5 = \mathbf{14g}$

(*ii*) **0.5 mole of N atoms**

1 mole of N atoms = Gram atomic mass of N

= 14g

Now, 1 mole of N atoms = 14g

0.5 mole of N atoms = 14 × 0.5 = **7g**

❑ Example 24. **What is the mass in grams of 3 moles of zinc (Zn) ?**

(atomic mass of Zn = 65.4)

Solution : Atomic mass of zinc = 65.4 u

We know that

1 mole of zinc = Gram atomic mass of zinc

= 65.4g

Now, 1 mole of zinc = 65.4g

3 moles of zinc = 65.4 × 3 = **196.2g**

❑ Example 25. **What is the mass of 2.5 moles of methane (CH_4) ? (atomic mass of C = 12, H = 1)**

Solution : Molecular mass of CH_4 = 12 + 4 × 1 = 16 u

We know that,

1 mole of CH_4 = Gram molecular mass of CH_4

= 16g

Now, 1 mole of CH_4 = 16g

2.5 moles of CH_4 = 16 × 2.5 = **40g**

❑ Example 26. **Convert into moles :**

(*a*) 90 g of water

(*b*) 12 g of oxygen

(*c*) 22 g of carbon dioxide.

Solution :

(*a*) Molecular mass $H_2O = 2 \times 1 + 16 = 18$ u

We know that,

1 mole water (H_2O) = 18g of water

Now, 18g of water = 1 mole

$$90\text{g of water} = \frac{1}{18} \times 90 = 5 \text{ mole}$$

(*b*) Molecular mass of oxygen = 2 × 16 = 32 u

We know that,

1 mole of oxygen = 32g of oxygen

Now, 32g oxygen = 1 mole

$$12 \text{ g of oxygen} = \frac{1}{32} \times 12 = \mathbf{0.375\ mole}$$

(*c*) Molecular mass of CO_2 = 12 + 2 × 16 = 44 u

We know that,

1 mole of CO_2 = 44g

Now, 44g of CO_2 = 1 mole

$$22\text{g of } CO_2 = \frac{1}{44} \times 22 = \mathbf{0.5\ mole}$$

B. Calculation of number of atoms or molecules from moles of substance.

We have learnt that

1 mole of a substance = 6.022×10^{23} particles (atoms, molecules or ions)

e.g., 1 mole of an element = 6.022×10^{23} atoms

1 mole of a compound = 6.022×10^{23} molecules.

Solved Examples

❑ Example 27. **Calculate the number of calcium atoms in 2.5 mole of calcium.**

Solution : 1 mole = 6.022×10^{23} particles

Now,

1 mole of calcium atoms = 6.022×10^{23} atoms

2.5 moles of calcium atoms = $6.022 \times 10^{23} \times 2.5$

= **15.055×10^{23} atoms**

❑ Example 28. **Calculate the number of water molecules and number of oxygen and hydrogen atoms in a drop of water containing 0.03 mole of water.**

Solution : 1 mole of water = 6.022×10^{23} molecules of water

0.03 mole of water = $6.022 \times 10^{23} \times 0.03$

= 1.81×10^{21} molecules of water

∴ Molecules of water = 1.81×10^{21}

Now 1 molecule of water contains two atoms of H and one atom of O

∴ Atoms of O = $1.81 \times 10^{21} \times 1 = 1.81 \times 10^{21}$

Atoms of H = $1.81 \times 10^{21} \times 2 = 3.62 \times 10^{21}$.

❑ Example 29. **Calculate the number of sulphur (S) atoms in one mole of S_8.**

Solution : 1 mole of $S_8 = 6.022 \times 10^{23}$ S_8 molecules

No. of atoms in one S_8 molecule = 8

No. of atoms in 6.022×10^{23} S_8 molecules =

$8 \times 6.022 \times 10^{23}$ = **4.818×10^{24}**

C. Calculation of number of atoms or molecules from mass of substance.

These types of calculations can be done by combining earlier types A and B.

Example 30. **Calculate the number of moles of 12.046×10^{23} number of He atoms.**

Solution :

$$1 \text{ mole} = 6.022 \times 10^{23}$$

$$1 \text{ mole of He atoms} = 6.022 \times 10^{23} \text{ He atoms}$$

Now, 6.022×10^{23} He atoms = 1 mole

$$12.046 \times 10^{23} \text{ He atoms} = \frac{1}{6.022 \times 10^{23}} \times 12.046 \times 10^{23}$$

$$= \textbf{2 mole}$$

Alternatively,

$$\text{No. of moles} = \frac{\text{Given number of particles}}{\text{Avogadro number}}$$

$$n = \frac{N}{N_0}, N = 12.046 \times 10^{23}, N_0 = 6.022 \times 10^{23}$$

$$\therefore \quad n = \frac{12.046 \times 10^{23}}{6.022 \times 10^{23}} = \textbf{2 mole}$$

Example 31. **Calculate the number of atoms in 0.1 mole of carbon atoms.**

Solution : We know that,

$$1 \text{ mole} = 6.022 \times 10^{23} \text{ particles}$$

$$1 \text{ mole of C atoms} = 6.022 \times 10^{23} \text{ C atoms}$$

$$0.1 \text{ mole of C atoms} = 6.022 \times 10^{23} \times 0.1$$

$$= \mathbf{6.022 \times 10^{22}} \textbf{ atoms}$$

Example 32. **Calculate the number of particles in each of the following:**

(*a*) 46 g of Na atoms (at mass of Na = 23 u)

(*b*) 8 g of O_2 molecules (at. mass of O = 16 u)

Solution :

(*a*) We know that,

$$1 \text{ mole of Na} = \text{Gram atomic mass} = 23\text{g}$$

$$= 6.022 \times 10^{23} \text{ particles (or Na atoms)}$$

Now, $23\text{g of Na} = 6.022 \times 10^{23}$ particles

$$46\text{g of Na} = \frac{6.022 \times 10^{23}}{23} \times 46$$

$$= 1.2044 \times 10^{24} \text{ atoms (or particles)}$$

This numerical problem can also be solved in two steps as:

(*i*) First calculate the number of moles from the mass and then

(*ii*) Calculate the number of Na atoms in the given mass as:

(*i*) 1 mole of Na = Gram atomic mass = 23g

Now, 23g of Na = 1 mole of Na

$$46\text{g of Na} = \frac{1}{23} \times 6 = 2 \text{ mole}$$

(*ii*) Now, 1 mole of Na = 6.022×10^{23} Na atoms

$$2 \text{ mole of Na} = 6.022 \times 10^{23} \times 2$$

$$= 1.2044 \times 10^{24} \text{ atoms}$$

(*b*) Atomic mass of oxygen = 16 u

Molecular mass of O_2 = $16 \times 2 = 32$ u

1 mole of O_2 = Gram molecular mass of O_2 = 32g

= 6.022×10^{23} molecules (particles)

Now, 32g of O_2 = 6.022×10^{23} molecules

$$8\text{g of } O_2 = \frac{6.022 \times 10^{23}}{32} \times 8$$

= **1.5055×10^{23} molecules**

❑ **Example 33. Calculate the mass of**

(*i*) 3.011×10^{23} atoms of N

(*ii*) 1.807×10^{24} molecules of N_2.

Solution : (*i*) Atomic mass of N = 14u

We know that,

1 mole of N = Gram atomic mass of N = 14g

= 6.022×10^{23} N atoms

Now, 6.022×10^{23} N atoms have mass = 14g

$$3.011 \times 10^{23} \text{ N atoms have mass} = \frac{14}{6.022 \times 10^{23}} \times 3.011 \times 10^{23}$$

= 7g

(*ii*) Molecular mass of N_2 = 14×2 = 28 u

We know that

1 mole of N_2 = Gram molecular mass of N_2 = 28g

= 6.022×10^{23} molecules of N_2

Now, 6.022×10^{23} molecules of N_2 = 28g

$$1.807 \times 10^{24} \text{ molecules of } N_2 = \frac{28}{6.022 \times 10^{23}} \times 1.807 \times 10^{24} = \mathbf{84g}$$

SOME ADDITIONAL NUMERICAL PROBLEMS (MISCELLANEOUS)

❑ **Example 34. Convert into moles**

(*i*) 12 g of oxygen gas

(*ii*) 20 g of water

(*iii*) 22 g of carbon dioxide.

Solution : (*i*) Molecular mass of O_2 gas = $16 \times 2 = 32$ u

We know that,

1 mole of O_2 gas = Gram molecular mass of O_2

= 32g

Now, 32g of O_2 gas = 1 mole

$$12\text{g of } O_2 \text{ gas} = \frac{1}{32} \times 12 = \mathbf{0.375 \ mole}$$

(*ii*) Molecular mass of water = $2 \times 1 + 16 = 18$u

We know that

1 mole of water = Gram molecular mass of H_2O

= 18g

Now, 18g of water = 1 mole

$$20\text{g of water} = \frac{1}{18} \times 20 = \mathbf{1.11 \ mole}$$

(*iii*) Molecular mass of CO_2 = $12 + 2 \times 16 = 44$ u

We know that

1 mole of CO_2 = Gram molecular mass of CO_2

= 44g

Now, 44g of CO_2 = 1 mole

22g of CO_2 = $\frac{1}{44} \times 22 =$ **0.5 mole**

Example 35. What is the mass of

(*i*) 0.5 mole of water molecules

(*ii*) 0.2 mole of oxygen atoms.

Solution : (*i*) Molecular mass of water (H_2O) = $2 \times 1 + 16 = 18u$

We know that,

1 mole of H_2O = Gram molecular mass of H_2O

= 18g

Now, 1 mole of H_2O = 18g

0.5 mole of H_2O = $18 \times 0.5 =$ **9g**

(*ii*) Atomic mass of oxygen = 16u

We know that,

1 mole of oxygen = Gram atomic mass of oxygen

= 16g

Now, 1 mole of oxygen atoms = 16g

0.2 mole of oxygen atoms = 16×0.2

= **3.2g**

Example 36. What is the mass of 1.20×10^{23} atoms of cobalt ? (atomic mass of cobalt = 58.9u)

Solution : Atomic mass of cobalt = 58.9u

We know that,

1 mole of cobalt atoms = Gram atomic mass of cobalt = 58.9g

= 6.022×10^{23} atoms

Now, 6.022×10^{23} atoms of cobalt have mass = 58.9g

1.20×10^{23} atoms of cobalt have mass = $\frac{58.9}{6.022 \times 10^{23}} \times 1.20 \times 10^{23}$

= 11.73g

Example 37. Calculate the actual mass of 1 atom of carbon if 12.0 g of carbon contains one mole of carbon atoms.

Solution : 1 mole of carbon atoms = 6.022×10^{23} atoms

Now, mass of 6.022×10^{23} atoms of carbon = 12.0 g

Mass of 1 atom of carbon = $\frac{12.0}{6.022 \times 10^{23}}$ g

= $\mathbf{1.99 \times 10^{-23}}$ **g**

Example 38. Calculate the mass of one molecule of water.

Solution : Molecular mass of water (H_2O) = $2 \times 1 + 16 = 18$ u

Gram molecular mass of water = 18 g

Now, 1 mole of water contains = 6.022×10^{23} molecules

Mass of 1 mole of water = 18 g

Thus, mass of 6.022×10^{23} molecules of water = 18 g

Mass of 1 molecule of water = $\frac{18}{6.022 \times 10^{23}} = \mathbf{2.99 \times 10^{-23}}$ **g**

Example 39. Calculate the mass of :

(*a*) 1.50 moles of N atoms **(*b*) 4 moles of Al atoms**

(*c*) 2.50 moles of Na^+ ions **(*d*) 10 moles of Na_2SO_3**

Solution : (*a*) Atomic mass of N = 14 u

We know that,

1 mole of N atoms = Gram atomic mass of N

= 14g

∴ Now, 1 mole of N atoms = 14g

1.50 mole of N atoms = 14 × 1.50

= **21g**

(*b*) Atomic mass of Al = 27 u

We know that,

1 mole of Al atoms = Gram atomic mass of Al

= 27g

Now, 1 mole of Al atoms = 27g

4 mole of Al atoms = 27 × 4

= **108g**

(*c*) Atomic mass of Na^+ = 23 u

We know that,

1 mole of Na^+ ions = Gram atomic mass of Na^+ ions

= 23g

Now, 1 mole of Na^+ ions = 23g

2.5 mole of Na^+ ions = 23 × 2.5

= **57.5g**

(*d*) Molecular mass of Na_2SO_3 = 2 × 23 + 32 + 3 × 16 = 126 u

We know that,

1 mole of Na_2SO_3 = Gram molecular mass of Na_2SO_3

= 126g

Now, 1 mole of Na_2SO_3 = 126g

10 moles of Na_2SO_3 = 126 × 10

= **1260g**

Example 40. What is the mass of the following :

(*a*) 0.40 mol of CO_2

(*b*) 2.00 mol of NH_3

(Atomic masses : H = 1, C = 12, N = 14, O = 16)

Solution : We know that

(*a*) Molecular mass of CO_2 = 12 + 2 × 12 = 44 u

We know that,

1 mole of CO_2 = Gram molecular mass of CO_2

= 44g

Now, 1 mole of CO_2 = 44g

0.40 mole of CO_2 = 44 × 0.40

= **17.6g**

(*b*) Molecular mass of NH_3 = 14 + 3 × 1 = 17 u

We know that,

1 mole of NH_3 = Gram molecular mass of NH_3

= 17g

Now, 1 mole of NH_3 = 17g

2.0 mole of NH_3 = 17 × 2.0

= **34.0g**

Example 41. Find the number of moles and number of particles of chloroform ($CHCl_3$) weighing 0.0239 g (C = 12, Cl = 35.5, H = 1).

Solution : Molecular mass of $CHCl_3$ = 12 + 1 + 3 × 35.5 = 119.5 u

We know that,

1 mole of $CHCl_3$ = Gram molecular mass of $CHCl_3$

= 119.5g

Now, 119.5g of $CHCl_3$ = 1 mole

0.0239g of $CHCl_3$ = $\frac{1}{119.5} \times 0.0239$

= 2.0×10^{-4} mole

We know that,

$$1 \text{ mole of } CHCl_3 = 6.022 \times 10^{23} \text{ particles of } CHCl_3$$

Now, $1 \text{ mole of } CHCl_3 = 6.022 \times 10^{23} \text{ particles of } CHCl_3$

$$2.0 \times 10^{-4} \text{ mole of } CHCl_3 = 6.022 \times 10^{23} \times 2.0 \times 10^{-4}$$

$$= \mathbf{1.2044 \times 10^{20}}$$

❑ Example 42. **Which has more atoms : 50 g of Fe or 50 g of Al ? (Atomic mass : Al = 27, Fe = 56)**

Solution : We know that

$$1 \text{ mole of Fe} = \text{Gram atomic mass of Fe} = 56\text{g}$$

$$= 6.022 \times 10^{23} \text{ Fe atoms}$$

Now, $56\text{g of Fe} = 6.022 \times 10^{23} \text{ atoms}$

$$50\text{g of Fe} = \frac{6.022 \times 10^{23}}{56} \times 50$$

$$= 5.38 \times 10^{23} \text{ Fe atoms}$$

Similarly, $1 \text{ mole of Al} = \text{Gram atomic mass of Al} = 27\text{g}$

$$= 6.022 \times 10^{23} \text{ Al atoms}$$

Now, $27\text{g of Al} = 6.022 \times 10^{23} \text{ Al atoms}$

$$50\text{g of Al} = \frac{6.022 \times 10^{23}}{27} \times 50$$

$$= 11.15 \times 10^{23} \text{ Al atoms}$$

∴ **50 g of Al contain more atoms than 50 g of Fe.**

❑ Example 43. **Calculate the number of moles in the following :**
(*i*) 4 g of oxygen (O_2) (*ii*) 11 g of CO_2 (*iii*) 17 g of H_2O_2.

Solution : (*i*) Molecular mass of $O_2 = 2 \times 16 = 32\text{u}$

We know that,

$$1 \text{ mole of } O_2 = \text{Gram molecular mass of } O_2$$

$$= 32\text{g}$$

Now, $32\text{g of } O_2 = 1 \text{ mole}$

$$4\text{g of } O_2 = \frac{1}{32} \times 4$$

$$= \mathbf{0.125 \text{ mole}}$$

(*ii*) Molecular mass of $CO_2 = 12 + 2 \times 16 = 44\text{u}$

We know that

$$1 \text{ mole of } CO_2 = \text{Gram molecular mass of } CO_2$$

$$= 44\text{g}$$

Now $44\text{g of } CO_2 = 1 \text{ mole}$

$$11\text{g of } CO_2 = \frac{1}{44} \times 11$$

$$= \mathbf{0.25 \text{ mole}}$$

(*iii*) Molecular mass of $H_2O_2 = 2 \times 1 + 2 \times 16 = 34 \text{ u}$

We know that

$$1 \text{ mole of } H_2O_2 = \text{Gram molecular mass of } H_2O_2$$

$$= 34\text{g}$$

Now, $34\text{g of } H_2O_2 = 1 \text{ mole}$

$$17\text{g of } H_2O_2 = \frac{1}{34} \times 17$$

$$= \mathbf{0.5 \text{ mole}}$$

❑ Example 44. **Arrange the following in the decreasing order of their masses :**

(*a*) 2.5 moles of water

(*b*) 3.012×10^{24} molecules of water

(*c*) 25 g of water.

Solution : Let us first calculate the mass of these water samples

(*a*) Molecular mass of $H_2O = 2 \times 1 + 16 = 18\text{u}$

We know that,

$$1 \text{ mole of water} = \text{Gram molecular mass of water}$$

$= 18g$

Now, 1 mole of water $= 18g$

2.5 moles of water $= 18 \times 2.5$

$= \mathbf{45g}$

(*b*) We know that

1 mole of water $=$ Gram molecular mass of water $= 18g$

$= 6.022 \times 10^{23}$ molecules of water

Now,

6.022×10^{23} molecues of water $= 18g$

$$3.012 \times 10^{24} \text{ molecules of water} = \frac{18}{6.022 \times 10^{23}} \times 3.012 \times 10^{24}$$

$= \mathbf{90g}$

(*c*) 25 g of water

Thus, decreasing order of mass is

3.012×10^{24} molecules of H_2O > 2.5 moles of water > 25 g of water.

Example 45. Calculate the number of aluminium ions in 0.056 g of aluminium oxide (Al_2O_3). (Atomic masses, Al = 27, O = 16)

Solution. Molecular mass of aluminium oxide (Al_2O_3) $= 27 \times 2 + 3 \times 16 = 102u$

Let us first calculate number of Al_2O_3 formula units.

We know that,

1 mole of Al_2O_3 $=$ Gram formula unit mass of $Al_2O_3 = 102g$

$= 6.022 \times 10^{23}$ Al_2O_3 formula units

Now, 102g of Al_2O_3 $= 6.022 \times 10^{23}$ Al_2O_3 formula units

$$0.056g \text{ of } Al_2O_3 = \frac{6.022 \times 10^{23}}{102} \times 0.056$$

$= 3.306 \times 10^{20}$ Al_2O_3 formula units

From the formula (Al_2O_3), it is clear that 1 formula unit of Al_2O_3 contains 2 Al^{3+} ions.

∴ Number of Al^{3+} ions $= 2 \times 3.306 \times 10^{20}$

$= \mathbf{6.612 \times 10^{20}}$ **ions.**

Example 46. The mass of single atom of silver is 1.794×10^{-22} g. What is the atomic mass of silver ?

Solution : The mass of 6.022×10^{23} atoms of any element is equal to its gram atomic mass.

Now, 1 atom of silver has mass $= 1.794 \times 10^{-22}$ g

6.022×10^{23} atoms of silver has mass $= 1.794 \times 10^{-22} \times 6.022 \times 10^{23}$ g $= 108.05$ g

Gram atomic mass of silver $= 108.05$ g

Atomic mass of silver $=$ **108.05 u.**

Example 47. Calculate the mass of nitrogen (N_2) which contains same number of molecules as are present in 4.4 g of CO_2.

Solution : Let us first calculate the number of molecules in 4.4g of CO_2.

Molecular mass of CO_2 $= 12 + 2 \times 16 = 44u$

We know that,

1 mole of CO_2 $=$ Gram molecular mass of $CO_2 = 44g$

$= 6.022 \times 10^{23}$ CO_2 molecules

Now, 44g of CO_2 $= 6.022 \times 10^{23}$ CO_2 molecules

$$4.4g \text{ of } CO_2 = \frac{6.022 \times 10^{23} \times 4.4}{44}$$

$= 6.022 \times 10^{22}$ CO_2 molecules

∴ 4.4 g of CO_2 contain molecules $= 6.022 \times 10^{22}$

Since number of molecules of N_2 are same, therefore,

Molecules of nitrogen (N_2) $= 6.022 \times 10^{22}$

Let us now calculate the mass of 6.022×10^{22} molecules of N_2.

Molecular mass of N_2 = $2 \times 14 = 28u$

We know that, 1 mole of N_2 = Gram molecular mass of $N_2 = 28g$

= 6.022×10^{23} N_2 molecules

Now, 6.022×10^{23} molecules of N_2 have mass = 28g

$$6.022 \times 10^{22} \text{ molecules of } N_2 \text{ have mass} = \frac{28}{6.022 \times 10^{23}} \times 6.022 \times 10^{22}$$

= **2.8g**

❑ **Example 48. How many grams of magnesium will have the same number of atoms as 40.5 g of aluminium ?**
(Atomic masses : Mg = 24, Al = 27)

Solution : Let us first calculate the number of atoms in 40.5 g of Al.

Atomic mass of Al = 27 u

We know that,

1 mole of Al = Gram atomic mass of Al = 27g

= 6.022×10^{23} atoms of Al

Now, 27g of Al contain atoms = 6.022×10^{23}

$$40.5\text{g of Al contain atoms} = \frac{6.022 \times 10^{23}}{27} \times 40.5$$

= **9.10×10^{23} atoms**

Since number of atoms of Mg are same, therefore,

Atoms of Mg = 9.10×10^{23} atoms

Let us now calculate the mass of 9.10×10^{23} atoms of Mg.

Atomic mass of Mg = 24 u

We know that

1 mole of Mg = Gram atomic mass of Mg = 24g

= 6.022×10^{23} atoms of Al

Now, 6.022×10^{23} atoms of Al = 24g

$$9.10 \times 10^{23} \text{ atoms of Al} = \frac{24}{6.022 \times 10^{23}} \times 9.10 \times 10^{23}$$

= **36.3g**

❑ **Example 49. Calculate the ratio of molecules present in 6.6 g of CO_2 and 3.2 g of SO_2.**
(atomic masses : C = 12, O = 16, S = 32).

Solution : Molecular mass of $CO_2 = 12 + 2 \times 16 = 44$ u

We know that,

1 mole of CO_2 = Gram molecular mass of $CO_2 = 44g$

= 6.022×10^{23} molecules of CO_2

Now, 44g of CO_2 = 6.022×10^{23} molecules

$$6.6\text{g of } CO_2 = \frac{6.022 \times 10^{23} \times 6.6}{44}$$

= 0.9033×10^{23} molecules

Molecular mass of SO_2 = $32 + 2 \times 16 = 64$ u

We know that,

1 mole of SO_2 = Gram molecular mass of $SO_2 = 64g$

= 6.022×10^{23} molecules of SO_2

Now, 64g of SO_2 = 6.022×10^{23} molecules

$$3.2\text{g of } SO_2 = \frac{6.022 \times 10^{23}}{64} \times 3.2$$

= 0.3011×10^{23}

$$\text{Ratio of molecules present in } CO_2 \text{ and } SO_2 = \frac{0.9033 \times 10^{23}}{0.3011 \times 10^{23}} = 3$$

∴ Ratio of molecules of CO_2 and SO_2 = **3:1.**

Practice Exercise 3B

Answers and Hints on Page 63

1. The atomic mass of lead is 207. How many times the atoms of lead are heavier than carbon atom ?
2. Calculate the molecular mass of the following :
   (*i*) Carbon dioxide (CO_2)
   (*ii*) Propane (C_3H_8)
   (*iii*) Sucrose (table sugar) $C_{12}H_{22}O_{11}$
   (*iv*) Nitric acid (HNO_3).
3. Copper is a metal known since ancient times and is used in electrical cables. How many grams are there in 0.352 mole of copper ?
   (atomic mass of Cu = 63.5)
4. Atomic mass of gold (Au) is 197 u. How many moles of gold are present in an ornament containing 88.65 g of gold ?
5. How many moles of water are present in a bucket of water containing 12 kg of water ?
6. How many moles of SO_2 have same mass as 3 moles of oxygen ? (atomic mass : S = 32, O = 16)
7. Which contains more molecules 0.5 mol of O_2 or 0.5 mol of O_3 ?
8. How many moles are there in 12.044×10^{24} atoms of phosphorus ?
9. Which contains more atoms of oxygen : 1 mole of CO or 1 mol of CO_2 ?
10. A glass of water contains 5 mole of water. How many molecules of water are present ?
11. What is the mass of :
    (*i*) an atom of oxygen (at. mass = 16)
    (*ii*) a molecule of CO_2 (at. mass C = 12, O = 16)
    (*iii*) a formula unit of Na^+Cl^- (at. mass Na = 23, Cl = 35.5)
12. How many atoms of silver are present in a silver wire weighing 5.4 g ?
13. 0.25 mole of sugar weighs 85.5 g. What is the molecular mass of sugar?
14. A flask P contains 0.5 mole of oxygen gas and another flask Q contains 0.4 mole of ozone (O_3) gas. Which of the two contains larger number of oxygen atoms ?
15. How many atoms of each element are there in 9.8 g of sulphuric acid, H_2SO_4? (atomic mass, H = 1, S = 32, O = 16).
16. Calculate the mass of sodium which contains same number of atoms as are present in 20 g of calcium. (atomic mass Ca = 40, Na = 23).
17. If 16 g of oxygen contains 1 mole of oxygen, calculate the mass of one atom of oxygen.
18. How many grams of neon will have the same number of atoms as 8 g of calcium ? (Atomic mass Ca = 40, Ne = 20).
19. Calculate the ratio of atoms present in 5 g of magnesium and 5 g of iron. (Atomic mass Mg = 24, Fe = 56).
20. Calculate the number of silver atoms in one milligram (0.001 g) of silver. (Atomic mass = 108).
21. Calculate the mass of 1 molecule of nitrogen (N_2). (Atomic mass of N = 14).
22. Calculate the ratio of molecules present in 16 g of methane (CH_4) and 16 g of oxygen. (Atomic masses : C = 12, H = 1, O = 16).
23. What mass of nitrogen, N_2 will contain the same number of molecules as in
    (*i*) 3.6 g of water ?
    (*ii*) 6.022×10^{22} molecules of methane ?
24. What is the mass in grams of 1.0×10^{12} lead (Pb) atoms ? (atomic mass of Pb = 207)
25. How many atoms of mercury are present in 1 g of mercury ? (atomic mass of mercury = 200.6)
26. Complete the missing spaces :
    (*a*) 3.5 moles of CO_2 = ... atoms
    (*b*) .... moles of SO_2 = 6.4g of SO_2
    (*c*) .... g of H_2SO_4 = 0.01 mole of H_2SO_4
    (*d*) .... g of $C_6H_{12}O_6 = 1.44 \times 10^{23}$ atoms
    (*e*) 1 molecule of H_2O = ... g of water.
27. What is the ratio of atoms by mass of
    (*i*) Ammonia (*ii*) Carbon dioxide
    (*iii*) Sulphur dioxide (*iv*) Magnesium sulphide
    (*v*) Sodium chloride.
28. Calculate the moles corresponding to the following :
    (*i*) 1.71g of sucrose $C_{12}H_{22}O_{11}$ = ...
    (*ii*) 1.2044×10^{23} Ag atoms = ...
    (*iii*) 1.2046×10^{21} atoms of He =
    (*iv*) 3.011×10^{20} molecules of CO_2 =
    (*v*) 108g of Al = ...
29. Aluminium oxide is electrolysed to produce aluminium. Oxygen gas is produced at the carbon anode which is then burnt according to the following reaction :
    $$C + O_2 \longrightarrow CO_2$$
    The relative atomic masses of Al = 27, C = 12 and O = 16.
    For each 16 kg of oxygen used calculate
    (*a*) mass of carbon burnt
    (*b*) the mass of carbon dioxide obtained
    (*c*) calculate the mass of aluminium produced from 10.2 kg of aluminium oxide according to the reaction :
    $$2Al_2O_3 \longrightarrow 4Al + 3O_2$$

30. How many electrons are there in 1 mole of electrons? If 1 electron carries a charge of 1.602×10^{-19} coulombs, what will be the charge of 1 mole of electrons?

31. Calculate the mass of 0.5 mol of water and 0.5 mol of ammonia. Which has larger mass?

32. What is the use of mole concept?

33. (*i*) What is the mass of 1 mol of water?

(*ii*) What is the volume of 1 mol of water (density = 1 gm/mL)

34. Which of the following are wrong masses in column B for the column A? Correct these.

Column A	Column B
(*a*) 1.07×10^{24} atoms of Fe	10 g
(*b*) 0.1 mole of Ca	4.0 g
(*c*) 0.001 mole of H_2SO_4	9.8 g
(*d*) 6.022×10^{22} molecules of N_2	5.6 g
(*e*) 1.16 mole of CO_2	51.2 g

35. Complete the following table:

Molecule	CH_4	SO_2	$C_6H_{12}O_6$	O_3
Mass	–	6.4g	–	–
No. of moles	2	–	–	–
No. of molecules	–	–	3.011×10^{22}	–
No. of atoms	–	–	–	9.033×10^{23}

What you have learnt

KEY TERMS

Atom : The ultimate particle of an element which shows all the properties of the element.

Molecule : The smallest particle of a substance (element or compound) which is capable of independent existence and shows all the properties of that substance.

Atomic mass unit : 1/12th the mass of a carbon-12 atom

Atomicity : Number of atoms in a molecule of an element

Mole : Represents 6.022×10^{23} particles

Chapter Summary

- The ultimate particle of all matter which cannot be further subdivided is atom.
- During a chemical reaction, the sum of the masses of the reactants and that of the products remains unchanged. This is law of conservation of mass.
- Law of definite proportion states that in a pure chemical compound, elements are always present in definite proportion by mass.
- An atom is the smallest particle of an element that may exist and retain all its chemical properties.
- A molecule is the smallest particle of an element or a compound capable of independent existence under ordinary conditions. It shows all the properties of the substance.
- A chemical formula of a compound gives its constituent elements and the number of atoms of each combining element.
- The chemical formula of a molecular compound is determined by the valency of each element.
- In ionic compounds, the chemical formula is written on the basis of charge on each ion.
- The masses of different atoms of elements may be compared on the basis of relative atomic mass scale.
- Atoms of carbon-12 isotope are assigned a relative atomic mass of 12 and relative atomic masses of all other atoms are obtained relative to the mass of carbon-12.
- One mole is 6.022×10^{23} particles. This number is known as Avogadro number (N_0)
- The mole is the amount of substance which contains the same number of particles (atoms, ions or molecules) as there are atoms in exactly 12 g of carbon-12.
- Mass of one mole molecules of a substance is its molecular mass.
- Mole is a counting unit for chemists.
- The atomic mass expressed in grams is gram atomic mass.
- The molecular mass expressed in grams is gram molecular mass.
- The formula unit mass expressed in grams is gram formula unit mass.

NCERT File *with* Answers & Hints

In-Text Questions

1. In a reaction, 5.3g of sodium carbonate reacted with 6g of ethanoic acid. The products were 2.2g of carbon dioxide, 0.9g of water and 8.2g of sodium ethanoate. Show that these observations are in agreement with the law of conservation of mass.

Sodium carbonate + Ethanoic acid ⟶ Sodium ethanoate + Water + Carbon dioxide

Ans. The chemical reaction is :

Sodium carbonate + Ethanoic acid ⟶ Sodium ethanoate + Water + Carbon dioxide

Mass of sodium carbonate = 5.3 g

Mass of ethanoic acid = 6.0 g

Total mass of reactants = 5.3 + 6.0 = 11.3 g

Mass of sodium ethanoate = 8.2 g

Mass of water = 0.9 g

Mass of carbon dioxide = 2.2 g

Total mass of products = 8.2 + 0.9 + 2.2 = 11.3 g

Since total mass of reactants is equal to total mass of products, these observations are in agreement with the law of conservation of mass.

2. Hydrogen and oxygen combine in the ratio 1 : 8 by mass to form water. What weight of oxygen gas would be required to react completely with 3 g of hydrogen gas.

Ans. 1 g of hydrogen reacts with oxygen = 8 g

∴ 3 g of hydrogen will react with oxygen = 8 × 3

= **24 g**

3. Which postulate of Dalton's atomic theory is a result of the law of conservation of mass ?

Ans. The postulate that atoms can neither be created nor destroyed in a chemical reaction.

4. Which postulate of Dalton's atomic theory can explain the law of definite proportions ?

Ans. The postulate that "atoms of various elements combine in simple whole number but fixed ratio to form compound atoms (molecules)", is the result of law of definite proportions.

5. Define the atomic mass unit.

Ans. One atomic mass unit is the mass of one twelveth $\left(\frac{1}{12}\right)$ of the mass of one atom of carbon (C^{12})

1 a.m.u. = $\frac{1}{12}$ th mass of carbon atom.

Its mass is 1.66×10^{-27} kg.

6. Why is it not possible to see an atom with a naked eye ?

Ans. An atom cannot be seen with a naked eye because its size is very verysmall. The radius of an atom is of the order of 10^{-10}m, which is too small to be seen with a naked eye.

7. Write down the formulae of
(i) sodium oxide
(ii) aluminium chloride
(iii) sodium sulphide
(iv) magnesium hydroxide

Ans. (*i*) Sodium oxide : Na (1+) ✕ O (2–) → Na_2O

(*ii*) Aluminium chloride : Al (3+) ✕ Cl (1–) → $AlCl_3$

(*iii*) Sodium sulphide : Na (1+) ✕ S (2–) → Na_2S

(*iv*) Magnesium hydroxide : Mg (2+) ✕ OH (1–) → $Mg(OH)_2$

8. Write down the names of the compounds represented by the following formulae :
(i) $Al_2(SO_4)_3$ (ii) $CaCl_2$ (iii) K_2SO_4
(iv) KNO_3 (v) $CaCO_3$

Ans. (*ii*) Aluminium sulphate (*ii*) Calcium chloride
(*iii*) Potassium sulphate (*iv*) Potassium nitrate
(*v*) Calcium carbonate

9. What is meant by the term chemical formula?

Ans. The chemical formula of a compound is the symbolic representation of its composition in terms of constituent elements and the number of atoms of each element present.

10. How many atoms are present in a
(i) H_2S molecule (ii) PO_4^{3-} ion ?

Ans. (i) H_2S molecule has two atoms of hydrogen and one atom of sulphur.

(ii) PO_4^{3-} ion has one atom of phosphorus and four atoms of oxygen.

11. Calculate the molecular masses of H_2, O_2, Cl_2, CO_2, CH_4, C_2H_6, C_2H_4, NH_3 and CH_3OH.

Ans. Molecular mass of H_2 : $2 \times 1 = 2$ u

Molecular mass of O_2 : $2 \times 16 = 32$ u

Molecular mass of Cl_2 : $2 \times 35.5 = 71$ u

Molecular mass of CH_4 : $12 + 4 \times 1 = 16$ u

Molecular mass of C_2H_6 : $2 \times 12 + 6 \times 1 = 30$ u

Molecular mass of C_2H_4 : $2 \times 12 + 4 \times 1 = 28$ u

Molecular mass of NH_3 : $1 \times 14 + 3 \times 1 = 17$ u

Molecular mass of CH_3OH : $12 + 3 \times 1 + 1 \times 16 + 1 \times 1 = 32$ u

12. Calculate the formula unit masses of ZnO, Na_2O, K_2CO_3 given atomic masses of Zn = 65u, Na = 23u, C = 12u, O = 16u, K = 39 u.

Ans. Formula unit mass of ZnO = 65 + 16 = 81 u

Formula unit mass of $Na_2O = 2 \times 23 + 1 \times 16 = 62$ u

Formula unit mass of $K_2CO_3 = 2 \times 39 + 1 \times 12 + 3 \times 16 = 138$ u

13. If one mole of carbon atoms weigh 12 g. What is the mass in gram of 1 atom of carbon ?

Ans. Mass of 1 mole of carbon atoms = 12 g

1 mole of carbon = 6.022×10^{23} atoms

6.022×10^{23} atoms of carbon has mass =12 g

$$1 \text{ atom of carbon will have mass } = \frac{12}{6.022 \times 10^{23}}$$

$$= 1.99 \times 10^{-23} \text{ g}$$

14. Which has more atoms, 100g of sodium or 100g of iron?
(at. mass : Na = 23 u, Fe = 56 u)

Ans. $$\text{No. of atoms} = \frac{\text{Given mass}}{\text{Molar mass}} \times 6.022 \times 10^{23}$$

Atomic mass of Na = 23 u

Molar mass of Na = 23 g

$$\text{No. of Na atoms} = \frac{100}{23} \times 6.022 \times 10^{23}$$

$$= 2.62 \times 10^{24}$$

Atomic mass of iron = 56 u

Molar mass of iron = 56 g

$$\text{No. of iron atoms} = \frac{100}{56} \times 6.022 \times 10^{23}$$

$$= 1.07 \times 10^{24} \text{ atoms}$$

∴ 100 g of sodium has more atoms.

Textbook Exercises

1. 0.24 g sample of compound of oxygen and boron was found by analysis to contain 0.096 g of boron and 0.144 g of oxygen. Calculate the percentage composition of the compound by weight.

Ans. Weight of the compound = 0.24 g

Weight of boron = 0.096 g

Weight of oxygen = 0.144 g

$$\text{Percentage by weight of boron} = \frac{0.096}{0.24} \times 100$$

$$= 40\%$$

$$\text{Percentage by weight of oxygen} = \frac{0.144}{0.24} \times 100$$

$$= 60\ \%$$

2. When 3.0 g of carbon is burnt in 8.00 g of oxygen, 11.00 g of carbon dioxide is produced. What mass of carbon dioxide will be formed when 3.00 g of carbon is burnt in 50.00 g of oxygen ? Which law of chemical combination will govern your answer ?

Ans. Carbon + Oxygen ⟶ Carbon dioxide

$$C + O_2 \longrightarrow CO_2$$

3.0 g of carbon + 8g of oxygen = 11g of CO_2

If 50 g of oxygen is there, only 8g of O_2 will react with 3.0 g of carbon. 50 – 8 = 42 g of oxygen will remain unreacted.

This is based on the law of constant composition.

3. What are polyatomic ions ? Give examples.

Ans. The ions which contain more than one atom and behave as a single unit are called polyatomic ions.

Examples : Ammonium ion, NH_4^+

Carbonate ion, CO_3^{2-}

4. Write the chemical formulae of the following :

(a) Magnesium chloride

(b) Calcium oxide

(c) Copper nitrate

(c) Aluminium chloride

(e) Calcium carbonate.

Ans. (a) Magnesium chloride :

Mg^{2+} Cl^- : $MgCl_2$

(b) Calcium oxide

Ca^{2+} O^{2-} : CaO

(c) Copper nitrate

Cu^{2+} NO_3^- : $Cu(NO_3)_2$

(d) Aluminium chloride

Al^{3+} Cl^- : $AlCl_3$

(e) Calcium carbonate

Ca^{2+} CO_3^{2-} : $CaCO_3$

5. Give the names of the elements present in the following compounds :

(a) Quick lime

(b) Hydrogen bromide

(c) Baking powder

(c) Potassium sulphate.

(e) Calcium carbonate.

Ans. (a) Quick lime is calcium oxide (CaO).

Elements present : Calcium (Ca) and oxygen (O).

(b) Hydrogen bromide is HBr.

Elements present : Hydrogen (H) and bromine (Br).

(c) Baking powder is sodium hydrogen carbonate ($NaHCO_3$).

Elements present : Sodium (Na), hydrogen (H), carbon (C) and oxygen (O).

(d) Potassium sulphate (K_2SO_4).

Elements present : Potassium (K), sulphur (S) and oxygen (O).

(e) Calcium carbonate is ($CaCO_3$).

Elements present : Calcium (Ca), carbon (C) and oxygen (O) :

6. Calculate the molar mass of the following substances.

(a) Ethyne, C_2H_2

(b) Sulphur molecule, S_8

(c) Phosphorus molecule, P_4 (Atomic mass of phosphorus = 31)

(d) Hydrochloric acid, HCl

(e) Nitric acid, HNO_3

Ans. (i) C_2H_2 = $2 \times 12 + 2 \times 1 = 26$ g mol^{-1}

(ii) S_8 = $8 \times 32 = 256$ g mol^{-1}

(iii) P_4 = $4 \times 31 = 124$ g mol^{-1}

(iv) HCl = $1 + 35.5 = 36.5$ g mol^{-1}

7. What is the mass of

(a) 1 mole of nitrogen atoms

(b) 4 moles of aluminium atoms (Atomic mass of aluminium = 27)

(c) 10 moles of sodium sulphite (Na_2SO_3) ?

Ans. (a) Mass of nitrogen atoms=Moles × Molar mass

$m = n \times M$

Atomic mass of N = 14 u

Molar mass of N = 14 g

$\therefore$ $m = 1 \times 14 = 14$ g

(b) Mass of Al atoms = Moles × Molar mass

$m = n \times M$

Atomic mass of Al = 27 u

Molar mass of Al = 27 g

Mass = $4 \times 27 = 108$ g

(c) Mass = No. of Moles × Molar mass

$m = n \times M$

Molecular mass of Na_2SO_3 = $2 \times 23 + 32 + 3 \times 16 = 126$ u

Molar mass of Na_2SO_3 = 126 g

Mass of Na_2SO_3 = $10 \times 126 =$ **1260 g**

8. Convert into mole.

(a) 12 g of oxygen gas

(b) 20 g of water

(c) 22 g of carbon dioxide.

Ans. *Refer Solved Example 29.*

9. What is the mass of

(a) 0.2 g of oxygen atoms ?

(b) 0.5 mole of water molecules ?

Ans. *Refer Solved Example 30.*

10. Calculate the number of molecules of sulphur (S_8) present in 16 g of solid sulphur.

Ans. Mass of 1 mole of S_8 = $8 \times 32 = 256$ g

256 of S_8 contains = 6.022×10^{23} molecules

$\therefore$ 16 g of S_8 contains = $\dfrac{6.022 \times 10^{23} \times 16}{256}$

= 3.76×10^{22} molecules.

11. Calculate the number of aluminium ions present in 0.051 g of aluminium oxide.

Ans. Molar mass of aluminium oxide, $Al_2O_3 = 2 \times 27 + 3 \times 16 = 102$ g

102 g of Al_2O_3 contains = $2 \times 6.022 \times 10^{23}$ Al^{3+} ions

0.051 g of Al_2O_3 contains = $\dfrac{2 \times 6.022 \times 10^{23}}{102}$

$= 6.022 \times 10^{20}$ Al^{3+} ions.

NCERT Exemplar Problems

Note: Multiple Choice Question (1–10) from Exemplar Problems are given Revision Exercise, Page 58

Short Answer Questions

11. Which of the following represents a correct chemical formula? Name it.

(a) CaCl **(b) $BiPO_4$**

(c) $NaSO_4$ **(d) NaS**

Ans. $BiPO_4$ represents correct formula. Its name is bismuth phosphate.

12. Write the molecular formulae for the following compounds

(a) Copper (II) bromide

(b) Aluminium (III) nitrate

(c) Calcium (II) phosphate

(d) Iron (III) sulphide

(e) Mercury (II) chloride

(f) Magnesium (II) acetate

Ans. (a) $CuBr_2$ (b) $Al(NO_3)_3$

(c) $Ca_3(PO_4)_2$ (d) Fe_2S_3

(e) $HgCl_2$ (f) $Mg(CH_3COO)_2$

13. Write the molecular formulae of all the compounds that can be formed by the combination of following ions:

Cu^{2+}, Na^+, Fe^{3+}, Cl^-, SO_4^{2-}, PO_4^{3-}

Ans. The compounds are :

$CuCl_2$, $CuSO_4$, $Cu_3(PO_4)_2$, NaCl, Na_2SO_4, Na_3PO_4, $FeCl_3$, $Fe_2(SO_4)_3$, $FePO_4$.

14. Write the cations and anions present (if any) in the following compounds:

(a) CH_3COONa **(b) NaCl**

(c) H_2 **(d) NH_4NO_3**

Ans.

	Anions	Cations
(a) CH_3COONa :	CH_3COO^-	Na^+
(b) NaCl :	Cl^-	Na^+
(c) H_2 : It is a covalent compound		
(d) NH_4NO_3	NO_3^-	NH_4^+

15. Give the formulae of the compounds formed from the following sets of elements:

(a) Calcium and fluorine

(b) Hydrogen and sulphur

(c) Nitrogen and hydrogen

(d) Carbon and chlorine

(e) Sodium and oxygen

(f) Carbon and oxygen

Ans. (a) CaF_2 (b) H_2S (c) NH_3

(d) CCl_4 (e) Na_2O (f) CO, CO_2.

16. Which of the following symbols of elements are incorrect? Give their correct symbols.

(a) Cobalt CO **(b) Carbon C**

(c) Aluminium AL (d) Helium He (e) Sodium So

Ans. (a) Incorrect, the correct symbol is Co

(b) Incorrect, the correct symbol is C

(c) Incorrect, the correct symbol is Al

(e) Incorrect, the correct symbol is Na

17. Give the chemical formulae for the following compounds and compute the ratio by mass of the combining elements in each one of them.

(a) Ammonia

(b) Carbon monoxide

(c) Hydrogen chloride

(d) Aluminium fluoride

(e) Magnesium sulphide

Ans.

(a) NH_3	$N : H \times 3$	or	$14 : 1 \times 3$	or	$14 : 3$
(b) CO	C : O	or	12 : 16	or	3 : 4
(c) HCl	H : Cl	or	1 : 35.5	or	2 : 71
(d) AlF_3	$Al : F \times 3$	or	$27 : 19 \times 3$	or	9 : 19
(e) MgS	Mg : S	or	24 : 32	or	3 : 4

18. State the number of atoms present in each of the following chemical species :

(a) CO_3^{2-} **(b) PO_4^{3-}**

(c) P_2O_5 **(d) CO**

Ans. (a) $1 + 3 = 4$ (b) $1 + 4 = 5$

(c) $2 + 5 = 7$ (d) $1 + 1 = 2$

19. What is the fraction of the mass of water due to neutrons?

Ans. No. of neutrons = 8

Mass of water = 18

Mass of 1 mole of neutrons $\simeq$ 1 g

Mass of 1 neutron = $\frac{1}{N_A}$ g

Mass of 1 molecule of water = $\frac{8}{N_A}$ g

Since there are 8 neutrons in one atom of oxygen.

Mass of 8 neutrons = $\frac{8}{N_A}$

Fraction of mass of water due to neutrons

$$= \frac{8}{N_A} \times \frac{N_A}{18} = \frac{8}{18} = \frac{4}{9}$$

20. Does the solubility of a substance change with temperature? Explain with the help of an example.

Ans. The solubility of a substance changes with temperature. The solubility, in general, increases with increase in temperature. For example, more sugar is dissolved in hot water than in cold water.

21. Classify each of the following on the basis of their atomicity.

(a) F_2 **(b)** NO_2 **(c)** N_2O **(d)** C_2H_6

(e) P_4 **(f)** H_2O_2 **(g)** P_4O_{10} **(h)** O_3

(i) HCl **(j)** CH_4 **(k)** He **(l)** Ag

Ans. (a) 2 (b) 3 (c) 3 (d) 8

(e) 4 (f) 4 (g) 14 (h) 3

(i) 2 (j) 5 (k) 1

(l) polyatomic because atoms in metals are bound to millions of atoms by metallic bonds.

22. You are provided with a fine white coloured powder which is either sugar or salt. How would you identify it without tasting?

Ans. On heating, if the powder chars, it is sugar. The other is salt.

23. Calculate the number of moles of magnesium present in a magnesium ribbon weighing 12 g. Molar atomic mass of magnesium is 24 g mol^{-1}.

Ans. Mass of magnesium ribbon = 12 g

Molar mass = 24 g mol^{-1}

No. of moles = $\frac{12}{24}$ = 0.5 mol

Long Answer Questions

24. Verify by calculating that

(a) 5 moles of CO_2 and 5 moles of H_2O do not have the same mass.

(b) 240 g of calcium and 240 g magnesium elements have a mole ratio of 3:5.

Ans. (a) Molar mass of CO_2 = 44 g mol^{-1}

Molar mass of 5 moles of CO_2 = 44 × 5 = 220 g

Molar mass of H_2O = 18 g mol^{-1}

5 moles of H_2O = 18 × 5 = 90 g

∴ 5 moles of CO_2 and 5 moles of H_2O do not have same mass.

(b) Molar mass of Ca = 40 g mol^{-1}

Moles of Ca = $\frac{240}{40}$ = 6

Molar mass of Mg = 24 g mol^{-1}

Molar of Mg = $\frac{240}{24}$ = 10

Molar ratio : 6 : 10 or 3 : 5.

25. Find the ratio by mass of the combining elements in the following compounds.

(a) $CaCO_3$ **(b)** $MgCl_2$ **(c)** H_2SO_4

(d) C_2H_5OH **(e)** NH_3 **(f)** $Ca(OH)_2$

Ans. (a) $CaCO_3$ = 40 : 12 : 16 × 3 or 40 : 12 : 48 or 10 : 3 : 12

(b) $MgCl_2$ = 24 : 35.5 × 2 or 24 : 71

(c) H_2SO_4 = 1 × 2 : 32 : 16 × 4 or 2 : 32 : 64 or 1 : 16 : 32

(d) C_2H_5OH = 12 × 2 : 1 × 6 : 16 or 24 : 6 : 16 or 12 : 3 : 8

(e) NH_3 = 14 : 1 × 3 or 14 : 3

(f) $Ca(OH)_2$ = 40 : 16 × 2 : 1 × 2 or 40 : 32 : 2 or 20 : 16 : 1

26. Calcium chloride when dissolved in water dissociates into its ions according to the following equation :

$$CaCl_2\,(aq) \longrightarrow Ca^{2+}\,(aq) + 2Cl^-\,(aq)$$

Calculate the number of ions obtained from $CaCl_2$ when 222 g of it is dissolved in water.

Ans. 1 mole of $CaCl_2$ = 111 g

Moles of $CaCl_2$ = $\frac{222}{111}$ = 2 mole

Since 1 formula unit of $CaCl_2$ gives 3 ions, 1 mole of $CaCl_2$ will give 3 moles of ions

∴ 2 moles of $CaCl_2$ would give ions = 3 × 2 = 6 mole

Now, 1 mole of ions = 6.022×10^{23}

6 mole of ions = $6.022 \times 10^{23} \times 6$

= 3.6132×10^{24} ions.

27. The difference in the mass of 100 moles each of sodium atoms and sodium ions is 5.48002 g. Compute the mass of an electron.

Ans. The difference of electrons between Na atom and Na^+ ion = 1

For 100 moles each of Na atoms and Na^+ ion, the difference will be of 100 moles of electrons.

Mass of 100 moles of electrons = 5.48002 g

Mass of 1 mole of electrons = $\frac{5.48002}{100}$

1 mole of electrons = 6.022×10^{23}

Mass of 1 electron = $\frac{5.48002}{100 \times 6.022 \times 10^{23}}$

$= 9.1 \times 10^{-28}$ g or 9.1×10^{-31} kg.

28. Cinnabar (HgS) is a prominent ore of mercury. How many grams of mercury are present in 225 g of pure HgS? Molar mass of Hg and S are 200.6 g mol^{-1} and 32 g mol^{-1} respectively.

Ans. Molar mass of HgS = 200.6 + 32 = 232.6 g

Mass of Hg in 232.6 g of HgS = 200.6 g

Mass of Hg in 225g of HgS = $\frac{200.6}{232.6} \times 225 = 194.04$ g.

29. The mass of one steel screw is 4.11g. Find the mass of one mole of these steel screws. Compare this value with the mass of the earth (5.98×10^{24} kg). Which one of the two is heavier and by how many times? *(Sample Paper 2010)*

Ans. Mass of 1 screw = 4.11 g

Mass of 1 mole or 6.022×10^{23} screws = $4.11 \times 6.022 \times 10^{23} = 2.475 \times 10^{24}$ g or 2.475×10^{21} kg

$$\frac{\text{Mass of earth}}{\text{Mass of 1 mole of screws}} = \frac{5.98 \times 10^{24} \text{kg}}{2.475 \times 10^{21} \text{kg}}$$

$= 2.4 \times 10^3$

Mass of earth is 2.4×10^3 times the mass of 1 mole of screws.

30. A sample of vitamic C is known to contain 2.58 $\times 10^{24}$ oxygen atoms. How many moles of oxygen atoms are present in the sample?

Ans. 6.022×10^{23} atoms of oxygen = 1 mole

2.58×10^{24} atoms of oxygen = $\frac{1}{6.022 \times 10^{23}} \times 2.58 \times 10^{24} = 4.28$ mol.

∴ 4.28 mole of atoms are present in the sample.

31. Raunak took 5 moles of carbon atoms in a container and Krish also took 5 moles of sodium atoms in another container of same weight. (a) Whose container is heavier? (b) Whose container has more number of atoms?

Ans. Molar mass of sodium = 23 g

Mass of 5 mole of sodium atoms = 23 × 5 = 115 g

Molar mass of carbon = 12 g

Mass of 5 moles of carbon atoms = 12 × 5 = 60 g

(*a*) Krish's container is heavier.

(*b*) Both the bags have same number of atoms because they have same number of moles of atoms.

32. Fill in the missing data in the given Table

Species	H_2O	CO_2	Na atom	$MgCl_2$
Property				
No. of moles	**2**	**—**	**—**	**0.5**
No. of particles	**—**	**3.011×10^{23}**	**—**	**—**
Mass	**36 g**	**—**	**115 g**	**—**

Ans.

Species	H_2O	CO_2	Na atom	$MgCl_2$
Property				
No. of moles	2	0.5	5	0.5
No. of particles	1.2044×10^{24}	3.011×10^{23}	3.011×10^{24}	3.011×10^{23}
Mass	36 g	22 g	115 g	47.5 g

33. The visible universe is estimated to contain 10^{22} stars. How many moles of stars are present in the visible universe?

Ans. 6.022×10^{23} stars = 1 mole

No. of moles of stars = $\frac{10^{22}}{6.022 \times 10^{23}} = 0.0166$ moles.

34. What is the SI prefix for each of the following multiples and submultiples of a unit?

(*a*) 10^3 **(*b*) 10^{-1}**

(*c*) 10^{-2} **(*d*) 10^{-6}**

(*e*) 10^{-9} **(*f*) 10^{-12}**

Ans. (*a*) kilo (*b*) deci

(*c*) centi (*d*) micro

(*e*) nano (*f*) pico

35. Express each of the following in kilograms:

(*a*) 5.84×10^{-3} mg **(*b*) 58.34 g**

(*c*) 0.584 g **(*d*) 5.873×10^{-21} g**

Ans. (*a*) 5.84×10^{-3} mg $= 5.84 \times 10^{-3} \times 10^{-3} \times 10^{-3} = 5.84 \times 10^{-9}$ kg

(*b*) 58.34 g $= 58.34 \times 10^{-3} = 5.834 \times 10^{-2}$ kg

(*c*) 0.584 g $= 0.584 \times 10^{-3} = 5.84 \times 10^{-4}$ kg

(*d*) 5.873×10^{-21}g $= 5.873 \times 10^{-21} \times 10^{-3} = 5.873 \times 10^{-24}$ kg.

36. Compute the difference in masses of 10^3 moles each of magnesium atoms and magnesium ions. (Mass of an electron = 9.1×10^{-31} kg)

Ans. Mg atoms and Mg^{2+} ions differ by 2 electrons

1 mole of Mg atoms and Mg^{2+} ions differ by 2 mole of electrons

10^3 moles of Mg atoms and Mg^{2+} ions differ by 2×10^3 mole of electrons

Mass of 1 mole of electrons = $6.022 \times 10^{23} \times 9.1 \times 10^{-31}$ kg

Mass of 2.0×10^3 mole of electrons = $6.022 \times 10^{23} \times 9.1 \times 10^{-31} \times 2.0 \times 10^3$ kg
$= 1.096 \times 10^{-3}$ kg

37. Which has more number of atoms? 100g of N_2 or 100 g of NH_3

Ans. Moles of $N_2 = \dfrac{100}{28}$

No. of molecules of $N_2 = \dfrac{100}{28} \times 6.022 \times 10^{23}$

No. of atoms $= \dfrac{100}{28} \times 6.022 \times 10^{23} \times 2 = 4.301 \times 10^{24}$

Moles of $NH_3 = \dfrac{100}{17}$ mole

No. of molecules of $NH_3 = \dfrac{100}{17} \times 6.022 \times 10^{23}$

No. of atoms $= \dfrac{100}{17} \times 6.022 \times 10^{23} \times 4 = 14.169 \times 10^{28}$

∴ NH_3 has more number of atoms.

38. Compute the number of ions present in 5.85 g of sodium chloride.

Ans. Molar mass of NaCl = 23 + 35.5 = 58.5

Moles of NaCl $= \dfrac{5.85}{58.5} = 0.1$ mole

Each NaCl contains two ions (one Na^+ and one Cl^-)

Total moles of ions in 0.1 mole of NaCl = 0.2

1 mole of ions = 6.022×10^{23}

0.2 mole of ions = $6.022 \times 10^{23} \times 2$
= 1.2042×10^{24} ions.

39. A gold sample contains 90% of gold and the rest copper. How many atoms of gold are present in one gram of this sample of gold?

Ans. 1 gram of gold sample will contain gold $= \dfrac{90}{100} = 0.9$ g

Molar mass of gold = 197 g

Moles of gold $= \dfrac{0.9}{197} = 0.0046$

1 mole of gold contains atoms = 6.022×10^{23}

0.0046 mole of gold will contain atoms = $6.022 \times 10^{23} \times 0.0046 = 2.77 \times 10^{21}$

40. What are ionic and molecular compounds? Give examples.

Ans. Ionic compounds are those which contain ions (charged particles) in their molecules. The ionic compounds contain positively charged and negatively charged ions in them. For example, sodium chloride, magnesium chloride, calcium oxide are ionic compounds. On the other hand, covalent compounds are those which contain atoms in their molecules of compounds. For example water, ammonia, carbon dioxide etc. are covalent compounds.

41. Compute the difference in masses of one mole each of aluminium atoms and one mole of its ions. (Mass of an electron is 9.1×10^{-28} g). Which one is heavier?

Ans. The difference in Al atom and Al^{3+} ion is of 3 electrons because an Al atom loses 3 electrons to become Al^{3+} ion.

Mass of 1 mole of Al atoms = 27 g

For one mole of Al^{3+}, 3 moles of electrons are to be lost.

The mass of 3 mole of electrons = $3 \times 9.1 \times 10^{-28} \times 6.022 \times 10^{23} = 1.64 \times 10^{-3}$ g or 0.00164 g

Molar mass of Al^{3+} = 27 – 0.00164 = 26.9984 g

∴ Difference in mass = 27 – 26.9984 = **0.0016 g**

42. A silver ornament of mass 'm' gram is polished with gold equivalent to 1% of the mass of silver. Compute the ratio of the number of atoms of gold and silver in the ornament.

Ans. Mass of silver = m g

Mass of gold $= \dfrac{m \times 1}{100} = \dfrac{m}{100}$ g

No. of atoms of silver $= \dfrac{\text{Mass}}{\text{At. mass}} \times N_0 = \dfrac{m}{108} \times N_0$

No. of atoms of gold $= \dfrac{m}{100 \times 197} \times N_0$

Ratio of no. of atoms of gold to silver

$$\frac{m}{100 \times 197} \times N_0 : \frac{m}{108} \times N_0$$

$$108 : 100 \times 197$$

$$108 : 19700$$

$$1 : 182.41$$

43. A sample of ethane (C_2H_6) gas has the same mass as 1.5×10^{20} molecules of methane (CH_4). How many C_2H_6 molecules does the sample of gas contain?

Ans. Mass of 1 molecule of $CH_4 = \dfrac{16}{N_0}$ g

Mass of 1.5×10^{20} molecules of $CH_4 = \dfrac{1.5 \times 10^{20} \times 16}{N_0}$

Mass of 1 molecule of $C_2H_6 = \frac{30}{N_0}$ g

Now mass of molecules of C_2H_6 = Mass of molecules of $CH_4 = \frac{1.5 \times 10^{20} \times 16}{N_0}$

$\therefore$ No. of molecules of $C_2H_6 = \frac{1.5 \times 10^{20} \times 16}{N_0} \times \frac{N_0}{30}$

$= 0.8 \times 10^{20}$

44. Fill in the blanks

(a) In a chemical reaction, the sum of the masses of the reactants and products remains unchanged. This is called............... .

(b) A group of atoms carrying a fixed charge on them is called ....

(c) The formula unit mass of $Ca_3(PO_4)_2$ is ....

(d) Formula of sodium carbonate is .... and that of ammonium sulphate is ....

Ans. (a) law of mass action

(b) polyatomic ion

(c) $3 \times 40 + 2 \times 31 + 8 \times 16 = 310$

(d) Na_2CO_3, $(NH_4)_2SO_4$

45. Complete the following crossword puzzle by using the name of the chemical elements. Use the data given in Table.

Across	Down
2. The element used by Rutherford during his α–scattering experiment 3. An element which forms rust on exposure to moist air 5. A very reactive non–metal stored under water 7. Zinc metal when treated with dilute hydrochloric acid produces a gas of this element which when tested with burning splinter produces a pop sound.	1. A white lustrous metal used for making ornaments and which tends to get tarnished black in the presence of moist air 4. Both brass and bronze are alloys of the element 6. The metal which exists in the liquid state at room temperature 8. An element with symbol Pb

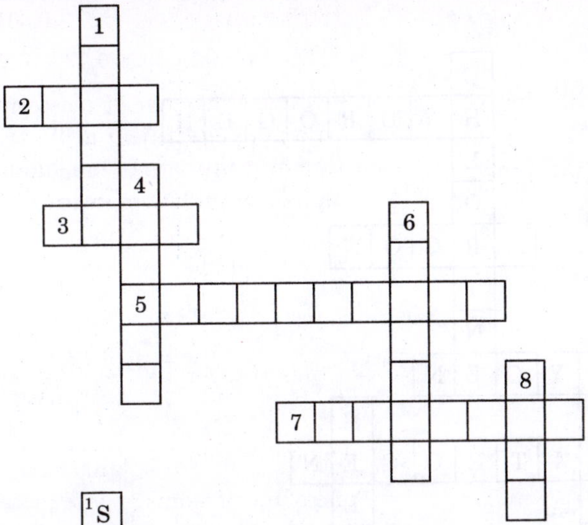

Ans.

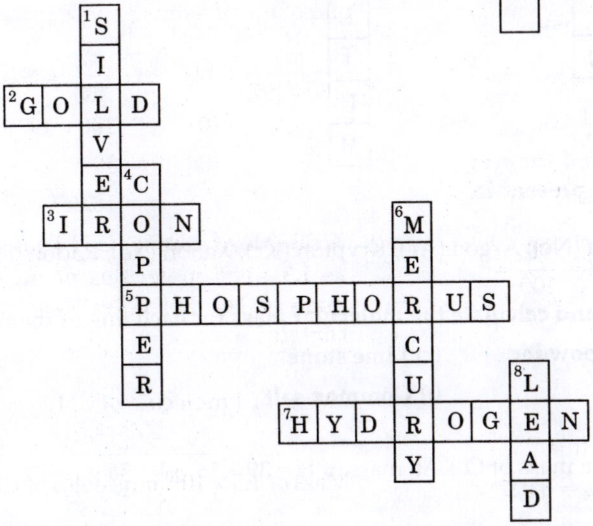

46. (*a*) **In following crossword puzzle names of 11 elements are hidden. Symbols of these are given below. Complete the puzzle.**

1. Cl 2. H 3. Ar 4. O 5. Xe 6. N 7. He
8. F 9. Kr 10. Rn 11. Ne

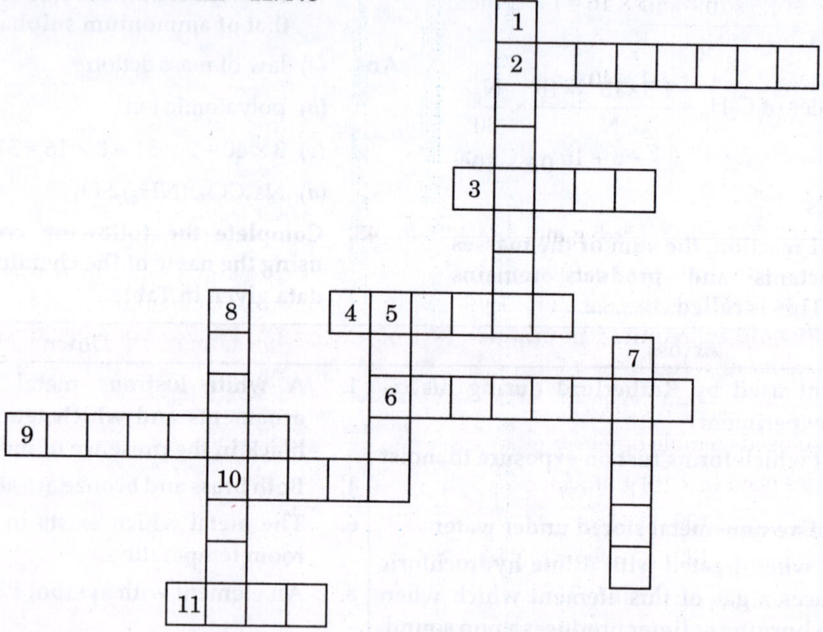

(*b*) **Identify the total number of inert gases, their names and symbols from this cross word puzzle.**

Ans. (*a*)

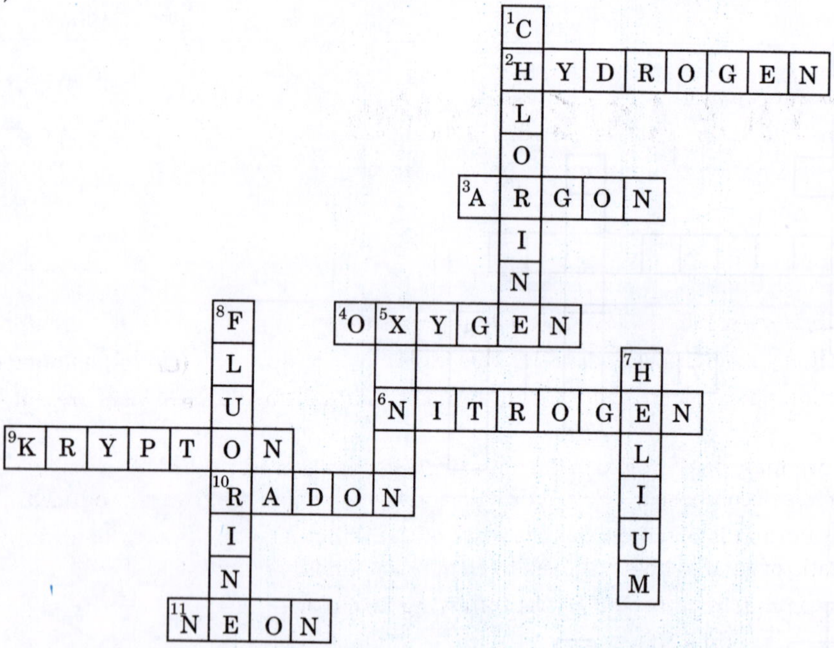

(*b*) Six noble gases. Helium (He), Neon (Ne), Argon (Ar), Krypton (Kr), Xenon (Xe); Radon (Rn)

47. **Write the formulae for the following and calculate the molecular mass for each one of them.**

(*a*) Caustic potash (*b*) Baking powder (*c*) Lime stone
(*d*) Caustic soda (*e*) Ethanol (*f*) Common salt

Ans. (*a*) Caustic potash, KOH

Molecular mass = At. mass of K + At. mass of O + At. mass of H = 39 + 16 + 1 = 56 g mol^{-1}

(*b*) Baking powder, $NaHCO_3$

Molecular mass = 23 + 1 + 12 + 3 × 16 = 84 g mol^{-1}

(*c*) Lime stone, $CaCO_3$

Molecular mass = 40 + 12 + 3 × 16 = 100 g mol^{-1}

(*d*) Caustic soda, NaOH

Molecular mass = 23 + 16 + 1 = 40 g mol^{-1}

(*e*) Ethanol, C_2H_5OH

Molecular mass = 2 × 12 + 1 × 6 + 16 = 46 g mol^{-1}

(*f*) Common salt, NaCl

Molecular mass = 23 + 35.5 = 58.5 g mol^{-1}

48. In photosynthesis, 6 molecules of carbon dioxide combine with an equal number of water molecules through a complex series of reactions to give a molecule of glucose having a molecular formula $C_6 H_{12} O_6$. How many grams of water would be required to produce 18 g of glucose? Compute the volume of water so consumed assuming the density of water to be 1 g cm^{-3}. ***(CBSE Sample Paper 2010)***

Ans. $6\,CO_2 + 6\,H_2O \longrightarrow C_6H_{12}O_6 + 6\,O_2$

1 mole of glucose needs 6 mole of water

or 180 g of glucose need (6 × 18) g of water

or 1 g of glucose needs = $\frac{108}{180}$

or 18 g of glucose would need = $\frac{108 \times 18}{180}$ = 10.8 g

Volume of water used = $\frac{\text{Mass}}{\text{Density}} = \frac{10.8\text{ g}}{1\text{ g cm}^{3}}$ = **10.8 cm³**

PRACTICE QUESTIONS

Some Solved CBSE Sample Questions

1. (*i*) State law of constant proportions.

(*ii*) Taking the example of water explain the law of constant proportions.

(*iii*) Which postulate of Dalton's atomic theory explains this law ? ***(CBSE Sample Paper 2010)***

Ans. (*i*) Law of constant proportion states that in a pure chemical substance the elements are always present in definite proportions by mass.

(*ii*) In water (H_2O), the ratio of mass of hydrogen to the mass of oxygen is always 2 : 16 or 1 : 8, whatever the source of it. Thus, if 9 g of water is decomposed, 1 g of hydrogen and 8 g of oxygen are always produced.

(*iii*) The law of constant proportion is based on the postulate of the Dalton's atomic theory, according to which atoms combine in the ratio of small whole numbers to form compounds.

2. (*i*) Write names of the compounds represented by the following formulae :

(*a*) Na_2S (*b*) KNO_3

(*ii*) Write the chemical formulae of (*a*) aluminium chloride (*b*) magnesium oxide.

(*iii*) Find out the mass of 12.044 × 10^{24} atoms of magnesium (Given the mass of Mg = 24u). ***(CBSE Sample Paper 2010)***

Ans. (*i*) (*a*) Sodium sulphide (*b*) Potassium nitrate.

(*ii*) (*a*) $AlCl_3$ (*b*) MgO

(*iii*) 6.022 × 10^{23} atoms of magnesium have mass = 24.0 g

12.044 × 10^{24} atoms of magnesium have mass = $\frac{24.0}{6.022 \times 10^{23}} \times 12.044 \times 10^{24}$ = **480 g**

3. Give the chemical formulae for the following compounds and compute the ratio by mass of the combining elements in each one of them.

(*a*) Ammonia **(*b*) Carbon monoxide**

(*c*) Hydrogen chloride **(*d*) Aluminium fluoride** ***(CBSE Sample Paper 2010)***

Ans. (*a*) Ammonia $N : H_3$

$14 : 1 \times 3$

$14 : 3$

(*b*) Carbon monoxide $C : O$

$12 : 16$

$3 : 4$

(*c*) Hydrogen chloride $H : Cl$

$1 : 35.5$

$2 : 71$

(*d*) $Al\,F_3$ $Al : F$

$27 : 19 \times 3$

$9 : 19$

4. Write the molecular formulae for the following compounds :

(*a*) Aluminium (III) nitrate

(*b*) Calcium (II) phosphate

(*c*) Mercury (II) chloride

(*d*) Magnesium (II) acetate ***(CBSE Sample Paper 2010)***

Ans. (*a*) $Al(NO_3)_3$ (*b*) $Ca_3(PO_4)_2$ (*c*) $HgCl_2$ (*d*) $Mg(CH_3COO)_2$

5. (*a*) Write chemical formula of aluminium sulphate.

(*b*) Give example each of a diatomic and tetra-atomic element molecule. ***(CBSE Sample Paper 2010)***

Ans. (*a*) Al^{3+} SO_4^{2-} or $Al_2\,(SO_4)_3$

(*b*) Diatomic element molecule : O_2

Tetra-atomic element molecule : P_4

6. A flask contains 4.4 g of CO_2 gas. Calculate

(*a*) How many moles of CO_2 gas does it contain?

(*b*) How many molecules of CO_2 gas are present in the sample?

(*c*) How many atoms of oxygen are present in the given sample? (Atomic mass of C = 12 u, O = 16 u). ***(CBSE Sample Paper 2010)***

Ans. 1 mol of CO_2 = $12 + 2 \times 16 = 44 \text{ g mol}^{-1}$

(*a*) No. of moles of CO_2 = $\dfrac{4.4\text{g}}{44\text{g mol}^{1}}$

= 0.1 mol

(*b*) No. of molecules of CO_2 = $0.1 \times 6.022 \times 10^{23}$

= 6.022×10^{22} molecules

(*c*) No. of atoms of oxygen = $2 \times 6.022 \times 10^{22}$

= 1.204×10^{23} atom

7. A sample of ammonia (NH_3) weighs 2.00 g. Calculate the mass of sulphur dioxide gas which will contain same number of molecules as 2.00 g of ammonia. (At. masses N = 14, H = 1, S = 32, O = 16). ***(CBSE 2011-12)***

Ans. Molar mass of NH_3 = $14 + 3 \times 1 = 17$ g/mol

17 g of NH_3 = 1 mol

$$2 \text{ g of } NH_3 = \frac{2}{17} \text{ mol}$$

$$\text{Molecules of } NH_3 \text{ in } \frac{2}{17} \text{ mol} = \frac{2}{17} \times 6.022 \times 10^{23} \text{ molecules}$$

$$\text{Now, molecules of } SO_2 = \text{Molecules of } NH_3$$

$$= \frac{2}{17} \times 6.022 \times 10^{23} \text{ molecules}$$

$$\text{Moles of } SO_2 = \frac{\frac{2}{17} \times 6.022 \times 10^{23}}{6.022 \times 10^{23}} = \frac{2}{17} \text{ mol}$$

$$\text{Molar mass of } SO_2 = 32 + 2 \times 16 = 64 \text{ g/mol}$$

$$\text{Now, 1 mol of } SO_2 = 64 \text{ g}$$

$$\frac{2}{17} \text{ mol of } SO_2 = \frac{64 \times 2}{17} = \mathbf{7.52 \text{ g.}}$$

8. (a) How many gram molecules of H_2SO_4 are present in 4.9 of the acid?

(b) What is the mass of 10 moles of water ? ***(CBSE 2011-12)***

Ans. (*a*)

$$\text{Gram molecular mass of } H_2SO_4 = 2 \times 1 + 32 + 4 \times 16 = 98\text{g}$$

$$98\text{g of } H_2SO_4 = 1 \text{ gram molecule}$$

$$4.9\text{g of } H_2SO_4 = \frac{1}{98} \times 4.9 = 0.05 \text{ gram molecule}$$

(*b*)

$$\text{Molecular mass of water } (H_2O) = 2 \times 1 + 16 = 18\text{u}$$

$$\text{1 mole of water} = \text{gram molecule mass of water} = 18\text{g}$$

Now,

$$\text{mass of 1 mole of water} = 18\text{g}$$

$$\text{Mass of 10 moles of water} = 18 \times 10 = 180\text{g}$$

9. (a) State the law of conservation of mass.

(b) How many atoms of hydrogen and oxygen are present in 0.15 mole of water? ***(CBSE 2011-12)***

Ans. (*a*) During any chemical change, the total mass of the products is equal to the total mass of the reactants.

(*b*)

$$\text{1 mole of water} = 6.022 \times 10^{23} \text{ molecules of } H_2O$$

$$\text{0.15 mole of water} = 6.022 \times 10^{23} \times 0.15$$

$$= 9.03 \times 10^{22} \text{ molecules of } H_2O$$

Now, 1 molecule of H_2O contains 2 hydrogen atoms and 1 oxygen atom

$\therefore$ Number of H atoms in 9.03×10^{22} molecules of H_2O

$$= 9.03 \times 10^{22} \times 2$$

$$= 1.806 \times 10^{23} \text{ H atoms}$$

Number of O atoms in 9.03×10^{22} molecules of H_2O

$$= 9.03 \times 10^{22} \times 1$$

$$= 9.03 \times 10^{22} \text{ Oxygen atoms.}$$

10. (a) Define atomic mass unit.

(b) Name a non-metal which is tetra-atomic. ***(CBSE 2011-12)***

Ans. (*a*) The quantity of mass equal to 1/12th of the mass of an atom of carbon (C-12) is called atomic mass unit.

(*b*) The non-metal is phosphorus. It exists as P_4 molecule and is tetra-atomic.

11. An element has valency 3. Write the formula of it oxide. ***(CBSE 2012-13)***

Ans. (*a*) If E is the element with valency 3 and valency of oxygen is 2 as

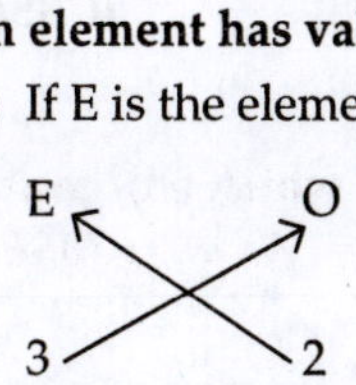

Therefore, formula of oxide of element E is E_2O_3

12. Calculate the formula unit mass of $Al_2(SO_4)_3$. *(CBSE 2012-13)*

Ans. Formula unit mass of $Al_2(SO_4)_3$

= 2 × At. mass of Al + 3 (At. mass of S + 4 × At. mass of O)

= 2 × 27 + 3 (32 + 4 × 16) = 342 u

13. What is meant by 1 amu? *(CBSE 2012-13)*

Ans. 1 amu is 1/12th the mass of an atom of carbon taken as 12 (C^{12}).

14. (a) Calculate the mass of 10 moles of sodium sulphite (Na_2SO_3).

(b) Calculate the number of molecules in 8g of oxygen gas.

(c) Convert 22g of CO_2 into moles. *(CBSE 2012-13)*

Ans. (a) Molecular mass of Na_2SO_3 = 2 × 23 + 32 + 3 × 16 = 126

We know that 1 mole of Na_2CO_3 = Gram molecular mass of Na_2CO_3

= 126g

Now, Mass of 1 mole of Na_2CO_3 = 126g

Mass of 10 moles of Na_2CO_3 = 126 × 10 = 1260g

(b) Molecular mass of O_2 = 2 × 16 = 32u

We know that,

1 mole of O_2 = Gram molecular mass of O_2

= 32g

Now, 32g of oxygen = 1 mole

8g of oxygen = $\frac{1 \times 8}{32}$ = 0.25 mole

Now, 1 mol of oxygen has 6.022×10^{23} molecules

0.25 mol of oxygen will have = $6.022 \times 10^{23} \times 0.25$

= 1.505×10^{23} molecules

(c) Molecular mass of CO_2 = 12 + 2 × 16 = 44u

We know that,

1 mole of CO_2 = Gram molecular mass of CO_2

= 44g

Now, 44g of CO_2 = 1 mol

22g of CO_2 = $\frac{1}{44} \times 22$ = 0.5 mole

15. (a) Define polyatomic ion. Give one example.

(b) Calculate the formula unit mass of $CaCO_3$ (Atomic mass of C = 12u, Ca= 40u, O = 16u)

(c) Calculate the molecular mass of the following:

(i) HNO_3 (ii) CH_3COOH *(CBSE 2013-14)*

Ans. (a) A group of atoms behaving as a single unit carrying a charge is called a polyatomic ion.

For example : SO_4^{2-} (sulphate) ion

(b) Formula unit mass of $CaCO_3$ = 40 + 12 + 3 × 16 = 100u

(c) (i) Molecular mass of HNO_3 = 1 + 14 + 3 × 16 = 63u

(ii) Molecular mass of CH_3COOH = 12 + 3 × 1 + 12 + 2 × 16 + 1 = 60u

16. How are given mass, molar mass and number of moles related to each other? *(CBSE 2013-14)*

Ans. No. of moles = $\frac{\text{Given mass}}{\text{Molar mass}}$

17. Write the formula and names of the compounds formed by the followig ions:

(a) Potassium ion and iodide ion

(b) Sodium ion and sulphide ion

(c) Aluminium ion and phosphate ion ***(CBSE 2014-15)***

Ans. (a) KI : Potassium iodide

(b) Na_2S : Sodium sulphide

(c) $AlPO_4$: Aluminium phosphate

18. What is atomicity of an element? Give two examples. ***(CBSE 2013-14)***

Ans. The atomicity of an element is the number of atoms present in one molecule of the element. For example,

Atomicity of oxygen in $O_3 = 3$

Atomicity of sulphur in $S_8 = 8$

19. A compound XH is formed by the combination of an element X with hydrogen. Find the valency of the element. Write the formula of the compound formed by the combination of

(a) X with nitrogen

(b) X with oxygen ***(CBSE 2014-15)***

Ans. In the compound XH, the valency of X is 1.

Formulae

(a) 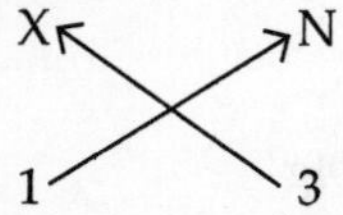

Formula : X_3N

(b) 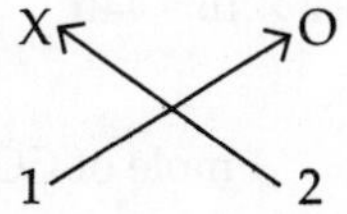

Formula : X_2O

20. Write chemical names of the following compounds:

(a) K_2SO_4 (b) $Mg_3(PO_4)_2$ (c) NH_4Cl (d) ZnS (e) Na_3N (f) AgBr ***(CBSE 2015-16)***

Ans. (a) Potassium sulphate (b) Magnesium phosphate (c) Ammonium chloride

(d) Zinc sulphide (e) Sodium nitride (f) Silver bromide

21. Calculate the formula unit mass of $Na_2CO_3.10H_2O$ ***(CBSE 2014-15)***

Ans. Formula unit mass of $Na_2CO_3.10H_2O$

$= 2 \times$ Atomic mass of Na + Atomic mass of C + $3 \times$ Atomic mass of O + $10 \times$ Molecular mass of H_2O

$= 2 \times 23 + 12 + 3 \times 16 + 10 \times 18 = 286u$

22. Calculate the number of molecules of S_8 in 128g of sulphur.

Ans. Gram molecular mass of sulphur (S_8) $= 32 \times 8 = 256g$

256g of sulphur (S_8) represent = 1 mole

128g of sulphur (S_8) represent $= \frac{1}{256} \times 128 = 0.5$ mole

1 mole of S_8 has molecules $= 6.022 \times 10^{23}$

0.5 mole of S_8 has molecules $= 6.022 \times 10^{23} \times 0.5$

$= 3.011 \times 10^{23}$

23. Calculate the number of molecules of SO_2 present in 44g of it. ***(CBSE 2014-15)***

Ans. Molecular mass of SO_2 $= 32 + 2 \times 16 = 64u$

1 mole of SO_2 = 64g

Gram molecular mass of SO_2 $= 6.022 \times 10^{23}$

64g of SO_2 have molecules $= 6.022 \times 10^{23}$

44g of SO_2 have molecules $= \frac{6.022 \times 10^{23}}{64} \times 44$

$= 4.14 \times 10^{23}$ molecules

24. What do you understand by the word 'mole'? ***(CBSE 2015-16)***

Ans. A mole represents Avogadro number i.e., 6.022×10^{23} particles.

25. (a) Calculate the molar mass of CH_3COOH.

(b) Write the molecular formula for

(i) Aluminium chloride

(ii) Ammonium nitrate ***(CBSE 2015-16)***

Ans. (*a*) Molar mass of $CH_3COOH = 12 + 3 \times 1 + 12 + 2 \times 16 + 1 = 60u$

(*b*) (*i*) Aluminium chloride : $AlCl_3$

(*ii*) Ammonium nitrate : NH_4NO_3

26. (*a*) State the law of constant proportion.

(*b*) In a compound, carbon and oxygen react in a ratio of 3 : 8 by mass to form carbon dioxide. What mass of oxygen is required to react completely with 9g of carbon? ***(CBSE 2015-16)***

Ans. (*a*) A pure chemical compound is always made up of same elements combined together in a fixed proportion by mass.

(*b*) Ratio of carbon and oxygen = 3:8

3g of carbon reacts with oxygen = 8g

9g of carbon will react oxygen = $\frac{8}{3} \times 9 = 24g$

27. (*a*) Calculate the number of molecules present in 4.4g of CO_2.

(*b*) What are polyatomic ions? Give one example. ***(CBSE 2015-16)***

Ans. (*a*) Molar mass of $CO_2 = 1 \times 12 + 2 \times 16 = 44u$

We know that,

$$1 \text{ mole of } CO_2 = \text{Gram molecular mass of } CO_2 = 44g$$
$$= 6.022 \times 10^{23} \text{ molecules}$$

Now,

$$44g \text{ of } CO_2 = 6.022 \times 10^{23} \text{ molecules}$$
$$4.4g \text{ of } CO_2 = \frac{6.022 \times 10^{23} \times 4.4}{44}$$
$$= \mathbf{6.022 \times 10^{22} \text{ molecules}}$$

(*b*) A group of atoms behaving as a single unit carrying a charge is called polyatomic ion.

For example, SO_4^{2-}, sulphate ion

28. Calculate the mass of 1 molecule of nitrogen gas. ***(CBSE 2015-16)***

Ans. (*a*) Molecular mass of nitrogen (N_2) = $2 \times 14 = 28u$

We know that,

$$1 \text{ mole of } N_2 \text{ gas} = \text{Gram molecular mass of } N_2 \text{ gas} = 28g$$
$$= 6.022 \times 10^{23} \text{ molecules}$$

Now,

$$6.022 \times 10^{23} \text{ molecules of } N_2 \text{ gas have mass} = 28 \text{ g}$$
$$\therefore \quad \text{Mass of 1 molecule of } N_2 = \frac{28}{6.022 \times 10^{23}}$$
$$= \mathbf{4.65 \times 10^{-23} g}$$

HOTS Higher Order Thinking Skill & Brain Twisting

Questions with Answers

1. Does NaCl represent the formula of sodium chloride molecule ? Why or why not ?

Ans. NaCl does not represent the formula of a sodium chloride molecule. This is because a crystal of sodium chloride consists of very large but equal number of Na^+ and Cl^- ions. The formula NaCl represents only the simplest formula of sodium chloride.

2. Suppose the chemists had selected 10^{20} as the number of particles in a mole, then what would be the molecular mass of hydrogen gas ?

Ans. According to present mole concept,

$$6.022 \times 10^{23} \text{ molecules of hydrogen weigh} = 2 \text{ g}$$

$$\text{Mass of 1 molecule of hydrogen} = \frac{2}{6.022 \times 10^{23}} = 3.32 \times 10^{-24} \text{ g}$$

If the mole contained 10^{20} particles

$$\text{Mass of 1 mole } i.e. \ 10^{20} \text{ molecules} = 3.32 \times 10^{-24} \times 10^{20} = 3.32 \times 10^{-4} \text{ g}$$

3. A sample of gold contains 12.70% of copper. What is the ratio of number of atoms of gold and copper in 1 g of gold sample. (At mass : gold = 197, copper = 63.5).

Ans.

$$\text{1 g of gold will contain copper} = \frac{12.70}{100} = 0.127$$

$$\text{Moles of copper} = \frac{0.127}{63.5} = 2 \times 10^{-3}$$

$$\text{100 g of gold contain gold} = 100 - 12.7 = 87.3$$

$$\text{1 g of gold contains gold} = \frac{87.3}{100} = 0.873\text{g}$$

$$\text{Moles of gold} = \frac{0.873}{197} = 4.43 \times 10^{-3}$$

$$\text{No. of atoms of copper} = 2 \times 10^{-3} \times 6.022 \times 10^{23}$$

$$\text{No. of atoms of gold} = 4.43 \times 10^{-3} \times 6.022 \times 10^{23}$$

Ratio of number of atoms of gold and copper

$$4.43 \times 10^{-3} \times 6.022 \times 10^{23} : 2 \times 10^{-3} \times 6.022 \times 10^{23}$$

$$4.43 : 2.0$$

$$2.215 : 1$$

4. The cost of sugar is ₹ 40 per kg. Calculate the cost of sugar per mole.

Ans.

$$\text{Molecular mass of sugar } (C_{12}H_{22}O_{11}) = 12 \times 12 + 22 \times 1 + 11 \times 16 = 342$$

Now,

$$\text{1000 g of sugar cost} = ₹\ 40$$

$$\text{342 g of sugar will cost} = \frac{40}{1000} \times 343 = ₹\ 13.68.$$

5. Calculate the total number of electrons present is 1.6 g of methane (CH_4).

Ans.

$$\text{16 g of methane contains} = 6.022 \times 10^{23} \text{ molecules}$$

$$\text{1.6 g of methane contains} = \frac{6.022 \times 10^{23}}{16} \times 1.6 = 6.022 \times 10^{22} \text{ molecules}$$

$$\text{No. of electrons in 1 molecule of methane} = 6 + 4 \times 1 = 10$$

$$\text{Total number of electrons in 1.6 g of methane} = 6.022 \times 10^{22} \times 10 = 6.022 \times 10^{23}.$$

Revision Exercise

Answers and Hints on Page 64

OBJECTIVE QUESTIONS (1 Mark each)

A. Multiple Choice Questions

I. NCERT Exemplar Problems

1. Which of the following correctly represents 360 g of water?
   (i) 2 moles of H_2O
   (ii) 20 moles of water
   (iii) 6.022×10^{23} molecules of water
   (iv) 1.2044×10^{25} molecules of water
   (a) (i) (b) (i) and (iv)
   (c) (ii) and (iii) (d) (ii) and (iv)
2. Which of the following statements is not true about an atom?
   (a) Atoms are not able to exist independently
   (b) Atoms are the basic units from which molecules and ions are formed
   (c) Atoms are always neutral in nature
   (d) Atoms aggregate in large numbers to form the matter that we can see, feel or touch
3. The chemical symbol for nitrogen gas is
   (a) Ni (b) N_2
   (c) N^+ (d) N
4. The chemical symbol for sodium is
   (a) So (b) Sd
   (c) NA (d) Na
5. Which of the following would weigh the highest?
   (a) 0.2 mole of sucrose ($C_{12}H_{22}O_{11}$)
   (b) 2 moles of CO_2
   (c) 2 moles of $CaCO_3$
   (d) 10 moles of H_2O
6. Which of the following has maximum number of atoms?
   (a) 18g of H_2O (b) 18g of O_2
   (c) 18g of CO_2 (d) 18g of CH_4
7. Which of the following contains maximum number of molecules?
   (a) 1g CO_2 (b) 1g N_2
   (c) 1g H_2 (d) 1g CH_4
8. Mass of one atom of oxygen is
   (a) $\frac{16}{6.023 \times 10^{23}}$ g (b) $\frac{32}{6.023 \times 10^{23}}$ g
   (c) $\frac{1}{6.023 \times 10^{23}}$ g (d) 8u
9. 3.42 g of sucrose are dissolved in 18g of water in a beaker. The number of oxygen atoms in the solution are:
   (a) 6.68×10^{23} (b) 6.09×10^{22}
   (c) 6.022×10^{23} (d) 6.022×10^{21}
10. A change in the physical state can be brought about
    (a) only when energy is given to the system
    (b) only when energy is taken out from the system
    (c) when energy is either given to, or taken out from the system
    (d) without any energy change

II. Additional Questions

1. The formula of silver sulphide is
   (a) AgS (b) Ag_2S
   (c) AgS_2 (d) Ag_2S_3
2. Iron exhibits the valency of
   (a) +1 (b) +2
   (c) +3 (d) +2 and +3
3. 1 mole of water is
   (a) 1g (b) 8g
   (c) 18g (d) 36g
4. What is the mass of an atom of carbon?
   (a) 12g (b) 1.2×10^{-6}g
   (c) 1.99×10^{-23}g (d) 1.99×10^{-22}g
5. Which of the formula is not correct?
   (a) Aluminium nitrate : $Al(NO_3)_3$
   (b) Aluminium sulphate : $Al_2(SO_4)_3$
   (c) Calcium phosphate : Ca_3PO_4
   (d) Chromium chloride: $CrCl_3$
6. The formula of the sulphate of an element X is XSO_4. The formula of its nitrate is
   (a) X_2NO_3 (b) $X(NO_3)_2$
   (c) $X_2(NO_3)_3$ (d) $X(NO_2)_2$
7. If 32g of sulphur has x atoms, then the number of atoms in 32g of oxygen will be
   (a) $2x$ (b) x
   (c) $\frac{x}{2}$ (d) $4x$
8. Which of the following has maximum number of atoms?
   (a) 10g of H_2O (b) 10g of O_2
   (c) 10g CH_4 (d) 10 g of CO_2

9. The total number of electrons present in 1.6g of methane (CH_4) is

(*a*) 6.022×10^{23} (*b*) 6.022×10^{24}

(*c*) 6.022×10^{22} (*d*) 6.022×10^{25}

10. Which of the following has largest number of oxygen atoms?

(*a*) 1.0 mole of O_2 (*b*) 1.0 mole of O_3

(*c*) 1.0 mole of H_2O_2 (*d*) 1.0 mole of SO_2

11. Which of the following has smallest mass ?

(*a*) 4 g of He (*b*) 6.022×10^{23} atoms of He

(*c*) 1 atom of He (*d*) 1 mole atoms of He

12. The number of moles in 6.4 g of SO_2 is :

(*a*) 1 (*b*) 0.1

(*c*) 10 (*d*) 6.4

13. The weight of 0.50 mole of CH_4 is :

(*a*) same as 0.50 mole of CO

(*b*) same as that of 0.50 mole of O_2.

(*c*) same as that of 0.125 mole of SO_2

(*d*) same as that of 1 mole of carbon.

14. The mass of a single atom of carbon is :

(*a*) 12g (*b*) $\frac{1}{12}$ g

(*c*) 1.99×10^{-23} g (*d*) 1.99×10^{23} g

15. A student wants to have 3.011×10^{23} atoms of each of sulphur and carbon elements. For this purpose, he will have to weigh

(*a*) 16g of S and 8g of C (*b*) 8g of S and 4g of C

(*c*) 16g of S and 6g of C (*d*) 32g of S and 12g of C

16. Which of the following is a polyatomic ion ?

(*a*) Zn^{2+} (*b*) PO_4^{3-}

(*c*) Mg^{2+} (*d*) Cr^{3+}

17. Which of the following is the correct symbol of an element ?

(*a*) SN (*b*) CO

(*c*) Cu (*d*) PB

18. 6.022×10^{20} atoms of silver (at. mass 108 u) weigh

(*a*) 108×10^3 g (*b*) 108 g

(*c*) 0.108 g (*d*) 10.8 g

19. Which of the following has largest number of particles?

(*a*) 8 g of CH_4 (*b*) 4.4 g of CO_2

(*c*) 34.2 g of $C_{12}H_{22}O_{11}$ (*d*) 2 g of H_2.

20. The mass of 1 u is

(*a*) $\frac{1}{12} \times \frac{1}{6.022 \times 10^{23}}$ g (*b*) $\frac{1}{6.022 \times 10^{23}}$ g

(*c*) $\frac{12}{6.022 \times 10^{23}}$ g (*d*) 6.022×10^{23} g

21. How many times 10^3 atoms of sulphur are heavier than 10^3 atoms of carbon ?

(*a*) 32 times (*b*) 6/5 times

(*c*) 8/3 times (*d*) 12 times

22. Correct formula of ferric sulphate is

(*a*) $FeSO_4$ (*b*) $Fe(SO_4)_2$

(*c*) $Fe_3(SO_4)_2$ (*d*) $Fe_2(SO_4)_3$

23. The charge on 1 electron is 1.602×10^{-19} coulombs. What will be the charge on 1 mole of electrons ?

(*a*) 1.602×10^4 coulombs (*b*) 96488 coulombs

(*c*) 964880 coulombs (*d*) 1.602×10^{-19} coulombs

24. Which of the formula is correct for an element ?

(*a*) CO (*b*) BR

(*c*) Ni (*d*) SN

25. In the formation of CO, it is found that 2.445 g of carbon combines with 3.260 g of oxygen. The atomic ratio of C and O which combines is

(*a*) 1 : 2 (*b*) 2 : 1

(*c*) 1 : 1 (*d*) 3 : 4

26. The ratio by mass of combining elements in aluminium fluoride is

(*a*) 1 : 3 (*b*) 9 : 19

(*c*) 3 : 7 (*d*) 1 : 2

27. Which of the following has largest moles ?

(*a*) 17 g of H_2O_2 (*b*) 16 g of SO_2

(*c*) 2.4 g of O_3 (*d*) 2.2 g of CO_2

29. Which has more number of atoms ?

(*a*) 10 g sodium (*b*) 10 g iron

(*c*) 10 g carbon dioxide (*d*) 10 g water

29. In carbon disulphide (CS_2), the mass of sulphur which combines with 1 g of carbon is

(*a*) 5.33 g (*b*) 8.36 g

(*c*) 10.66 g (*d*) 15.99 g

30. Match the substance in Column I with its atomicity in Column II

Column I	Column II
(P) Argon	1. Diatomic
(Q) Phosphorus	2. Triatomic
(R) Ozone	3. Monoatomic
(S) Nitrogen	4. Tetraatomic

(*a*) P–3, Q–4, R–2, S–1 (*b*) P–3, Q–1, R–2, S–4

(*c*) P–4, Q–3, R–2, S–1 (*d*) P–3, Q–2, R–1, S–4

31. Match the amount of substance in Column I with number of oxygen atoms in Column II

Column I	Column II
(P) 1 mol H_2O	1. 1.204×10^{24}
(Q) 1 mol O_2	2. 1.806×10^{24}
(R) 1 mol SO_3	3. 3.612×10^{24}

(S) 1 mol glucose ($C_6H_{12}O_6$) 4. 6.02×10^{23}

(*a*) P–4, Q–3, R–2, S–1 (*b*) P–3, Q–4, R–2, S–1

(*c*) P–4, Q–1, R–2, S–3 (*d*) P–1, Q–4, R–2, S–3

32. Match the mass of the substance in Column I with its moles in Column II

Column I	Column II
(P) 3.2 g of oxgyen gas	1. 0.25
(Q) 20 g water	2. 0.1
(R) 11 g CO_2	3. 2.5
(S) 42.5 g NH_3	4. 1.11

(*a*) P–2, Q–4, R–1, S–3 (*b*) P–3, Q–4, R–1, S–2

(*c*) P–4, Q–1, R–3, S–2 (*d*) P–2, Q–4, R–3, S–1

33. Match the molecule in Column I with the ratio of atoms by mass of elements in Column II

Column I	Column II
(P) Carbon dioxide	1. 1:8
(Q) Water	2. 14:3
(R) Sulphur dioxide	3. 3:8
(S) Ammonia	4. 1:1

(*a*) P–3, Q–2, R–4, S–1 (*b*) P–3, Q–1, R–2, S–4

(*c*) P–2, Q–3, R–4, S–1 (*d*) P–3, Q–1, R–4, S–2

B. Assertion–Reason Type Questions

For the following questions, two statements are given- one labeled *Assertion* (A) and the other labeled *Reason* (R). Select the correct answer to these questions from the codes (*a*), (*b*), (*c*) and (*d*) as given below:

(*a*) *Both A and R are true and R is correct explanation of the assertion.*

(*b*) *Both A and R are true but R is not the correct explanation of the assertion*

(*c*) *A is true but R is false.*

(*d*) *A is false but R is true.*

1. **Assertion:** Pure water obtained from different sources such as well, spring, river or sea, always contains hydrogen and oxygen combined in the ratio of 1 : 8 by mass.

   Reason: A chemical compound always contains same elements combined in same fixed proportions by mass.

2. **Assertion:** Atomic mass of sulphur is 32u.

   Reason: Carbon–12 isotope was selected as a standard.

3. **Assertion:** The formula of a metal oxide is M_2O but the formula of metal nitride is M_3N.

   Reason: The valency of metal is +1 and that of oxide and nitride are –2 and –3 respectively.

4. **Assertion:** Ammonium ion is a polyatomic ion.

   Reason: The valency of ammonium ion is +3.

5. **Assertion:** A molecule is smallest particle of a substance which is capable of independent existence.

   Reason: A molecule of H_2SO_4 contains 7 atoms.

6. **Assertion:** Molecular mass of SO_2 is double to that of O_2.

   Reason: One mole of SO_2 contains double the number of molecules present in one mole of O_2.

7. **Assertion:** Both 16 g of CH_4 and 44 g of CO_2 have same number of atoms.

   Reason: Both contain 1 g atom of carbon.

8. **Assertion:** The atomicity of sulphur is 8.

   Reason: Sulphur has 8 atoms in its molecule.

9. **Assertion:** 1 amu is $\frac{1}{12}$ th the mass of carbon –12 atom.

   Reason: The scale of relative masses of atoms is called atomic mass unit scale.

10. **Assertion:** Carbon and oxygen combine in the ratio of 3 : 8 to form carbon dioxide.

    Reason: A pure chemical compound is always made up of same elements combined together in a fixed proportions by mass.

C. Fill in the Blanks

1. The quantity of mass equal to $\frac{1}{12}$ th of the mass of an atom of carbon (C – 12) is ________.
2. The atomicity of ozone molecule is ________.
3. The valency of phosphate ion is ________.
4. An element E forms an oxide with formula E_2O_3, the formula of its sulphate is ________.
5. The molecular mass of glucose ($C_6H_{12}O_6$) is ______ u.
6. Actual mass of 1 atom of C is ________ g.
7. The ratio of molecules present in 4.4 g CO_2 and 3.2 g of SO_2 is ________.
8. The mass of 1 mol of water is ________ g.
9. The formula of sodium sulphide is ________.
10. ________ mol of NH_3 weigh 3.4 g.

D. Paragraph Based Questions

1. Answers questions 1(*a*) to 1(*d*) on the basis of your understanding of the following paragraph and the related studied concepts:

   The mass of an atom is too small to be measured even with most sensitive balance. Chemists use average relative mass to compare the atomic masses of different elements. Relative atomic mass is the weighed average mass of an atom of an element compared with one-twelfth of the mass of an atom of carbon-12. A relative atomic mass is measured using a mass spectrometer. The mass spectrometer provides the relative isotopic masses of the isotopes in an element and the isotopic abundances. The mass spectrum of an element is shown below :

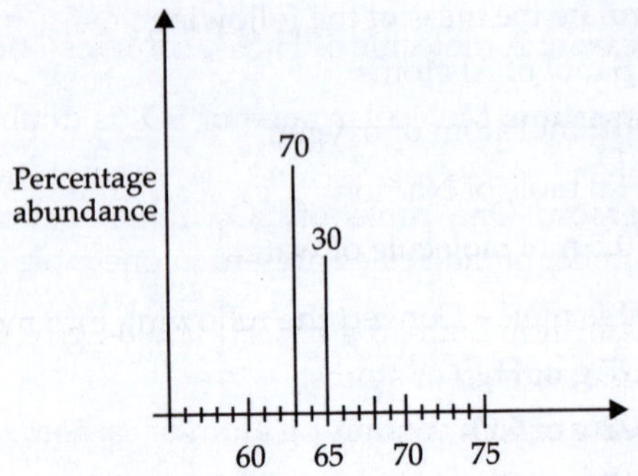

Like atomic masses, the molecular masses are also expressed relative to stable isotope of carbon (carbon-12).

1(*a*) Define atomic mass unit.

1(*b*) What is the relative atomic mass of the element whose mass spectrum is shown in the figure?

1 (*c*) Calculate the formula unit mass of $Al_2(SO_4)_3$. (atomic masses; Al = 27, S = 32)

1 (*d*) Which of the following is higher:

(*i*) Atomic mass of N

(*ii*) Molecular mass of CO_2

(*iii*) Formula unit mass of NaCl

(*iv*) Atomic mass of S

2. Atoms and molecules are too small to be seen. We cannot pick two atoms of hydrogen and one atom of oxygen to form 1 molecule of water. But we can prepare water by weighing and combining 2 g of hydrogen and 16 g of oxygen. Chemists used the term mole, which has same number of atoms as in 12 g of carbon – 12. The actual number of atoms in carbon – 12 is 6.02×10^{23}, which is a constant known as Avogadro number. The mass of 1 mole of a substance is also fixed. It is equal to the relative atomic mass of an element or relative molecular mass of a compound in grams.

2(*a*) A sample of vitamin C contain 3.10×10^{24} oxygen atoms. How many moles of oxygen atoms are present in the sample?

2(*b*) How are given mass, molar mass and moles related to each other?

2(*c*) If 1 g of carbon contains *x* atoms, what will be the number of atoms in 1 g of H_2O ?

2(*d*) Which of the following has larger mass:

(*i*) 2 mol H_2O (*ii*) 2 mol CO_2 (*iii*) 2 mol O_3

Very Short Answer Questions

1. State law of conservation of mass.
2. State law of constant proportions.
3. Name the building block of all matter.
4. What are the symbols of copper and cobalt ?
5. Name two elements whose symbols are derived from Latin names. Give their symbols.
6. What is the mass of 1 mole of water ?
7. Give symbols of lead and aluminium.
8. If 1 g of carbon contains *x* atoms, what will be the number of atoms in 1 g of magnesium ? (At. mass of C = 12, Mg = 24).
9. What is meant by 1 mol of carbon atoms ?
10. What is the molecular mass of H_2SO_4 ?
11. Which contains more molecules ?
    4 g of CH_4 or 4 g of O_2.
12. Sodium carbonate ($Na_2CO_3.10H_2O$) is an important industrial compound. Calculate its formula mass.
13. What is the mass of 1 atom of sulphur ?
14. Which of the following is tetraatomic molecule ?
    CH_3OH, CH_4, H_2O_2
15. Helium gas consists of single atoms. What mass of helium contains 6.022×10^{23} atoms ?
16. What is atomic mass unit ?
17. What is a molecule ?
18. What is the ratio by mass of nitrogen and hydrogen in ammonia ?
19. Give two examples of trivalent metal ions.
20. What is the chemical formula of calcium oxide ?
21. Complete the statement :
    1 mole of water molecules has .... molecules of water and has mass .... g.
22. Which of the following has larger mass ?
    (*i*) a mole of ammonia (NH_3)
    (*ii*) a mole of methane (CH_4)
23. How many moles of helium are present in 104 g of He ?
24. How many atoms of calcium are present in 2 g of calcium ? (at. mass of Ca = 40)
25. What is the molar mass of sulphur molecule (S_8) ?

Short Answer Questions

1. (*a*) State the following laws
   (*i*) law of conservation of mass
   (*ii*) law of constant proportions
   (*b*) Taking the example of water explain the law of constant proportions.
2. (*a*) What is mole ? How is it related to molar mass ?
   (*b*) Correct the following symbols and formulae of elements and compounds
   Lead : PB; Mercury : Me;
   Water : H_2O_2; Ammonia : HN_3
3. (*a*) Define the following :
   (*i*) Gram atomic mass
   (*ii*) Gram molecular mass.
   (*b*) Calculate the number of aluminium ions in 0.056 g of aluminium oxide (Al_2O_3).

4. Write the chemical formulae of the following :
   (i) Calcium nitrate
   (ii) Copper sulphate
   (iii) Aluminium carbonate
   (iv) Magnesium chloride
   (v) Sodium sulphate
   (vi) Silver sulphide
5. Write the names of the following compounds :
   (i) $AlPO_4$ (ii) $Ba(NO_3)_2$
   (iii) Na_2O (iv) $CuCO_3$
   (v) $CaCl_2$ (vi) $(NH_4)_2SO_3$
6. Arrange the following in the increasing order of mass :
   (i) One atom of silver
   (ii) one mole atoms of N
   (iii) 2 g of sodium
   (iv) 6.022×10^{22} atoms of calcium
7. The formula of a compound of radium is $RaBr_2$. Write the formulae of
   (i) radium carbonate
   (ii) radium sulphate
   (iii) radium nitrate
8. What are the main postulates of Dalton's atomic theory ?
9. What is an atom ? How big are atoms ?
10. Define a molecule. How many molecules are present in
   (a) 9 g of water
   (b) 17 g of ammonia ?
11. Calculate the mass of oxygen which contains same number of atoms as are present in 4.6 g of sodium. (At. mass of Na = 23, O = 16)
12. Define the following :
   (i) atom
   (ii) molecule
   (iii) atomic mass
   (iv) molecular mass.
13. What is an atom ? Give symbols for the atoms of the following elements :
   Aluminium, sodium, potassium, gold, cadmium.
14. Calculate the molar mass of the following substances :
   (i) Phosphorus molecule, P_4
   (ii) Nitric acid, HNO_3
   (iii) Sulphuric acid, H_2SO_4
   (iv) Sulphur molecule, S_8
   (v) Ethene, C_2H_4
15. Calculate the mass of the following :
   (i) 5 mol of Al atoms
   (ii) 0.2 mol atom of oxygen
   (iii) 1.5 mole of Na^+ ion
   (iv) 0.5 mol molecule of water.
16. What is mole ? Convert the following into mole :
   (i) 27 g of H_2O
   (ii) 22 g of CO_2
   (ii) 12 g of O_2
17. Write the molecular formula of the following and give the ratio by mass of atoms present.
   (i) Ammonia (ii) Water
   (iii) Carbon dioxide (iv) Sulphur dioxide
   (v) Methane
18. Calculate the number of moles in
   (i) 17 g of H_2O_2 (ii) 2.2 g of CO_2
   (iii) 16 g of SO_2 (iv) 2.4 g of O_3

Long Answer Questions

1. Explain the following terms :
   (a) Atomic mass (b) Molecular mass
   (c) Mole (d) Avogadro constant
   (e) Polyatomic ions
2. What is Dalton's atomic theory ? Give its main postulates. Which postulate of Dalton's atomic theory explain the law of conservation of mass ?
3. (a) State law of conservation of mass and law of constant proportions.
   (b) What are atoms ? How big are atoms ? How do atoms occur ?
4. Write the chemical formulae of the following compounds :
   (i) Magnesium bromide
   (ii) Sodium nitrate
   (iii) Copper sulphite
   (iv) Ammonium bicarbonate
   (v) Zinc phosphate
5. Calculate the following :
   (i) Number of S atoms in 3.2 g of S_8.
   (ii) Number of molecules of CH_4 in 80.0 g of it.
   (iii) The mass of 1 molecule of NH_3.
   (iv) The mass of 0.25 moles of calcium
   (v) Number of bromide ion in 0.2 mole of $MgBr_2$.

Solution File

Answer & Solutions to Selected Questions

Practice Exercise 3A

1. 5.8 g.

2. Mass of reactants = 14.2g; Mass of products = 14.2g

3. Both contain Cu and O in the ratio 4:1.

4. In first compound, % of metal = $\frac{2.0}{3.2} \times 100 = 62.5\%$

% of oxygen = $\frac{1.2}{3.2} \times 100 = 37.5\%$

In second compound, % of metal = $\frac{1.42}{2.27} \times 100 = 62.55\%$

% of oxygen = $\frac{0.85}{2.27} \times 100 = 37.45\%$

The percentage of metal and oxygen in metal oxide obtained from two experiments are nearly same. Hence, the data illustrates the law of definite proportions.

5. (*a*) K_2CO_3 (*b*) Na_2S (*c*) $(NH_4)_3PO_4$

6. (*i*) SO_3 (*ii*) N_2O_3 (*iii*) NH_3 (*iv*) CCl_4

7. (*i*) $CuCO_3$ (*ii*) $Ca_3(PO_4)_2$ (*iii*) $(NH_4)_2CO_3$ (*iv*) $BaSO_4$

8. (*i*) Chromium sulphate (*ii*) Potassium sulphate (*iii*) Magnesium nitrate (*iv*) Nickel sulphide

9. (*i*), (*iv*), (*v*), (*vii*)

10. (*i*) CrF_3 (*ii*) HgS (*iii*) $Pb_3(PO_4)_2$

11. (*i*) MCl (*ii*) M_2SO_4

12. (*i*) ZCl_4 (*ii*) $Z(SO_4)_2$ (*iii*) ZO_2 (*iv*) $Z(CO_3)_2$ (*v*) $Z(NO_3)_4$

13. (*i*) Na_3X (*ii*) AlX

14. 3

15. FeO, Fe_2O_3

16. $HgNO_3$, $Hg(NO_3)_2$

17. XCl_2, XCO_3

18. CuCl, $CuCl_2$

19. (*i*) +2 (*ii*) +2 (*iii*) +3 (*iv*) +2

20. (*i*) $BaCl_2$ (*ii*) $Al(NO_3)_3$ (*iii*) $Pb(MnO_4)_2$ (*iv*) NaCl (*v*) $CuSO_4$ (*vi*) $MgSO_4$ (*vii*) $Ca(NO_3)_2$ (*viii*) Ag_2S

21. (*a*) Ag_3PO_4 (*d*) $Al_2(SO_4)_3$ (*e*) Ag_2S (*f*) Cd I_2

22. (*a*) $Zn_3(PO_4)_2$ (*b*) Al (*c*) Ni (*d*) $BiPO_4$ (*e*) Ag_2S (*f*) NH_4HCO_3 (*g*) Ca (*h*) $CaCl_2$ (*i*) CaO

23. It was observed that the composition of a pure compound is always same no matter which sample of the compound is taken. For example, CO_2 obtained by different methods always contain carbon and oxygen in the ratio of 3 : 8 by weight. This led to the formulation of the law of constant composition. It is also known as law of definite composition.

24. (*i*) ammonium carbonate (*ii*) $Fe_2(SO_4)_3$ (*iii*) $Al_2(SO_3)_3$ (*iv*) potassium permanganate (*v*) $Mg_3(PO_4)_2$

25. (*i*) $Ca(ClO_3)_2$ (*ii*) $AlPO_4$ (*iii*) Mg_3N_2 (*iv*) NH_4Cl (*v*) $NaHSO_3$ (*vi*) $Al_2(SO_4)_3$

Practice Exercise 3B

1. 17.25 times
2. (*i*) 44 (*ii*) 44 (*iii*) 342 (*iv*) 63
3. 22.352 g
4. 0.45 mole
5. 666.67 mole
6. 1.5 mol of SO_2
7. Both contain same number of molecules.
8. 20 mol
9. CO_2
10. 3.01×10^{24}
11. (*i*) 2.66×10^{-23} g (*ii*) 7.31×10^{-23} g (*iii*) 9.71×10^{-23} g
12. 3.01×10^{23}
13. 342
14. Number of O atoms in P = 6.022×10^{23}, Number of O atoms in Q = 7.2×10^{23}, Flask Q contains larger number of atoms.
15. 1.2044×10^{23} H, 0.6022×10^{23} S, 2.4088×10^{23} O.
16. 11.5 g
17. 2.66×10^{-23} g
18. 4 g
19. 2.33
20. 5.54×10^{18}
21. 4.65×10^{-23} g
22. 2 : 1
23. (*i*) 5.6 g (*ii*) 2.8 g
24. 3.44×10^{-10} g
25. 3.00×10^{21}
26. (*a*) 6.323×10^{24} (*b*) 0.1 (*c*) 0.98 (*d*) 1.80 g (*e*) 2.99×10^{-23}
27. (*i*) 14 : 3 (*ii*) 3 : 8 (*iii*) 1 : 1 (*iv*) 3 : 4 (*v*) 23 : 35.5
28. (*i*) 0.005 (*ii*) 0.2 (*iii*) 0.002 (*iv*) 0.005 (*v*) 4
29. (*a*) 6 kg (*b*) 22 kg (*c*) 5.4 kg

30. 1 mol of electrons = 6.022×10^{23} electrons

Charge on 1 electron = 1.602×10^{-19} coulomb

Charge on 6.022×10^{23} electrons = $1.602 \times 10^{-19} \times 6.022 \times 10^{23}$ = 96488 coulombs

$\therefore$ Charge on 1 mol of electrons = **96488 coulombs.**

31. Molecular mass of H_2O = 18

Mass of 1 mol of H_2O = 18 g

Mass of 0.5 mol of H_2O = $18 \times 0.5 = 9$ g

Molecular mass of NH_3 = 17

Mass of 1 mol of NH_3 = 17 g

Mass of 0.5 mol of NH_3 = $17 \times 0.5 = 8.5$ g

0.5 mol of H_2O has larger mass than 0.5 mol of NH_3.

32. Mole concept gives a relationship between the number of particles (atoms, molecules, ions) and their masses. The mass of one mole of atoms in grams is one gram atomic mass and it contains 6.022×10^{23} number of atoms. The mass of one mole of molecules in grams is equal to its gram molecular mass and contains 6.022×10^{23} molecules. Similarly, in case of ionic compounds, the mass of 1 mole of formula units of the compound in grams is equal to its gram formula unit and contains 6.022×10^{23} formula units.

33. (*i*) Mass of 1 mol of water = 18 g
(*ii*) Volume of 1 mol of water = 18 mL

34. (*a*) 100 g (*c*) 0.098 g (*d*) 2.8 g

35. **line 1** : 32 g, 9 g, 24 g, **line 2** : 0.1, 0.05, 0.5, **line 3** : 12.044×10^{23}, 6.022×10^{23}, 3.011×10^{23},
line 4 : 30.11×10^{23}, 18.066×10^{22}, 72.264×10^{22}

Revision Exercise

OBJECTIVE QUESTIONS

A. Multiple Choice Questions

I. NCERT Exemplar Problems

1. (*d*) (*ii*) 20 moles of water = 20 × 18 = 360 g

(*iv*) Moles of water = $\dfrac{1.2044 \times 10^{25}}{6.022 \times 10^{23}}$ = 20 moles

20 moles of water = 20 × 18 = 360 g

2. (*a*) Noble gases exist as monoatomic.
3. (*b*) 4. (*d*)
5. (*c*) (*a*) $0.2 \times 342 = 68.4$ g (*b*) $2 \times 44 = 88$ g
(*c*) $2 \times 100 = 200$ g (*d*) $10 \times 18 = 180$ g
6. (*d*) : (*a*) $\frac{18 \times 3}{18} \times N_0 = 3\,N_0$
(*b*) $\frac{18 \times 2}{32} \times N_0 = 1.12\,N_0$
(*c*) $\frac{18 \times 3}{44} \times N_0 = 1.23\,N_0$
(*d*) $\frac{18 \times 5}{16} = 5.63\,N_0$
7. (*c*) 8. (*a*)
9. (*a*) Moles of sucrose = $\frac{3.42}{342} = 0.01$ mole
1 mol of $C_{12}H_{22}O_{11}$ contains = $11 \times N_0$ atoms of oxygen
0.01 mol of $C_{12}H_{22}O_{11}$ contains = $0.01 \times 11 \times N_0$ = $0.11\,N_0$ atoms of oxygen
Moles of water = $\frac{18}{18} = 1$ mol
1 mol of water contains = $1 \times N_0$ atoms of oxygen
Total no. of O atoms = $0.11 + 1.0 = 1.11\,N_0$
No. of O atoms in solution = $1.11 \times 6.022 \times 10^{23}$
= 6.68×10^{23}
10. (*c*)

II. Additional Questions

1. (*b*) 2. (*d*)
3. (*c*) 1 mole of water = 18 g
4. (*c*) 6.022×10^{23} atoms of C = 12 g
1 atom of C = $\frac{12}{6.022 \times 10^{23}} = 1.99 \times 10^{-23}$ g
5. (*c*) Calcium phosphate
Ca^{2+} PO_4^{3-} : $Ca_3(PO_4)_2$
6. (*b*) Valency of X is +2
Formula of nitrate is NO_3^-
∴ Formula $X^{2+}\,(NO_3^-) \Rightarrow X(NO_3)_2$
7. (*a*) 32 g of S = 1 mole = X atoms
32 g of oxygen = 2 mole = 2*x* atoms
8. (*c*) (*a*) 10 g of $H_2O = \frac{10}{18} \times N_0 \times 3$ atoms
(*b*) 10 g of $O_2 = \frac{10}{32} \times N_0 \times 2$ atoms
(*c*) 10 g of $CH_4 = \frac{10}{16} \times N_0 \times 5$ atoms
(*d*) 10 g of $CO_2 = \frac{10}{44} \times N_0 \times 3$ atoms
∴ (*c*) has maximum number of atoms.
9. (*a*) Moles of methane (CH_4) = $\frac{1.6}{16} = 0.1$ mole
No. of molecules of $CH_4 = 0.1 \times 6.022 \times 10^{23}$
One molecule of CH_4 contains = 6 + 4
=10 electrons
No. of electrons = $0.1 \times 6.022 \times 10^{23} \times 10$
= 6.022×10^{23}
10. (*b*) (*a*) 1 mole of $O_2 = 6.022 \times 10^{23} \times 2$
(*b*) 1 mole of $O_3 = 6.022 \times 10^{23} \times 3$
(*c*) 1 mole of $H_2O_2 = 6.022 \times 10^{23} \times 2$
(*d*) 1 mole of $SO_2 = 6.022 \times 10^{23} \times 2$
∴ (*b*) has largest number of oxygen atoms.
11. (*c*);
12. (*b*): 64 g of SO_2 = 1 mole
6.4 g of $SO_2 = \frac{1}{64} \times 6.4 = 0.1$ mole
13. (*c*): 1 mole of CH_4 = 16 g
0.5 mole of $CH_4 = 16 \times 0.5 = 8.0$ g
(*a*): 0.50 mole of CO = $0.50 \times 28 = 14$ g
(*b*): 0.50 mole of $O_2 = 0.5 \times 32 = 16$ g
(*c*): 0.125 mole of $SO_2 = 0.125 \times 64 = 8$ g
(*d*): 1 mole of carbon = 12 g
14. (*c*);
15. (*c*) 6.022×10^{23} atoms of S = 32g
3.011×10^{23} atoms of S = 16g
6.022×10^{23} atoms of C = 12g
3.011×10^{23} atoms of C = 6g
16. (*b*)
17. (*c*)
18. (*c*) 6.022×10^{23} atoms of Ag = 108g
6.022×10^{20} atoms of Ag = 0.108g
19. (*d*) (*a*) 16 g of $CH_4 = 6.022 \times 10^{23}$ particles
8g of $CH_4 = 3.011 \times 10^{23}$ particles
(*b*) 44g of $CO_2 = 6.022 \times 10^{23}$ particles
4.4g of $CO_2 = 6.022 \times 10^{22}$ particles
(*c*) 342 g of $C_{12}H_{22}O_{11} = 6.022 \times 10^{23}$ particles
34.2g of $C_{12}H_{22}O_{11} = 6.022 \times 10^{22}$ particles
(*d*) 2g of $H_2 = 6.022 \times 10^{23}$ particles

20. (*b*)

21. (*c*) $\frac{32}{12}$ times or $\frac{8}{3}$ times

22. (*d*) 23. (*b*) 24. (*c*)

25. (*d*) C : O

2.445 : 3.260 or 3 : 4

26. (*b*) Al : 3F

27 : 3 × 19 or 9 : 19

27. (*a*) 34g of H_2O_2 = 1 mole

17 g of H_2O_2 = 0.5 mole

(*b*) 64g of SO_2 = 1 mole

16g of SO_2 = 0.25 mole

(*c*) 48g of O_3 = 1 mole

2.4g of O_3 = 0.05 mole

(*d*) 44g of CO_2 = 1 mole

2.2g of CO_2 = 0.05 mole

28 (*d*) (*a*) 23g of Na = 6.022×10^{23} atoms

$$10\text{g of Na} = \frac{6.022 \times 10^{23}}{23} \times 10 \text{ atoms}$$

(*b*) 56g of Fe = 6.022×10^{23} atoms

$$10\text{g of Fe} = \frac{6.022 \times 10^{23}}{56} \times 10 \text{ atoms}$$

(*c*) 44g of CO_2 = 6.022×10^{23} molecules

= $6.022 \times 10^{23} \times 3$ atoms

$$10\text{g of } CO_2 = \frac{6.022 \times 10^{23} \times 3}{44} \times 10 \text{ atoms}$$

(*d*) 18 g of H_2O = 6.022×10^{23} molecules

= $6.022 \times 10^{23} \times 3$ atoms

$$10\text{g of } H_2O = \frac{6.022 \times 10^{23} \times 3}{18} \times 10 \text{ atoms}$$

∴ 10g of H_2O has maximum number of atoms.

29. (*a*) In CS_2

12g of C combines with 2 × 32g of S

$$1\text{g of C combines with S} = \frac{2 \times 32}{12} = 5.33\text{g}$$

30. (*a*) **31.** (*c*) **32.** (*a*) **33.** (**d**)

B. Assertion–Reason Type

1. (*a*) **2.** (*b*) **3.** (*a*)

4. (*c*) The valency of ammonium ion (NH_4^+) is + 1.

5. (*b*)

6. (*c*) One mole of SO_2 and 1 mol of O_2 contain same number of molecules.

7. (*a*) 16 g of CH_4 = 1 mol = 1 g atom of C

44 g of CO_2 = 1 mol = 1 g atom of C

8. (*a*) **9.** (*b*) **10.** (*a*)

C. Fill in the Blanks

1. atomic mass unit **2.** three **3.** –3

4. $E_2(SO_4)_3$ **5.** 180 **6.** 1.99×10^{-23}

7. 2:1 **8.** 18 **9.** Na_2S **10.** 0.2

D. Paragraph Based Questions

1.(*a*) The quantity of mass equal to $^1/_{12}$ th of the mass of an atom of carbon (C-12)

$$1.(b)\ \frac{70 \times 63 + 30 \times 65}{100} = 63.6$$

1.(*c*) 2 × 27 + 3 (32 + 4 × 16) = 342 u

1.(*d*) (*iii*)

2.(*a*) 6.02×10^{23} atoms of oxygen = 1 mole

$$3.01 \times 10^{24} \text{ atoms of oxygen} = \frac{1}{6.02 \times 10^{23}} \times 3.01 \times 10^{24}$$

= 5 mole

$$2(b)\ \text{No. of moles} = \frac{\text{Mass}}{\text{Molar mass}}$$

2(*c*) 2*x*

2(*d*) (*iii*)

Very Short Answer Questions

3. Atoms **4.** Cu and Co

5. (*i*) Fe for iron from ferrum

(*ii*) Na for sodium from natrium

6. 18 g **7.** Pb, Al **8.** x/2

9. 12 g **10.** 98 u **11.** CH_4

12. 286 u **13.** 5.31×10^{-23} g

14. H_2O_2 **15.** 4 g

16. 1/12th the mass of atom of carbon-12 isotope.

18. 14 : 3 **19.** Al^{3+}, Fe^{3+} **20.** CaO

21. 6.022×10^{23}, 18 g **22.** (*i*) NH_3

23. 26 **24.** 3.01×10^{22} **25.** 256 g

Short Answer Questions

2(*b*). Pb, Hg ; H_2O, NH_3 **3(*b*).** 6.612×10^{20}

4. (*i*) $Ca(NO_3)_2$ (*ii*) $CuSO_4$ (*iii*) $Al_2(CO_3)_3$ (*iv*) $MgCl_2$ (*v*) Na_2SO_4 (*vi*) Ag_2S

5. (*i*) Aluminium phosphate (*ii*) Barium nitrate (*iii*) Sodium oxide (*iv*) Copper carbonate (*v*) Calcium chloride (*vi*) Ammonium sulphite

6. (*i*) < (*ii*) < (*iii*) < (*iv*)

7. (*i*) $RaCO_3$ (*ii*) $RaSO_4$ (*iii*) $Ra(NO_3)_2$

10. (*a*) 3.01×10^{23} (*b*) 6.022×10^{23} **13.** Al, Na, K, Au, Cd.

14. (*i*) 124 (*ii*) 63 (*iii*) 98 (*iv*) 256 (*v*) 28

15. (*i*) 135g (*ii*) 6.4 (*iii*) 34.5 (*iv*) 9 g

16. (*i*) 1.5 (*ii*) 0.5 (*iii*) 0.375

17. NH_3 (14 : 3) (*ii*) H_2O (1 : 8) (*iii*) CO_2 (3 : 8) (*iv*) SO_2 (1 : 1) (*v*) CH_4 (3 : 1)

18. (*i*) 0.5 (*ii*) 0.05 (*iii*) 0.25 (*iv*) 0.05

Competition File

NTSE-SAT—Target: Scholastic Aptitude Test

1. The ratio by mass of C and O in CO_2 is
   (*a*) 1 : 2 (*b*) 3 : 14
   (*c*) 3 : 8 (*d*) 3 : 11 *(NTSE 2012-13)*

2. Which of the following is a triatomic molecule ?
   (*a*) carbon dioxide (*b*) ammonia
   (*c*) helium (*d*) sugar.

3. Which of the following has maximum number of molecules ?
   (*a*) 4 g of H_2 gas (*b*) 1 mole of H_2O
   (*c*) 3 mole of CO (*d*) 22 g of CO_2.
   (NTSE 2011-12)

4. The number of carbon atoms in 1 g of $CaCO_3$ is :
   (*a*) 6.022×10^{23} (*b*) 6.022×10^{21}
   (*c*) 3.0125×10^{22} (*d*) 1.204×10^{23}.

5. Which of the following weighs maximum ?
   (*a*) 1 mole of NH_3 (*b*) 0.5 mole of C_2H_6
   (*c*) 0.1 mole of CO_2 (*d*) 0.5 mole of H_2O.

6. The percentage of oxygen in ozone molecule is :
   (*a*) 33.3 % (*b*) 50.0%
   (*c*) 75.0% (*d*) 100.0%

7. Mg has three natural isotopes whose isotopic masses and relative abundances are respectively 23.98 (78.60%), 24.98 (10.11%) and 25.98 (11.29%). The atomic mass of Mg will be
   (*a*) 23.42 (*b*) 24.31
   (*c*) 24.95 (*d*) 23.95 *(NTSE 2012-13)*

8. Which of the following contains maximum number of molecules?
   (*a*) 1g of CO_2 (*b*) 1g of N_2
   (*c*) 1g of H_2 (*d*) 1g of CH_4
   (NTSE 2013-14)

9. Which of the following correctly represent 360g of water?
   (*i*) 2 moles of H_2O
   (*ii*) 20 moles of H_2O
   (*iii*) 6.022×10^{23} molecules of water
   (*iv*) 1.2044×10^{25} molecules of water
   (*a*) (*i*) (*b*) (*i*) and (*iv*)
   (c) (*ii*) and (*iii*) (*iv*) (*ii*) and (*iv*)
   (NTSE 2013-14)

10. The mass of neon having same number of atoms as present in 4g of calcium is (at masses : Ne = 20u, Ca = 40u)
    (*a*) 8g (*b*) 2g
    (*c*) 5g (*d*) 12g *(NTSE 2013-14)*

11. The formula of a compound is M_3X. The valencies of elements M and X are respectively
    (*a*) 1 and 3 (*b*) 3 and 1
    (*c*) 2 and 4 (*d*) 2 and 3

12. What mass of carbon dioxide (CO_2) will contain 3.01×10^{22} molecules ?
    (*a*) 22 g (*b*) 8.8 g
    (*c*) 2.2 g (*d*) 4.4 g
    (NTSE 2012-13)

13. Number of molecules in 14g of carbon monoxide is
    (*a*) 12.044×10^{23} (*b*) 6.022×10^{23}
    (*c*) 3.011×10^{23} (*d*) 1.5050×10^{23}
    (NTSE 2014-15)

14. A certain sample of element Z contains 60% of ^{69}Z and 40% of ^{71}Z. What is the relative atomic mass of element Z in the sample?
    (*a*) 69.2 (*b*) 69.8
    (*c*) 70.0 (*d*) 70.2
    (NTSE 2015-16)

15. The law of conservation of mass is valid for which of the following?
    (*i*) Reactions involving oxidation
    (*ii*) Nuclear reactions
    (*iii*) Endothermic reactions
    (*a*) (*i*) and (*iii*) (*b*) (*i*) and (*ii*)
    (*c*) (*ii*) and (*iii*) (*d*) (*ii*) only
    (NTSE 2015-16)

16. Total number of atoms in 44g of CO_2 is

(*a*) 6.02×10^{23} (*b*) 6.02×10^{24}

(*c*) 1.806×10^{24} (*d*) 18.06×10^{22}

(NTSE 2015-16)

17. Number of molecules present in 14 gm of N_2 molecule is

(*a*) 6.022×10^{23} (*b*) 3.011×10^{23}

(*c*) 1.51×10^{23} (*d*) 6.022×10^{22}

(NTSE 2017-18)

18. Formula of aluminium carbonate is

(*a*) $Al_2(CO_3)_3$ (*b*) Al_2CO_3

(*c*) Al_2HCO_3 (*d*) $AlCO_3$ *(NTSE 2017-18)*

19. The formula of sulphate of element X is $X_2(SO_4)_3$. The formula of nitride of element X is

(*a*) X_3N (*b*) XN_3

(*c*) XN (*d*) X_3N_3 *(NTSE 2018-19)*

20. Calculate the number of atoms in 0.2 mole of sodium carbonate (Na_2CO_3).

(*a*) 7.2264×10^{23} atoms (*b*) 12.044×10^{23} atoms

(*c*) 6.022×10^{23} atoms (*d*) 1.505×10^{23} atoms

(NTSE 2018-19)

ANSWERS AND HINTS (NTSE) : SAT

1. (*c*) C : O

12 : 32 or 3 : 8

2. (*a*)

3. (*a*) $2g$ of $H_2 = 6.022 \times 10^{23}$

$\therefore$ $4g$ of $H_2 = 12.044 \times 10^{23}$

(*b*) 1 mole of $H_2O = 6.022 \times 10^{23}$

(*c*) 3 mole of $CO = 3 \times 6.022 \times 10^{23}$

$= 18.066 \times 10^{23}$

(*d*) 44g of $CO_2 = 6.022 \times 10^{23}$

22g of $CO_2 = 3.011 \times 10^{23}$

4. (*b*) 100g of $CaCO_3 = 6.022 \times 10^{23}$ molecules of $CaCO_3$

$$1 \text{ g of } CaCO_3 = \frac{6.022 \times 10^{23}}{100} \times 1$$

$= 6.022 \times 10^{21}$

Since 1 molecule of $CaCO_3$ = 1 C atom

No. of carbon atoms $= 6.022 \times 10^{21}$

5. (*a*) 1 mole of NH_3 = 17 g

0.5 mole of $C_2H_6 = 0.5 \times 30 = 15$ g

0.1 mole of $CO_2 = 0.1 \times 44 = 4.4$ g

0.5 mole of $H_2O = 0.5 \times 18 = 9$ g

6. (*d*)

7. (*b*) $$\frac{23.98 \times 78.60 + 24.98 \times 10.11 + 25.98 \times 11.29}{100}$$

$= 24.31$

8. (*c*)

9. (*d*) (*i*) 1 moles of H_2O = 18g

2 moles of $H_2O = 18 \times 2 = 36$g

(*ii*) 1 mole of H_2O = 18g

20 moles of $H_2O = 18 \times 20 = 360$g

(*iii*) 6.022×10^{23} molecules of H_2O = 18g

(*iv*) 6.022×10^{23} molecules of H_2O = 18g

1.2044×10^{25} molecules of H_2O

$$= \frac{18}{6.022 \times 10^{23}} \times 1.2044 \times 10^{25}$$

$= 360$ g

10. (*b*) 40g of Ca contain atoms $= 6.022 \times 10^{23}$

$$4\text{g of Ca contain atoms} = \frac{6.022 \times 10^{23}}{40} \times 4$$

$= 6.022 \times 10^{22}$

Mass of 6.022×10^{23} atoms of Ne = 20g

Mass of 6.022×10^{22} atoms of Ne = 2g

11. (*a*)

12. (*c*) 6.022×10^{23} molecules of CO_2 has mass = 44g

3.011×10^{22} molecules of CO_2 has mass = 2.2 g

13. (*c*) 28 g of CO has molecules $= 6.022 \times 10^{23}$

14g of CO has molecules $= 3.011 \times 10^{23}$

14. (*b*) $$\text{Relative atomic mass} = \frac{60 \times 69 + 40 \times 71}{100} = 69.8$$

15. (*a*)

16. (*c*) 44g of $CO_2 = 6.022 \times 10^{23}$ molecules

Since a molecule of CO_2 contains three atoms then

No. of atoms in 44g of $CO_2 = 6.022 \times 10^{23} \times 3$

$= 1.806 \times 10^{24}$

17. (*b*) **18.** (*a*)

19. (*c*) Formula of sulphate of X = $X_2(SO_4)_3$

Valency of X = 3+

Formula of nitride of element X,

$X^{3+}N^{3-}$ = XN

20. (*a*) 1 mol of $Na_2CO_3 = 6.022 \times 10^{23}$ molecules

0.2 mol of $Na_2CO_3 = 6.022 \times 10^{23} \times 0.2$

$= 1.2044 \times 10^{23}$ molecules

1 molecule of Na_2CO_3 has 6 atoms (2Na + 1C + 3O)

No. of atoms in 0.2 mol of Na_2CO_3

$= 1.2044 \times 10^{23} \times 6$

$= 7.2264 \times 10^{23}$

TEST YOURSELF

CHAPTER PRACTICE TEST

Time allowed : 1 Hour **Maximum Marks : 20**

1. Define atomic mass unit. 1

2. Read the following paragraph and answer questions 2(*a*) – 2(*d*) on the basis of your understanding of the paragraph and the related studied concepts.

   The compounds containing metal and non-metals consist of charged particles called ions. In ionic compounds, the ions are present in a fixed ratio by mass. The formula of an ionic compound gives the simplest whole number ratio of ions present in it. The valency of an atom may be used to find out how many atoms of one element will combine with other to form a chemical formula. Three elements A, B and C exhibit the following valencies :

A	A′	B	B′	C	C′
+1,	+3	+2,	+3	+ 2,	+ 4

   (*a*) Write the chemical formula of B′ phosphate. 1

   (*b*) Which out of A or A′ has larger atomic mass 1

   (*c*) Which out of C sulphate and C′ sulphate has larger molecular mass. 1

   (*d*) Which out of A nitrate or A′ nitrate has larger number of oxygen atoms. 1

3. What mass of sulphur dioxide will contain 3.01×10^{22} molecules ? 1

   (*a*) 3.2 g (*b*) 2.2 g (*c*) 320 g (*d*) 24 g

4. Formula of aluminium phosphate is

   (*a*) $Al_2(PO_4)_3$ (*b*) $AlPO_4$ (*c*) $Al(PO_4)_3$ (*d*) $Al_3(PO_4)_2$ 1

5. The mass of single atom of carbon is

   (*a*) 1.99×10^{23} g (*b*) 12 g (*c*) $\frac{1}{12}$ g (*d*) 1.99×10^{-23} g 1

6. For the following questions two statements are given- one labeled *Assertion* (A) and the other labeled *Reason* (R). Select the correct answer to these questions from the codes (*a*), (*b*), (*c*) and (*d*) as given below:

   (*a*) Both A and R are true and R is correct explanation of the assertion

   (*b*) Both A and R are true and R is not the correct explanation of the assertion

   (*c*) A is true but R is false

   (*d*) A is false but R is true.

   Assertion : Nitrogen and oxygen combine in the ratio of 7:8 to form nitrogen dioxide..

   Reason : Atomic mass of oxygen is more than that of nitrogen. 1

7. (*a*) What is the mass of 1 mole of water.

   (*b*) Carbon and oxygen combine in the ratio of 3 : 8 by mass to form carbon dioxide. What mass of oxygen will be required to combine completely with 12g of carbon?

   (*c*) Define law of conservation of mass. Which postulate of Dalton's atomic theory is the basis of this law? 3

8. Define the following:

   (*i*) Atomic mass (*ii*) Molecular mass (*iii*) Gram atomic mass 3

9. (*a*) Explain the term 'mole' and Avogadro's number. How are they related?

   (*b*) Why is it not correct to speak a molecule of sodium chloride?

   (*c*) Correct the symbols and formulae of the following:

   (*i*) KCO_3 (*ii*) CDI_2 (*iii*) CR (*iv*) $AL(PO_4)_3$ (*v*) $CuCl_3$ (*vi*) Fe_2 5

Chapter 4

Structure of Atom

We have learnt in previous chapters that every thing is made up of atoms and molecules. The atoms and molecules are regarded as the fundamental building blocks of matter. These atoms are so small particles that they cannot be seen by naked eye or under a microscope. Naturally, many questions came to our mind. Some of these questions are :

(*i*) What is an atom made up of ?

(*ii*) What makes the atom of one element different from the atom of another element ?

(*iii*) Are the atoms indivisible as proposed by Dalton ?

To answer these questions, it would be worth while to learn the most curious question. *"What is there inside an atom?"* These questions led scientists to perform experiments and search evidences to understand the structure of atom and explain its important properties.

As we have studied, John Dalton proposed that atoms are structureless hard spherical particles. Dalton's atomic theory remained undisputed upto the end of 19th century. However, the discoveries towards the end of 19th century and early 20th century showed that atom has a complex structure and is not indivisible. These studies also showed that an atom is composed of smaller particles such as **electron, proton and neutron.** These particles are regarded as **fundamental particles** because these are the main constituents of all atoms. The presence of fundamental particles in an atom is also shown by the electrical nature of matter.

EXISTENCE OF CHARGED PARTICLES IN MATTER

We are all familiar with the electrical nature of matter. It has been known since ancient times that materials attract small objects like the bits of the paper after they have been rubbed with certain other material. For example, it was known that amber when rubbed with a piece of flannel attracts small pieces of paper. Any substance showing such attractive force was said to be electrified or to have acquired some **electric charge.**

In this chapter

To understand electric nature of matter, observe the following activities :

Activity 1

To show the existence of charged particles in matter

(*i*) Comb dry hair with a plastic comb and bring it near small pieces of paper.

Observe what happens?

(*ii*) Rub a glass rod with a silk cloth and bring it near an inflated balloon.

What do you observe ?

You will find that the plastic comb after combing dry hair will attract the small pieces of paper. Similarly, the glass rod after rubbing with silk cloth will attract the inflated balloon. These activities show that after rubbing two articles with each other, they become electrically charged.

From the above activities, we can conclude that when two bodies are rubbed together, they became electrically charged. Where does this charge come from ? Since all matter is made up of atoms, this suggests that atoms consist of charged particles.

Many scientists contributed in revealing the presence of charged particles in an atom. Among these, experimental works carried out with a device known as discharge tube led to many historic discoveries about 100 years ago.

DISCOVERY OF CATHODE RAYS AND ELECTRON

The cathode rays were discovered by J. J. Thomson, an English Physicist, at the end of 19th century during the studies of passage of electricity through gases at extremely low pressures. These studies were known as **discharge tube experiments.**

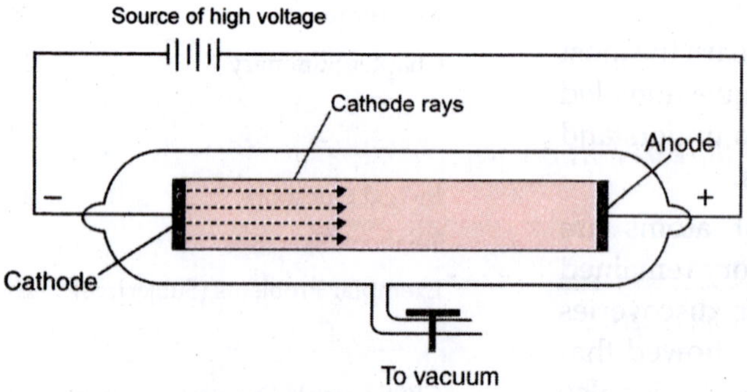

Fig. 1. Formation of cathode rays.

Under ordinary pressure, gases are bad conductors of electricity. However, when a high voltage is applied to the gases at very low pressure, the gases become conductors and electricity begins to flow in the form of rays. These rays are called **cathode rays.** The studies of cathode rays show that these rays consist of negatively charged particles known as **electrons.**

The experiment in its simplest form consists of a cylindrical hard glass tube (about 50 cm long) closed at both ends as shown in Fig. 1. It is known as discharge tube or Crookes tube. It is fitted with two metallic electrodes. The electrode connected to negative terminal of the battery is called **cathode** while the other connected to positive terminal of the battery is called **anode**. The tube is connected to a side tube, through which it can be evacuated to any desired pressure with the help of a vacuum pump. The discharge tube is filled with air or the gas under study and the two electrodes are connected to a source of high voltage. During these experiments, the following observations are made :

(*i*) A current of high voltage (about 10,000 volts) was passed through the discharge tube under normal pressure of one atmosphere. It was observed that no electricity flows through the gas.

(*ii*) The pressure of the gas inside the tube is slowly decreased by pumping out the gas with the help of a vacuum pump. When the pressure of the gas is decreased to about 10^{-2} atm, electricity started flowing through the tube. As a result, light is emitted in the tube. The colour of the light depends upon the nature of the gas taken.

(*iii*) When the pressure of the gas in the discharge tube is further reduced to about 10^{-4} atm pressure, the emission of light in the tube stops. The walls of the discharge tube opposite to the cathode started glowing with a greenish light called **fluorescence.**

It was discovered that the glowing of the tube is due to the bombardment of the glass by certain rays emitted from the cathode. These rays moved from the cathode towards the anode in the form of streaks of light. These rays were named **cathode rays** because they originate from the cathode. Further studies of cathode rays led to the conclusion that cathode rays consist of negatively charged particles. These negatively charged particles constituting the cathode rays were named **electrons.**

Thus, an **electron** ***is a negatively charged particle found in the atoms of all the elements.***

In general, an electron is represented as e or e^-

Mass and Charge of an Electron

Mass of electron. The mass of an electron is about $\frac{1}{1840}$ of the mass of a hydrogen atom. Since mass of a hydrogen atom is $\frac{1}{1840}$ *u*, we can say that the mass of an electron is u. The absolute mass of an electron is 9.1×10^{-31} kg. This mass is very small and therefore, **the mass of an electron is assumed** to be **negligible.**

Charge of electron. The absolute charge of an electron is 1.602×10^{-19} coulomb of negative charge. This charge is the smallest negative charge carried by any particle. This has been taken to be 1 unit of negative charge. Thus, an electron has **1 unit of negative charge (–1).**

An **electron** may be defined as

a subatomic particle having mass equal to $\frac{1}{1840}$ th of that of a hydrogen atom and carrying one unit negative charge.

In addition to discharge tube experiments (as discussed above) many other discoveries were made, which suggested the existence of electrons.

DISCOVERY OF CANAL RAYS OR ANODE RAYS AND PROTON

The presence of negatively charged electrons in an atom suggests that there must be some positively charged particles because the atom on the whole is electrically neutral. The existence of positively charged particles in an atom was observed by E. Goldstein in 1886. He repeated the discharge tube experiments using special perforated cathode as shown in Fig. 2. When the pressure in the tube is decreased, it was observed that in addition to cathode rays, a new kind of rays are also found. These rays travelled in opposite direction to the cathode rays and were also called **anode rays** or **canal rays** because they move from the anode. It was found that the anode rays consist of positively charged particles. Therefore, these rays were also called **positive** rays.

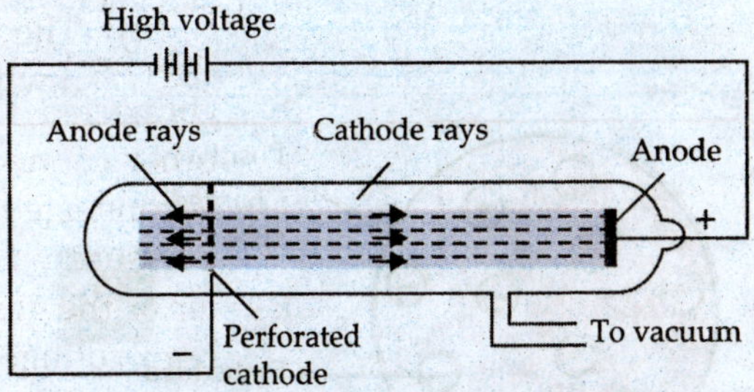

Fig. 2. Production of canal rays or anode rays (protons)

This lightest positively charged particle was named proton and is also regarded as a fundamental particle. In general, proton is represented as *p* or p^+.

It has been observed that the positively charged particles obtained from other gases are also made up of protons. This means that the atoms of other gases also contain two or more protons.

Thus, **proton** ***is a positively charged particle found in the atoms of all elements.***

Mass and Charge of a Proton

Mass of proton. The mass of proton has been found to be almost equal to that of an atom of hydrogen. Since the mass of a hydrogen atom is 1 *u*, therefore, the relative mass of a proton is also 1 *u*. If we compare the mass of a proton with that of an electron, then the mass of a proton is 1840 times that of an electron. The absolute mass of a proton is 1.67×10^{-27} kg.

Charge of proton. The charge of proton is equal and opposite to the charge of an electron. The value of charge on proton is 1.602×10^{-19} coulomb of positive charge. This is also the smallest positive charge carried by any particle. It is regarded as *one unit of positive charge.* Thus, the mass of proton is one unit positive charge (+1).

Thus, a **proton** may be defined as :
a subatomic particle having mass equal to that of a hydrogen atom (1 a.m.u.) and carrying one unit positive charge.

Thus, the formation of negatively charged cathode rays and positively charged anode rays from a gas in discharge tube suggests that an atom consists of two types of particles : electrons and protons.

The above studies showed that the atom is not indivisible as proposed by Dalton. On the other hand, it is composed of at least two types of particles namely electrons and protons. Electrons are negatively charged while protons are positively charged. Moreover, *the number of protons had to be equal to the number of electrons because the atom as a whole is electrically neutral.*

WHAT IS THE STRUCTURE OF ATOM ?

After the discovery of electron and proton, the scientists started thinking of arranging these particles in an atom. The first simple model was proposed by J.J. Thomson known as Thomson's model of an atom.

Thomson's model of an atom

In 1899, Thomson proposed that

(*i*) An atom consists of a positively charged sphere with electrons embedded in it.

(*ii*) The negative and positive charges balance each other. So the atom as a whole is neutral.

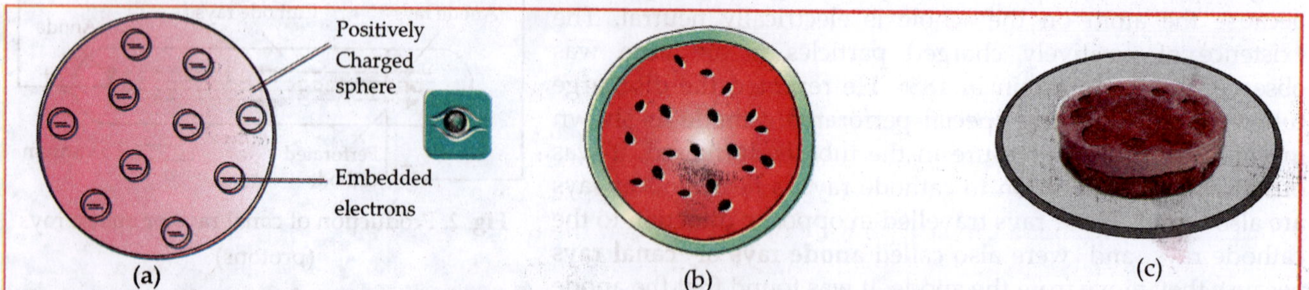

Fig. 3. (a) Thomson's model of an atom. The positively charged particles are uniformly distributed and electrons are embedded in them. Similarity of model with watermelon (b) and pudding (c).

The size of the atom had been independently established as about 10^{-10} m or 1 Å. This has been shown in Fig. 3, in which positive charge is shown uniformly distributed in a sphere of radius of about 1 Å and electrons are shown embedded in the positive charge. This model looks like a **watermelon** (*tarbooz*) or **Christmas pudding.** The electron in a sphere of positive charge were linked to currants (dry fruits) in a spherical Christmas pudding. That is why, the model was also named as *plum pudding model.*

This model explains some of the properties of atoms. It also explained that atoms are neutral. However, it was soon discarded, when Rutherford and his co-workers observed some unusual scattering of α-particles by thin metal foils. These observations are discussed below.

RUTHERFORD MODEL OF AN ATOM

Rutherford and his co-workers made a fundamental contribution in understanding the structure of the atom and establishing the presence of a small **nucleus** in the atom. They performed a number of experiments known as **scattering experiments.** They took very thin sheets of gold foil (about 1000 atoms thick) and bombarded it with a stream of alpha (α) particles. The alpha particles are positively charged helium ions (He^{2+}) which carry two units of positive charge and mass four times that of an atom of hydrogen (*i.e.,* mass of helium ions = 4 u). These are emitted from radioactive elements such as radium. Since the α-particles have a mass of 4u, the fast moving α-particles have a considerable energy.

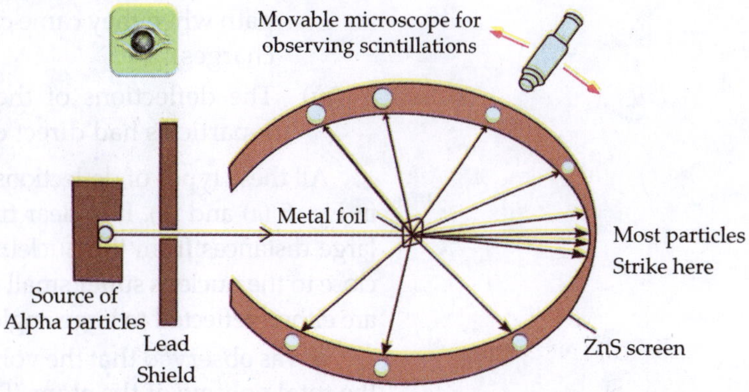

Fig. 4. Rutherford scattering experiment

The experiment employs a piece of radioactive substance (radium) placed in a lead block as shown in Fig. 4. The block is constructed in such a way with slits that only a narrow beam of α-particles could escape. The beam then passes through a thin gold foil. In order to detect the deflection of α-particles, a movable screen coated with zinc sulphide was placed around the gold foil. When α-particles strike the zinc sulphide screen, there produce flashes of light (called scintillation) which can be detected. By examining different proton of the screen, it was possible to determine the proportions of α-particles which got deflected through various angles.

Now, if our picture of uniformly packed atom is correct (as proposed by Dalton), we would expect the α-particles to pass undeflected or bend only slightly. The deflection of all the particles would have been almost same. But, what Rutherford found was amazing. He made the following important observations :

(*i*) Most of the fast moving α-particles passed straight through the gold foil without any deflection from their original path.

(*ii*) Some of the α-particles were deflected from their path through small angles.

(*iii*) Very few (about 1 in 12,000) did not pass through the foil at all but suffered large deflections (more than 90°) or even came back in the direction from which they came (just as a ball rebounds after hitting a hard wall).

Since α-particles are highly energetic particles, their scattering at large angles reflected that they had direct collision with the entire mass of the atom of the material. In the words of Rutherford, *"this result was almost as incredible as if you fire a 15 inch shell (artillery shell) at a piece of tissue paper and it cames back and hits you."*

From these observations, Rutherford guessed that the atom of gold may have a tiny part in its centre and the remaining part is mostly empty. The main conclusions of Rutherford's experiment are :

(*i*) Most of the space inside the atom is empty. Therefore, most of the α-particles went through the gold foil without deflecting from their path.

(*ii*) There is a positive tiny part in the atom in its centre, which deflects or repels the α-particles. This must be containing the whole mass of the atom. Moreover, this mass must be occupying a very small space within the atom because only a few α-particles suffered large deflections. This positively charged heavy mass in the centre of the atom is called **nucleus.** The α-particles get deflected from their normal path when they came close to nucleus due to force of repulsion (similar charges).

(*iii*) The deflections of the α-particles to large angles indicate that the α-particles had direct collision with the positively charged nucleus.

All these types of deflections of α-particles from atoms of gold foil are shown in Fig. 5 (*a*) and (*b*). It is clear from the figure that the α-particles which pass at large distances from the nucleus do not suffer any deflection, those which pass close to the nucleus suffer small deflections, while very few which hit the nucleus are either deflected to large angles or they return back to their original path.

It was observed that the volume of the nucleus is very small as compared to the total volume of the atom. The radius of the atom is of the order of 10^{-10} m, while the radius of the nucleus has been estimated to be of the order of 10^{-15} m. This means that the size of the nucleus is extremely small *i.e.,* about 10^5 times less than the size of the atom.

On the basis of the above experiment and observations, Rutherford proposed a new model known as Rutherford's nuclear model of an atom.

Rutherford's Atomic Model

The main features of Rutherford's model of an atom are :

1. The atom consists of a positively charged centre called the **nucleus.**
2. Most of the mass of the atom is concentrated in the nucleus.

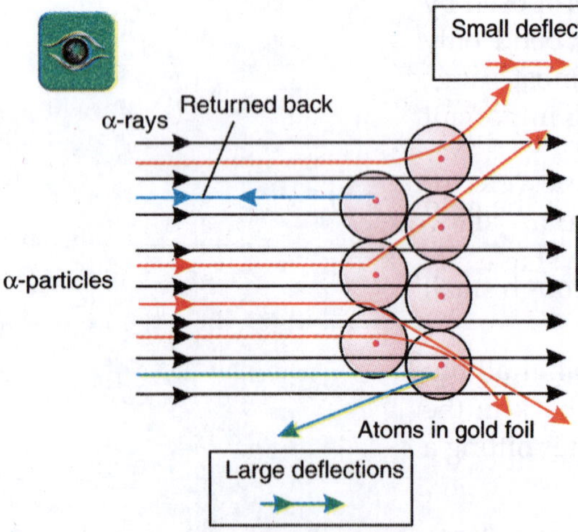

Fig. 5 (*a*). Scattering of α-particles from gold foil as proposed by Rutherford.

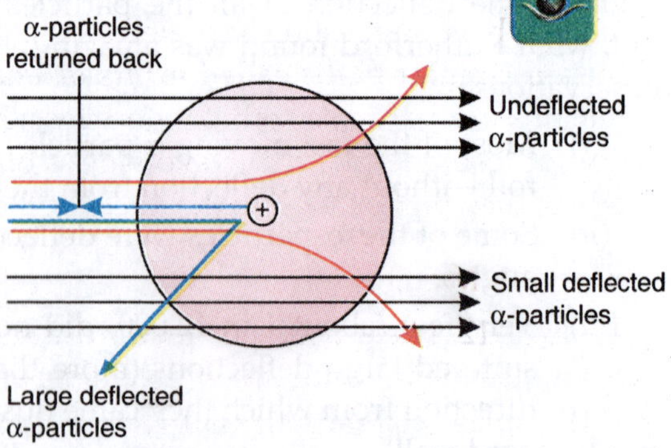

Fig. 5 (*b*). Scattering of α-particles from a single gold atom.

3. The size (or volume) of the nucleus is very small as compared to the size (or total volume) of the atom.
4. The nucleus is surrounded by the negatively charged electrons. The electrons balance the positive charge of the nucleus. Therefore, the number of electrons in an atom is equal to the number of protons in it.
5. The magnitude of the positive charge on the nucleus is different for different atoms.
6. The electrons are not stationary but they are revolving around the nucleus at very high speeds like planets revolving around the sun. As a result, the electrons are also known as *planetary electrons*.

DRAWBACK OF RUTHERFORD'S MODEL

A major drawback of Rutherford's model of an atom is that it does not explain the stability of the atom. According to Rutherford model, an atom consists of a heavy positively charged nucleus and the negatively charged electrons are revolving around it in circular path.

Rutherford suggested that electrons are revolving around the nucleus. When a particle moves in a circle it experiences a force in a direction away from the centre called centrifugal force of electron that counter balances the force of attraction between the moving electron and the nucleus.

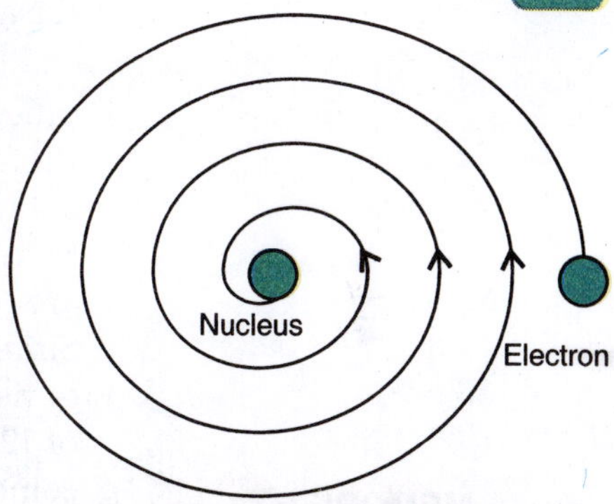

Fig. 6. Decrease in the distance between the electron and the nucleus.

However, the circular revolution of a charge is not expected to be stable. If an object moves in a circular path, its motion is said to be accelerated. According to electromagnetic theory of physics, if a charged particle undergoes accelerated motion, then it radiates energy (or loses energy) continuously. Now, if we apply this electromagnetic theory to the Rutherford model of an atom, it will mean that the negatively charged electrons revolving around the nucleus will also radiate energy continuously. The electron will lose energy at every turn and move closer and closer to the nucleus. It will take a spiral path (as shown in Fig.6) and will ultimately fall into the nucleus. In other words, atom should collapse. However, **this never happens.** We all know that electrons do not fall into the nucleus of the atom. Rather, atoms are very stable and do not collapse of their own. Therefore, Rutherford's model cannot explain the stability of an atom.

To overcome the drawback of Rutherford's model of an atom, Niels Bohr proposed a new model of the atom which was based on new concepts. He made a bold suggestion that electrons **could revolve around the nucleus in certain circular paths called orbits or energy levels.** As long as the electron remains in a particular orbit, it does lose or radiate energy. Since the electrons do not lose energy while revolving around the nucleus in certain allowed orbits, they do not fall into the nucleus. Hence the atoms remain stable.

BOHR'S MODEL OF AN ATOM

In 1912, Niels Bohr put forward a model to explain the structure of an atom. The main postulates of the model are :

1. Atom has central nucleus surrounded by electrons. The nucleus is situated at the centre of the atom.
2. The electrons in an atom revolve around the nucleus in certain fixed circular paths. These circular paths are known as **orbits** or **shells.**

3. Each orbit has fixed energy. Therefore, these orbits are also known as ***energy levels*** or ***energy shells.***
4. The orbits or energy shells are numbered as 1, 2, 3, 4, or K, L, M, N (from the nucleus). These are shown in Fig. 7.
5. As long as an electron remains in a particular orbit, it does not lose or gain energy.
6. The change in energy of an electron takes place only when it jumps from one energy level to another energy level. If the electron gains energy from outside, it jumps from lower to higher energy level. On the other hand, when it jumps from higher to lower energy level, it loses energy.

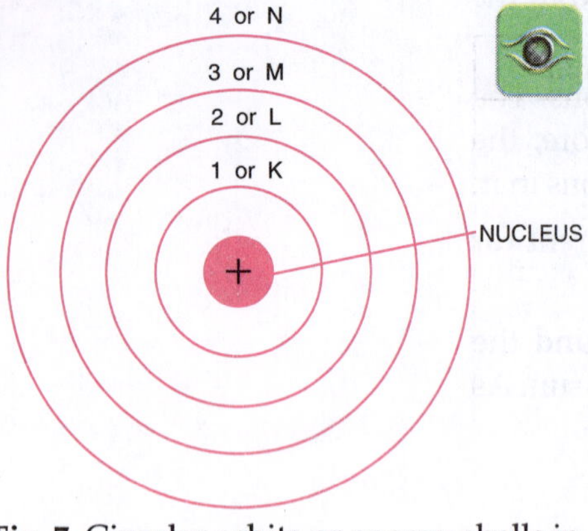

Fig. 7. Circular orbits or energy shells in an atom.

HOW WAS NEUTRON DISCOVERED?

Till 1930, it was believed that the mass of an atom is due to the mass of protons only because electron are of negligible mass.

The hydrogen atom is lightest of all atoms. It has one proton and one electron. Since the electrons are of negligible mass, the whole of the mass of the atom should be due to the protons.

The atomic mass of hydrogen is the same as that of a proton. However, in other cases, the mass of an atom cannot be accounted for on the basis of only protons present in it. For example, the next element, helium has two protons and two electrons. This means that a helium atom should be two times heavier than hydrogen. Its atomic mass should be 2, which is mass of protons (electrons are of negligible mass). This is wrong because the atomic mass of helium is 4. Similarly, magnesium has 12 protons and 12 electrons. Since the electrons are of negligible mass, the atomic mass of magnessium should be 12 (total mass of 12 protons). But the atomic mass of magnesium is 24. Naturally, a question comes to our mind, why the atomic masses of these elements are almost twice the total mass of all the protons present in the atom.

To solve the problem, it was thought that the balance of mass may be due to some neutral particles because the positive charge is already balanced by negative electrons. The neutral particle called **neutron,** was discovered by Chadwick.

In 1932, Chadwick discovered the fundamental particle neutron. Atoms of all elements contain neutrons except hydrogen atom which does not contain any neutron.

In general, neutron is represented as *n*.

MEMORISE

- All atoms except hydrogen contain neutrons.
- Hydrogen does not contain neutron.
- Neutron was discovered by Chadwick.

Characteristics of neutron

(*i*) **Mass.** The mass of the neutron is nearly equal to the mass of the proton. Since mass of proton is regarded as 1 *u*. Therefore, the mass of neutron is also 1 *u*. Its absolute mass is 1.67×10^{-27} kg equal to that of a hydrogen atom.

(*ii*) **Charge.** Neutron has no charge. It is electrically neutral.

Thus,

a neutron is a subatomic particle having mass equal to that of a hydrogen atom (1 a.m.u.) and carrying no electrical charge.

From the above discussion, it may be concluded that an atom consists of three fundamental particles. These are summarised ahead:

Table 1. Three fundamental particles

	Electron	Proton	Neutron
(*i*) Symbol	*e*	*p*	*n*
(*ii*) Nature	Negatively charged	Positively charged	Neutral
(*iii*) Relative mass	1/1840 of a H atom	equal to H atom	equal to H atom
(*iv*) Actual mass	9.1×10^{-31} kg	1.67×10^{-27} kg	1.67×10^{-27} kg
(*v*) Charge	–1 (1.602×10^{-19} C)	+1 (1.602×10^{-19} C)	No charge

ATOMIC NUMBER AND MASS NUMBER

Atoms of different elements have different number of protons in their nuclei.

The number of protons present in the nucleus of an atom of an element is known as its atomic number.

For example, an atom of carbon has 6 protons so, the atomic number of carbon is 6. The atomic number is denoted by Z. Now positive charge on the nucleus is due to the presence of protons in it and each proton carries one unit of positive charge. Therefore, the atomic number of an element is equal to number of positive charges carried by the nucleus of an atom of the element.

Thus,

Atomic number of an element (Z) = Number of protons (*p*)
= Number of positive charges carried by the nucleus of the atom

We have also learnt that the number of protons in an atom is equal to the number of electrons, since an atom, on the whole is electrically neutral. Thus, the atomic number is also equal to the number of electrons for a neutral atom. It is very important to remember that atomic number of an element is equal to the number of electrons only in a neutral atom and not in an ion. This is because only a neutral atom contains equal number of protons and electrons. On the other hand, an ion is formed by the removal of electrons from a normal atom or by the addition of electrons to a normal atom. Therefore, an ion contains either less or more electrons than protons. For example, sodium has 11 protons and 11 electrons. Therefore, atomic number of sodium is 11, which is the same as the number of protons or the number of electrons. In case of Na^+ ion, there are still 11 protons but 11 – 1 = 10 electrons. The atomic number of Na^+ ion is 11 which is equal to number of protons, but it is not equal to number of electrons in case of ions.

Sodium (Z = 11), Na : No. of protons = 11
: No. of electrons = 11

Sodium ion, Na^+ : No. of protons = 11
(one electron less than atom) No. of electrons = 10

Net charge on ion = +1

Similarly, chlorine (Z = 17), Cl : No. of protons = 17
No. of electrons = 17

MEMORISE

For positive ions

No. of protons > No. of electrons

For negative ions

No. of protons < No. of electrons

For neutral atoms

No. of protons = No. of electrons

Chloride ion, Cl^-	:	No. of protons	= 17
(One electron more than atom)		No. of electrons	= 18
		Net charge on ion	= –1

All the atoms of the same element have the same number of protons in their nuclei and therefore, they have the same atomic number. Atoms of different elements have different number of protons in their nuclei, so they have different atomic numbers. No two elements can have the same atomic number. Since each element has its own fixed atomic number, therefore, atomic number is used to identify an element. For example, atomic number 8 tells us that it is oxygen element. No other element can have atomic number of 8. Thus, it is the atomic number (or number of protons) which distinguishes the atoms of one element from the atoms of another element.

Moreover, during chemical reactions, only the electrons of an atom take part. As a result, the number of electrons may change during a chemical reaction, but the number of protons remains the same. Since the number of protons is equal to atomic number of the element, the atomic number of an element does not change during a chemical reaction.

MEMORISE

Nucleus contains protons and neutrons.

Electrons revolve outside the nucleus.

The number of protons is equal to the **Atomic number (Z)**

$Z = e = p$

The sum of neutrons and protons is equal to **Mass number (A)**

$A = p + n$

Mass Number

An atom consists of protons, neutrons and electrons. Since the mass of electrons is negligible, the mass of an atom is due to the protons and neutrons only. The mass of the atom is represented by mass number. The **mass number** is defined as :

The sum of the number of protons and neutrons in an atom of the element.

Mass number (A) = No. of protons (*p*) + No. of neutrons (*n*)

For example, helium atom has 2 protons, 2 neutrons and 2 electrons. Its mass number is equal to 2 + 2 = 4. Similarly, oxygen has 8 protons, 8 neutrons and 8 electrons. Its mass number is 16. In some cases, particularly heavier elements, the number of neutrons is more than, the number of protons. For example, mercury has atomic number equal to 80. So, it has 80 protons and 80 electrons. But the mass number of mercury is 200. Therefore, the number of neutrons in mercury is

	Mass number	=	No. of protons + No. of neutrons
	200	=	80 + No. of neutrons
∴	No. of neutrons	=	200 – 18 = 120

Generally, an atom is represented by its symbol for the element.

Atomic number is written on the lower side of the symbol and the mass number is written on the upper side.

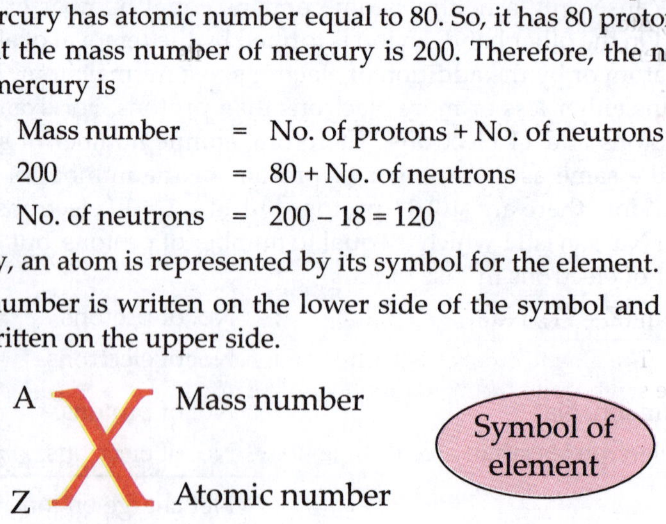

For example, $^{7}_{3}Li$ indicates that lithium has atomic number equal to 3 and mass number equal to 7.

The atomic number, mass number and the number of protons, electrons and neutrons of some elements are given in Table 2.

Table 2. Atomic number, number of electrons, protons and neutrons of some elements

Element	Atomic No. (Z)	Mass number (A)	Number of		
			Protons (*p*) = Z	Electrons (*e*) = Z	Neutrons *n* = A – Z
Hydrogen (H)	1	1	1	1	0
Helium (He)	2	4	2	2	2
Lithium (Li)	3	7	3	3	4
Beryllium (Be)	4	9	4	4	5
Boron (B)	5	11	5	5	6
Carbon (C)	6	12	6	6	6
Nitrogen (N)	7	14	7	7	7
Oxygen (O)	8	16	8	8	8
Fluorine (F)	9	19	9	9	10
Sulphur (S)	16	32	16	16	16
Mercury (Hg)	80	200	80	80	120

Solved Examples

❑ **Example 1. The atomic nucleus of an element has mass number 23 and number of neutrons 12. What is the atomic number of the element ? What is the symbol of the element ?**

Solution : We know that

Mass No. = No. of protons + No. of neutrons

23 = No. of protons + 12

∴ No. of protons = 23 – 12 = 11

Now, Atomic No. = No. of protons = 11.

The element having At. No. 11 is sodium and its symbol is Na.

❑ **Example 2. The mass number and atomic number of some elements are :**

Oxygen	**Mass No. = 16**	**Atomic No. = 8**
Chlorine	**Mass No. = 35**	**Atomic No. = 17**
Magnesiumm	**Mass No. = 24**	**Atomic No. = 12**
Mercury	**Mass No. = 200**	**Atomic No. = 80**

Give their correct representations.

Solution : The atomic number is written on the lower side of the symbol and the mass number on the upper side. Therefore,

Oxygen : $^{16}_{8}O$ Chlorine : $^{35}_{17}Cl$

Magnesium : $^{24}_{12}Mg$ Mercury : $^{200}_{80}Hg$

❑ **Example 3. Calculate the number of :**

(*i*) electrons (*ii*) protons

(*iii*) neutrons and (*iv*) nucleons in $^{39}_{19}K$.

Solution : Mass No. = 39

Atomic No. = 19

(*i*) We know that Atomic No. = No. of protons = No. of electrons

No. of electrons = 19

(*ii*) No. of protons = 19

(*iii*) Mass No. = No. of neutrons + No. of protons

No. of neutrons = Mass number – No. of protons

= 39 – 19 = 20

(*iv*) Nucleons = No. of protons + No. of neutrons

= 19 + 20 = 39

❑ **Example 4. (*i*) An atom has 13 protons and 14 neutrons. How many electrons does it contain ?**

(*ii*) Calculate the atomic number of an element E, whose atomic nucleus has mass number 39 and neutron number 20.

(*iii*) Name an atom whose nucleus does not contain neutrons.

(*iv*) An atom has 9 protons, 9 electrons and 10 neutrons. What is the symbol of the element ?

Solution :

(*i*) No. of protons = 13

No. of neutrons = 14

No. of electrons = No. of protons

∴ No. of electrons = 13

(*ii*) Mass No. $= n + p = 39$

Neutron No. $= n = 20$

∴ No. of protons $= p = 39 - 20 = 19$

∴ Atomic No. = 19

(*iii*) Hydrogen has only one electron and one proton. It does not contain neutrons.

(*iv*) No. of protons = 9

No. of electrons = 9

No. of neutrons = 10

Atomic No. = 9

Mass No. = 19

Thus, atom is fluorine and its symbol is F.

Practice Exercise 4A

Answers and Hints on Page 40

1. How many times an atom of hydrogen is heavier than an electron ?
2. What is the nature of charge on :
   (*i*) cathode rays (*ii*) anode rays ?
3. Which of the two has larger mass : electron or proton ?
4. Which of the following statements are true ?
   (*a*) In an electrical field, the cathode rays are deflected towards the negatively charged plate.
   (*b*) All atoms except hydrogen contain electrons.
   (*c*) The charges of electrons and protons are of equal magnitude.
5. What is the approximate ratio of mass of proton and electron ?
6. Give one property in which cathode rays and anode rays differ.
7. Complete the following sentences :
   (*a*) Cathode rays consist of beam of fast moving ....
   (*b*) The charge of proton is .... coulomb.
   (*c*) The mass of proton is .... times that of an electron.
   (*d*) Anode rays consist of .... charged particles.
8. Are electrons present in all matter ?
9. How does a proton differ from an electron ?
10. What is a absolute mass and charge of a proton ?
11. The nucleus of an element contains 17 protons and 18 neutrons. What is its mass number and atomic number ?
12. The atomic mass of an element is 197 and its atomic number is 79. Find the number of protons, neutrons and electrons.
13. Fill in the blanks :
    (*i*) An atom contains 22 neutrons in its nucleus and 18 electrons around it. It contains .... protons in its nucleus, its atomic number is .... and mass number is ....
    (*ii*) The neutrons and protons are collectively called ....
    (*iii*) The size of nucleus is of the order of .... m.
14. Complete the following table.

Element	*n*	*p*	*e*	Mass number	Atomic number
Be	–	4	–	9	–
Mg	12	–	12	–	–
Si	14	–	–	–	14
P	–	15	–	31	–

15. Consider the following table in which the elements from A to E are hypothetical :

Element	Protons	Neutrons	Electrons
A	9	10	9
B	17	18	17
C	10	10	10
D	6	6	6
E	17	20	17

Choose from the letters which represent :
(*i*) an element with mass number 19
(*ii*) an element having atomic number 10.

16. What does the symbol stand for ?
17. Name the fundamental particle whose relative charge is
    (*i*) +1 (*ii*) –1 (*iii*) 0
18. Complete the statement :
    The total number of protons and neutrons in the nucleus of an atom is called its ....
19. Sodium atoms have 11 electrons but 12 neutrons. Will it have any charge ?
20. Name the particles which actually determine the mass of an atom.
21. The symbol of helium atom is $^{4}_{2}He$. How many neutrons are present in He^{2+} ion ?
22. Do all atoms have same number of electrons and protons ?
23. A species contains 10 electrons and 12 protons. Is it an atom or cation or anion ?
24. An ion X^- contains 18 electrons and 18 neutrons. What is the atomic number of the element X ?

25. Who discovered neutron experimentally ?
26. (a) What is the source of α-particles in Rutherford scattering experiment ?
(b) Why did most of the α-particles pass through the gold foil undeflected ?
27. An ion M^{2+} contains 10 electrons. What is the atomic number of M?
28. Out of neutron and proton which is slightly heavier?
29. How many neutrons are present in $^{18}_{8}O$?
30. Name an element which does not contain neutrons.
31. Which metal was used by Rutherford in making thin foils?
32. In Rutherford experiment of scattering of alpha particles can we take foil of any other metal instead of gold ?
33. Who discovered the nucleus of the atom and how ?
34. Name the subatomic particles present in an atom of (i) hydrogen (ii) sodium.
35. If number of electrons in an atom are 8 and number of protons are also 8, then will the atomic number of the atom be eight or zero ?
36. What problem of atomic structure was solved by the discovery of neutron ?
37. What does $^{14}_{7}N$ represent ?
38. Name the scientists who were responsible for the following scientific development:
(a) the theory that atoms consist of small positive nuclei surrounded by electrons
(b) the theory that all substances are composed of tiny, structureless hard indestructible particles
(c) the theory that the electrons move in circular orbits around the nucleus of an atom
(d) the discovery of the existence of neutrons
(e) the existence of protons in an atom
39. We can represent an atom by the symbol $^{A}_{Z}X$. Give the meaning of
(i) X (ii) A (iii) Z
40. Complete the following table :

Particle	Mass number	Atomic number	Protons	Neutrons	Electrons
O		8		8	
Al	27				13
Cl^-	35		17		
Mg^{2+}				12	10

DISTRIBUTION OF ELECTRONS IN DIFFERENT ORBITS (SHELLS)

As studied in Bohr's model, the electrons revolve around the nucleus in certain orbits or shells. According to Bohr model, the number of electrons that can be accommodated in different orbits or shells is fixed. Now, let us come back to the question of how electrons are arranged around the nucleus in the orbits. The distribution of electrons in different orbits or shells is governed by a scheme known as **Bohr Bury scheme.** According to this scheme :

1. *The maximum number of electrons that can be present in any shell is given by the formula $2n^2$, where n is the number of energy level. Thus,*

The first orbit ($n = 1$, known as K-shell) can contain $2 \times 1^2 = 2$ electrons.

Similarly, for second orbit ($n = 2$ or L shell)

maximum number of electrons $= 2 \times (2)^2 = 8$

for third orbit ($n = 3$ or M shell)

maximum number of electrons $= 2 \times (3)^2 = 18$

for fourth orbit ($n = 4$ or N shell)

maximum number of electrons $= 2 \times (4)^2 = 32$

The distribution of electrons in first four orbits is given in Table 3.

Table 3. Maximum number of electrons in different orbits

Orbit	Value of n	Maximum no. of electrons in the orbit
K	1	$2 \times 1^2 = 2$
L	2	$2 \times 2^2 = 8$
M	3	$2 \times 3^2 = 18$
N	4	$2 \times 4^2 = 32$

2. *The maximum number of electrons that can be accommodated in the outermost shell is 8.*

This means that the outeremost orbit can take a maximum of 8 electrons only, though its maximum capacity may be 18 electrons. This is because 8 electrons in the outermost shell makes the atoms very stable. For example, if M shell is the outermost shell of an atom then it can have a maximum of 8 electrons only though its maximum capacity is 18 electrons.

3. *Electrons in an atom donot occupy a new shell unless all the inner shells are completely filled.* This means that the shells are filled in a stepwise manner (n = 1, 2, 3, 4 ..... or K, L, M, N . . . .)

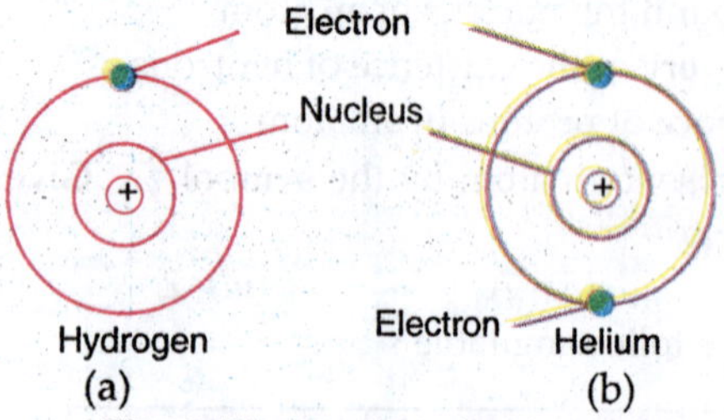

Fig. 8. Electronic arrangements in (a) Hydrogen (b) Helium

With the help of above rules, we can start building up the electrons in different energy shells for atoms. The systematic distribution of electrons in different energy shells is called the ***electronic configuration*** of the atom. Let us consider the electronic configuration of first 18 elements.

First element : hydrogen. It consists of one electron revolving around the nucleus containing one proton. Thus, one electron is present in the first (or K) shell. The distribution is shown in Fig. 8 (*a*). The electronic configuration may be written as :

Hydrogen (Z = 1, one electron) : 1 electron in 1st shell

or simply written as 1.

Second element : helium. The atomic number of helium is 2 and it contains 2 electrons in the first shell. In other words, the first shell becomes full [Fig. 8(*b*)]. The electronic configuration is:

Helium (Z = 2, two electrons) : 2 electrons in 1st shell or simply written as 2.

Since the first orbit cannot have more than 2 electrons, from lithium onwards, the next electron is added to second shell till neon, when second shell becomes completely full. From sodium onwards, the electrons are added to 3rd shell. The electronic distribution in the first 18 atoms is given in Fig. 9.

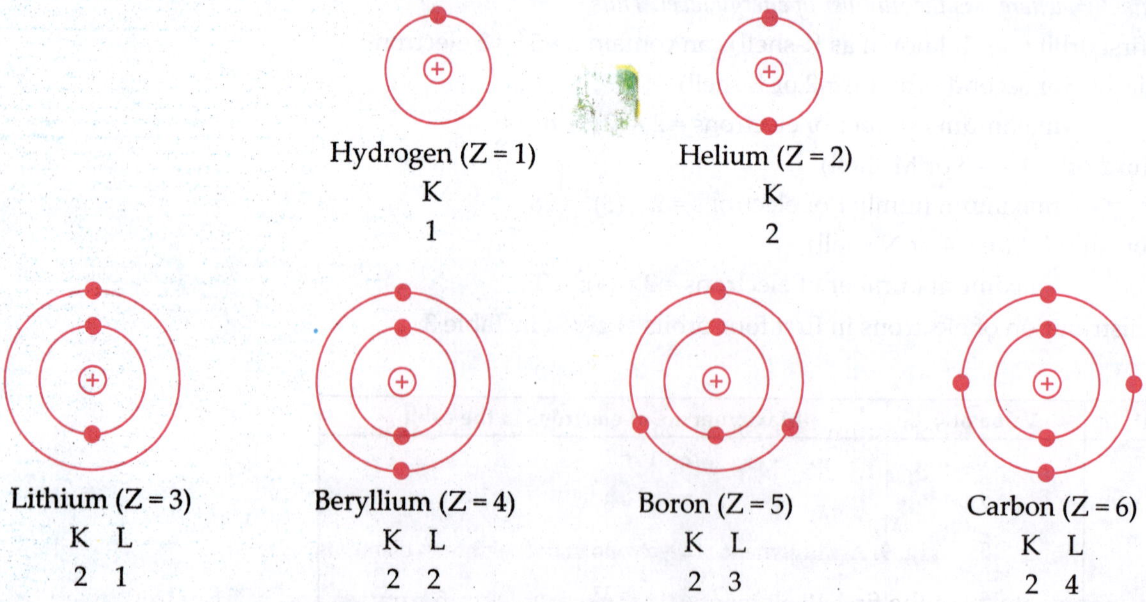

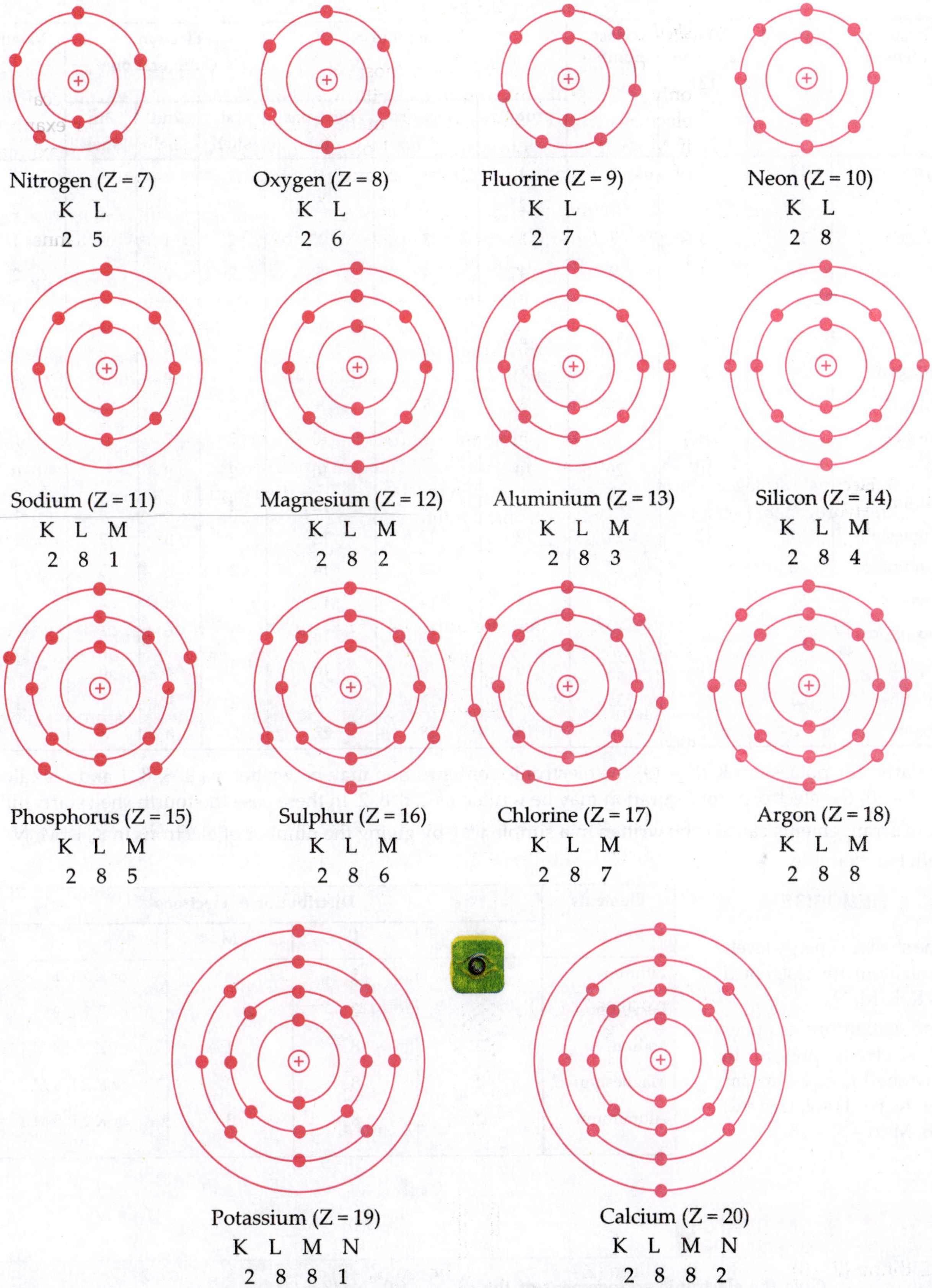

Fig. 9. Arrangement of electrons in first eighteen elements.

The composition of atoms of the first 18 elements, their electronic configuration and valency (discussed later) are given in Table 4.

Table 4. Composition of atoms of the first eighteen elements with their electronic configuration and valency.

Name of element	Symbol	Atomic number (Z)	Mass number (A)	Number of			Electronic configuration			Valency
				protons (*p*)	electrons (*e*)	neutrons (*n*)	1st shell	2nd shell	3rd shell	
Hydrogen	H	1	1	1	1	0	1			1
Helium	He	2	4	2	2	2	2			2
Lithium	Li	3	7	3	3	4	2	1		1
Beryllium	Be	4	9	4	4	5	2	2		2
Boron	B	5	11	5	5	6	2	3		3
Carbon	C	6	12	6	6	6	2	4		4
Nitrogen	N	7	14	7	7	7	2	5		3
Oxygen	O	8	16	8	8	8	2	6		2
Fluorine	F	9	19	9	9	10	2	7		1
Neon	Ne	10	20	10	10	10	2	8		0
Sodium	Na	11	23	11	11	12	2	8	1	1
Magnesium	Mg	12	24	12	12	12	2	8	2	2
Aluminium	Al	13	27	13	13	14	2	8	3	3
Silicon	Si	14	28	14	14	14	2	8	4	4
Phosphorus	P	15	31	15	15	16	2	8	5	3, 5
Sulphur	S	16	32	16	16	16	2	8	6	2
Chlorine	Cl	17	35	17	17	18	2	8	7	1
Argon	Ar	18	40	18	18	22	2	8	8	0

Similarly, for potassium K (Z = 19) the electronic configuration may be written as 2, 8, 8, 1 and for calcium Ca (Z = 20) the electronic configuration may be written as 2, 8, 8, 2. In these case the fourth shell starts filling. These arrangements can also be written in a simple way by giving the number of electrons in K, L, M, N shell. For example,

MEMORISE

The shells or energy levels in an atom are designated as K, L, M, N...

The maximum number of electrons present in any shell is equal to $\mathbf{2n^2}$ e.g. K (n = 1) = 2, L (n = 2) = 8, M (n = 3) = 18.

Elements	Distribution of electrons			
	K	L	M	
Lithium	2	1		or K 2 L 1
Beryllium	2	2		or K 2 L 2
Sodium	2	8	1	or K 2 L 8 M 1
Magnesium	2	8	2	or K 2 L 8 M 2
Aluminium	2	8	3	or K 2 L 8 M 3

Solved Examples

❑ **Example 5.** **Give the electronic arrangement of the following elements in terms of K, L, M...... shells :**

(*i*) **Cl (Z = 17)**

(*ii*) **Na (Z = 11)**

(*iii*) **F (Z = 9)**

(*iv*) **P (Z = 15)**

Solution :

Electronic arrangement

Element	At. Number	No. of electrons in			
		K	L	M	
(*i*) Cl	17	2	8	7	or 2, 8, 7
(*ii*) Na	11	2	8	1	or 2, 8, 1
(*iii*) F	9	2	7		or 2, 7
(*iv*) P	15	2	8	5	or 2, 8, 5

❑ **Example 6. The four elements A, B, C and D have the following arrangements :**

A : 2, 3 B : 2, 6 C : 2, 8, 5 D : 2, 8, 8

Name the elements.

Solution :

A : 2, 3 Element = Boron (B)
B : 2, 6 Element = Oxygen (O)
C : 2, 8, 5 Element = Phosphorus (P)
D : 2, 8, 8 Element = Argon (Ar).

❑ **Example 7. Write the electronic arrangement in aluminium. How many neutrons does an atom of aluminium contain ?**

(At. mass = 27, At. no. = 13)

Solution : Atomic number of aluminium is 13. Therefore, there are 13 electrons and electronic arrangement is:

K	L	M
2	8	3

Now atomic mass = No. of neutrons + No. of protons

At. mass = 27

No. of protons = No. of electrons = 13

or 27 = No. of neutrons + 13

∴ No. of neutrons = 27 – 13 = 14

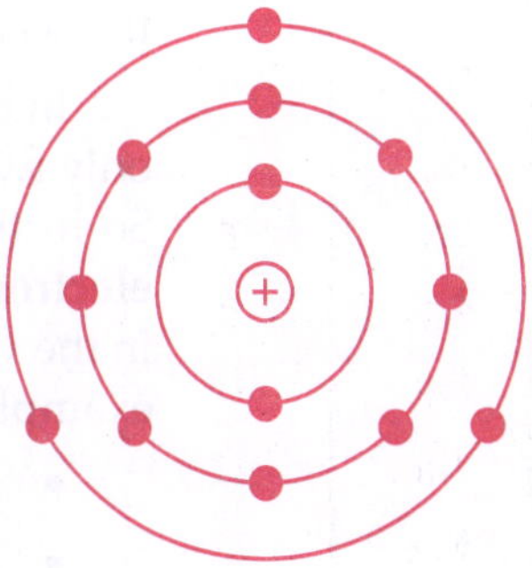

VALENCE ELECTRONS AND VALENCY

1. Valence shell

We have learnt that electrons in an atom are present in different orbits. The outermost orbit (or shell) of an atom is called its **valence shell.** *The electrons present in the outermost orbit* (or *valence shell*) *are called* **valence electrons.** For example, the electronic configuration of lithium is 2, 1 or it may be represented as :

K	L
2	1

The outermost orbit is L shell and the number of electrons in its valence shell is one. In other words, the valence electrons present in lithium is 1.

Similarly, the valence electrons in beryllium (2, 2, or $\begin{matrix} K & L \\ 2 & 2 \end{matrix}$) is 2, in boron (2, 3, or $\begin{matrix} K & L \\ 2 & 3 \end{matrix}$) is 3, in carbon (2, 4, or $\begin{matrix} K & L \\ 2 & 4 \end{matrix}$) is 4 and so on. The number of valence electrons can easily be calculated by writing the electronic configurations as given in Table 5.

Table 5. Valence electrons in some atoms of the elements

Element	Atomic No.	Distribution of electrons			Valence electrons
		K	L	M	
Nitrogen	7	2	5		5
Oxygen	8	2	6		6
Fluorine	9	2	7		7
Sodium	11	2	8	1	1
Magnesium	12	2	8	2	2
Aluminium	13	2	8	3	3
Silicon	14	2	8	4	4
Phosphorus	15	2	8	5	5
Sulphur	16	2	8	6	6

2. Valency

The valency of an atom depends upon the number of electrons present in the outermost shell. For example, the valency of hydrogen is 1 because it has only one electron in its valence shell. Similarly, lithium (2, 1) has one electron in its valence shell. Therefore, valency of lithium is **one**. Similarly beryllium (2, 2) has two electrons in its valence shell and therefore, its valency is **two.** Valency of boron (2, 3) and carbon (2, 4) is **three** and **four** because they have three and four electrons in their valence shell. Therefore, **valency of these elements is equal to the number of electrons present in their valence shell.**

In some cases, when the number of valence electrons of an atom is close to its full capacity, valency is determined differently. In this case, valency is equal to number of electrons by adding which the shell gets completed. For example, the second shell has a maximum capacity of 8 electrons.

In case of oxygen (2, 6), there are 6 electrons in the valence shell and needs only two electrons to completely fill its valence shell. Hence, its valency is two. So in these cases, **the valency is equal to 8 minus the number of valence electrons.** For example, elements after carbon having more than 4 electrons in the valence shell have valency equal to 8 – number of valence electrons. For example,

- nitrogen (2, 5) has valency **three** (8 – 5 = 3),
- oxygen (2, 6) has valency **two** (8 – 6 = 2),
- fluorine (2, 7) has valency **one** (8 – 7 = 1).
- Neon (2, 8) has valency **zero** (8 – 8 = 0).

Similarly, for elements from sodium to argon, the valency increases from 1 to 4 and then decreases from 4 to 1. It may be noted that valency of Na atom has integrated values only. It cannot be fractional. Therefore an atom of each element has a definite combining capacity called valency. Valency of first eighteen elements is given in last column of Table 4.

ISOTOPES

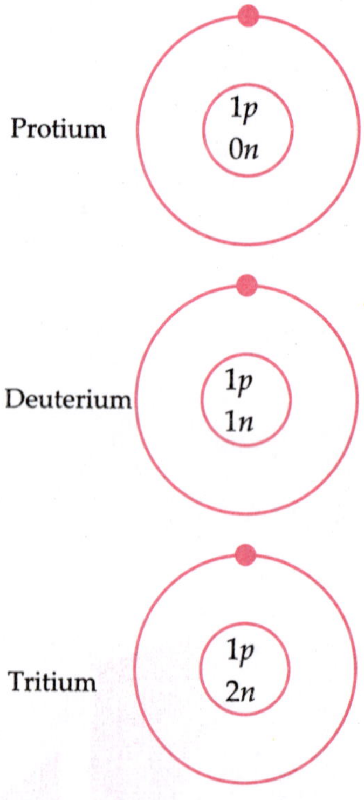

Isotopes of hydrogen

All the atoms of certain elements do not have same mass number. For example, in nature two different types of chlorine atoms are known which have mass numbers 35 and 37. Such atoms of the same element are called isotopes. Thus,

isotopes are atoms of the same element which have the same atomic number but different mass numbers.

In other words, isotopes differ in mass but have same electrical charge on their nuclei and same chemical properties. Since the atomic number of different isotopes of the same element is same, it means that they have same number of electrons and protons. The difference in their mass numbers is due to different number of neutrons present in their nuclei. Atomic number being the same, the isotopes will have an identical electronic distribution in shells. The isotopes have similar chemical properties but different physical properties.

Hydrogen is the common example which has three isotopes. These have the same atomic number, one, but different mass numbers 1, 2 and 3. These three isotopes are commonly known as hydrogen or protium, deuterium (D) and tritium (T) respectively. Since atomic number is same for all the three, they all have one electron (present in the 1st shell) and therefore, one proton but different neutrons. Their atomic structures are given below :

(*i*) Hydrogen At. No. = 1, Mass No. = 1
Electrons = 1, Protons = 1, Neutrons = 0

It is also represented as ^1_1H or H

(*ii*) Deuterium	At. No. = 1,	Mass No. = 2
Electrons = 1,	Protons = 1,	Neutrons = 1

It is also represented as ^2_1H

(*iii*) Tritium	At. No. = 1,	Mass No. = 3
Electrons = 1,	Protons = 1	Neutrons = 2.

It is also represented as ^3_1H or T.

Similarly, chlorine has two isotopes having same atomic number 17 whereas their mass numbers are 35 and 37. They have same distribution of electrons in shells and the electron distribution may be written as 2, 8, 7. They differ in the number of neutrons in their nucleus as:

First isotope of chlorine ($^{35}_{17}Cl$).	At. No. = 17,	Mass No. = 35
Electrons = 17,	Protons = 17 and	Neutrons = 18
Second isotope of chlorine ($^{37}_{17}Cl$).	At. No. = 17,	Mass No. = 37
Electrons = 17,	Protons = 17 and	Neutrons = 20

Some more examples of isotopes are :

(*i*) Carbon : $^{12}_{6}12$ (protons = 6, electrons = 6 and neutrons = 6)

$^{14}_{6}C$ (protons = 6, electrons = 6 and neutrons = 8)

(*ii*) Oxygen: $^{16}_{8}O$ (protons = 8, electrons = 8 and neutrons = 8)

$^{17}_{8}O$ (protons = 8, electrons = 8 and neutrons = 9)

$^{18}_{8}O$ (protons = 8, electrons = 8 and neutrons = 10)

Let us **summarise** some important points regarding isotopes :

1. Isotopes are atoms of same element having the same atomic number but different mass numbers.
2. Isotopes have same number of protons and electrons but different neutrons.
3. Isotopes have same electrical charge on their nuclei.
4. Since all the isotopes contain same number of electrons, they have same chemical properties.

MEMORISE

Isotopes : Atoms of same element which have different mass numbers.

Isotopes have same number of protons and electrons but different number of neutrons.

Fractional atomic masses of isotopes

The mass of an atom is due to the masses of protons and neutrons in the nucleus. The relative masses of protons and neutrons are almost equal to one. Therefore, the atomic mass of an element should be nearly a whole number. This is correct only in a few cases. But in many cases, the atomic masses are fractional. For example, the atomic mass of chlorine is 35.5. The main reason for these fractional atomic masses is that these elements occur in nature as mixtures of several isotopes. The atomic mass of an element is the average of the atomic masses of these isotopes in the ratio of their proportion of occurrence. For example, chlorine occurs in nature in the form of two isotopes with atomic masses 35 u and 37u in the ratio of 3 : 1 respectively. Therefore,

$$\text{Atomic mass} = \frac{35 \times 3 + 37 \times 1}{3 + 1} = \frac{142}{4} = 35.5 \text{ u}$$

Applications of Isotopes

Isotopes are used in almost all the fields such as medicines, agriculture, biology, chemistry, engineering and industry. Some important uses of isotopes are given below :

1. In nuclear reactors. Isotopes of uranium are used as fuel in nuclear reactors.

2. In carbon dating. One of the important application of radio isotopes is radio isotope dating or popularly known as **carbon dating.** It is intensively used to estimate the age of fosssils like dead plants, animals and rocks. It is based on the measuring of levels of carbon in the fossils.

3. Tracer techniques. Radioactive isotopes are used as tracers in many processes, in medicines, surgery, agriculture, industry and chemistry. In this method, a small amount of radioactive isotope is mixed and its movement is studied by measuring radioactivity in different parts. For example, in medical diagnosis, it is used to find out if blood is circulating to a wound or not. A small amount of radioactive isotope is injected into the blood stream. After suitable time gap, the blood from the wound is examined for its radioactivity. If no radioactive isotope is detected, it means that the passage of blood is hindered.

4. In treatment of diseases. Some radioisotopes are useful in treatment of diseases, particularly in radiotherapy. For example,

(*i*) Radio-cobalt (Co-60) is used for treatment of cancerous tumours

(*ii*) Iron- 59 is used for detecting cases of anaemia.

(*iii*) Phosphorus-32 is used for blood cancer known as leukaemia.

(*iv*) Iodine-131 is used for detection and cure of disorders of thyroid glands.

ISOBARS

Isobars are the atoms of different elements having same mass number but different atomic numbers.

MEMORISE

Isobars : Atom of different elements having same mass number.

Isobars have same number of protons and electrons but different number of neutrons.

Since isobars have the same mass number, therefore sum of the protons and neutrons in the nucleus of each is the same. These atoms differ in their atomic number and therefore, they have different number of protons and also different number of neutrons. Due to different atomic numbers, the isobars will have different atomic structures and therefore, will differ in chemical properties. For example, argon (atomic number 18) and calcium (atomic number 20) are isobars because they have same mass number 40. Thus, their atomic structures are :

Argon ($^{40}_{18}Ar$)	Calcium ($^{40}_{20}Ca$)
At. No. = 18, Mass No. = 40	At. No. = 20, Mass No. = 40.
No. of electrons = 18	No. of electrons = 20
No. of protons = 18	No. of protons = 20
No. of neutrons = 22	No. of neutrons = 20

Another common example of isobars is $^{22}_{10}Ne$ and $^{22}_{11}Na$ because both have same mass number 22. But their atomic numbers are different.

Practice Exercise 4B

Answers and Hints on Page 41

1. Write the distribution of electrons in an atom of element whose atomic number is 13.
2. State the number of electrons present in the outermost shell of the atoms of the following elements :
   (*i*) Neon (Z = 10) (*ii*) Sodium (Z = 11)
   (*iii*) Chlorine (Z = 17)
3. Write the electronic arrangement for :
   (*i*) Carbon (at. mass = 12, at. no. = 6)
   (*ii*) Magnesium (at. mass = 24, at. no. = 12)
4. What is the maximum number of electrons that can be accommodated in the M shell of the atom ?
5. An element has an atomic number of 19 and atomic mass of 39.
   (*i*) How many electrons are there in each atom of the element ?

(*ii*) How are these arranged in the atom ?

6. What are the names and symbols of elements having the electronic configuration ?

	K	L	M	N
(*i*)	2	3		
(*ii*)	2	8		
(*iii*)	2	8	8	1

7. Draw the electronic distribution for (i) sodium (Z = 11) (*ii*) silicon (Z = 14) (*iii*) fluorine (Z = 9).

8. How many valence electrons are present in nitrogen having atomic number 7 ?

9. What is the valency of an element having the electronic arrangement as : 2, 8, 7 ?

10. Which of the following have same valency ?
A (2, 8, 2) B (2, 8, 4) C (2, 2) D (2, 8)

11. Which of the following represent isotopes and which represent isobars?
(*i*) $^{10}_{5}B$, $^{11}_{5}B$ (*ii*) $^{40}_{19}K$, $^{40}_{20}Ca$ (*iii*) $^{235}_{92}U$, $^{238}_{92}U$
(*iv*) $^{22}_{10}Ne$, $^{22}_{11}Na$ (*v*) $^{3}_{1}H$, $^{3}_{2}He$ (*vi*) $^{28}_{14}Si$, $^{29}_{14}Si$

12. Boron occurs in nature in the form of two isotopes having mass number 10 and 11. Their relative abundance is 20% and 80% respectively. What is the average atomic mass of boron?

13. The two carbon atoms represented below are isotopes: The atoms of both isotopes have six protons.
(*i*) Give one other way in which the isotopes are similar.
(*ii*) Give two ways in which they are different.

14. $^{222}_{86}Rn$ is an isotope of the noble gas radon.
(*i*) How many protons, neutrons and electrons are present in one atom of the element ?
(*ii*) What is the valency of radon ?
(*iii*) What will be the atomic number of another isotope of radon ?

15. A diagram of nucleus of an atom is shown below :

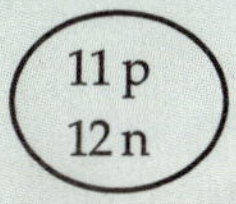

(*i*) Draw a diagram to show the electronic arrangement of this atom.
(*ii*) What is the mass number of this atom ?
(*iii*) How many neutrons will be present in unipositive ion of this atom ?

16. Find out of the valency of the atoms A and B represented below :

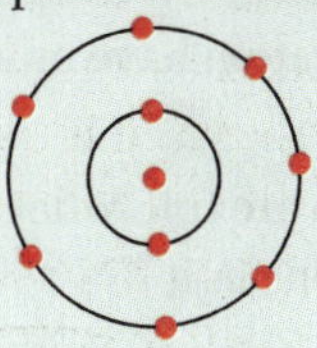
A

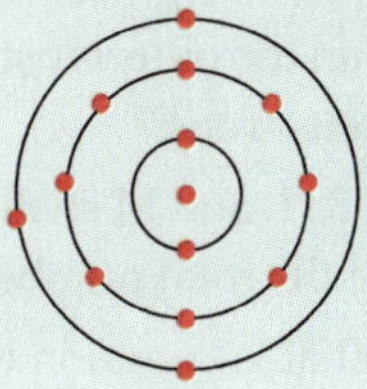
B

17. An element Z consists of three types of atoms:
$^{11}_{22}Z$, $^{11}_{23}Z$ and $^{11}_{24}Z$
(*i*) How many protons does each atom have ?
(*ii*) How many neutrons does each atom have ?
(*iii*) How many electrons does each atom have ?
(*iv*) How many nucleons does each atom have ?
(*v*) Give the word we use to describe the atoms of this element.

18. What is the number of valence electrons in
(*i*) the atoms of element having atomic number 14 ?
(*ii*) the atom having the electronic arrangement 2, 8, 2.
(*iii*) the atom of oxygen ?

19. From the symbol $^{40}_{20}Ca$ state
(*i*) Mass number of Ca
(*ii*) Atomic number
(*iii*) Electronic distribution of Ca.

20. Boron occurs in nature in the form of two isotopes having atomic mass 10 and 11. Calculate the percentage abundances of two isotopes in a sample having atomic mass 10.80.

21. Two isotopes of iron are ^{56}Fe and ^{59}Fe. Complete the following table by putting in missing numbers.

Isotope	Mass number	No. of protons	No. of neutrons	No. of electrons
^{56}Fe	56	26		
^{59}Fe	59			

22. The electronic arrangements of atoms A, B, C and D are given below :

Atom	No. of subatomic particles		
	protons	neutrons	electrons
A	8	8	8
B	10	12	10
C	11	11	11
D	8	10	8

(*i*) Which two of these represent isotopes ?
(*ii*) Which two of these represent isobars ?

23. Describe the distribution of electrons in different shells of the following atoms :
lithium, nitrogen, neon, magnesium and silicon.
24. What is the maximum number of electrons that can be accommodated in the outermost orbit ?
25. Do isotopes represent different elements ?
26. Can the outermost shell in an atom have more than 8 electrons ?
27. If K, L and M shell of an atom are full, what would be the total number of electrons in it ?
28. What is common between the following atoms? $^{40}_{18}Z$ and $^{40}_{20}Z$
29. What is the maximum number of electrons that can be present in a given shell according to Bohr-Bury scheme?
30. Predict which of the following statements are true :
(*i*) The total number of neutrons and protons in isobars are same.
(*ii*) The valency of an element having atomic number 7 is three.
(*iii*) Magnesium and beryllium have same number of electrons in valence shell.
(*iv*) The electronic arrangement of nitrogen is 2, 7.
(*v*) The species $^{231}_{90}Z$ and $^{233}_{90}Z$ represent isobars.

What you have learnt

KEY TERMS

Fundamental particles	:	Electron, proton and neutron are fundamental particles because these are the main constituents of all atoms.
Nucleus	:	The positively charged centre of an atom.
Atomic number	:	The number of protons present in the nucleus of an atom of an element.
Mass number	:	The sum of the number of protons and neutrons in an atom of the element.
Valence electrons	:	The electrons present in the outermost orbit (or valence shell).
Isotopes	:	Atoms of the same element which have same atomic number but different mass number.
Isobars	:	Atoms of different elements having same mass number but different atomic numbers.

Chapter Summary

- Experimental studies have shown that matter is electrical in nature and neutral.
- Discharge tube studies by J.J. Thomson and other led to the discovery of electron.
- J.J. Thomson determined the value of charge/mass ratio, e/m of the electron.
- R.A. Millikan determined the value of charge on the electron.
- Positive rays were discovered by E. Goldstein and these are also called **canal rays.**
- Rutherford and his co-workers performed α-particle scattering experiments which led to the discovery of **atomic nucleus.**
- Atoms of the same element which have the same atomic number but different mass number are called **isotopes.**
- Atoms of different elements having same mass number but different atomic number are called **isobars.**
- Bohr's model of an atom gave the concept of **orbits** or **shells.** These are designeted as K, L, M, N, ...
- Each orbit has a definite energy and that is why these are also called **energy levels** or **energy shells.**
- Neutron was discovered by Chadwick.
- The number of protons in an atom of an element is known as **atomic number.**

- The sum of the number of protons and neutrons in an atom of the element is called **mass number.**
- In general, the maximum number of electrons that can be present in any shell is $2n^2$ where n is the number of energy shell.
- The distribution of electrons in different energy shells is called **electronic configuration.** Electronic configuration of atoms are written with the help of K, L, M, etc.
- The electrons present in the outermost orbit (or valence shell) are called **valence electrons.**
- The valency of atom is either no. of electrons in valence shell or 8 – no. of electrons in the valence shell.

NCERT File *with* Answers & Hints

In-Text Questions

1. What are canal rays ?

Ans. A beam of rays or a stream of particles which travel in a direction away from anode towards cathode when a gas taken in a discharge tube is subjected to the action of high voltage under low pressure are called canal rays. These were discoverd by E. Goldstein.

2. If an atom contains one electron and one proton, will it carry any charge or not ?

Ans. No, it will not carry any charge because the negative charge (–1) of an electron will be neutralised by the positive (+1) charge of a proton.

3. Name the three sub-atomic particles of an atom.

Ans. These are :

(*a*) Electron (*b*) Proton and (*c*) Neutron.

4. Helium atom has an atomic mass of 4u and two protons in its nucleus. How many neutrons does it have ?

Ans. Atomic mass of Helium = 4u

No. of protons = 2

No. of neutrons = 4 – 2 = 2

5. On the basis of Thomson's model of an atom explain how the atom is neutral as a whole.

Ans. Thomson's model of atom

(*i*) According to Thomson model, an atom may be regarded as a uniform sphere of positive charge (protons) in which negatively charged electrons are embedded like the seeds in a water-melon.

(*ii*) The total positive charge is equal to the total negative charge on all the electrons so that atoms on the whole is electrically neutral.

6. On the basis of Rutherford's model of an atom which sub-atomic particle is present in the nucleus of an atom ?

Ans. Proton, the positively charged subatomic particle is present in the nucleus of an atom.

7. Draw a sketch of Bohr's model of an atom with three shells.

Ans.

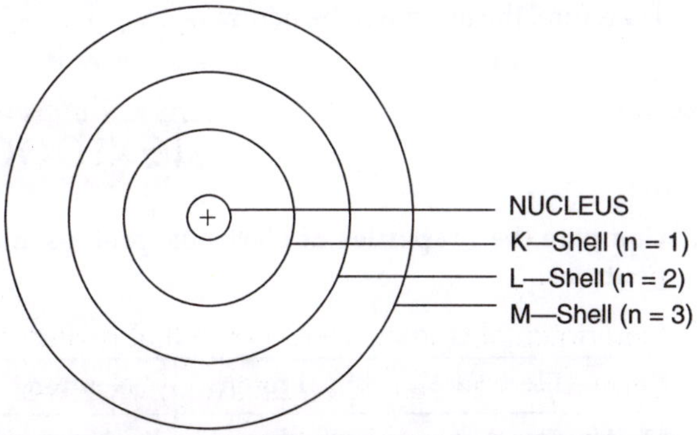

8. What do you think would be the observation if the α-particle scattering experiment is carried out using a foil of metal other than gold ?

Ans. Almost same behaviour if the metal is heavy metal.

9. Write the electronic configuration of carbon and sodium.

(*i*) Carbon (At. No. = 6) : K L

2 4 or 2, 4

(*ii*) Sodium (At. No. = 11) : K L M

2 8 1 or 2, 8, 1

10. If K and L shell of an atom are full, then what would be the total number of electrons in it ?

Ans. No. of electrons in K- shell= 2

No. of electrons in L- shell = 8

Total number of electrons = 2 + 8 = 10

11. How will you find the valency of chlorine, sulphur and magnesium ?

Ans. Valency of an atom is the number of electrons gained, lost or shared so as to complete the octet of electrons in the valence shell.

(*i*) Chlorine : Its electronic configuration is 2, 8, 7.

It needs one electron to complete its octet and hence its valency is 1.

(*ii*) Sulphur : Its electronic configuration is 2, 8, 6.

It needs two electrons to complete its octet and hence its valency is 2.

(*iii*) Magnesium : Its electronic configuration is 2, 8, 2

It can lose two electrons to attain octet in the valence shell. Therefore, its valency is 2.

12. If the number of electrons in an atom are 8 and number of protons are also 8, then

(*i*) What is the atomic number of the atom and

(*ii*) What is the charge on the atom ?

Ans. (*i*) No. of protons = 8

Atomic number of atom = 8

(*ii*) No. of electrons = No. of protons.

Therefore, the atom will be neutral.

13. The number of electrons, protons and neutrons in oxygen and sulphur are 8, 8, 8 and 16, 16, 16 respectively. Calculate the mass number of oxygen and sulphur.

Ans. Mass number of oxygen = $n + p = 8 + 8 = 16$

Mass number of sulphur = 16 + 16 = 32

14. For the symbol H, D and T tabulate three fundamental particles found in each of them.

Ans.

Symbol	*p*	*e*	*n*
H	1	1	0
D	1	1	1
T	1	1	2

Q.15. Write the electronic configuration of any one pair of isotopes and isobars.

Ans. Pair of Isotopes : $^{35}_{17}Cl$ and $^{37}_{17}Cl$

Electronic configuration of these isotopes

= K L M or 2, 8, 7
2 8 7

Pair of isobars : $^{40}_{18}Ar$ and $^{40}_{20}Ca$

Electronic Configuration of $^{40}_{18}Ar$

= K L M or 2, 8, 8
2 8 8

Electronic Configuration of $^{40}_{20}Ca$

= K L M N or 2, 8, 8, 2
2 8 8 2

Textbook *Exercises*

1. Compare the properties of electrons, protons and neutrons.

Ans.

Electron	Proton	Neutron
1. It has mass of $\frac{1}{1837}$ th of H atom. Its absolute mass is 9.1×10^{-31} kg	Its absolute mass is 1.67 $\times 10^{-27}$ kg	Its mass is almost equal to that of a proton i.e., 1.675×10^{-27} kg
2. It is negatively charged	It is positively charged	It is neutral

2. What are the limitations of J. J. Thomson's model of the atom ?

Ans. (*i*) It could not explain the stability of an atom.

(*ii*) It could not explain hydrogen spectrum.

3. What are the limitations of Rutherford's model of the atom ?

Ans. (*i*) Rutherford model could not explain the stability of atom. This is because when a charged particle revolves in a circular orbit, it continuously radiates energy. The electron would lose energy and finally may fall into the nucleus.

(*ii*) Rutherford model could not explain the spectrum of hydrogen and other atoms.

4. Describe Bohr's model of the atom.

Ans. Refer Text.

5. Compare all the proposed models of distribution of electrons in various shells for the first eighteen elements.

Ans. Refer Text.

6. Summarise the rules for writing of distribution the electrons in various shells for the first eighteen elements.

Ans. Refer Text.

7. Define valency by taking examples of silicon and oxygen.

Ans. Valency is the combining tendency of an atom and is equal to number of electrons lost, gained or shared by it.

Silicon has 4 valence electrons, it can share four electrons and therefore, its valency is 4,

Oxygen has 6 valence electrons, so it can gain two electrons to complete its octet. Hence its valency is 2.

8. Explain with examples (*i*) Atomic number, (*ii*) Mass number, (*iii*) Isotopes and (*iv*) Isobars. Give any two uses of isotopes.

Ans. (*i*) **Atomic number.** It is defined as the number of protons present in the nucleus of an atom.

(*ii*) **Mass number.** It is the sum of the number of protons and neutrons present in the nucleus of an atom.

(*iii*) **Isotopes.** These are the atoms of the same element having same atomic number but different mass numbers. For example $^{35}_{17}Cl$ and $^{37}_{17}Cl$.

(*iv*) **Isobars.** These are the atoms of different elements having same mass number but different atomic numbers. For example $^{40}_{20}Ca$ and $^{40}_{18}Ar$.

(*v*) **Uses of isotopes :**

(*a*) Isotope of uranium (U-235) is used as a fuel in nuclear reactor.

(*b*) Isotope of cobalt (Co-60) is used in the treatment of cancer.

9. Na^+ has completely filled K and L shells. Explain.

Ans. Atomic number of sodium = 11

No. of electrons in Na = 11

No. of electrons in Na^+ = 11 – 1 = 10

Electronic configuration of Na^+ : K L

2, 8

In Na^+, K and L shells are completely filled.

10. If bromine atom is available in the form of, say, two isotopes $^{79}_{35}Br$ (49.7%) and $^{81}_{35}Br$ (50.3%), calculate the average atomic mass of bromine atom.

Ans. Percentage of $^{79}_{35}Br$ isotope = 49.7

Percentage of $^{81}_{35}Br$ isotope = 50.3

$$\text{Average atomic mass} = \frac{49.7 \times 79 + 50.3 \times 81}{100}$$

$$= \frac{3926.3 + 4074.3}{100}$$

$$= \frac{8000.6}{100}$$

$$= 80.006.$$

11. The average atomic mass of a sample of an element X is 16.2 u. What are the percentage of isotopes $^{16}_{8}X$ and $^{18}_{8}X$ in the sample.

Ans. Let the percentage abundance of $^{16}_{8}X$ = x

Percentage abundance of $^{18}_{8}X$ = $100 - x$

Average atomic mass = 16.2

Average atomic mass =

$$\frac{\text{Mass of } ^{16}_{8}X \text{ isotope} + \text{Mass of } ^{18}_{8}X \text{ isotope}}{100}$$

$$16.2 = \frac{x \times 16 + (100 - x) \times 18}{100}$$

$$1620 = 16x + 1800 - 18x$$

$$2x = 1800 - 1620 = 180$$

$$x = 90$$

Abundance of $^{16}_{8}X$ = 90%, Abundance of $^{18}_{8}X$ = 10%

12. If Z = 3, what would be the valency of the element ? Also name the element.

Ans. Electronic configuration : 2, 1

Valency = 1, Name : Lithium

13. Composition of the nuclei of two atomic species X and Y are :

	X	Y
Protons	6	6
Neutrons	6	8

Give the mass numbers of X and Y. What is the relation between two species.

Ans. Mass No. of X = 12

Mass No. of Y = 14

These are isotopes because they have same atomic number but different mass numbers.

14. For the following statements, write T for True and F for False.

(*a*) J.J. Thomson proposed that the nucleus of an atom contains only nucleons.

(*b*) A neutron is formed by an electron and a proton combining together. Therefore, it is neutral.

(*c*) The mass of an electron is about $\frac{1}{2000}$ times that of proton.

(*d*) An isotope of iodine is used for making tincture of iodine, which is used as a medicine.

Ans. (*a*) F (*b*) F (*c*) T (*d*) T

15. Rutherford's alpha-particle scattering experiment was responsible for the discovery of

(*a*) Atomic Nucleus (*b*) Electrons
(*c*) Proton (*d*) Neutron

Ans. (*a*)

16. Isotopes of an element have

(*a*) the same physical properties
(*b*) different chemical properties
(*c*) different number of neutrons
(*d*) different atomic number.

Ans. (*c*)

17. Number of valence electrons in Cl^- ion are :

(*a*) 16 (*b*) 8 (*c*) 17 (*d*) 18

Ans. (*b*)

18. Which one of the following is a correct electronic configuration of sodium ?

(*a*) 2, 8 (*b*) 8, 2, 1 (*c*) 2, 1, 8 (*d*) 2, 8, 1.

Ans. (*d*)

19. Complete the following table :

Atomic number	Mass number	Number of neutrons	Number of protons	Number of electrons	Name of the atomic species
9	-	10	-	-	-
16	32	-	-	-	Sulphur
-	24	-	12	-	-
-	2	-	1	-	-
-	1	0	1	0	-

Ans.

Atomic No.	Mass No.	No. of neutrons	No. of protons	No. of electrons	Name of atomic species
9	19	10	9	9	Fluorine
16	32	16	16	16	Sulphur
12	24	12	12	12	Magnesium
1	2	1	1	1	Deuterium
1	1	0	1	0	Protium

NCERT Exemplar Problems

Note: Multiple Choice Question (1-18) from Exemplar Problems are given in Revision Exercise, Page 34.

Short Answer Questions

19. Is it possible for the atom of an element to have one electron, one proton and no neutron. If so, name the element.

Ans. It is possible for an atom of the element to have one electron, one proton and no neutron. The element is hydrogen and can be represented as ^1_1H.

20. Write any two observations which support the fact that atoms are divisible.

Ans. (*i*) The discovery of electrons shows that atoms are divisible.

(*ii*) The discovery of protons shows that atoms are divisible.

21. Will ^{35}Cl and ^{37}Cl have different valencies? Justify your answer.

Ans. Both ^{35}Cl and ^{37}Cl are isotopes and have the same atomic number 17. Since their atomic numbers are same, their electronic configuration is same (2, 8, 7) and therefore their valencies are same.

22. Why did Rutherford select a gold foil in his α–ray scattering experiment?

Ans. Gold is highly malleable in nature and can be beaten into very fine sheets or foils. Rutherford used a very thin foil of gold.

23. Find out the valency of the atoms represented by the figures (*a*) and (*b*).

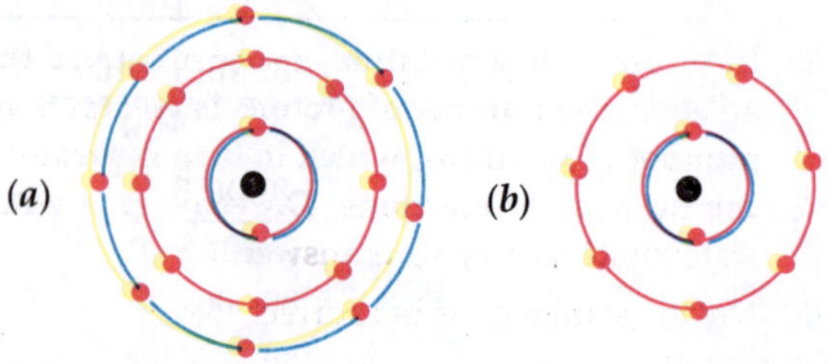

Ans. (*a*) Valency of (*a*) is zero because it has full M shell.

(*b*) Valency of (*b*) is one because it has 7 electrons in L shell (8 – 7 = 1).

24. One electron is present in the outermost shell of the atom of an element X. What would be the nature and value of charge on the ion formed if this electron is removed from the outer most shell? ***(CBSE Sample Paper 2010)***

Ans. X will get one unit of positive charge. It can be represented as X^+.

25. Write down the electron distribution of chlorine atom. How many electrons are there in the L shell? (Atomic number of chlorine is 17).

Ans. Chlorine :

	K	L	M
	2	8	7

It has 8 electrons in L shell.

26. In the atom of an element X, 6 electrons are present in the outermost shell. If it acquires noble gas configuration by accepting requisite number of electrons, then what would be the charge on the ion so formed?

Ans. It can acquire noble gas configuration by accepting 2 electrons. It will get 2 unit of negative charge and can be represented as X^{2-}.

27. What information do you get from the following figures about the atomic number, mass number and valency of atoms X, Y and Z? Give your answer in a tabular form. ***(CBSE Sample Paper 2010)***

(X)

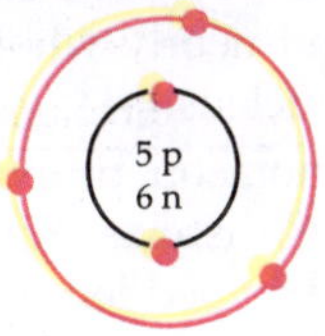

(Y)

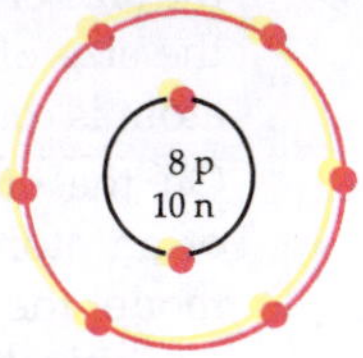

(Z)

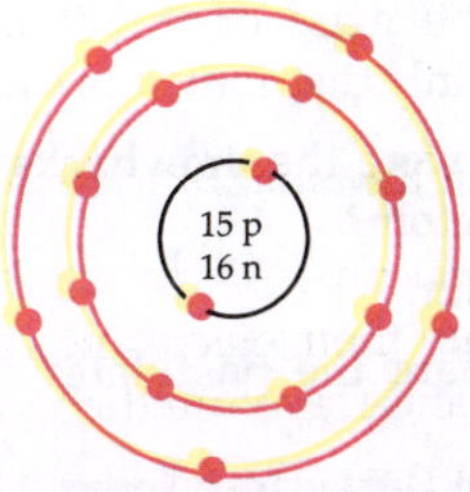

Ans.

Atom	Atomic no.	Mass no.	Valency
X	5	11	3
Y	8	18	2
Z	15	31	3, 5

28. In response to a question, a student stated that in an atom, the number of protons is greater than the number of neutrons, which in turn is greater than the number of electrons. Do you agree with the statement? Justify your answer.

Ans. No, the statement is not correct.

In a neutral atom, number of protons cannot be greater than number of electrons because an atom as a whole must be neutral. Therefore, number of electrons must be equal to number of protons in an atom.

29. Calculate the number of neutrons present in the nucleus of an element X which is represented as $^{31}_{15}X$

Ans. $^{31}_{15}X$ No. of electrons = 15

No. of protons = 15

No. of neutrons = 31 – 15 = 16

30. Match the names of the scientists given in column A with their contributions towards the understanding of the atomic structure as given in column B

(A)	(B)
(*a*) Ernest Rutherford	(*i*) Indivisibility of atoms
(*b*) J.J.Thomson	(*ii*) Stationary orbits
(*c*) Dalton	(*iii*) Concept of nucleus
(*d*) Neils Bohr	(*iv*) Discovery of electrons
(*e*) James Chadwick	(*v*) Atomic number
(*f*) E. Goldstein	(*vi*) Neutron
(*g*) Mosley	(*vii*) Canal rays

Ans. (*a*) – (*iii*), (*b*) – (*iv*), (*c*) – (*i*), (*d*) – (*ii*), (*e*) – (*vi*), (*f*) – (*vii*), (*g*) – (*v*).

31. The atomic number of calcium and argon are 20 and 18 respectively, but the mass number of both these elements is 40. What is the name given to such a pair of elements?

Ans. These atoms are called isobars because they have same mass number but different atomic numbers. These isobars represent atoms of different elements.

32. Complete the given table on the basis of information available in the symbols given below:

(*a*) $^{35}_{17}Cl$ (*b*) $^{12}_{6}C$ (*c*) $^{81}_{35}Br$

Table

Element	n_p	n_n

Ans.

Element	n_p	n_n
(a) $^{35}_{17}Cl$	17	18
(a) $^{12}_{6}C$	6	6
(a) $^{81}_{35}Br$	35	46

33. Helium atom has 2 electrons in its valence shell but its valency is not 2.Explain.

(*CBSE Sample Paper 2010*)

Ans. Valency of helium is zero because it has two electrons in K shell. It is full shell and has no combining capacity. Hence its valency is zero.

34. Fill in the blanks in the following statements

(*a*) Rutherford's α-particle scattering experiment led to the discovery of the..................

(*b*) Isotopes have same .... but different ....

(*c*) Neon and chlorine have atomic numbers 10 and 17 respectively. Their valencies will be .... and .... respectively.

(*d*) The electronic configuration of silicon is .... and that of sulphur is ....

Ans. (*i*) atomic nucleus

(*ii*) atomic number, mass number

(*iii*) zero, 1

(*iv*) 2, 8, 4, 2, 8, 6.

35. An element X has a mass number 4 and atomic number 2. Write the valency of this element?

Ans. Zero because K shell (K) is completely full.

Long Answer Questions

36. Why do helium, neon and argon have a zero valency?

Ans. The electronic configuration of three elements are :

	K	L	M
Helium (He)	2	–	–
Neon (Ne)	2	8	–
Argon (Ar)	2	8	8

These elements have full capacity of outermost shell and therefore, they have no tendency to gain or lose electrons. Hence they donot have any tendency to comine with other elements and thus have valency equal to zero.

37. The ratio of the radii of hydrogen atom and its nucleus is ~ 10^5. Assuming the atom and the nucleus to be spherical, (*i*) what will be the ratio of their sizes? (*ii*) If atom is represented by planet earth 'R_e' = 6.4×10^6 m, estimate the size of the nucleus.

Ans. (*i*) Volume of the sphere $= \frac{4}{3}\pi r^3$

Let R be the radius of the atom and *r* be the radius of the nucleus.

Since $\frac{R}{r} = 10^5$ or $R = 10^5 r$

Volume of atom $= \frac{4}{3}\pi R^3$

$= \frac{4}{3}\pi (10^5 r)^3 = \frac{4}{3}\pi r^3 \times 10^{15}$

Volume of the nucleus $= \frac{4}{3}\pi r^3$

Ratio of the size of the atom to the nucleus

$$\frac{\frac{4}{3}\pi r^3 \times 10^{15}}{\frac{4}{3}\pi r^3} = 10^{15} : 1$$

(*ii*) If the atom is represented by the planet earth, $R_e = 6.4 \times 10^6$ m

then radius of the nucleus would be, $r_n = \frac{R_e}{10^5}$

$$r_n = \frac{6.4 \times 10^6}{10^5} = 64 \text{ m}$$

38. Enlist the conclusions drawn by Rutherford from his α-ray scattering experiment.

Ans. *Refer Text.*

39. In what way is the Rutherford's atomic model different from that of Thomson's atomic model?

Ans. Rutherford proposed a model in which there is a positively charged nucleus and the electrons revolve around the nucleus. He also proposed that the size of the nucleus is very small as compared to the size of the atom and nearly whole mass of an atom is centred in the nucleus.

On the other hand, Thomson proposed a model of an atom similar to Christmas pudding. In this model the electrons are embedded like currants in a positively charged sphere like christmas pudding and the mass of the atom was supposed to be uniformly distributed in the sphere.

40. What were the drawbacks of Rutherford's model of an atom?

Ans. *Refer Text.*

41. What are the postulates of Bohr's model of an atom?

Ans. *Refer Text.*

42. Show diagramatically the electron distributions in a sodium atom and a sodium ion and also give their atomic number.

Ans.

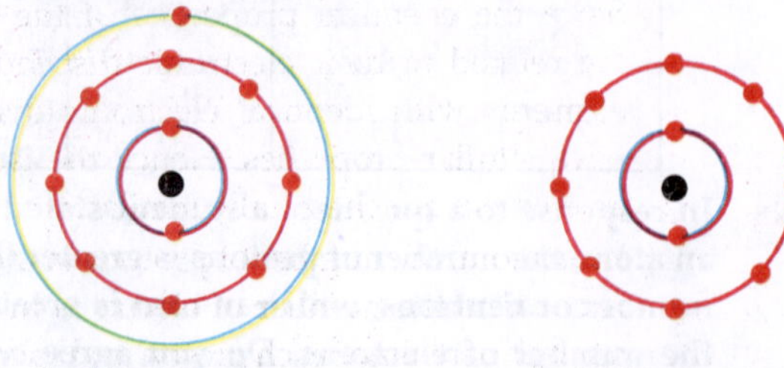

Sodium atom Sodium ion

Atomic number of sodium and sodium ion = 11

43. In the Gold foil experiment of Geiger and Marsden, that paved the way for Rutherford's model of an atom, ~ 1.00% of the α-particles were found to deflect at angles > 50°.

If one mole of α-particles were bombarded on the gold foil, compute the number of α-particles that would deflect at angles less than 50°.

Ans. 1 mole of α-particles = 6.022×10^{23} particles

No. of α-particles deflected at angle < 50°

$= 100 - 1 = 99\%$

No. of α-particles deflected at angle < 50°

$$= \frac{6.022 \times 10^{23} \times 99}{100}$$

$$= 5.96 \times 10^{23}$$

PRACTICE QUESTIONS

Some Solved CBSE Sample Questions

1. The average atomic mass of a sample of an element 'X' is 16.2u. What is the percentage of each isotope $^{16}_{8}X$ and $^{18}_{8}X$ in the sample ?

(CBSE Sample Paper 2010)

Ans. Let the percentage of $^{16}_{8}X$ isotope $= x$

Percentage of $^{16}_{8}X$ isotope $= 100 - x$

Average atomic mass $= 16.2$

$$\frac{16 \times x}{100} + \frac{18\,(100 - x)}{100} = 16.2$$

$$16\,x + 1800 - 18\,x = 1620$$

$$-2x = 1620 - 1800 = -180$$

$$x = 90$$

Percentage of $^{16}_{8}X$ isotope $= 90$

Percentage of $^{18}_{8}X$ isotope $= 10$

2. Give reasons for the following :

(*a*) Isotopes of an element are chemically similar.

(*b*) An atom is electrically neutral.

(*c*) Noble gases show least reactivity.

(*d*) Nucleus of an atom is heavy and positively charged.

(*e*) Ions are more stable than atoms.

(CBSE Sample Paper 2010)

Ans. (*a*) Isotopes of an element have same atomic number and have same electronic distribution. Since the chemical properties of the elements are related to their electronic distribution, the elements with identical electronic distribution have similar properties. Hence the isotopes of an element are chemically similar.

(*b*) In an atom, the number of protons in the nucleus is equal to the number of electrons in the extra nuclear part. Since each proton and each electron has the same charge but opposite magnitude, therefore, an atom is electrically neutral.

(*c*) The atoms of noble gases have complete outermost shells. With the exception of helium (He) which has two electrons in its only shell (K-shell), the other members of the family have eight electrons in their outermost or valence shell. This means that the atoms of noble gases have no tendency to gain or lose electrons. In other words, they donot take part in chemical combination and therefore, they have least reactivity.

(*d*) Nucleus of an atom contains protons and neutrons. Since electrons which are revolving in extra nuclear part have negligible mass, the whole mass of the atom is concentrated in the nucleus. Because of positive charge of protons, it is positively charged. Hence, nucleus of an atom is heavy and positively charged.

(*e*) When an atom forms ions by loss or gain of electrons, the valence shell of the ions has complete octet configuration. Since these octet configurations are stable, the ions are more stable than atoms.

3. Helium has two electrons in its valence shell but its valency is not 2. Explain.

(CBSE Sample Paper 2010)

Ans. Helium has 2 electrons in its outermost first (K) shell. In this its duplet is complete and it has no tendency to lose or gain electrons. Hence the valency of helium is zero.

4. The following data represents the distribution of electrons, protons and neutrons in atoms of four elements A, B, C and D.

Elements	Protons	Neutrons	Electrons
A	19	21	19
B	17	18	17
C	17	20	17
D	18	22	18

Answer the following questions :

(*i*) Describe the electron distribution in atom of element B.

(*ii*) Is element B a metal or a non-metal? Why?

(*iii*) Which two elements form a pair of Isotopes?

(*iv*) Which two elements form a pair of Isobars? ***(CBSE Sample Paper 2010)***

Ans. (*i*) B(17) :

	K	L	M
	2	8	7

(*ii*) Non-metal. It contains one electron less to complete the octet.

(*iii*) B and C

(*iv*) A and D

5. What are isotopes ? Give one example. ***(CBSE 2011-12)***

Ans. Isotopes are the atoms of the same elements having same atomic number but different mass number. Hydrogen has three isotopes having mass number 1, 2 and 3 but all have same atomic number 1. These are called protium (mass no. = 1), deuterium (mass no. = 2) and tritium (mass no.= 3). These are represented as ^1_1H, ^2_1H and ^3_1H respectively.

6. Which of the two would be chemically more reactive : element X of atomic number 18 or element Z of atomic number 16 ? ***(CBSE 2011-12)***

Ans. The electronic configuration of elements X and Z are :

X (Atomic no. = 18) : 2, 8, 8

Z (Atomic no. = 16) : 2, 8, 6

Since X has 3rd shell full, it behaves as chemically inert. Z has two electrons less than the full capacity of 3rd shell, so it is more reactive than X.

7. For chlorine, Z = 17 and A = 35 give the number of protons, electrons and neutrons in

(*i*) Chlorine atom

(*ii*) Chloride ion ***(CBSE 2011-12)***

Ans. (*i*) Chlorine, Cl atom

No. of protons = 17

No. of electrons = 17

No. of neutrons = A – Z = 35 – 17 = 18

(*ii*) Chloride, Cl^- ion

No. of protons = 17

No. of electrons = 17 + 1 = 18

No. of neutrons = 35 – 17 = 18

8. The composition of two atoms X and Y is given as:

	X	Y
Protons	8	8
Electrons	8	8
Neutrons	8	9

(*i*) What is the mass number of X?

(*ii*) What is the mass number of Y?

(*iii*) What is the relation between X and Y?

(*iv*) Which element/elements do they represent? ***(CBSE 2012-13)***

Ans. (*i*) Mass number of X = 8 + 8 = 16

(*ii*) Mass number of Y = 8 + 9 = 17

(*iii*) These represent a pair of isotopes.

(*iv*) The element X and Y is oxygen.

9. Write the electronic configuration of carbon, oxygen and magnesium. ***(CBSE 2012-13)***

Ans.

Carbon (Z = 6)	2, 4
Oxygen (Z = 8)	2, 6
Magnesium (Z = 12)	2, 8, 2

10. An element X has mass number 4 and atomic number 2. Find the valency of X. ***(CBSE 2012-13)***

Ans. Its electronic configuration is K(2). Since K shell is filled, the valency of X is zero.

11. Describe the essential differences between the cathode rays and the canal rays. Why are the canal rays called so ? ***(CBSE 2013-14)***

Ans. The essential differences between cathode rays and canal rays are :

Cathode rays	Canal rays
1. These consist of negatively charged particles.	1. These consist of positively charged particles.
2. *e*/*m* value of cathode rays is same irrespective of the nature of the gas.	2. *e*/*m* value depends upon the nature of the gas taken in the discharge tube.

The canal rays are called so because they pass through the holes or the canals in the cathode.

12. If K and L shells of an atom are completely filled then, what would be

(*i*) Total number of electrons in an atom?

(*ii*) Valency? ***(CBSE 2013-14)***

Ans. K can have maximum of 2 electrons and L can have maximum of 8 electrons. If both K and L are filled then

(*i*) Number of electrons = 2 + 8 = 10

(*ii*) Valency of the atom = zero because outer shell is completely filled.

13. You are given an element $^{16}_{8}Z$. Find out

(*i*) Protons, electrons and neutrons in Z.

(*ii*) Write its electronic configuration.

(*iii*) Valency of Z.

(iv) Write the formula of the compound when P reacts with hydrogen and carbon. ***(CBSE 2012-13)***

Ans. (i) No. of protons = 8

No. of electrons = 8

No. of neutrons = 16 – 8 = 8

(ii) Electronic configuration : 2, 6 or K (2) L (6)

(iii) Valency = 2

(iv) The element Z is O and its compounds with hydrogen and carbon are H_2O and CO_2.

14. Define the term isotopes. Name the element whose isotope is used in

(i) treatment of cancer.

(ii) nuclear reactor. ***(CBSE 2012-13)***

Ans. Isotopes are the atoms of the same element having different mass number.

Element used in

(i) treatment of cancer : Cobalt-60

(ii) nuclear reactor : Uranium-235

15. The atomic number and mass number of an element are 16 and 32 respectively. Find the number of protons, electrons and neutrons in it. Write its electronic configuration. ***(CBSE 2014-15)***

Ans. (i) No. of protons = Atomic number = 16

No. of electrons = Atomic number = 16

No. of neutrons = Mass number– Atomic number

= 32 – 16 = 16

Electronic configuration : 2, 8, 6

16. What were the observations that led to the conclusion that cathode rays are negatively charged? ***(CBSE 2013-14)***

Ans. When an electric field is applied to the cathode rays, they are deflected towards the positively charged plate. This shows that cathode rays are negatively charged. Similarly, when the cathode rays are made to pass through magnetic field, these are deflected. The direction of the deflection suggests that these rays are negatively charged.

17. Show the distribution of electrons in magnesium atom and magnesium ion diagrammatically. Atomic number of magnesium is 12. ***(CBSE 2014-15)***

Ans. Atomic number of Mg is 12 and its electronic distribution is 2, 8, 2. Magnesium ion is formed by the loss of two electrons from the valence shell of the atom. Therefore, its electronic distribution is 2, 8. These are shown as:

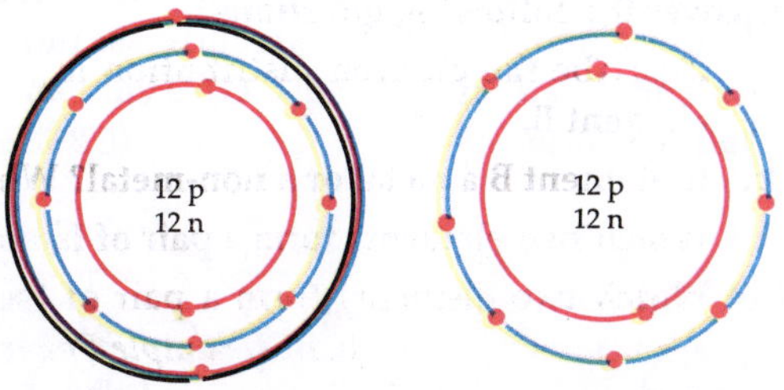

Mg atom Mg^{2+} ion

18. Which two of the following species are isotopes of each other and which two are isobars.

$^{231}_{90}X$ $^{230}_{91}Y$ $^{230}_{88}Z$ $^{233}_{90}X$ ***(CBSE 2013-14)***

Ans. $^{231}_{90}X$ and $^{233}_{90}X$ are isotopes.

$^{230}_{91}Y$ and $^{230}_{88}Z$ are isobars.

19. Define isobars. Give one example. *(CBSE 2014-15)*

Ans. The atoms of different elements having same mass number are called isobars.

For example : $^{40}_{18}Ar$ and $^{40}_{20}Ca$ are isobars because they have same mass number (40).

20. Write the electron distribution of oxygen and sodium atom. How many valence electrons do they have ? ***(CBSE 2015-16)***

Ans. Atomic no. of oxygen = 8

Electron distribution : 2, 6

No. of valence electrons = 6

Atomic no. of Na = 11

Electron distribution : 2, 8, 1

No. of valence electrons = 1

21. An element X has 13 protons, 13 electrons and 14 neutrons. Answer the following questions:

(a) What is the atomic number of X ?

(b) Identify the element.

(c) What is its valency ? What is the number of valence electrons in X ?

(d) What is the type of ion formed by X ? Why ?

(e) Name the scientists who discovered electrons and protons. ***(CBSE 2015-16)***

Ans. (a) Atomic number of X = 13.

(b) Element is aluminium, Al.

(c) Valency = 3, No. of valence electrons = 3 (2, 8, 3)

(d) X can form X^{3+} i.e. Al^{3+} ion because it can lose 3 electrons to acquire noble gas configuration.

(e) Proton was discovered by E. Goldstein

Electron was discovered by J.J. Thomson

22. What information do you get from the figure given below about the atomic number, mass number and valency of atoms X, Y and Z. Give your answer in a tabular form. ***(CBSE 2015-16)***

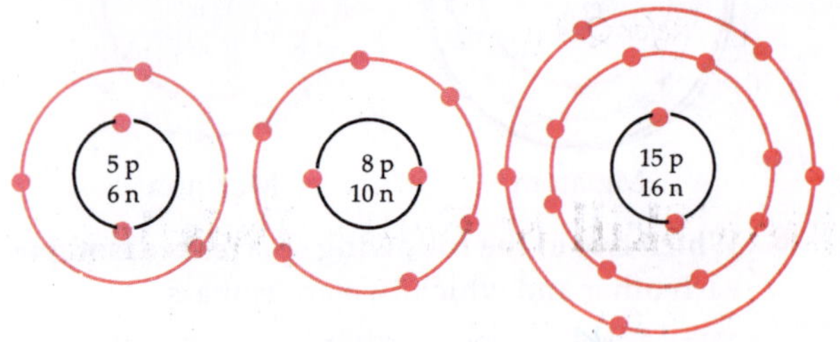

Ans.

Atom	Atomic number	Mass number	Valency
X	5	11	3
Y	8	18	2
Z	15	31	3 or 5

23. (*a*) Why are the shells in which the electron revolve are called energy shells ?

(*b*) Name the shells.

(*c*) How many electrons can be there in M shell ? ***(CBSE 2015-16)***

Ans. (*a*) Each shell has a fixed energy. Therefore, the shells are called energy shells.

(*b*) Shells can be named as K, L, M, N (from the nucleus)

(*c*) M shell can have maximum of 18 electrons.

24. (*a*) What is the relationship between two elements X and Y whose atomic numbers are 18 and 20 respectively but their mass numbers are the same 40.

(*b*) Are their chemical properties same or different ?

(*c*) Which has more number of electrons Na or Na^+ ? ***(CBSE 2015-16)***

Ans. (*a*) The elements X and Y are isobars.

(*b*) Since the atomic numbers of the elements are different, their chemical properties are also different.

(*c*) Na^+ ion is formed by the loss of one electron. Therefore, Na has more electrons (11) than Na^+ ion (10).

25. What is the number of valence electrons in

(*i*) Sodium ion (Na^+)

(*ii*) Oxide ion O^{2-} ***(CBSE 2015-16)***

Ans. (*i*) Sodium (Na^+) ion

Atomic number = 11

No. of electrons in Na atom = 11

No. of electrons in Na^+ ion = 11–1 = 10

Electronic configuration: 2, 8

No. of valence electrons in Na^+ ion = 8

(*ii*) Oxide ion O^{2-}

Atomic number of O atom = 8

No. of electrons in O atom = 8

No. of electrons in O^{2-} ion = 8 + 2 = 10

Electronic configuration: 2, 8

No. of valence electrons in O^{2-} ion = 8

26. (*a*) How many neutrons are present in C-14 isotope of carbon ?

(*b*) How many protons does He^{2+} ion possess ?

(*c*) How many electrons can be filled in the third orbit of an atom at the maximum ? ***(CBSE 2015-16)***

Ans. (*a*) C-14 isotope has atomic no. 6 and mass no. 14

No. of neutrons = Mass no. – Atomic no.

= 14 – 6 = 8

(*b*) He^{2+} ion (atomic no. = 2) has 2 protons.

(*c*) The third orbit of an atom can have maximum of 18 electrons.

27. From the given table answer the following:

Element	Mass number	Atomic number
A	3	2
B	9	4
C	11	5
D	19	9
E	23	11

(*a*) How many electrons are present in B ?

(*b*) Which is an inert gas ? Why ?

(*c*) Which atom will form a negatively charged ion ?

(*d*) Which element has 12 neutrons ? Why ?

(*e*) Which atom will form a cation with one positive charge. ***(CBSE 2015-16)***

Ans. (*a*) 4

(*b*) A is an inert gas because it has completely filled (K) shell.

(*c*) D because it has 7 valence electrons (2, 7).

(*d*) E

(*e*) E

28. **(a) How did Rutherford came to the conclusion that most of the space in an atom is empty ?**

(b) Why do isotopes of an element have similar properties ? ***(CBSE 2015-16)***

Ans. (*a*) During Rutherford's scattering experiments, most of the α-particles passed through the foil without any deflection from their original path. This means that most of the α-particles donot suffer any collision with the mass of the atom. Thus, most of the space in an atom is empty.

(*b*) *Refer Q. 4 (a)*

HOTS Higher Order Thinking Skill & Brain Twisting Questions with Answers

Q 1. Give one point of similarity and one point of difference between :

(*i*) isotopes $^{14}_{6}C$ and $^{12}_{6}C$

(*ii*) isobars $^{40}_{20}Ca$ and $^{40}_{18}Ar$

Ans. (*i*) Both $^{14}_{6}C$ and $^{12}_{6}C$ have same atomic number.

Both $^{14}_{6}C$ and $^{12}_{6}C$ have different atomic mass.

(*ii*) Both $^{40}_{20}Ca$ and $^{40}_{18}Ar$ have same mass number $(n + p)$.

Both $^{40}_{20}Ca$ and $^{40}_{18}Ar$ have different atomic number.

Q 2. In Rutherford's experiment, generally thin foils of heavy atoms like gold and platinum etc. have been used for bombardment by α-particles. If thin foil of light atoms like aluminium is used, what difference would be observed in the results ?

Ans. Heavy atoms such as gold and platinum have heavy nucleus and large positive charge. Therefore, number of α-particles deflected are significant. However, if light atoms are used, they will have light nuclei and small positive charge. Therefore, the number of a-particles deflected will be almost negligible.

Q 3. An element with mass number 81 has 31.7% more neutrons as compared to protons. Calculate the atomic number of the element.

Ans. Mass number = No. of protons + No. of neutrons = 81

i.e $p + n = 81$

Let number of protons $= x$

$$\text{No. of neutrons} = x + \frac{x \times 31.7}{100} = 1.317x$$

Now $x + 1.317x = 81$

$$x = \frac{81}{2.317} = 34.96 \text{ or } 35$$

Atomic number = 35.

Q 4. How many neutrons (*n*), protons (*p*) and electrons (*e*) are present in each of the following :

(*i*) $^{88}_{38}Sr$ (*ii*) $^{35}_{17}Cl^-$ (*iii*) $^{56}_{26}Fe^{2+}$

Ans. (*i*) $^{88}_{38}Sr$ $p = 38, e = 38, n = 88 - 38 = 50$

(*ii*) $^{35}_{17}Cl^-$ $p = 17, e = 17 + 1 = 18, n = 35 - 17 = 18$

(*iii*) $^{56}_{26}Fe^{2+}$ $p = 26, e = 26 - 2 = 24, n = 56 - 26 = 30$

Q 5. An isotope of $^{112}_{50}Sn$ contains 68 neutrons. What will be its mass number?

Ans. No. of protons = 50

No. of neutrons = 68

Mass number = 50 + 68 = 118

Q 6. An ion with mass number 37 possesses one unit of negative charge. If the ion contains 11.1% more neutrons than electrons, find the symbol of the ion.

Ans. Since the ion carries 1 unit of negative charge, it will have one electron more than the number of protons.

Mass number $= n + p = 37$

Let no. of electrons $= x$

No. of protons $= x - 1$

$$\text{No. of neutrons} = x + \frac{x \times 11.1}{100} = 1.111x$$

Now $x - 1 + 1.111x = 37$

$2.111x = 38$

$x = 18$

No. of electrons = 18

No. of protons = 18 − 1 = 17

No. of neutrons = 35 − 17 = 18

Since atomic number is 17 it is chlorine.

Symbol $^{35}_{17}Cl^-$.

Revision Exercise

Answers and Hints on Page 41

OBJECTIVE QUESTIONS

A. Multiple Choice Questions

I. NCERT Exemplar Problems

1. Which of the following correctly represent the electronic distribution in the Mg atom?
   (*a*) 3, 8, 1 (*b*) 2, 8, 2
   (*c*) 1, 8, 3 (*d*) 8, 2, 2

2. Rutherford's alpha (α) particles scattering experiment resulted in the discovery of
   (*a*) electron (*b*) proton
   (*c*) nucleus in the atom (*d*) atomic mass

3. The number of electrons in an element X is 15 and the number of neutrons is 16. Which of the following is the correct representation of the element?
   (*a*) ${}^{31}_{15}X$ (*b*) ${}^{31}_{16}X$
   (*b*) ${}^{16}_{15}X$ (*d*) ${}^{15}_{16}X$

4. Dalton's atomic theory successfully explained
   (*i*) Law of conservation of mass
   (*ii*) Law of constant composition
   (*iii*) Law of radioactivity
   (*iv*) Law of multiple proportion
   (*a*) (*i*), (*ii*) and (*iii*) (*b*) (*i*), (*iii*) and (*iv*)
   (*c*) (*ii*), (*iii*) and (*iv*) (*d*) (*i*), (*ii*) and (*iv*)

5. Which of the following statements about Rutherford's model of atom are correct?
   (*i*) considered the nucleus as positively charged
   (*ii*) established that the α–particles are four times as heavy as a hydrogen atom
   (*iii*) can be compared to solar system
   (*iv*) was in agreement with Thomson's model
   (*a*) (*i*) and (*iii*) (*b*) (*ii*) and (*iii*)
   (*c*) (*i*) and (*iv*) (*d*) only (*i*)

6. Which of the following are true for an element?
   (*i*) Atomic number = number of protons + number of electrons
   (*ii*) Mass number = number of protons + number of neutrons
   (*iii*) Atomic mass = number of protons = number of neutrons
   (*iv*) Atomic number = number of protons = number of electrons
   (*a*) (*i*) and (*ii*) (*b*) (*i*) and (*iii*)
   (*c*) (*ii*) and (*iii*) (*d*) (*ii*) and (*iv*)

7. In the Thomson's model of atom, which of the following statments are correct?
   (*i*) the mass of the atom is assumed to be uniformaly distributed over the atom
   (*ii*) the positive charge is assumed to be uniformaly distributed over the atom
   (*iii*) the electrons are uniformaly distributed in the positively charged sphere
   (*iv*) the electrons attract each other to stabilise the atom
   (*a*) (*i*), (*ii*) and (*iii*) (*b*) (*i*) and (*iii*)
   (*c*) (*i*) and (*iv*) (*d*) (*i*), (*iii*) and (*iv*)

8. Rutherford's α–particle scattering experiment showed that
   (*i*) electrons have negative charge
   (*ii*) the mass and positive charge of the atom is concentrated in the nucleus
   (*iii*) neutron exists in the nucleus
   (*iv*) most of the space in atom is empty
   Which of the above statements are correct?
   (*a*) (*i*) and (*iii*) (*b*) (*ii*) and (*iv*)
   (*c*) (*i*) and (*iv*) (*d*) (*iii*) and (*iv*)

9. The ion of an element has 3 positive charges. Mass number of the atom is 27 and the number of neutrons is 14. What is the number of electrons in the ion?
   (*a*) 13 (*b*) 10
   (*c*) 14 (*d*) 16

10. Identify the Mg^{2+} ion from the given figures where, ***n*** and ***p*** represent the number of neutrons and protons respectively

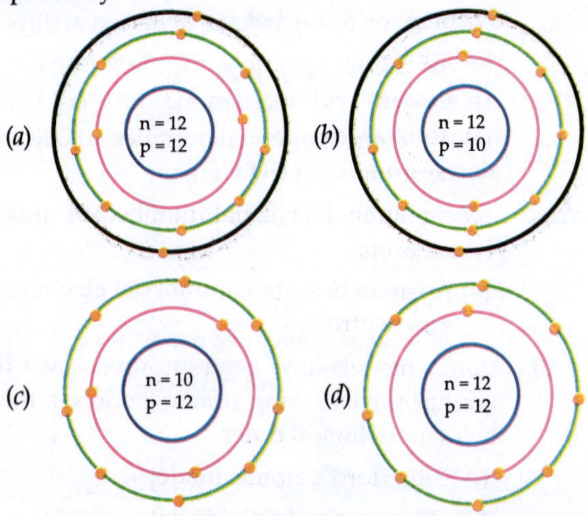

11. In a sample of ethyl ethanoate ($CH_3COOC_2H_5$) the two oxygen atoms have the same number of electrons but different number of neutrons. Which of the following is the correct reason for it?

(*a*) One of the oxygen atoms has gained electrons

(*b*) One of the oxygen atoms has gained two neutrons

(*c*) The two oxygen atoms are isotopes

(*d*) The two oxygen atoms are isobars.

12. Elements with valency 1 are

(*a*) always metals

(*b*) always metalloids

(*c*) either metals or non-metals

(*d*) always non-metals

13. The first model of an atom was given by

(*a*) N. Bohr (*b*) E. Goldstein

(*c*) Rutherford (*d*) J.J. Thomson

14. An atom with 3 protons and 4 neutrons will have a valency of

(*a*) 3 (*b*) 7

(*c*) 1 (*d*) 4

15. The electron distribution in an aluminium atom is

(*a*) 2, 8, 3 (*b*) 2, 8, 2

(*c*) 8, 2, 3 (*d*) 2, 3, 8

16. Which of the following in figure do not represent Bohr's model of an atom correctly?

(*i*)

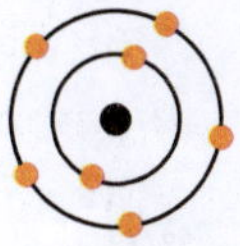

(*ii*)

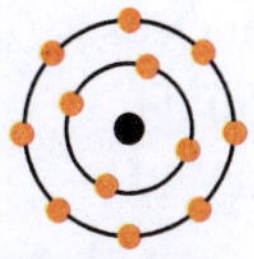

(*iii*)

(*iv*)

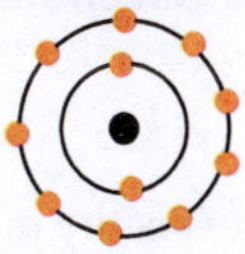

(*a*) (*i*) and (*ii*) (*b*) (*ii*) and (*iii*)

(*c*) (*ii*) and (*iv*) (*d*) (*i*) and (*iv*)

17. Which of the following statements is always correct?

(*a*) An atom has equal number of electrons and protons.

(*b*) An atom has equal number of electrons and neutrons.

(*c*) An atom has equal number of protons and neutrons.

(*d*) An atom has equal number of electrons, protons and neutrons.

18. Atomic models have been improved over the years. Arrange the following atomic models in the order of their chronological order

(*i*) Rutherford's atomic model

(*ii*) Thomson's atomic model

(*iii*) Bohr's atomic model

(*a*) (*i*), (*ii*) and (*iii*) (*b*) (*ii*), (*iii*) and (*i*)

(*c*) (*ii*), (*i*) and (*iii*) (*d*) (*iii*), (*ii*) and (*i*)

II. Additional Questions

1. Rutherford's alpha particle scattering experiment led to the discovery of

(*a*) neutron (*b*) nucleus

(*c*) proton (*d*) electron

2. The number of protons in $^{31}_{15}P^{3-}$ ion is

(*a*) 15 (*b*) 16

(*c*) 18 (*d*) 3

3. The electron distribution of Al^{3+} ion is

(*a*) 2, 8, 3 (*b*) 2, 8, 6

(*c*) 2, 8 (*d*) 2, 8, 8

4. The number of valence electrons is O^{2-} (Z = 6) ion is

(*a*) 6 (*b*) 4

(*c*) 8 (*d*) 2

5. The four atomic species can be represented as given below. Which of these are isobars?

(*i*) $^{201}_{60}X$ (*ii*) $^{200}_{61}X$

(*iii*) $^{200}_{58}X$ (*iv*) $^{203}_{60}X$

(*a*) (*i*) and (*ii*) (*b*) (*ii*) and (*iv*)

(*c*) (*ii*) and (*iii*) (*d*) (*i*) and (*iv*)

6. An atom has mass number 209 and atomic number 82. The number of electrons in it is

(*a*) 82 (*b*) 209

(*c*) 127 (*d*) 129

7. Which isotope of oxygen has more number of protons : $^{16}_{8}O$, $^{17}_{8}O$ and $^{18}_{8}O$

(*a*) $^{16}_{8}O$ (*b*) $^{17}_{8}O$

(*c*) $^{18}_{8}O$ (*d*) all have same

8. Neutron was discovered by

(*a*) Rutherford (*b*) Goldstein

(*c*) Chadwick (*d*) Thomson

9. The number of valence electrons in argon (Z = 18) is

(*a*) 8 (*b*) 6

(*c*) 4 (*d*) 0

10. The ion of an element has 3 positive charge. The mass of the atom of this element is 27 and the number of neutrons is 14. What is the number of electrons in the ion?

(*a*) 4 (*b*) 13

(*c*) 10 (*d*) 16

11. Lithium has 3 electrons, 4 neutrons and 3 protons. Its mass number is :

(*a*) 3 (*b*) 4

(*c*) 7 (*d*) 1

12. Isotopes have :

(*a*) same number of neutrons.

(*b*) same number of electrons but different number of protons.

(*c*) same number of protons and neutrons.

(*d*) same number of electrons and protons.

13. An atom has the arrangement of electrons in shells as : 1st and 2nd shells full and 2 electrons in 3rd shell. The atom is:
(a) carbon (b) magnesium
(c) sulphur (d) fluorine

14. Which of the following configuration of electrons represent sodium ?
(a) 2, 8, 4 (b) 2, 8, 5
(c) 2, 3 (d) 2, 8, 1

15. Which of the following statements is not correct regarding cathode rays ?
(a) These rays are deflected towards the positive pole of electricity.
(b) These rays consist of particles having mass equal to mass of proton.
(c) The charge/mass ratio of all cathode rays is same.
(d) These rays travel in straight lines.

16. Which of the following does not have neutrons ?
(a) H (b) He
(c) Ne (d) C

17. The maximum number of electrons in second shell are :
(a) 2 (b) 8
(c) 18 (d) 32

18. The valency of aluminium (2, 8, 3) is :
(a) 2 (b) 3
(c) 5 (d) 1

19. Which of the following has maximum valence electrons ? (Atomic numbers are given in brackets)
(a) Na (11) (b) N (7)
(c) Mg (12) (d) Si (14)

20. Which of the following elements (atomic number given in brackets) have valency 2?
(a) C (6) (b) P (15)
(c) Mg (12) (d) Ar (18)

21. The mass number of an element is 39 and it has 20 neutrons. The atomic number of the element is
(a) 20 (b) 39
(c) 19 (d) 59

22. Mass number of atom is 27 and the number of neutrons is 14. The number of electrons in its tripositive ion will be
(a) 13 (b) 14
(c) 10 (d) 17

23. The four atomic species can be represented as:
(i) $^{130}_{52}X$ (ii) $^{31}_{15}Y$
(iii) $^{130}_{56}Z$ (iv) $^{32}_{15}Y$
The isobars among these are
(a) (i) and (ii) (b) (iii) and (iv)
(c) (i) and (iii) (d) (ii) and (iii)

24. The number of valence electrons in S^{2-} (Z = 16) is
(a) 8 (b) 6
(c) 2 (d) 10

25. Rutherford's alpha scattering experiment was responsible for the discovery of
(a) Atomic nucleus (b) Electron
(c) Proton (d) Neutron

26. Positive ions are formed from the neutral atom by
(a) loss of protons (b) gain of electrons
(c) loss of electrons (d) loss of neutrons

27. The alpha particles are the same as
(a) protons (b) helium nuclei
(c) helium atoms (d) lithium nuclei

28. Which of the following elements has same number of protons, electrons and neutrons ?
(a) Magnesium (b) Beryllium
(c) Helium (d) All of these

29. Which of the following elements has same number of protons, electrons and neutrons ?
(a) $^{27}_{13}Al$ (b) $^{24}_{12}Mg$
(c) $^{35}_{17}Cl$ (d) $^{23}_{11}Na$

30. The electronic configuration of an ion M^{2+} is 2, 8. If its mass number is 24, the number of neutrons in its nucleus is
(a) 14 (b) 12
(c) 10 (d) 24

31. Number of valence electrons in $^{27}_{13}Al$ is
(a) 5 (b) 3
(c) 7 (d) 2

32. If A is the mass number and Z is the atomic number of an element, then the number of neutrons are
(a) A + Z (b) Z – A
(c) A – Z (d) A / Z

33. Which of following will have equal number of electrons ?
(a) Cl^- and Br^- (b) Na^+ and Mg^{2+}
(c) Ar and Ne (d) Mg^{2+} and Ca^{2+}

34. Match the element given in Column I with its property given in Column II.

Column I	Column II
(P) Sodium	1. 9 protons
(Q) Fluorine	2. 32 mass number
(R) Magnesium	3. 12 neutrons
(S) Sulphur	4. 11 electrons

(a) P–4, Q–1, R–3, S–2 (b) P–4, Q–2, R–3, S–1
(c) P–3, Q–1, R–2, S–4 (d) P–4, Q–3, R–2, S–1

35. Match the electrons distribution in Column I with element as given in Column II.

Column I	Column II
(P) 2, 8, 6	1. Beryllium
(Q) 2, 2	2. Aluminium
(R) 2, 6	3. Sulphur
(S) 2, 8, 3	4. Oxygen

(*a*) P–2, Q–1, R–4, S–3 (*b*) P–3, Q–2, R–4, S–1

(*c*) P–3, Q–1, R–4, S–2 (*d*) P–3, Q–1, R–2, S–4

36. Match Column I with Column II

Column I	Column II
(P) Oxygen	1. technique to know age of fossils
(Q) Radio Co–60	2. Valency 2
(R) Carbon–dating	3. 2, 8, 8 configuration
(S) Chloride ion	4. treatment of tumours

(*a*) P–3, Q–4, R–1, S–2 (*b*) P–1, Q–2, R–4, S–3

(*c*) P–2, Q–1, R–4, S–3 (*d*) P–2, Q–4, R–1, S–3

37. Match the electronic configuration of element in Column I with its valency in Column II

Column I	Column II
(P) 2, 8, 2	1. 0
(Q) 2, 3	2. 1
(R) 2, 8	3. 2
(S) 2, 8, 1	4. 3

(*a*) P–3, Q–4, R–1, S–2 (*b*) P–2, Q–3, R–1, S–4

(*c*) P–2, Q–4, R–3, S–1 (*d*) P–2, Q–4, R–3, S–1

B. Assertion–Reason Type Questions

For the following questions two statements are given-one labeled *Assertion* (A) and the other labeled *Reason* (R). Select the correct answer to these questions from the codes (*a*), (*b*), (*c*) and (*d*) as given below:

(*a*) Both A and R are true and R is correct explanation of the assertion

(*b*) Both A and R are true and R is not the correct explanation of the assertion

(*c*) A is true but R is false

(*d*) A is false but R is true.

1. **Assertion:** An atom of an element is electrically neutral.
   Reason: It contains equal number of protons and neutrons.
2. **Assertion:** Bohr's orbits are also called stationary orbits.
   Reason: Electrons remain stationary in these orbits.
3. **Assertion:** Cathode rays get deflected towards the positive plate of electric field.
   Reason: Cathode rays consist of negatively charged particles known as electrons.
4. **Assertion:** The atoms of different elements having same mass number but different atomic numbers are known as isobars.
   Reason: The sum of protons and neutrons in the isobars is also same.
5. **Assertion:** Isotopes of an element have almost similar properties.
   Reason: Isotopes have same electronic distributions which determine the chemical properties.
6. **Assertion:** During Rutherford's scattering experiments, the α-particles passing very close to nucleus also got slightly deflected.
   Reason: Because of the positive charge of the nucleus, α-particles suffered repulsion.
7. **Assertion:** $^{35}_{17}Cl$ and $^{37}_{17}Cl$ are pair of isobars.
   Reason: Isobars have same mass number.
8. **Assertion:** Hydrogen, deuterium and tritium are isotopes of hydrogen.
   Reason: Hydrogen, deuterium and tritium have same atomic number but different mass numbers.
9. **Assertion:** Na^+ has completely filled shells.
   Reason: In Na^+, K(2) and L(8) are completely filled.
10. **Assertion:** In Rutherford's experiment, most of the α-particles passed through the gold foil undeflected.
    Reason: Most of the space inside the atom is empty.

C. Fill in the Blanks

1. Cathode rays consist of beam of fast moving ________.
2. The total number of protons and neutrons in the nucleus of an atom is called its ________.
3. The maximum number of electrons in L shell is ________.
4. Phosphorus has ________ electrons in M shell.
5. Rutherford's α–particle scattering experiment led to the discovery of the ________.
6. No. of neutrons in $^{56}_{26}Fe^{2+}$ is ________.
7. Mercury contains 80 protons, 80 electrons and 120 neutrons. Its mass number is ________.
8. The maximum number of electrons in 1st shell is ________.
9. The α-particles carry ________ units of positive charge.
10. An atoms has atomic mass number 23 and atomic number 11. The atom has ________ electrons.

D. Paragraph Based Questions

1. Answer questions 1(*a*)-1(*d*) on the basis of your understanding of the following data and its related studied concepts.

The following data represents four atoms A, B, C and D:

Element	Electron distribution	Mass number
A	2, 8, 7	37
B	2, 8, 5	31
C	2, 8, 8, 1	40
D	2, 8, 7	35

Answer the following questions :

1(*a*) Which two elements form a pair of isotopes ?

1(*b*) Which of these elements has maximum and minimum number of neutrons ?

1(*c*) What will be electron distribution of B^{3-} ion ?

1(*d*) Which of these can show maximum negative valency ?

2. Answer questions 2(*a*) - 2(*d*) on the basis of following table in which the elements W, X, Y and Z are hypothetical.

Element	Protons	Neutron	Electrons
W	9	10	10
X	19	20	18
Y	26	30	26
Z	3	7	3

2(*a*) What is mass number? What is the mass number of Y?

2(*b*) Which of these elements is (*i*) cation and (*ii*) anion?

2(*c*) Give the electronic distribution of neutral W and Z

2(*d*) Name the elements X and Z.

Very Short Answer Questions

1. How many times a proton is heavier than an electron ?
2. Who was the first to discover neutrons ?
3. What are cathode rays ?
4. How will you explain that the electron is a negatively charged particle ?
5. Compare the properties of electron, proton and neutron.
6. What are the limitation of J. J. Thomson model of atom ?
7. The atomic number of oxygen and sulphur are 8 and 16 respectively. What will be the number of electrons in these ?
8. How do the charges on electron and proton differ ?
9. Complete the following sentence :
   The anode rays obtained from hydrogen gas consist of particles called ....
10. What is a proton ? How does it differ from a neutron ?
11. What are the limitations of Rutherford model of atom ?
12. An element may be represented as $^{40}_{18}X$. Find the number of electrons, protons and neutrons in this atom. Give its electronic configuration.
13. Is it possible to write down the electronic configuration of an atom if we know its atomic number ? Why is this so ?
14. Will the element F(Z = 9) and Cl(Z = 17) show similar properties ? Why ?
15. Out of O–16 and O–18 isotopes, which has more number of neutrons ?
16. What determines the number of positive charges on the nucleus ?
17. What is nucleus ?
18. What is an orbit ?
19. The mass number and atomic number of an element is 23 and 11 respectively. What is the number of nucleons present in it ?
20. Define valency and valence shell.
21. An element has atomic number 19 and mass number 39. How many electrons and protons are present in its unipositive ion ?
22. Give the nuclear composition of $^{18}_{8}O$.
23. Define the term isotope with a suitable example.
24. Give one example of isobars.
25. Find the atomic number of an element whose atom has the electronic configuration 2, 8, 4.

Short Answer Questions

1. Define : (*i*) Mass number, (*ii*) Atomic number (*iii*) Isotopes
2. How was neutron discovered ? Explain.
3. (*a*) What are isotopes? Write three isotopes of hydrogen.
   (*b*) Isotopes have same chemical properties but different physical properties. Explain.
4. (*a*) How do the two isotopes of chlorine differ ?
   (*b*) Give two applications of isotopes.
5. Write the electronic configurations of $^{27}_{13}Al$, $^{32}_{16}S$ and $^{35}_{17}Cl$.
6. Explain :
   (*i*) Nucleus of an atom carries positive charge.
   (*ii*) Most of the space in an atom is empty.
7. What are the characteristic features of Rutherford model of an atom ? What is the limitation of this model ?
8. Write the Bohr Bury scheme to fill the electrons in various energy levels of an atom. Using these rules, write the electron arrangement of the elements having atomic numbers 11 and 18.
9. What are the main postulates of Bohr's atomic theory ?
10. What are the maximum number of electrons that can be present in the K, L and M shells ?
11. What is mass number of an element ? How is the mass number related to the protons and neutrons present in the nucleus of an atom ? Is it same as atomic number ?
12. Write electronic configuration for the following elements:
    $^{16}_{8}O$, $^{28}_{14}Si$, $^{40}_{18}Ar$.

13. What were the conclusions drawn from Rutherford's experiment of α-particles scattering by a gold foil ?

14. Name the elements which have the following electronic configuration :

(i) 2, 6 (ii) 2, 7 (iii) 2, 8, 1

(iv) 2, 8, 7 (v) 2, 8 (vi) 2, 4

Which of these is chemically inert ?

15. Oxygen has three isotopes having mass number 16, 17 and 18. How do atoms of these isotopes differ ?

16. Consider an atom of manganese, represented as $^{55}_{25}Mn$ and Mn^{2+} ion. Give the number of

(i) electrons

(ii) protons

(iii) nucleons present in these.

17. What was bold new concept incorporated by Neils Bohr in the model of atom proposed by him ?

18. What experiment established the presence of atomic nucleus ? What features of the nucleus were deduced from this experiment ?

19. You have learnt that the value of e/m for electron is 2000 times that of the proton or H^+. Calculate the charge to mass ratio for He^+ and He^{2+} in comparison to e/m of the electron. Mass of helium is four times that of hydrogen.

20. Match the description in Column B with the term/statement in Column A.

Column A	Column B
(a) Atomic number	(i) shells in an atom.
(b) Isotopes	(ii) positively charged particles having mass equal to that of a hydrogen atom.
(c) Valence electrons	(iii) number of positive charge on the nucleus.
(d) Protons	(iv) electrons present in outermost shell.
(e) K, L, M	(v) a technique to know the age of dead bodies.
(f) Carbon dating	(vi) atoms having same atomic number but different mass numbers.

21. What are the main applications of isotopes ?

Long Answer Questions

1. Who discovered the presence of electrons in an atom ? Discuss detailed experiment connected with it. How is its mass and charge determined ?

2. Discuss in brief the Bohr's model of atom.

3. Describe Rutherford's experiment to establish the position of electrons and protons in an atom.

4. What observations in scattering experiment led Rutherford to make the following conclusions :

(i) The most of the space in an atom is empty.

(ii) The whole mass of an atom is present in the centre of the atom.

(iii) Nucleus has positive charge.

5. Write brief notes on :

(i) Isotopes (ii) Isobars (iii) Application of isotopes

6. The following table lists mass number and atomic number of five elements A, B, C, D and E.

Element	Mass number	Atomic number
A	3	1
B	7	3
C	35	17
D	40	18
E	37	17

(i) How many protons are there in an atom of B ?

(ii) How many neutrons are there in an atom of A ?

(iii) How many electrons are there in an atom of E ?

(iv) How many nucleons are there in an atom of D ?

(v) Which atoms are isotopes of the same element ?

7. Define isotopes. What are the essential characteristics of isotopes ? Give important applications of isotopes.

8. Give important differences between :

(i) Canal rays and cathode rays

(ii) Atomic number and mass number

(iii) Isotopes and isobars.

Solution File

Answer & Solutions to Selected Questions

Practice Exercises

Practice Exercise 4A

1. About 1840 times 2. (i) negative (ii) positive 3. Proton 4. True statement (c) 5. 1840 : 1 (c)

6. Cathode rays are negatively charged while anode rays are positively charged.
7. (*a*) electrons (*b*) 1.60×10^{-19} (*c*) 1840 (*d*) positively.
8. Yes.
9. (*i*) Proton is positively charged while electron is negatively charged.
(*ii*) Proton is heavier than electron. Proton is about 1840 times heavier than an electron.
10. 1.67×10^{-27} kg, 1.602×10^{-19} C
11. 35, 17
12. 79, 118, 79
13. (*i*) 18, 18, 40 (*ii*) nucleons (*iii*) 10^{-15}
14. 5, 4, 4; 12, 24, 12; 14, 14, 28; 16, 15, 15
15. (*i*) A is an element with mass number 19 (*ii*) C
16. It indicates atomic number of element X is 13 and its mass number is 27.
17. (*i*) proton (*ii*) electron (*iii*) neutron
18. Nucleons
19. No charge
20. neutrons and protons
21. 2
22. Yes, all atoms have the numbers of electrons and protons same because these are electrically neutral.
23. Cation
24. 17
25. James Chadwick discovered neutron. He bombarded a thin sheet of beryllium element with fast moving α-particles and neutrons were produced.

$${}^{9}_{4}Be + {}^{4}_{2}He \longrightarrow {}^{12}_{6}C + {}^{1}_{0}n$$

Beryllium Carbon Neutron

26. (*a*) Radium (*b*) Most of the space in an atom is empty.
27. 12
28. Neutron
29. 10
30. Hydrogen
31. Gold
32. Yes, of a heavy metal.
33. Rutherford discovered the nucleus of the atom by bombarding a thin gold foil by fast moving α-particles. His experiments were called Rutherford's scattering experiments.
34. (*i*) In hydrogen, two subatomic particles namely *electron* and *proton* are present.
(*ii*) In sodium, three subatomic particles namely *electron, proton* and *neutron* are present.
35. 8, because atomic number is equal to number of protons.
36. The discovery of neutron has helped to account for the mass of the atom.
37. It stands for the atom of nitrogen. The number on the lower side of the symbol represents atomic number and the number on the upper side represents mass number. Thus, ${}^{14}_{7}N$ represents nitrogen atom having atomic number 7 and mass number 14.
38. (*a*) E. Rutherford (*b*) James Dalton (*c*) Niels Bohr (*d*) James Chadwick (*e*) E. Goldstein
39. (*i*) Symbol of the element
(*ii*) Mass number of the element (no. of protons and neutrons in the nucleus)
(*iii*) Atomic number of the element (no. of protons in the nucleus)
40. First row : 16, 8, 8; second row : 13, 13, 14, third row : 17, 18, 18, fourth row : 24, 12, 12.

Practice Exercise 4B

1. K L M
2 8 3 or 2, 8, 3
2. (*i*) 8 (*ii*) 1 (*iii*) 7
2. (*i*) 8 (*ii*) 1 (*iii*) 7
3. (*i*) K 2, L 4 or 2, 4 (*ii*) K 2, L 8, M 2 or 2, 8, 2
4. 18
5. (*i*) 19 (*ii*) K L M N
2 8 8 1
6. (*i*) Boron, B (*ii*) Neon, Ne (*iii*) Potassium, K
8. 5
9. 1
10. A and C
11. (*i*) isotopes (*ii*) isobars (*iii*) isotopes (*iv*) isobars (*v*) isobars (*vi*) isotopes
12. 10.8 u
14. (*i*) 86, 136, 86 (*ii*) zero (*iii*) 86.
15. (*i*)

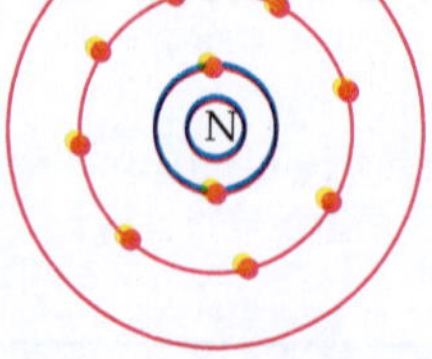

(*ii*) 23 (*iii*) 12
16. A : 1 B : 3
17. (*i*) 11 (*ii*) 11, 12, 13 (*iii*) 11 (*iv*) 22, 23, 24 (*v*) isotopes
18. (*i*) 4 (*ii*) 2 (*iii*) 6

19. (*i*) Mass number = 40 (*ii*) Atomic number = 20

(*iii*) Electronic distribution :

K	L	M	N
2	8	8	2

or 2, 8, 8, 2

20. Let percentage abundance of 1st isotope (^{10}B) = x

Percentage abundance of 2nd isotope (^{11}B) = $100 - x$

Average atomic mass = 10.80

$$\text{Average atomic mass} = \frac{\text{Mass of 1st isotope} + \text{Mass of 2nd isotope}}{100}$$

$$10.80 = \frac{x \times 10 + (100 - x) \times 11}{100}$$

or $1080 = 10x + 1100 - 11x$

or $x = 1100 - 1080 = 20$

Abundance of ^{10}B = 20%

Abundance of ^{11}B = 100 – 20 = **80%.**

21. (**line 1**), 30, 26, (**line 2**), 26, 33, 26.

22. isotopes : A and D, isobars : B and C.

23.

	K	L	M
Lithium (Z = 3)	2	1	
Nitrogen (Z = 7)	2	5	
Neon (Z = 10)	2	8	
Magnesium (Z = 12)	2	8	2
Silicon (Z = 14)	2	8	4

24. 8

25. No, isotopes represent same element.

26. No

27. 18

28. Mass number and are called isobars.

29. $2n^2$

30. (*i*) True (*ii*) True (*iii*) True (*iv*) False (*v*) False

Revision Exercise

OBJECTIVE QUESTIONS

A. Multiple Choice Questions

I. NCERT Exemplar Problems

1. (*b*) Mg has atomic number 12 and its electronic configuration is 2, 8, 2.

2. (*c*)

3. (*a*) No. of electrons = No. of protons = 15

Mass number = No. of protons + No. of neutrons = 15 + 16 = 31

$\therefore$ $^{31}_{15}X$

4. (*d*) Dalton's atomic theory explained all laws of chemical combination.

5. (*a*) Both the statements (*i*) and (*iii*) are correct.

6. (*d*) **7.** (*a*)

8. (*b*) Statements (*ii*) and (*iv*) are correct. During Rutherford scattering experiment neutron was not discovered and hence statement (*iii*) is not correct.

9. (*b*) It is Al^{3+} and has 13 protons and 10 electrons.

10. (*d*) It has 12 protons, 12 neutrons and 10 electrons.

11. (*c*)

12. (*c*) Elements with +1 valency are metals and those with –1 valency are non-metals.

13. (*d*)

14. (*c*) It has three electrons and its electronic distribution is 2, 1.

15. (*a*) The atomic number of Al is 13 and its electronic distribution is 2, 8, 3.

16. (*c*) First shell (K) cannot have more than 2 electrons and second shell (L) cannot have more than 8 electrons.

17. (*a*)

18. (*c*) The correct order is Thomson, Rutherford and Bohr.

II. Additional Questions

1. (*b*); **2.** (*a*); **3.** (*c*); **4.** (*c*); **5.** (*c*);
6. (*a*); **7.** (*d*); **8.** (*c*); **9.** (*d*); **10.** (*c*).

11. (*c*) Mass no. = n + p = 4 + 3 = 7

12. (*d*); **13.** (*b*); **14.** (*d*); **15.** (*b*);

16. (*a*) Hydrogen does not have neutrons

17. (*b*); **18.** (*b*);

19. (*b*) Na (2, 8, 1), N (2, 5), Mg (2, 8, 2), Si (2, 8, 4)

20. (*c*);

21. (*c*) No. of protons = 39 – 20 = 19, Atomic number = 19

22. (*c*) No. of electrons = No. of protons = 27 – 14 = 13

23. (*c*) (*i*) and (*iii*) are isobars because these have same mass number (130).

24. (*a*) Electron distribution of S^{2-} ion : 2, 8, 8

No. of valence electrons = 8.

25. (*a*); **26.** (*c*); **27.** (*b*); **28.** (*d*); **29.** (*b*);

30. (*b*) Mass number = n + p = 24

No. of electrons in M = 10 + 2 = 12

No. of protons = 24 – 12 = 12

31. (*b*) electron distribution of Al ; 2, 8, 3

No. of valence electrons = 3

32. (*c*); **33.** (*b*). **34.** (*a*) **35.** (*c*) **36.** (*d*)

37. (*a*)

B. Assertion–Reason Type

1. (*c*) An atom contains equal number of protons and electrons and hence is electrically neutral.
2. (*c*) Electrons are not stationary in an orbit.
3. (*a*) **4.** (*b*) **5.** (*a*) **6.** (*a*)
7. (*d*) $^{35}_{17}Cl$ and $^{37}_{17}Cl$ are isotopes.
8. (*a*) **9.** (*a*) **10.** (*a*).

C. Fill in the Blanks

1. electrons **2.** mass number **3.** 8
4. 5 **5.** nucleus **6.** 30
7. 200 **8.** 2 **9.** 2
10. 11

D. Paragraph Based Questions

1(*a*). A and D

1(*b*). Maximum no. of neutrons : C

Minimum no. of neutrons : B

1(*c*) 2, 8, 8

1(*d*) B

2(*a*) 56

2(*b*) (i) X^+ (ii) W^-

2(*c*) 2, 7 : 2, 1

2(*d*) X : Potassium; Z : Lithium

Very Short Answer Questions

1. 1840 times **2.** James Chadwick

7. 8 and 16 **9.** protons

12. $e = 18, p = 18, n = 20$, electronic configuration : 2, 8, 8

15. O–18 **16.** Number of protons

19. 23 **21.** $p = 19, e = 18$

22. proton = 8, neutron = 10

Short Answer Questions

4(*a*). They have different mass numbers and number of neutrons.

8. 2, 8, 1; 2, 8, 8 **10.** 2, 8, 18

12. $^{16}_{8}O$: 2, 6; $^{28}_{14}Si$: 2, 8, 4; $^{40}_{18}Ar$: 2, 8, 8

14. (*i*) oxygen (*ii*) fluorine (*iii*) sodium (*iv*) chlorine (*v*) neon; neon is chemically inert (*vi*) carbon

16. (*i*) 25, 23 (*ii*) 25, 25 (*iii*) 55, 55

20. (*a*) (*iii*), (*b*) (*vi*), (*c*) (*iv*), (*d*) (*ii*), (*e*) (*i*), (*f*) (*v*)

Competition File

NTSE -SAT—Target: Scholastic Aptitude Test

1. The electronic configuration of an element with atomic number 19 will be

(*a*) 2, 9, 8 (*b*) 2, 8, 9
(*c*) 2, 8, 8, 1 (*d*) 2, 10, 7 (*NTSE 2015-16*)

2. Proton was discovered by

(*a*) J.J. Thomson (*b*) Chadwick
(*c*) E. Goldstein (*d*) Rutherford (*NTSE 2015-16*)

3. What is the electronic configuration of Cl^- ?

(*a*) 2, 8, 7 (*b*) 2, 8, 8
(*c*) 2, 8, 6 (*d*) 2, 8, 8, 1 (***NTSE 2015-16***)

4. If there are 12 neutrons in an atom and its atomic number is 11. How many protons are present in it ?

(*a*) 11 (*b*) 12
(*c*) 23 (*d*) 1 (***NTSE 2015-16***)

5. How many subatomic particles are present in an α-particle used in Rutherford scattering experiment ?

	No. of protons	No. of neutrons	No. of electrons
(*a*)	4	0	0
(*b*)	2	0	2
(*c*)	2	2	0
(*d*)	2	2	1

4(*a*). Which of the following element has an electronic configuration 2, 8, 6?

(*a*) Sulphur (*b*) Oxygen
(*c*) Phosphorus (*d*) Chlorine.

7. Which of the following element show variable valency?

(*a*) Na (*b*) Mg
(*c*) Fe (*d*) Zn.

8. Electron was discovered by

(*a*) J.J. Thomson (*b*) Chadwick
(*c*) E. Goldstein (*d*) Rutherford.

9. Electronic configuration of Na^+ is

(*a*) 2, 8, 1 (*b*) 2, 8, 8

(*c*) 2, 8 (*d*) 2, 8, 8, 1

10. Valency of sulphur atom in SO_2 is

(*a*) 3 (*b*) 2

(*c*) 4 (*d*) 6

11. If there are 12 neutrons in an atom and its atomic number is 11. Then how many electrons are present in it?

(*a*) 23 (*b*) 12

(*c*) 10 (*d*) 11

12. Isotopes of an element has

(*a*) Same physical properties

(*b*) Different chemical properties

(*c*) Different number of neutrons

(*d*) Different atomic number (*NTSE 2018-19*)

13. Number of valence electrons in Cl^- ion are

(*a*) 16 (*b*) 8

(*c*) 17 (*d*) 18 (*NTSE 2018-19*)

14. Which of the following is correct electronic configuration of sodium

(*a*) 2, 8, 1 (b) 8, 2, 1

(*c*) 2, 1, 8 (*d*) 2, 8, 2 (*NTSE 2018-19*)

15. What is the maximum number of electrons that can be accommodated in the outermost orbit?

(*a*) 2 (*b*) 8

(*c*) 3 (*d*) 18 (*NTSE 2018-19*)

16. Distribution of electrons in carbon is as follows :

(*a*) 2, 4 (*b*) 2, 2, 2

(*c*) 4, 2 (*d*) None of the these

(*NTSE 2018-19*)

17. The electronic configuration of an atom is 2, 8. Which of the following element has similar chemical properties with it?

(*a*) N (7) (*b*) F (9)

(*c*) P (15) (*d*) Ar (18) (*NTSE 2018-19*)

18. Which of the following radioactive isotope is used in the treatment of Cancer?

(*a*) Iodine–131 (*b*) Uranium–235

(*c*) Sodium–24 (*d*) Cobalt–60

(*NTSE 2018-19*)

19. The ion of an element has 3 positive charge, 27 mass number and 14 neutrons. Find the number of electrons in this ion.

(*a*) 13 (*b*) 10

(*c*) 14 (*d*) 16 (*NTSE 2018-19*)

20. Which one of the following is cation

(*a*) Na^+ (*b*) Cl^-

(*c*) H_2 (*d*) None of these

(*NTSE 2018-19*)

ANSWERS AND HINTS (NTSE) : SAT

1. (*c*); **2.** (*c*);

3. (*b*) Electronic configuration of Cl^- : 2, 8, 8

4. (*a*) Atomic no = No. of protons = No. of electrons in neutral atom.

5. (*c*) α – particles are He^{2+} (helium nuclei)

No. of protons = 2, No. of neutrons = 4 – 2 = 2,

No. of electrons = 0

6. (*a*) **7.** (*c*) **8.** (*a*) **9.** (*c*) **10.** (*c*)

11. (*d*) **12.** (*c*);

13. (*b*) Electron distribution of Cl^- ion : 2, 8, 8

No. of valence electrons = 8

14. (*a*); **15.** (*b*) **16.** (*a*) **17.** (*d*) **18.** (*d*)

19. (*b*) Mass number = 27

No. of protons + No. of neutrons = 27

No. of protons + 14 = 27

No. of electrons = 27 – 14 = 13

No. of electrons in element with 3 positive charge = 13 – 3 = 10

20. (*a*)

TEST YOURSELF

CHAPTER PRACTICE TEST

Time allowed : 1 Hour **Maximum marks : 30**

1. Name the scientist who showed the existence of protons in an atom. 1

2. On the basis of the following table, answer questions 2(*a*) - 2(*d*)

Element	Atomic no.	No. of neutrons
A	3	4
B	9	10
C	13	14
D	17	18
E	18	22

2(*a*) How many protons are there in an atom of D ? 1

2(*b*) What is the mass number of B ? 1

2(*c*) Write electron distribution of C. 1

2(*d*) What is the number of electrons present in a monovalent positive cation of A and a monovalent anion of D ? 1

3. The number of protons in $^{32}_{16}S^{2-}$ ion is

(*a*) 16 (*b*) 18 (*c*) 14 (*d*) 32 1

4. The electronic distribution of an ion M^{3+} is 2, 8. If its mass number is 27, the number of neutrons in its nucleus is

(*a*) 13 (*b*) 14 (*c*) 10 (*d*) 24 1

5. Neutron was discovered by

(*a*) Bohr (*b*) Goldstein (*c*) Thomson (*d*) Chadwick 1

6. For the following questions two statements are given- one labeled *Assertion* (A) and the other labeled *Reason* (R). Select the correct answer to these questions from the codes (*a*), (*b*), (*c*) and (*d*) as given below:

(*a*) Both A and R are true and R is correct explanation of the assertion

(*b*) Both A and R are true and R is not the correct explanation of the assertion

(*c*) A is true but R is false

(*d*) A is false but R is true.

Assertion : Magnesium (+2) ion has completely filled 1st and 2nd shell.

Reason : Magnesium has equal number of neutrons and protons. 1

7. Explain :

(*i*) Nucleus of an atom carries positive charge.

(*ii*) Most of the space in an atom is empty.

(*iii*) The whole mass of an atom is present in the centre of the atom. 3

8. Complete the following :

(*i*) Mercury (+2) ion contains 80 protons, 78 electrons and 120 nucleons. Its mass number is ....

(*ii*) The element $^{17}_{9}F$ has .... valence electrons.

(*iii*) The maximum number of electrons that can be present in the outermost shell of an atom is 3

9(*a*). Explain three main postulates of Bohr's model of an atom.

(*b*). The average atomic mass of a sample of an element 'X' is 16.2 u. What is the percentage of each isotope $^{16}_{8}X$ and $^{18}_{8}X$ in the sample ? 5